SOCIALIST REGISTER 2022

THE SOCIALIST REGISTER

Founded in 1964

To get online access to all Register volumes visit our website
http://www.socialistregister.com

SOCIALIST REGISTER 2022

NEW POLARIZATIONS OLD CONTRADICTIONS

THE CRISIS OF CENTRISM

Edited by GREG ALBO, LEO PANITCH, & COLIN LEYS

THE MERLIN PRESS
MONTHLY REVIEW PRESS
FERNWOOD PUBLISHING

First published in 2021
by The Merlin Press Ltd
Central Books Building
Freshwater Road
London
RM8 1RX

www.merlinpress.co.uk

British Library Cataloguing in Publication Data is available from the British Library

ISSN. 0081-0606

Published in the UK by The Merlin Press
ISBN. 978-0-85036-773-7 Paperback
ISBN. 978-0-85036-772-0 Hardback

Published in the USA by Monthly Review Press
ISBN. 978-1-58367-937-1 Paperback

Published in Canada by Fernwood Publishing
ISBN. 978-1-77363-489-0 Paperback

Printed and bound in the UK on behalf of Stanton Book Services

CONTENTS

CONTRIBUTORS

Walden Bello is currently the International Adjunct Professor of Sociology at the State University of New York at Binghamton and Co-Chairperson of the Bangkok-based research and advocacy institute Focus on the Global South.

Bill Fletcher Jr. is a long-time trade unionist, writer, and a past president of TransAfrica Forum.

Virginia Fontes is Professor at the Graduate Program in History at Fluminense Federal University and at the Florestan Fernandes National School – MST.

Samir Gandesha is Professor and Director of the Institute for the Humanities at Simon Fraser University in Vancouver.

Ana Garcia is Assistant Professor at the International Relations Institute of the Pontifical Catholic University of Rio de Janeiro, and the Graduate Program in Social Sciences at the Federal Rural University of Rio de Janeiro.

Jayati Ghosh is the Chairperson of the Centre for Economic Studies and Planning at Jawaharlal Nehru University, New Delhi, and is also teaching at the University of Massachusetts, Amherst.

Marcus Gilroy-Ware is Senior Lecturer in digital journalism at the School of Film and Journalism at the University of the West of England.

Sam Gindin is former research director of the Canadian Auto Workers and co-author of *The Making of Global Capitalism: The Political Economy of American Empire*.

David Harvey is Distinguished Professor of Anthropology and Geography at the Graduate Center of the City University of New York.

Rejane Hoeveler is Lecturer at the School of Social Service at Federal University of Rio de Janeiro and has a PhD in History from the Fluminense Federal University.

Ilya Matveev teaches Russian politics at the Russian Presidential Academy of National Economy and Public Administration in St. Petersburg. He is a member of the Public Sociology Laboratory.

Simon Mohun is Professor Emeritus of Political Economy at Queen Mary, University in London.

Adolph Reed Jr. is Professor Emeritus of Political Science at the University of Pennsylvania.

Touré F. Reed is a professor in the Department of History at Illinois State University.

Vishwas Satgar is an Associate Professor of International Relations and principal investigator for Emancipatory Futures Studies in the Anthropocene at the University of Witwatersrand, South Africa.

James Schneider is the communications director of Progressive International, co-founder of Momentum, and a former spokesperson for Jeremy Corbyn.

Ingar Solty is Senior Research Fellow in Foreign, Peace and Security Policy at the Rosa Luxemburg Foundation's Institute for Critical Social Analysis in Berlin.

Samir Sonti has worked as a union organizer in the US and now teaches at the City University of New York School of Labor and Urban Studies.

Hilary Wainwright is an editor of *Red Pepper* magazine. She is a Fellow of the Transnational Institute, and an Honorary Associate of the Institute of Development Studies, Sussex University.

Oleg Zhuravlev is a researcher at the Public Sociology Laboratory based at the Center for Independent Social Research in St. Petersburg.

PREFACE

Leo Panitch, the most brilliant student and long-time friend of Ralph Miliband, who founded the *Socialist Register* with John Saville in 1964, edited or co-edited it from 1985 until his tragic death in December last year from Covid-19. The shock to us, along with all his friends, colleagues, students, and comrades around the world, was momentarily paralysing. This volume was in preparation; it was hard enough to bring it to completion on time without Leo, let alone to write anything about him that could begin to do justice to his 35 years as the Register's editor, not to mention his place in the history of the left. Some considered appreciations have already appeared, notably the book edited by Leo's *Register* colleagues Greg Albo, Steve Maher and Alan Zuege, entitled *State Transformations: Classes, Strategy, Socialism* (Brill 2021), in honour and memory of Leo's contribution to a critical political science.

Of course, there have already been many commemorations of Leo's life and work in a wide range of publications of the left around the world, as well as in the mainstream press. More will be taking place over the coming year, and the next volume of the *Register* will include several essays reflecting on Leo's contributions to socialist thought and politics. Here, we would just like to quote from three of the dozens of heartfelt and moving tributes that appeared in the weeks after Leo's death, which convey well the emotions, comradeship, and loss we feel ourselves.

From Michalis Spourdalakis, Leo's former student and close friend, in Athens, writing soon after Leo died:

Leo's tragic end reminded us of the unpredictable and often gloomy whims of the end that each of us eventually face, but it also shocked those who knew him. Hard to accept. It is difficult to swallow that he, with his invincible passion for life, and his unwavering commitment and mobilization for the cause of the socialist perspective, is no longer with us. It is not so much the hundreds of statements, interventions, and stories that fill not only social media but also the mainstream media in many languages, but the number of people who were stunned by the unexpected news, struck dumb by the shock.

I also belong to this last category ... Suspended, puzzled ... How do I squeeze into one article forty-two years of acquaintance, apprenticeship, friendship, and companionship in the movement for socialist transform-ation? How can I include all his work, his contribution to the social sciences, his contribution to the Marxist tradition, his international and internationalist presence, his ties and passion for our country, our struggles and our culture, and finally his life and his personality?

Exactly so, and we profoundly share the feeling that Michalis also expresses here:

Even though I am a former speed-walker, he was always one step ahead. It was as if he wanted to anticipate tomorrow, to approach it, to understand it, and to project it through teaching. That is why his memory and his example weigh heavily upon us now, so much so that I feel I will never be able to cover that step that always separated us, even in our quiet walks.

But impossible as it seems now, we are bound to do everything we can to carry forward the project Leo left us, a project that Ingar Solty, also a former student of Leo's now located in Berlin, expressed very well:

Frankfurt Schoolers like Adorno are often credited with sending a 'message in a bottle', allowing Marxism to survive the near-successful effort to physically eliminate it in the Nazi period ... The same metaphor extends to the role Panitch and his colleagues played after 1989. York's political science department – probably the biggest cluster of Marxist scholars and innovation in the world – kept Marxism alive through the difficult 1990s and 2000s, only for it to be taken up by a new generation of socialists, faced with today's deep civilizational crisis ...

Panitch's special role also had to do with his ability to write accessibly. While his thinking was deeply entrenched in social complexities and theoretical debates, his prose was crystal clear. He resisted the kind of academic jargon which became fashionable during the 1980s ...

And that way of writing was also a quality that Leo, like Miliband, always wanted the *Register* to have – combining serious analytical thought with clear, accessible prose and a close connection to the politics of activists. This called for exceptional editorial skills and an extraordinary range of knowledge, as Ursula Huws, a contributing editor of the *Register* over many years, also noted:

> It is indeed hard to imagine anyone else on the planet with such a vast overview. He did not just have a horizon-to-horizon knowledge of the literature but was also personally acquainted with many of the greatest political thinkers of our time. He used to boast about how rarely anyone turned down an invitation to contribute to *Socialist Register*, attributing that to its history as a non-sectarian source of quality analysis. In fact, I suspect, it was Leo himself they did not want to say no to. The warmth and charisma that he radiated made everyone want to be included in it. And he bore no grudges, often inviting people with whom he might have had serious disagreements on some issues to contribute their ideas if he thought these ideas deserved a hearing.

All this and more is reflected in the thinking behind the present volume, which Leo planned and commissioned with Greg Albo, and which he had been corresponding about with some of the contributors until his last days. The commissioning letter he and Greg sent to contributors set out the task as follows: 'With the word polarization now on the lips of commentators on the left as well as mainstream journalists everywhere, we feel it is the responsibility for the *Register* to undertake a deeper analysis of the current political and economic moment by addressing the underlying social contradictions that are producing these polarizations. It is one of the great ironies of our time that, just two decades after capitalism became the singular global mode of production, as capitalist accumulation and social relations finally penetrated every corner of the earth over 150 years after the *Communist Manifesto* predicted this, that polarizations of politics, income and wealth, gross consumption alongside abysmal poverty, of ecological destruction, are there for all to see. What Philip Roth wrote about the personality of his Mickey Sabbath character in his novel, *Sabbath's Theater*, seems to apply to 21st century capitalism: "What's clinically denoted by the word 'bi-polarity' is something puny … Imagine, rather, a multitudinous intensity of polarities, polarities piled shamelessly upon polarities, polarities to comprise not a company of players, but this single existence, this theatre of one." Our aim is that the essays will conceptually and analytically yield the kind of global survey that will help to uncover the generative mechanisms behind the multiplication of new and old "identities", and not least nationalist and racial identities, as well as party and class polarizations amidst growing income and wealth inequalities, new forms of rural and urban divides, as well as of imperial and sub-imperial "rivalries".'

A second year of the Covid-19 pandemic is adding to the polarities in its unequal impact on the global north and the global south, on the zones and classes with access to vaccines and those without, and on public health systems that have weathered decades of austerity with some remaining operational capacities and those on the brink of collapse. As well, the global lockdown to contain the virus brought about the deepest and most abrupt recession capitalism has experienced in decades, reinforcing pre-existing divisions in the world market. The emergency economic stimulus, with both fiscal and monetary policy adopting exceptional policy stances, is now approaching wartime levels, leading many pundits to suggest a 'return of the state' (as if it had ever disappeared). But after so many declarations in the past of the replacement of market-driven politics by a new centrist politics of Keynesian economic guidance, more than a little scepticism is warranted. Despite daily reports of unprecedented 'weather events' – heat domes, flash floods, raging fires, droughts, constant hurricanes – it is still market ecology and the pricing of carbon that frames the prevailing policy accord on climate change. And in this multi-dimensional crisis, the centre-right consensus that was struck around the neoliberal policy regime has been steadily splintering, with a phalanx of far right and neo-fascist groups inserting themselves into electoral politics and gaining prominence 'in the streets' (not least in motley demonstrations against pandemic measures of any kind, from lockdowns to masking).

The observation that capitalism is always characterized by just such economic and political polarizations has preoccupied – even haunted – socialist analysis from its very origins: in Marx's and Engels' memorable phrase of revolutionary optimism in *The Communist Manifesto*, 'the more or less open civil war, raging within existing society, up to the point where that war breaks out into open revolution, and ... lays the foundation for the sway of the proletariat'. In the much picked-over chapter in Marx's *Capital* on 'The General Law of Capitalist Accumulation', the language is just as vibrant but now stark in its imagery: 'The greater the social wealth, the functioning capital, the extent and energy of its growth, and therefore also the greater the absolute mass of the proletariat and the productivity of its labour, the greater is the industrial reserve army.... Accumulation of wealth at one pole is, therefore, at the same time the accumulation of misery, the torment of labour, slavery, ignorance, brutalization at the opposite pole, i.e. on the side of the class that produces its own product as capital.' Absent from this passage, of course, is the organized working class struggling in the opposite direction. Yet in stating his 'General Law' in this absolute fashion

Marx allows us to see that the very 'inner nature' of capital is constantly pushing toward a polarization to secure the conditions for extracting value and profits irrespective of the social consequences. That is the system, Marx is insisting, that the working-class movement is up against.

The point here can be made more general. Capitalist development is in a constant process of forming new political conjunctures, as inter-connected forces are locked in mutual struggle within their antagonistic social relations. Such 'contradictions' contain many possibilities, as their antagonisms and conflicts develop and intensify – continued reproduction in ever more complex and baroque forms, crises, reconstructions, and even revolutions. The contradictory patterns and conflicts of capital accumulation push the capitalist state into a role of constant mediation of shifting alliances in the turmoil of events and shifting strategies. In the chapter in *Capital* on the struggle over the 'Working Day', with the state arbitrating the length of the work day in the general interest of capital, Marx identifies the class relation of conflict and struggle: 'The capitalist maintains his rights as a purchaser when he tries to make the working day as long as possible, and, when possible, to make two working days out of one. On the other hand, ... the worker maintains his right as a seller when he wishes to reduce the working day to a particular normal length .... Between equal rights, force decides.'

It is this alertness to the inter-connectedness of struggles that we wanted to foreground in this volume: the 'new' polarizations arising from the actual struggles and divisions of contemporary capitalism, understood in terms of the 'old' contradictions embedded in the class relations – in all their diversity – of capitalism. We hope such a perspective assists in understanding the forces of reaction that are mobilizing today and contribute to a socialist movement that is actively exploring alternatives in radical organization and democracy. It is to the essays in this volume that we now turn.

The *Register* has been preoccupied since the early 1980s with the policy regime of neoliberalism, the economic and social contradictions of market regulation, and the politics of the 'new right'; and the left's political impasse, and the need for organizational experimentation in unions and parties, in the search for new paths to socialism, has run as a constant, equally pressing, concern. It is thus entirely appropriate that this volume on 'new polarizations' begins with Simon Mohun's remarkable 'Portrait of Contemporary Neoliberalism'. With the massive growth of inequalities in income and wealth being perhaps the most commonly agreed-upon polarization today, Mohun argues that most 'important for understanding the structure and dynamic of neoliberalism has been the large and sustained increase in income share' accruing to the richest one per cent. In calling for radical state action that breaks with neoliberalism to address inequalities and climate change, Mohun draws the blunt conclusion that the 'divergence between social interest and individual profitability has never been as great as it is today'.

Within the context of the compounding contradictions of 'late neoliberalism', a brace of essays that follow also pick up themes of earlier volumes of the *Register*. The 2019 volume, *A World Turned Upside Down?*, explored the new geo-political conjuncture, as Donald Trump sowed confusion about the US's continued role in 'superintending' the world market, while Xi Jinping made China's claim for leadership in guiding global capitalism. Walden Bello writes from within the social movements of Southeast Asia and from the Philippines, a particularly auspicious location from which to evaluate the growing rivalry between the US and China. His essay, 'At the Summit of Global Capitalism', provides a judicious assessment of the growing polarizations and contradictions in the inter-state system as the phase of US unilateral power gives way to a much more variegated world order as part of 'China's push for global political and ideological leadership'.

Ingar Solty's 'Market Polarization Means Political Polarization' offers yet a third assessment of this particular moment, in this case echoing themes on the global growth of hard right forces presented in the 2016 *Register* on *The Politics of the Right*. Solty's contention is that the social polarizations that result from the market processes set in motion by neoliberalism bring with them a political polarization in the form of fissures in the party systems of liberal democracies, allowing the hard right new political space to occupy and permitting varied forms of authoritarian nationalism to take hold. After analyzing the dynamics of this political polarization, he concludes with the gravest of warnings that unless a new organized working-class politics emerges, current political forces 'are bound to move the world further and further down the slippery slope of liberalism into fascism'.

The market and digital dystopias explored in the last two volumes of the *Socialist Register* have at their analytical centre the longstanding state practices of neoliberalism which promote pro-market ideologies and extend markets and prices into every possible institution and sphere of life. These policies fundamentally alter the ways and means by which we communicate, and replace the old social compromises of collective bargaining, welfare provisioning, and social justice with the 'inclusionary' neoliberal practices of diversity and ESG (environment, social, governance) mandates. Many countries have seen authoritarian nationalisms of the right grow and gain power – even win hegemony – in this environment. How these processes have played out in the US during the presidency of Donald Trump, and the extent to which the Biden administration will accommodate or reverse them, is a matter of some importance for the global left.

Bill Fletcher's essay on the 'Danger of Right-Wing Populism in the US' presents a careful appraisal of the forces marshalled on the right over the course of the Trump presidency, leading to the insurrection of January 2021. Fletcher's longstanding contention, put forth in his widely-noted 'Stars and Bars' essay in the *Politics of the Right* volume, was of the dangers of a right-wing mass movement emerging in the US. Under Trump, Fletcher argues, this indeed occurred as the Republican Party became 'the party of the White Republic'. For the American left, this 'political polarization' means, Fletcher contends, united front work and tactical alliances to combat the far right, but also a left that is 'organized around an alternative set of politics and an alternative practice'. The role that 'fake news' and social media have played in these events in the US, and in the making of the new far right every where, is constantly bewailed. Marcus Gilroy-Ware provides, however, an authoritative and sceptical assessment of 'what is wrong with social media', and places the social pathologies they reflect and amplify within the capitalist imperatives that drive the 'misdeeds of the tech companies'. He argues, together with other recent *Register* contributors, for a democratic communications system that would 'cultivate forms of communicative capacity and bottom-up truth-telling' as an indispensable project for the left.

From a quite different point of departure, Adolph Reed Jr. and Touré Reed locate the foundations of the hard right today in the US in the marginalization of the progressive pole in US politics as the link between economic justice and racial justice formed in the 1963 March on Washington steadily eroded, and 'the black political class' became embedded within 'the processes that shaped the Democratic Party's commitment to a programme of retrenchment'. An alternative path to racial justice, addressing black poverty, housing problems, and inequalities, depends not only on 'the continued value of anti-discrimination policies' but also 'building a broad working-class based movement … [that] might successfully defeat the reactionary right wing'. It is to the prospects and strategies for rebuilding the US labour movement and the left after Trump that Samir Sonti and Sam Gindin also turn their attention in their respective essays. Whatever political space may have opened up with the defeat of Trump, the finance capital that still dominates American capitalism, and the limits of Biden's 'Keynesian' reflation, still constitute a difficult terrain for organizing American workers. Indeed, it is because the obstacles still loom so large that a left that is just re-emerging needs to take steps not to slip into spending all its energies in aligning itself with the liberal-progressive forces backing Biden as opposed to organizing workers and independent campaigns. For Sonti, this is the challenge of rebuilding the American union movement, notably through campaigns that 'align the interests of workers who provide vital public services with those of communities that depend upon them'. For Gindin, the US left faces 'polarized options'; the challenge it faces is 'to conceive of reforms that change the terrain of the struggle [and] contribute to working-class formation'.

The volume then turns to a series of regional studies of the major states most often invoked as leading examples of the social polarization and of authoritarian nationalisms. Jayati Ghosh provides a penetrating analysis of 'pandemic polarizations' amidst the contradictions of Indian capitalism. Guided by the 'Hindutva authoritarianism' of Narendra Modi and the BJP, India has gone through 'the worst health calamity … for at least a century', with much of the damage resulting 'from government action and inaction, in a context of an extremely frail and inadequate public health infrastructure created by decades of underspending'. The consequence, Ghosh argues, is 'major setbacks to … the broader development project in India'. Writing as both a campaign activist and a university researcher, Vishwas Satgar sets out the Covid-19 pandemic in South Africa as an example of the polarization within the infected population, and of polarized access to vaccine being shamelessly piled on top of the acute polarizations of income and employment, on top of the inequities of housing, on top of ecological vandalism. The judgement Satgar passes on the ANC-led state and ruling class is severe: 'The Covid-19 pandemic revealed the limits of more than two decades of neoliberalization. A corrupt and failing state was unable, or unwilling, to adequately cushion the shock to a deeply unequal society.' But the extreme social polarization of South Africa, compounded by the government's neoliberal pandemic response, 'has also unleashed a new cycle of post-apartheid progressive resistance'.

The post-Soviet economic and social polarizations in Russia have long been observed, but the political form they now take is less known and perhaps even less understood. Ilya Matveev and Oleg Zhuravlev offer a compelling account of how these developments are registered in urban–rural and core-periphery regional divisions under the authoritarian nationalism of Vladimir Putin. The Russian president rose to power at a unique moment, when 'political polarization receded at the cost of widespread public apathy towards politics', which allowed an authoritarian regime to emerge. Until recently the Putin regime was able to rely on the 'apathetic indifference of the population and general appeals to social stability'. But with the protest movements that have now emerged, even if they have been inchoate, the

Kremlin has not sought to create a counter populism of its own: its objective 'has been to prevent independent political activity of any kind, even ones that might benefit the regime'.

'Brazilianization' was a term adopted by sociologists decades ago to capture the sharpening of income and social polarizations that came with neoliberalism. Under the far-right rule of Jair Bolsonaro, polarization has taken on multiple meanings and Ana Garcia, Virginia Fontes, and Rejane Hoeveler carefully unpack the 'fictitious polarizations' involved in the electoral opposition between the right and the 'centre' an opposition that is being pulled to the right in quarrels over 'cultural values', while remaining within the confines of the hegemony of the corporate sector. This contrasts, they argue, with real polarizations resulting from an organized and combative working class that develops, invoking Gramsci's term, a 'spirit of cleavage', in being conscious of, and determined to pursue, its class interests. That is the challenge from an insurgent far right that confronts the Brazilian and Latin American working classes today.

These cases all point to the contradictions and strategic limits of the 'actually-existing' left today, as it confronts ever more confusing neoliberal policy regimes in states that are turning to authoritarian measures under pressure from a radicalizing right. What is the agenda, then, for constructing viable anti-capitalist alternatives in both organization and programme? This is a question that the final contributions to the volume take-up. Samir Gandesha seeks an answer in what he identifies as 'a fragmentation of the universalism that had historically underwritten the struggle for socialism', leading to a what he terms a 'politics of false concreteness' centred on forms of identity politics on both the left and the right. Indeed, in the absence of a 'left universalism', Gandesha argues, 'we can only expect the logic of polarization to drive an already accelerating authoritarianism, as right-wing demagogues mobilize support based on racialized grievances'. This can only be met by a '*class* identity' that seeks a universalism 'in its own self-dissolution', that is, in the struggle against classes as such and thus capitalism. For his part, David Harvey returns to Marx in the *Grundrisse* and, in an interesting and unexpected move, to W.E.B. Du Bois on 'double consciousness', to locate a tension in the making of an anti-capitalist politics. This is the tension between the possibilities – and polarization – found in the creative destruction and technological revolutions that capitalism brings, and the alienation and the loss of 'human potentiality' that occurs alongside them. Navigating the contradictions of this double consciousness is, Harvey insists, 'critical for socialism to have some future'.

Finally, Hilary Wainwright engages in a remarkable discussion with

James Schneider on the lessons to be gained from the experience of forming Momentum as a national campaigning organization, and from the achievements and ultimate defeat of the Corbyn project in the UK. Schneider and Wainwright are optimists in their accounting of the gains that have been made from these struggles and the new spaces that are now open for a radical democratic politics. Schneider's conclusion, to the extent one can be made at this moment in the history of the left, is that 'we need to have a party in the Gramscian sense of the term: a political organization that stretches into society, that has real and organic links with different forms of ongoing struggle – trade union, environmental, feminist, anti-racist, and so on – and has some parliamentary representation and can speak in the country – it has the ability to communicate in a mass way'.

This volume of the *Socialist Register* has been produced in the most difficult of circumstances. We need to thank in particular the support offered by Hilary Wainwright, Ursula Huws, Michalis Spourdalakis, Sam Gindin, Nicole Aschoff, Alfredo Saad-Filho, Barbara Harriss-White, and Bryan Palmer. It would have been far more difficult without their encouragement and solidarity. Alan Zuege and Steve Maher used their editorial skills and political insights to improve the volume, and helped us keep our nerve in the darkest days. Our gratitude is also once again extended to our publishers at the Merlin Press, Tony Zurbrugg and Adrian Howe, especially for their understanding of the difficulties we suddenly faced. The theme of this year's *Register* is not an easy one to grasp in aesthetic terms, but Louis MacKay has as usual provided us with an inventive cover that adroitly captures the political antagonisms we asked the essayists to address.

It is necessary to return, finally, to the sad note we opened the preface with. As well as Leo we also lost several other of the left's most important public intellectuals, contributors to socialist thought, and friends of the *Socialist Register* in the past year: Neil Davidson in Scotland, John Loxley and Mel Watkins in Canada, and David Graeber and Stanley Aronowitz in the US. Stanley published his classic account of the state of the US labour movement at the outset of Reaganism in the 1980 *Register*, and it well bears re-reading in light of the essays on the US left in this volume. All these deaths, coinciding with Leo's, underscore, indirectly, the difficult generational transition the *Register* faces. Keeping constantly in mind the steadfast commitment of these socialists to a world beyond the social polarizations and ecological degradations of capitalism will surely keep us pointed in the right direction.

GA
CL
September 2021

A PORTRAIT OF CONTEMPORARY NEOLIBERALISM:
THE RISE AND ECONOMIC CONSEQUENCES OF THE ONE PER CENT

SIMON MOHUN

The 'golden age' of capitalism ended in the early 1970s, and the remainder of the decade was marked by turmoil as to what should replace it. There were two broad but rather different capitalist approaches. One, a managerialist approach, had prospered during the golden age in a de facto alliance with the organized working class, and was generally supportive of (or at least not hostile to) collective bargaining, the expansion (or at least maintenance) of the welfare state, the regulation of industry and finance, and a mix of fiscal and monetary policies in pursuit of low unemployment and a high level of aggregate demand. The second approach harked back to a market fundamentalism which had dominated before the Great Depression but had been rolled back in the US, initially by the New Deal, and then more generally by wartime planning and continued state intervention during the post-war recovery. This market-fundamentalist approach saw its opportunity in the collapse of the golden age to challenge managerialism and its associated (often rather mild) forms of social democracy.

The context for these competing approaches was one of an accumulation of problems. The inflationary financing of the Vietnam War, the breaking of the link between the dollar and gold in 1971, the collapse of the Bretton Woods exchange rate system in 1973, the commodities price boom culminating in the OPEC price rise of 1973, and rises in unemployment combined to create a situation to which the golden age type policies of high employment rates and low interest rates seemed an ineffectual response. With collective bargaining blamed both for profit-squeezing wage rises and for the inflation that was eroding the returns from bondholding, the golden age alliance between managerialism and the organized labour movement became increasingly insecure. But it took some time to break apart. If the rate of surplus value is interpreted as a measure of the outcome of class struggle, its graph against time through the 1970s is a horizontal line, indicating a stalemate: the golden age alliance might be in the process of breaking down, but the political and economic structures established in the golden age were too strong to allow market fundamentalism to take advantage.[1]

The stalemate was ended by the Fed's anti-inflationary large interest rate rise in October 1979, and the election of Reagan to the US presidency the following year, on a programme in large part promising deregulation and a more laissez-faire economy. This followed the election of Thatcher's Conservatives in the UK in 1979 on a similar programme and was succeeded by Mitterand's turn away from his own attempt at a more thoroughgoing social democracy in France. What followed is well known: a sustained assault on the institutions of the organized labour movement, both in the public sector (for example, in the US on the air traffic controllers' union and in the UK on the miners' union), and more generally through significant alterations in the legal framework under which labour unions operated. At the same time, in place of the post-war consensus in favour of full employment, much higher levels of unemployment were tolerated. Deregulation and privatization of nationalized industries proceeded apace, alongside 'reforms' of the welfare state which variously concentrated on real cuts in entitlements and stricter eligibility criteria. And there were substantial tax reductions for the rich.

The policies pursued after about 1980, and the outcomes achieved by those policies, cemented in place a politics and economics in which financial interests increasingly dominated. Because of suggestive historical parallels to the pre-1929 and even pre-1914 periods, the current period since around 1980 has come to be called 'neoliberal'. There are three distinctive but intertwined economic features of the current neoliberal period: the rise of 'the one per cent', globalization, and financialization. Many have used these terms, but in what follows they are given precise and distinctive meanings which are less commonly encountered in the existing literature.

POLARIZATION: THE RISE OF THE ONE PER CENT

Associated with deregulating the market was a very large and sustained shift in income distribution.[2] While much discussion on the left focuses on what has happened in the lower half of the income distribution, arguably more important for understanding the structure and dynamic of neoliberalism has been the large and sustained increase in income share at the top.

Table 1. National Income Shares(%) Accruing to the One Per Cent

	1985	2007	2019
Anglo-Saxon countries			
Australia	6.1	11.5	12.4
Canada	8.9	15.8	14.3
New Zealand	6.4	8.7	11.4
United Kingdom	8.6	14.9	12.7
United States	12.0	18.4	18.7
Mainland Europe			
France	6.9	10.8	10.0 (2018)
Germany	9.4	13.5	13.0
Ireland	7.9	11.9	11.6 (2018)
Italy	5.0	8.1	8.8
Netherlands	6.0	7.8	7.0 (2018)
Portugal	9.6	10.9	11.6
Spain	12.1	11.2	12.2
Switzerland	10.4	12.0	10.9
Scandinavia			
Denmark	10.1	10.7	11.2
Finland	5.3	11.1	10.0
Norway	8.1	12.7	10.4
Sweden	9.3	12.0	10.9
Ex-USSR and satellites			
Czech Republic	2.4	10.6	10.0
Hungary	2.6	11.4	12.4
Poland	4.7 (1984)	15.7	14.6
Russian Federation	4.4	26.8	21.3
South and East Asia			
China	8.0	15.3	13.9 (2015)
India	10.5	20.1	21.4 (2016)
Indonesia	11.1 (1993)	12.1	10.7 (2017)
Japan	9.2	13.4	12.4 (2017)
South Korea	9.4 (1984)	13.1	14.1
Vietnam	15.2 (1992)	14.7	15.2 (2016)
Miscellaneous			
Brazil	n.a.	23.4	27.7
Mexico	n.a.	23.6	28.7
South Africa	9.9 (1990)	20.1	19.2 (2012)

Source: World Inequality Database, at: https://wid.world/, downloaded 18 February 2021.

This tends not to be captured in official statistics of income distribution, because household surveys leave out the very richest households on the grounds that they are unrepresentative. Consequently, data on the richest have to be estimated from tax returns, so that the results are generally pre-tax.[3] Tax return data create further difficulties; they are not as timely as household survey or national accounts data, and the results depend on how the data are collected in individual countries. For example, in the UK individuals are taxed but households receive benefits, and in the US the basic unit of taxation is not an individual but a 'tax-unit' (since married couples can file together). Moreover, not all data are available for every year. While such calculations from tax statistics must therefore be treated with caution, they are nevertheless widely accepted.

Table 1 collects data on thirty countries which together account for between 74 per cent and 77 per cent of world national income (depending on the date), for three sample years: 1985 (it took a few years for neoliberalism to be established), 2007 (just before the financial crisis) and 2019 (the latest year for which data are available). The data are the percentages of national income accruing to the top 1 per cent in each country.[4] The increase in share from 1985 to 2007 for every country (except Denmark, Spain, and Vietnam) is substantial; comparing 2019 with 2007 the record is more erratic, with some countries showing small increases in their one per cent income shares and others small falls. National income grows over time, so that Table 1 implicitly shows that the top one per cent in each country obtained a growing share of a growing total from 1985 to 2007, and a roughly constant share of a growing total from 2007 to 2019. Further, while these data are pre-tax, another feature of neoliberalism has been sharply falling tax rates on the rich, so that the 2007 and 2019 data are closer to post-tax outcomes than the 1985 data. In sum, the data show a very large increase in income accruing to the one per cent. By 2019 (at constant 2019 dollar prices), in these thirty countries the top one per cent received an *extra* $11.6 trillion over what they received in 1985, an amount corresponding to more than four and a half times the entire 2019 national income for the UK.

Before examining the implications of the rising income share of the one per cent for the structure of neoliberal capitalist economies, it is worth exploring what the top one per cent income share has to do with the capitalist class. The history of neoliberalism is certainly one of sustained defeat of the labour movement and its allies, a defeat in which social democratic parties have either actively colluded or been paralyzed by an inability to propose any coherent progressive alternative. So, in a society which is structured by social class and driven by class conflict, one might expect to see rewards going to the winners, and it is a short step to seeing the rise of the income share of the one per cent as a precise reflection of those rewards.

This raises several analytical issues. In the simplest and most abstract view, if class struggle is the motor of history, then in the capitalist era that struggle is between capitalist class and working class. The definition of the working class is relatively straightforward: the working class is all those who are forced into the labour market because they do not have sufficient assets to remain out of it, assets which they could trade in order to acquire the money needed to gain access to consumer goods and services. At the extreme, they have no assets to sell, other than their capacity to work (labour power). This is not affected by the twentieth-century growth of social security provision, because it was purposely never set at levels which seriously threatened the supply of workers into the labour market. So, it is (fairly) clear who are the working class.[5]

But who the capitalist class are is not at all obvious. Those who solely live off income from non-labour assets (rents, bond payments and share dividends) are a tiny fraction of contemporary capitalist society, and anyway have few if any decision-making powers that can influence events. Almost everybody is on an employment contract, including those who own private jets, luxury yachts, luxury apartments and houses in many countries, and large holdings of stocks and bonds. The top executives of multinational (financial and nonfinancial) corporations are employees (in the sense of having an employment contract) just as much as those who clean their offices and empty their garbage for a minimum wage. So, selling labour power doesn't work as an abstract criterion for determining class position. Neither does ownership of and control over the means of production. Compared with, say, a nineteenth-century cotton mill, asset ownership in contemporary capitalist economies is much more widely distributed (for example, in sovereign wealth funds, pension funds, insurance companies, investment and unit trusts and so on), and much of that ownership does not confer control.

Two different (but not necessarily alternative) approaches are then possible. One is to try to identify people who are capitalists. The other is to work with the idea that capital is a social relation which is not reducible to a collection of its top functionaries.

Consider first capitalists as people. Suppose a distinction could be made between, on the one hand, those who are *compelled* to sell their labour-power because they have insufficient income-generating non-labour assets, and, on the other hand, those who continue to sell their labour-power even though they do have sufficient income-generating non-labour assets. The former are forced by economic necessity to sell their labour power, and the latter are not, even though in fact they do so. This entails identifying a threshold income such that all whose non-labour incomes exceed this threshold are voluntary sellers of labour power ('capitalists'), whereas all those whose non-labour incomes are below this threshold are forced into the labour market in the classical manner.[6] This latter group can be further divided into those who have no essential supervisory function in the production process ('workers') and those who are supervisory employees ('managers').[7]

For the US, over the period 1973-2012, in terms of round numbers, about 83 per cent were workers, 16 per cent were managers, and 1 per cent were capitalists. The data are in tax units (singles and married couples with a dependent child), and there is some variability over time especially for capitalists (because the non-labour income used as a criterion of separation is sensitive to business cycle fluctuations). For the period 1987-2012, capitalist numbers averaged 1.25 per cent (of all tax units), peaking at 1.5 per cent in 1999-2000 (the dotcom bubble) and 1.8 per cent in 2007 (just before the financial crisis). So, while the data should be treated cautiously, a focus on the one per cent (at least for the US) is not a bad approximation for looking at who could meaningfully choose not to enter the labour market.

Figure 1. US Income Shares, 1973–2012
Source: Mohun (2016)

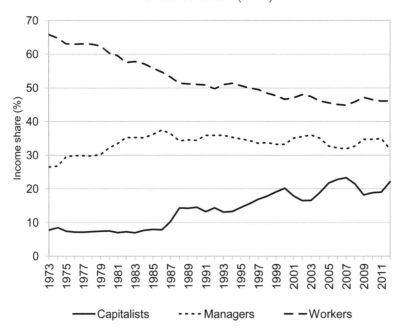

Figure 1 shows how income shares have changed over the period. The data in Figure 1 divide into two periods, from 1973 to 1986 (from the end of the golden age through the initial establishment of neoliberalism to the Reagan tax reductions of 1986), and from 1986 onwards (the consolidation of neoliberalism). In the first period, the capitalist income share was flat, barely changing at all over the period; workers' income share fell from 65.8 per cent in 1973 to 54.7 per cent in 1986, and that share was entirely taken by managers, whose share rose from 26.5 per cent in 1973 to 37.5 per cent in 1986. To the extent, therefore, that there was a wage squeeze on profits in the later 1970s, it was not increases in the wages of workers that were squeezing profits but increases in the labour incomes of managers. But after 1986 the managerial income share changed little. Workers' income share continued to fall to a low of 44.8 per cent in 2007. This fall was matched by the increasing income share of capitalists, from 7.8 per cent in 1986 to a peak of 23.7 per cent in 2007, before falling back a little.

The increasing income share of capitalists was not solely due to increases in non-labour incomes (distributed profits, interest, and rent). Indeed, over the whole neoliberal period, the proportions of capitalist income deriving from an employment contract (about 60 per cent) and from non-labour incomes (about 40 per cent) hardly changed. That is, as the capitalist income share rose, increases in their labour income were no less important than increases in their non-labour income. Prior to the neoliberal era, large corporations were largely run by insiders, internally promoted, fairly easily substitutable one for another, and with an ethos of a team committed to the corporation. Consequently, they were not paid the extraordinary amounts that became common in the neoliberal era, because that would have been internally divisive. Neoliberalism changed this by incentivizing managers through stock options, tying remuneration to share price performance. Whereas the idea was to reward managerial performance that increased the company's share price by more than its rivals, in practice a rising stock market rewarded all managers regardless of their relative performance. Large increases in top managerial pay were arguably necessary to lock in managerial loyalties much more to the interests of capital, because globalized profit-maximizing strategies increasingly entailed the destruction of local economic environments through off-shoring and down-sizing and were incompatible with notions of stake-holding.[8]

However, there are some obvious difficulties with this approach to identifying classes. One concerns the (non-uniform) distinction between supervisory and non-supervisory employees in different industries. A second is an obvious difficulty with tax statistics regarding (legal) tax avoidance and (illegal) tax evasion. Third, many very highly paid individuals (such as actors, entertainers and sports stars, accountants, lawyers, and highly paid medical professionals) will be included as 'capitalists', which does not quite capture the meaning of the term. That is, the data depict highly stratified labour market outcomes, but it is difficult to feel confident that these map neatly into class structure, rather than emerging as a consequence of class relations.

Thus tax data investigations report the consequences of capitalist class relations for income distribution: a very large shift of income share to the top of the income distribution through the neoliberal era. But since it is difficult to identify with precision that this is a shift to capitalists as a defined group of people, the second approach is to treat capital as a social relation which is not simply reducible to a collection of its top functionaries, although they are the bearers of that relation. Rather than focus on these top functionaries, the following sections focus on 'globalization' and 'financialization', key structural characteristics of the neoliberal era that are completely intertwined with the shift of income share to the one per cent.

GLOBALIZATION

Globalization means increasing international flows of people, goods, services, and investment, both direct (the construction of production facilities overseas, and the off-shoring of production from developed to developing economies) and indirect (the purchase of foreign financial securities). One of the consequences of the off-shoring of production to lower wage economies has been wage stagnation for large portions of the metropolitan working class: relatively well-paid industrial jobs have disappeared overseas, and for large numbers of people what has remained in metropolitan countries has been lower-skilled service sector employment, generally much less well paid than the jobs that have vanished. Indeed, working conditions have so deteriorated in parts of the industrial structures of metropolitan capitalism that the differences between the insecurities generated by unemployment and those generated by low-paid and insecure employment are disappearing. The combination in the same income distribution of an élite that has done spectacularly well, and a large number of people who have been 'left behind', resentful and seemingly powerless to do anything about their situation, is one of the drivers behind the populism that has characterized recent years.

A striking feature of globalization has been the development of the economies of south and east Asia, which have been the recipients of much of the off-shoring capital flows. The rapid economic growth of China in particular, beginning with the turn to the market in 1978, has proceeded alongside neoliberalism. The result has been a very large increase in the world's working class, which under capitalist relations entails a concomitant increase in the world's pool of surplus value.

The metaphor that a corporation contributes to the world pool of surplus value through the exploitation of its own employees, but takes from the world pool as profit whatever the forces of competition allow, is central to the understanding of how capitalism works.[9] In ideal circumstances of frictionless free trade and free entry into industries, this competitive mechanism would tend to equalize rates of profit (for given technologies and levels of consumer demand). Such tendential equalization would require corporations with more labour-intensive production processes to lose value in the marketplace to corporations with less labour-intensive production processes. But there isn't frictionless free trade and free entry. Firms are always trying to build barriers around their products and processes so that they can insulate themselves from competitive forces. To be effective, these barriers have to be relatively impregnable to legislative ways of enforcing competition, and so they generally rely on some technological feature of a product or production process that discourages potential competitors from entry into the industry.

Barrier-building examples are numerous in information technology (generally due to economies of scale associated with network externalities), to such an extent that there is a tendency to see the corporations involved as somehow defining the nature of contemporary capitalism. These corporations have a significant impact on ordinary everyday life, but they use rather different business models: thus Apple is a consumer electronics corporation, Facebook is a social networking platform, Alphabet (Google) uses its search engine expertise to promote online advertising, Amazon is a business-to-consumer e-commerce platform (with an online entertainment streaming service competing with Netflix, Walt Disney and others), and Microsoft is a computing software and electronics company. All that they have in common is the use of information technology to acquire and retain customers.

While barriers protect what corporations manage to extract from the world pool of surplus value, the mechanism remains one of contribution to the pool according to labour employed, and extraction from the pool of the maximum possible profit. A corollary of this perspective is that it is not possible to look at an individual corporation's profit and attribute it to its success in exploiting its own labour force. So the profits that accrue to Apple, for example, do not derive from the exploitation of Apple employees, who are a tiny proportion of the world working class; they derive from Apple's success in extracting a large share of the world pool of surplus value, which derives from the world's working class. The mechanism whereby this happens is through Apple's success in charging high prices for its products without losing market share to competitors. And it is very successful: every single second of its latest fiscal year Apple recorded $1,752 of profit (rather more per second than Microsoft's $1,244, Alphabet's $1,089, and Facebook's $586). Successful barriers to competition thus mean that the profits that accrue to successful corporations include a large component of rent (that is, the profit due to their barriers), so that rent-seeking is a large part of the determination of the paths of their development.

Back-of-the-envelope calculations can give some approximate idea of orders of magnitude of this central mechanism of globalized capitalism. Consider the largest 500 corporations in the world by sales revenue, and calculate for each the size of its workforce as a percentage of the world's workforce (its workforce ratio) and the size of its profits as a percentage of world profits (its profits ratio).[10] If for some company its workforce ratio is equal to its profits ratio, then (in proportional terms) that company is taking from the pool exactly what it contributes. If its workforce ratio is less than its profits ratio, it is taking out proportionately more profit than its workforce is contributing; and if its workforce ratio is more than its profits ratio, then the opposite. So divide each company's profits ratio by its workforce ratio, and use this to rank all 500 corporations from highest to lowest. At the top of this ranking are eight corporations which take out of the pool more than ten times what they put in; one is Apple, and the other seven are in mining, oil production and pipelines, all classic areas for rent extraction. There are 188 corporations which put more in than they take out and 114 corporations which take out more than they put in. And then there are 198 corporations which are unproductive in the Marxian sense, taking something out but putting nothing in. Of these, 80 are in wholesale and retail trade, and 118 are in finance. Ranking these 198 unproductive corporations by profit mark-up (the ratio of profits to total sales revenues less profits), out of the top 50, four are in internet services and retailing (Alibaba, Alphabet, Facebook, Tencent), four are in wholesale and retail trade, and 42 are in finance (banking, insurance and diversified financials). Finance is an industry concerned with the management of risk, and in the management of risk size really matters because the pooling of uncorrelated risks enables overall risk reductions. That is, there are increasing returns to scale, which is a very difficult barrier for new entrants to surmount. So finance is different.

Gains through risk pooling have always existed. But through the post-war years until the 1970s, finance was heavily regulated; with little autonomous power, it was treated as an auxiliary to capitalist development, necessary but subordinate to industry and industrial development. Yet nothing is forever. Technologies change and industries can change dramatically as an innovating technology disrupts existing industrial structures. This is what happened to banking through the 1980s, and, together with the growth of the one per cent, it is this change that underpins the financialization of the neoliberal era.

FINANCIALIZATION

Financialization is a contested term, but minimally concerns the growing weight of finance in all economies, at both macro and micro levels. One way in which to render it more specific and concrete is to interpret it as a summary description of how the banking sector changed in the 1980s and what the consequences of those changes were. The neoliberal emphasis on deregulation posed a potential threat to the legal protections enjoyed by US banking since the New Deal.[11] But it was financial innovation that posed the more immediate threat. For the moat around banking was not so secure. The industry was vulnerable not to major competitive entry, but rather to piecemeal attacks on elements of its balance sheet from bank-like institutions and activities. And the more successful this was, the greater was the pressure for legislative change, from both incumbents and competitors. No firm, even a monopoly, is completely secure from the threat of technological innovation by competitors attempting to undermine incumbents' positions. Innovation in pursuit of market share and profitability is how competition works. If it is successful, then that success forces a generalization of the innovation throughout the industry, which restructures the industry: laggards go to the wall, and innovators dominate as the whole industry is reorganized. Such reorganizations tend to extend the existing division of labour by creating new specialized areas of activity. So disruptive innovation yields competitive advantage and eventually generalization of the innovation across the industry, via a rebalancing between capitals that are competitively strong and those that are weak.

In the early 1980s, US banking faced three separate threats. First, its depositor base was eroded by competition from Money Market Mutual Funds (MMMFs), which did not face the same legislative ceilings on interest rates and so could offer higher interest rates to depositors. When these legislative ceilings were repealed, banks were still under a disadvantage because they had to finance the costs of deposit insurance either by absorbing them, or by passing them on to their depositors. MMMF accounts were, in contrast, not insured, but to their depositors, their deposits were as good as a deposit in a bank. In fact the deposits were shares in the MMMF business, and as long as everything went well each share was translatable into a dollar on withdrawing the deposit. The typical MMMF made its profit on the difference between the interest it received from investing its deposits in short term money market instruments, and the interest it paid out to its depositors. The second threat to US banking was to its loan business. Needing large funds for capital investment, large companies had always issued their own bonds directly into the market, bypassing banks because they were not large enough to supply the needed funds. But in the early 1980s medium-sized companies began to do the same thing, raising funds not for capital investment but for speculative mergers and acquisitions. Companies were targeted for takeover, and if the acquisition was successful the target company was loaded up with the debt, burdened with large payouts to the acquiring company, and often asset stripped to pay for the debt. Issuing debt directly into the market to finance buyouts attacked a core loan-making part of the banking industry. And the third threat to US banking was to its overdraft business, for at the short end of the market firms also began issuing their own debt in the commercial paper market. (Major purchasers of such debt were MMMFs.) So banks were in trouble in three parts of their balance sheet: deposits, medium-term loans to industry, and short-term overdrafts.

The unsurprising result was a serious problem of relative profitability as banks lost market share. The response was typical of capitalism: the industry was restructured in a way that enabled it to compete more successfully. What emerged from this restructuring was fundamental to the nature and structure of the neoliberal economy.

Loan-making is the core business activity of a bank. Prior to the neoliberal era, when a bank made a loan, it held it on its balance sheet until maturity when the loan was repaid, a model known as 'originate and hold'. It was this model that was restructured in response to falling relative profitability. Every separate aspect of the loan-making process was made a separate market activity, conducted by specialized profit-making intermediaries. Loan origination, the screening of customers for credit risk, the warehousing of loans made, the monitoring of loans and the packaging of loans into complex debt instruments to be sold to end-investors as bonds – all of these became separate market activities. The process of packaging up the expected income streams from loans into a bond and selling on is called 'securitization'. To reduce risk, collections of such bonds were combined into an asset (a 'security') which could be divided up and sold in different slices, or tranches, according to the degree of risk attached to the underlying income streams and to the eventual repayment of the original debt – tranches with higher risk paying a higher rate of return. In this manner, the fundamental model of banking was transformed from 'originate and hold' into 'originate and distribute'.

Each stage of the process is financed by debt. An institution borrows funds to process its stage in the securitization process and repays them with the funds obtained from selling its 'output' to the next stage, also charging a fee for its services. So there is a daisy-chain of transactions linking the original debt and its income stream of repayments with the final bond, tranched according to risk, for sale to a variety of end-purchasers. The final bond is a derivative, because it entirely depends upon the underlying income stream (at the other end of the daisy-chain). The whole process is financed by borrowing in wholesale money markets, so that the process can be described as 'money market borrowing to finance capital market lending'.[12]

But borrowing in money markets requires that someone is lending; equally, selling securitized bonds requires purchasers, and so another feature of financialized capitalism has been the growth in asset-management industries. Banks, insurance companies, pension funds, hedge funds, fund managers, family offices, legal and accountancy firms, non-financial corporations, institutions of the local and central government, the central bank – all are involved in a spider's web of lending and borrowing securities, buying and selling derivatives-based assets, and managing large-scale cash holdings. Focusing on this last, Zoltan Pozsar reports that in 2010 institutional cash pools (two-thirds of which derived from asset-management industries and one-third from corporations and other entities) had an average size of some $10 billion each, and a total size of $3.5 trillion.[13] Managing these pools in a way that preserves their safety means that the funds cannot be placed in banks (because US deposit insurance is limited to $250,000, and cash pool risk mandates limit exposure to uninsured bank deposits). These funds could purchase government-guaranteed debt (Treasury Bills issued by the US government, or triple-A-rated debt securities issued by any of the Federal Home Loan Banks), but that debt is in short supply.[14] So the only safe home is in a money market instrument that is privately guaranteed, that is, a sale and repurchase agreement, or 'repo' for short.

A repo is a pair of transactions in which a security owner sells the security for cash and at the same time commits to buying the security back after some short term (often overnight). The small positive price difference between selling price and buying price renders this equivalent to borrowing cash and paying an interest rate for the borrowing: the percentage difference in price is the repo rate. The securities act as collateral for the cash owner; if the second leg of the transaction fails, the cash-owner can sell the securities to recover their initial cash position. For this reason, the value of the securities sold in the first leg is generally greater than the cash received (the difference is called the 'haircut'). The pair of transactions gives the cash owner a return (the repo rate) on the cash, and protection in the event of default (because the bonds can then be sold).[15] So cash holders seek safety in repo; at the same time, the bond holder gains cash for the defined period and pays the repo rate for the use of the cash. The system works as long as the quality of the collateral securities is not called into question.

So at the core of financialization is a market-based system of finance. At one end are both those seeking risk (for example, hedge funds) and those seeking to fund long-term investments. At the other end are those seeking safety (for example municipal authorities with cash that is committed to future expenditure projects and needing to do something with the cash in the meantime). Cash hoards derive ultimately from the increasing income share of the one per cent; securities derive from the securitization process (private debt transformed into saleable securities) and from state debt (Treasuries). Then, facing one way, the dealing desks of the major banks sell securities to short-term investors (such as MMMFs), and facing the other way, use the cash to buy securities – securities, for example, borrowed by hedge funds from insurance companies and pension funds. In all of this, repo markets are central to the transformation of short-term deposits in money markets into long-term debt.

INSTABILITIES

The scale of these activities is both enormous and largely invisible in everyday life, because the activities occur in wholesale markets. These activities constitute the fabric of neoliberal capitalism, and they require three conditions for their successful operation. First, they require a continual supply of cash. Second, they require a continual supply of securities. And third, they require financial markets to work.

The income shift to the one per cent has provided a great deal of cash for financial markets. One cloud on the horizon is the threat of increased taxation, both of multinational corporations that aggressively manage in which jurisdiction they declare their profits, and of individuals in the one per cent. While there might be some movement on the former, as tax competition is not in the interest of national states seeking increased tax revenues, and while there is talk of future increases in personal taxation, there is currently no serious movement towards any dramatic increase in tax progressivity. So the flow of cash into financial markets looks set to continue for the foreseeable future.

As regards the supply of securities, financial engineering around securitization is hardly likely to disappear. With the neoliberal transformation of banking, banking assets are no longer long-term loans held to maturity, but tradeable securitized debt. The most important raw materials for securitization are residential mortgages, automobile debt, credit card debt, and student debt, but financial engineering will always search for further forms of debt to securitize. The other factor to consider is state debt, the safest form of debt (in particular US Treasuries). The Covid-19 pandemic has involved very large increases in state debt. But at the same time, central banks (particularly the Fed and the Bank of England) have bought very large amounts of state debt from the private sector in quantitative easing programmes to support aggregate demand through lower interest rates. While the direct financing of state debt by central bank creation of money is supposed to be eschewed, that financing is close to what has happened through 2020, and it remains to be seen how these tensions between state finance and private sector finance will play out.

Thirdly, financial markets have to work. In pre-neoliberal days, banks collected up the small amounts of deposits of lots of individuals and lent them out in much larger amounts as loans (to industry for capital investments and to households for residential mortgages). The success of this transformation of short-term cash available on demand into long-term illiquid loans depended upon the confidence of depositors that their cash was indeed available on demand, and as long as everyone did not demand their money at the same time, the system could function. The risks of maturity mismatches between more liquid short-term liabilities and less liquid long-term assets always existed, if rarely realized; in the neoliberal world the risks not only remain, but have spread far beyond traditional banks, so that the danger of runs on institutions or markets is correspondingly wider.

In particular, the perceived quality of the collateral offered in repo is crucial. In the 2007-08 financial crisis, highly leveraged financial institutions depended on continually rolling over their debt in repo, effectively borrowing cash overnight against the collateral of mortgage debt packaged into very complex securities. Once the collateral was called into question (as flows of mortgage payments dried up in the wake of the house price bubble collapse), liquidity concerns morphed into solvency concerns, and the system was only saved by very large-scale state intervention.

That financial crisis was not a one-off event. For the state had to step in again in March 2020. On 21 February 2020, in response to the spread of the Covid-19 virus, local lockdowns were announced in northern Italy, and volatility suddenly increased in global financial markets. From 21 February to around 11 March there was a 'flight to safety', as investors favoured more liquid assets. On 11 March, the World Health Organization declared a pandemic, and the flight to safety became a 'dash for cash'. Unlike in

2007-09, banks remained solvent and continued to lend to creditworthy borrowers. But the dash for cash created financial distress for nonbank financial institutions (about half of the US financial sector) which abruptly stopped lending, threatening severe effects. The turmoil spread through the commercial paper market, through MMMFs and into US Treasuries, with bid-ask spreads widening dramatically, and with dealers effectively beginning to withdraw from markets. If dealers were to stop dealing, market disintegration would follow. So the state intervened, the Fed substituting itself for private sector dealers, just as in 2007-09. In addition to establishing a number of emergency lending facilities, the Fed purchased securities, and as a consequence increased the total size of its balance sheet from $4.3 trillion in mid-March to almost $7.2 trillion in early June. To get an idea of the scale, consider the ratio of Fed assets to US GDP. In the second quarter of 2008, the ratio was 6.5 per cent; in the third quarter (when Lehman collapsed) it was 10.5 per cent, and by the fourth quarter it was 15.7 per cent. Through quantitative easing, by the fourth quarter of 2019 it stood at 20.2 per cent. The first quarter of 2020 saw it climb to 28.7 per cent and by the end of the second quarter of 2020 it had risen to 37.8 per cent. This very large increase did in the event succeed in stabilizing markets.

But it also demonstrates the fragility of the private market-based financial system infrastructure. Because the largest financial institutions were considered too big to fail, during the 2007-09 financial crisis they were explicitly bailed out. Being systemically important, they remain too big to fail, and that implicit subsidy encourages more risky behaviour than would otherwise be the case.[16] When systemic fragility is thereby exposed, the Fed has further demonstrated that it will substitute for private market dealers, as dealer of last resort to support the private market system of finance. Yet the interplay between state and private market is complex. For example, one consequence of the last decade of quantitative easing has been asset price inflation; while that was the point of the policy, those elevated prices have in turn exposed asset-holders to greater risk of a downturn, which has intensified the search for safe assets as a hedge against market falls. Completing the loop, the safest assets are US Treasuries. Yet quantitative easing withdraws some of these from the market and into the central bank. So this increased demand for, and reduced supply of, US Treasuries, maintains downward pressure on long-run interest rates, which further encourages risk-seeking behaviour.

NEOLIBERAL CAPITALISM AGAINST
ITS OWN CONDITIONS OF EXISTENCE

The neoliberal economy reached its apogee in 2007, was then nearly destroyed by the financial crisis, and was only rescued by a massive commitment of state resources. This commitment was repeated during the Covid-19 pandemic. These sorts of state intervention are not what market fundamentalism is supposed to be about. Because the world economy has become so dependent on large-scale financial state interventions, it is not surprising that neoliberalism has been drifting in a directionless manner.

In all of capitalism's historical phases, the accumulation of capital has tended to destroy the conditions of its own existence, and the crises thereby produced tend to lead to political change. To date such change has fallen well short of an emancipatory socialism. Rather, it has been limited to enabling an economic restructuring that can support the renewed accumulation of capital. In the neoliberal era, one consequence of globalization has been the increasing indifference of multinational corporations to the conditions of reproduction of national working classes. But however globalized, capital still requires a working class, and so cannot in fact make itself independent of the conditions of social reproduction. The conditions created by the social pressures of low-wage, low-productivity austerity since the financial crisis have prompted a neoliberal political response favouring some sort of Keynesian expansionism, combined (in declining countries) with an aggressive social conservatism, the particular balance depending upon recent national histories.

Such expansionism will entail some sort of re-industrialization. For global just-in-time systems of logistics have not managed at all well at the social level through the 2020-21 pandemic, however much they have proved efficient for individual corporations. There will therefore be some social pressure for more precautionary, more nationally based, just-in-case logistical systems. Similarly, some national effort will be put into constructing and maintaining pharmaceutical capacity; for some, this will involve the construction of new capacity, and for others, the contracting out to existing pharma companies. More generally, the national requirements for a more precautionary approach express a divergence between the individual interests of corporations in profitability and the social interest, but whether the pressure for change will be sufficient to over-ride corporate profitability concerns – to over-ride, that is, the anarchy of the market – has yet to be determined.

Capitalism has always been replete with examples of divergence between social interest and individual profitability. Thus Marx analyzed the nineteenth-century struggle to limit the hours of the working day in similar terms. But that divergence between social interest and individual profitability has never been as great as it is today. For capitalism has to confront climate change, the result of past capital accumulation which has paid no regard to its effects on the physical environment. The changes required are massive, pervading every sphere of human existence, and the earlier capital embraces carbon neutrality, the less socially costly the changes will be. But the scope for corporate inaction, free riding on the commitments of others, is all too significant.

Adaptation to climate change requires major state action to force capital to bear the full costs of its drive to accumulate, and hence to completely alter its calculus of risk and return in making investments. This means much more than setting targets for carbon reduction; it means coherent planning for how those targets are to be achieved. However, as neoliberal state responses to the Covid-19 pandemic have shown, there is only limited neoliberal state capacity for serious planning. The required shifts of diet away from meat and dairy, the rapid phasing out of fossil fuels for domestic heating and industrial power, the electrification of transport – all of these are in their infancy and are proceeding too slowly. Given the hollowing out of the administrative capacities of the neoliberal state, and the political unwillingness to contemplate the huge tax changes required to incentivise private capital to move significantly towards carbon neutrality, the challenge presented to neoliberal capitalism by the climate emergency is immense and may be insuperable.

The basic features of contemporary capitalism – globalization and a financialization driven by the processes of securitization and the growth of the one per cent – will remain, even as the neoliberal politics around them change. But existing financial instabilities will be compounded by the additional shocks arising out of increasingly frequent extreme climatic events. In these circumstances, it has never been more important to oppose the ways in which neoliberalism privatizes its gains and socializes its losses.

NOTES

1   See for example Simon Mohun 'Unproductive Labour in the US Economy 1964–2010', *Review of Radical Political Economics*, 46(3), 2014, pp. 355-79. Throughout, while examples are largely drawn from the US economy, the thematic portrait drawn of neoliberalism has broad applicability.

2   Income distribution should not be confused with wealth distribution. Wealth distribution measures the ownership of assets (property – net of loans or mortgages, physical household contents, pension, financial, and business). Income distribution measures incomes, an annual flow: income from employment and self-employment, and non-labour incomes (distributed profits, interest, and rent). Wealth distributions are more concentrated than income distributions. For example, in the US the wealthiest 1 per cent own about 40 per cent of all wealth, and in the UK the wealthiest 1 per cent own around 23 per cent of all wealth. These percentages are much greater than the income figures reported in Table 1. Of course, wealth and income distributions

are related, because non-labour incomes derive from stocks of wealth. But what is remarkable about the changes at the top of the income distribution in the neoliberal period is that they do *not* derive from an increase in non-labour income relative to labour income. For the top 1 per cent, the source of their income (about 60 per cent income from employment and 40 per cent non-labour income) hardly changed at all from 1980 to 2012.

For the US wealth distribution see: 'The Distribution of Wealth in the United States and Implications for a New Worth Tax,' Washington Center for Equitable Growth, 21 March 2019, available at equitablegrowth.org. For the UK, see Arun Advani, George Bangham, and Jack Leslie, 'The UK's Wealth Distribution and Characteristics of High-Wealth Households', Resolution Foundation, 3 January 2021, available at www.resolutionfoundation.org.

3   Using methods based on the Pareto distribution. This work seeks its inspiration largely in Thomas Piketty and Emmanuel Saez, 'Income Inequality in the United States, 1913–1998', *Quarterly Journal of Economics*, CXVIII, 2003, pp. 1–39. The dataset is regularly updated by Saez at eml.berkeley.edu/~saez. It reached a wider readership with Thomas Piketty, *Capital in the Twenty-First Century,* Cambridge, MA: Harvard University Press, 2014. Scholars working in this area currently maintain an interactive and downloadable world-wide database at https://wid.world.

4   National income is measured at constant 2019 prices in purchasing power parity US dollars.

5   There is a complication: workers live in households of varying composition, raising issues of how many people the wage is supposed to support. That ambiguity is not pursued here.

6   See Simon Mohun, 'Class Structure and the US Personal Income Distribution, 1918-2012', *Metroeconomica*, 67(2), 2016, pp. 334-63, for a discussion of possible thresholds.

7   Supervisory roles on the shop floor itself – as for example with foremen – are performed by workers.

8   Some of the argument in this paragraph is due to correspondence with Duncan Foley.

9   This mechanism means that it is quite possible to conceive of a corporation which produces no value at all and yet is very profitable. That is, there is a meaningful theoretical space to consider issues of productive and unproductive labour in a coherent manner.

10   The data are from the *Fortune* Global 500 list for 2020. The world's workforce is a World Bank figure, of which 80 per cent are assumed to be private sector workers. Using Mohun, 'Unproductive Labour in the US Economy', some 52 per cent of these are assumed to be productive workers. World national income is from the World Income Database, and 40 per cent of this is assumed to be profits. Unproductive labour is defined as circulation labour, overwhelmingly wholesale and retail trade, and finance. Supervisory labour in productive sector corporations is assumed unproductive and is assumed to be 17.7 per cent of the workforce of those corporations. Huge though these top 500 global corporations are, together they account for only 5.7 per cent of the world's profits and employ 2.6 per cent of the world's productive labour.

11   Following waves of bank failures, US banking emerged from the Great Depression in a weakened state and was heavily regulated. One effect of these regulations was to protect the banking industry from new entrants. Hence it was quipped that the industry was run

on a 3-6-3 basis: take in deposits at 3 per cent, lend at 6 per cent, and be on the golf course at 3 p.m.

12   Perry Mehrling, *The New Lombard Street: How the Fed Became the Dealer of Last Resort,* Princeton N.J.: Princeton University Press, 2010.

13   Zoltan Pozsar, 'Institutional cash pools and the Triffin dilemma of the U.S. banking system,' Working Paper WP 11/190, 2011, International Monetary Fund, available at www.imf.org.

14   Partly because so much of it is held by Southeast and East Asian central banks as a liquidity guarantee against any repetition of the late-1990s currency crises, and partly because of Fed purchases of Treasuries in the open market (quantitative easing).

15   The cash owner also gains the use of the bonds over the same time period, using them as collateral in further transactions (as long as those latter can be unwound – or rolled over – at the end of the defined time period) in a process called 'rehypothecation'.

16   The successive Basel rules of the Bank for International Settlements attempt to confront this.

AT THE SUMMIT OF GLOBAL CAPITALISM: ACCOMMODATION, RIVALRY, OR CONFRONTATION BETWEEN THE US AND CHINA?

WALDEN BELLO

At the beginning of the third decade of the twenty-first century, China was not only the world's second biggest economy. It had become the centre of global capital accumulation or, in the popular image, the 'locomotive of the world economy', accounting for 28 per cent of all growth worldwide in the five years from 2013 to 2018, more than twice the share of the United States, according to the International Monetary Fund.[1]

True, its growth rate was down to 6 per cent from the blistering 10-12 per cent rates in the 2000s, but that was far superior to the performance of the US economy, which had been, for all intents and purposes, in the grip of stagnation for almost a decade following the 2008 financial crisis. In 2020, China's economic recovery from the impact of the coronavirus pandemic earlier in the year made it the only major economy to register a positive growth rate.[2]

But beyond economics, Beijing was making a bid for global political and ideological leadership as Washington 'turned away' from the world during the Trump years, faulting the US's traditional allies with taking advantage of its 'generosity', radically tightening immigration rules, and declaring a trade war on China. Donald Trump as president was a purveyor of fake news, a master of exaggeration, and a promoter of conspiracy theories, but there was one thing he and ideological allies, such as his former adviser Steve Bannon, and his right-hand man on trade issues, Peter Navarro, were right about: US political and economic elites had played a central role in turning China from the outcast of the capitalist world into the biggest threat to America's hegemony over that world, not, like the defunct Soviet Union, as an outsider, but as an insider – or perhaps, more accurately, as an insider that retained many of the traits of an outsider.

The US has a new president, but Joe Biden is not likely to change course from Trump's when it comes to China. Democrats and Republicans may be at each other's throats on other issues but they are united in militantly confronting China.

There are many facets to the story of China's rise to the top rank of global capitalism. This account will focus on the evolution of China's relationship with US capital, choosing, for reasons of space, not to cover some other key dimensions, such as China's relations with the global South and the much discussed Belt and Road Initiative (BRI).[3] Our narrative begins in the early seventies, with two concurrent but unconnected crises: a severe crisis of profitability in the US economy, and a crisis of political legitimacy in China.

THE COLLAPSE OF THE SOCIAL DEMOCRATIC COMPROMISE

Through all the turbulent years of the Kennedy and Johnson administrations in the 1960s, a prosperous America anchored in a social compromise between capital and labour, and a political regime dominated by Big Government, Big Capital, and Big Labour, as these actors were popularly known, seemed destined to endure. This regime served, in turn, as the axis of a global hegemony that also seemed secure.

The defeat of the US in Vietnam in 1975 was an important ideological and political set-back, but it was economic troubles, beginning with Richard Nixon's taking the dollar off the gold-dollar standard, and the deep crisis that the economy entered beginning in the early seventies, that were more consequential. 'We are all Keynesians now', Nixon said, invoking the informal ideology of the system, as he imposed wage-and-price controls in the early seventies, but Keynesianism ended up being discredited as the coincidence of high inflation and weak growth, or 'stagflation', which was not supposed to happen in the Keynesian scheme, dragged the US into its most severe crisis since the Great Depression.

What the central cause of stagflation was continues to be debated, with the likely chain of events being more intense competition globally, leading to overcapacity, indicating an overaccumulation of capital, and resulting in cost-push inflation, as 'Big Capital and Big Labour' engaged in a contest of strength, with one side deploying price increases to overcome the advantage of the other's wage gains via union power, to maintain or increase their respective shares of decreasing rates of profit.[4] The period leading up to this, however, had been marked by high marginal tax rates on the rich, the steady growth of wages, and a decreasing rate of profitability. This was the basis of the social contract known as the 'New Deal', which the French economist Thomas Piketty characterized as a 'bargain basement social democracy'.[5] Though it was 'bargain basement', the deal was not inconsequential for labour and capital, with the latter being hardly indifferent to the decline in the rate of profit, which plunged from about 14 per cent in 1963 to 6 per cent in the early 1980s.[6]

Conservative economists saw the social democratic New Deal constraints on corporate profitability as the central cause of stagflation, and their narrative provided legitimacy to the rising ideology of neoliberalism, whose main objective was to radically raise the rate of profit by reversing wage growth, cutting transfer payments from the rich to social security programmes for workers, and destroying the political power of labour.

THE NEOLIBERAL OFFENSIVE

The neoliberal response to the crisis of profitability also included financialization, or shifting much investment to the speculative sector of the economy, where much greater profits could be made and globalization, a key thrust of which was shifting manufacturing operations to places where capital could extract much greater value from workers who could be exploited at much lower wages than in the US.

Income redistribution included lowering the marginal tax rate on the highest incomes from 91 per cent in 1950-63 to 39.6 per cent in 1987-2002,[7] and a decline in the share of wages in national income from close to 60 per cent in 1977 to around 55 per cent in 2011.[8] Financialization resulted in a situation where the financial sector (with the appropriately named acronym FIRE – finance, insurance, and real estate) accounted for only 8 per cent of US gross domestic product – but raked in 30 per cent of the profits, with some analysts saying the actual figure was 50 per cent.[9] Among the three ways of shoring up the rate of profit, however, globalization of the productive process, or the marriage of capital with labour not located in the home economy, appears to have been the most decisive.

CRISIS OF LEGITIMACY IN CHINA

Compared to the growth of its East Asian neighbours, China in the 1970s was experiencing modest growth. But its economic performance was related to a much bigger problem. After over 25 years of 'line struggles' that had caused tremendous social upheavals, people were exhausted with politics: the Chinese Communist Party (CCP) was experiencing a crisis of legitimacy, and key people in the leadership were seeking an alternative to the Maoist utopianism that had led to the chaos of the Cultural Revolution. When the Cultural Revolution began in early 1965, nothing much appeared to have changed in neighbouring Asia since the Communists had come to power in 1949. But by the time it ended in 1976, with Deng's assumption of power (a second time),

[T]he Japanese miracle had been emulated in South Korea and Taiwan. The sleepy entrepots of Singapore and Hong Kong had become flourishing industrial centers. The rampant East Asian tigers had proved that being part of the old Chinese cultural area, let alone Chinese, need not condemn one to poverty. Yet at the historic heart of the area, China itself now lay spread-eagled, this time by its own hand, not as a result of foreign invasion or conventional civil war.[10]

'For the Chinese leaders the message was clear', according to two of the most authoritative students of the Cultural Revolution, 'they had to embark upon a policy of rapid economic growth to make up for lost time and to relegitimize CCP rule. They had to abandon Maoist utopianism in favor of building the strong and prosperous nation of which they had dreamed when they joined the nascent CCP in the 1920s. Otherwise the CCP itself might not last. So "practice," not ideology – not Marxism-Leninism, not Mao Zedong Thought – became the "sole criterion of truth." If it worked, it would be done.'[11]

The theoretical explanation of what would become the practical connection between an American capitalism suffering a crisis of profitability, and a Communist leadership battered by a self-inflicted crisis of legitimacy, is provided by Rosa Luxemburg.

ROSA LUXEMBURG AND THE CHINESE PUZZLE

In her book, *The Accumulation of Capital*, Luxemburg argued that a central dynamic of capitalism is to integrate pre-capitalist or non-capitalist areas of the world, for three reasons: to acquire sources of raw materials for industry, to serve as markets to absorb surplus production from the central capitalist economies, and to access cheap labour to counter the rising cost of labour in the central economies. Of the three, the third is the most critical since labour-power is the source of surplus value and profits.

'The existence and development of capitalism requires an environment of non-capitalist forms of production,' Luxemburg wrote. 'Capitalism needs non-capitalist social strata as a market for its surplus value, as a source of supply for its means of production and as a reservoir of labour power for its wage system.'[12] Capitalism's relationship to non-capitalist modes of production is contradictory: it needs them, even as their destruction is necessary for its survival:

Capital needs other races to exploit territories where the white man cannot work. It must be able to mobilise world labour without restriction in order to utilize all productive forces of the globe – up to the limits imposed by a system of producing surplus value. This labour power, however, is in most cases rigidly bound by the traditional pre-capitalist organization of production. It must be 'set free' in order to be enrolled in the active army of capital. The emancipation of labour power from primitive social conditions and its absorption by the capitalist wage system is one of the indispensable historical bases of capitalism. Obtaining the necessary labour power from non-capitalist societies, the so-called 'labour problem' is ever more important for capital … All possible methods of 'gentle compulsion' are applied to transfer labour from former social systems to the command of capital.[13]

The post-Second World War New Deal and social democratic-inspired restrictions on the free flow of capital at home, and nationalist laws on portfolio and direct investment in developing countries, discouraged capital from the centre economies from moving aggressively abroad in search of cheap labour in the sixties. But the crisis of the Keynesian economy and ideology that had promoted social compromise in a national context led to the erosion of Big Labour's power to constrain Big Capital's determination to liberalize portfolio capital and investment flows.

The 'runaway shop' phenomenon began in the seventies, with transnational corporations setting up operations to exploit cheap labour in the largely non-unionized American South and in developing countries like Mexico, Central America, South Korea, the Philippines, and Thailand. But rural labour reserves in these countries were too limited to depress urban wages for an extended period of time, and they were integrated into a global economy where there were strong market pressures to equalize wage rates across countries, so that the ability of TNCs to extract super-profits abroad to counter the decline in the rate of profit at home by moving to these areas was limited. The entry of China into the global labour market in the late 1980s was, however, a different story.

China was a massive non-capitalist enclave sealed off politically and economically from global capitalism from 1949 to the late seventies. The focus on egalitarian income distribution and on building a social infrastructure apparently did not conflict with the achievement of not insubstantial GDP growth; Angus Maddison, regarded as the authority on comparative historical statistics, estimated China's average annual GDP growth rate between 1950 and 1976 at 4.7 per cent, compared to 4.5 per cent for Western Europe, 4.6 per cent for East and South Asia, and 4.7 per cent for the world.[14] By the end of the Mao era, as the progressive economist

Ho-Fung Hung points out, 'China was already endowed with a network of state industries and infrastructure; a large, educated, and healthy labor force; and a state autonomous from foreign governments and international financial institutions'.[15] This achievement is usually overshadowed by the social and political crises that accompanied intense 'line struggles' during the time of the Great Leap Forward from the late fifties to the Cultural Revolution in the late sixties. But it 'laid the foundation for the success of the subsequent market reform'.[16]

Be that as it may, China began moving away from socialist priorities towards a guarded embrace of market incentives after the death of Mao in 1976. Market relations were tried out first in the countryside, and when these promoted quickening rural growth, the focus shifted, in 1984, to subjecting state enterprises to market reform, and then, in the late eighties and early nineties, to opening the country to international market forces and foreign investment.

THE BIRTH OF THE CHINA-TNC ALLIANCE

There is a school of thought that heaps the blame for the woes of US labour on China.[17] What these economists forget is that US TNCs played an active, central role in creating the Chinese economic dragon. As pointed out above, US TNCs had begun moving industrial processes in earnest to cheap labour areas like the American South, Mexico, and Southeast Asia in the mid-seventies. From their perspective, China in the late 1980s was merely their latest potential pawn in their struggle with US labour. But as they witnessed adventurous overseas Chinese enterprises from Hong Kong, Taiwan, and Southeast Asia begin to invest in Southeastern China and reap huge profits from cheap mainland Chinese labour, US corporations gradually became aware of the momentous implications of China's trade and investment opening for the problem of their declining profits.

First of all, here was a large labour pool, previously un-integrated into capitalism, which was starting from a very low wage base and was relatively sealed off from immediate market pressures for wage increases, and whose mere existence and impact on investment decisions could exert significant downward pressure on global wage rates in manufacturing. In the first decade of the twenty-first century, China was to release no less than 121 million new workers into its manufacturing and service sectors.[18]

Second, China had a large reservoir of rural labour that, via migration, would serve as an internal check on wage rates in the cities.[19] In the 2000 decade, more than 80 million rural people went to the cities to fill urban jobs. As Hung points out, '[O]ne indispensable fuel for China's export-oriented success has been the protracted low-wage labor released from the countryside since the mid-1990s'.[20]

Looking back from the end of the second decade of the twenty-first century, one cannot overstate the importance of the fact that in slightly over thirty-five years, Luxemburg's insight was translated into an overwhelming reality. As Lin Chun put it in her essay in the *Socialist Register 2019*: '[By] fueling global capitalism with its enormous workforce and vast market for capitalist expansion and financialization, China actually helped extend and sustain the global capitalist system.'[21]

Beginning in the early 1990s US TNCs moved into China in force, establishing either subsidiaries or sub-contractual arrangements with small and medium Chinese suppliers, determined to access both the huge mainland market and cheap labour for export-oriented production. China did not disappoint. From 1985 to 2005, the hourly manufacturing wage there was less than 5 per cent of that in the US.[22] Investment in China, along with neoliberal restructuring and financialization at home, contributed to halting the precipitous decline of profitability, with profit rates for US corporations climbing from a post-war nadir of 6 per cent in the early eighties to close to 9 per cent in the early mid-2000s.[23] What TNC executives came to call enthusiastically the 'China price' made a major difference to the corporate bottom line, and from $30 to $40 billion a year in the mid-1990s, the stock of US investment in China had climbed to $107.6 billion by 2019.[24]

Nor did the transnational corporations disappoint China. While investment directed at production for local consumption accounted for the bulk of total investment, investment from abroad for production for export was a decisive element in China's capital accumulation. Foreign Direct Investment (FDI) played a much larger role in the capitalist industrialization of China not only than in Europe and the United States, but also in its East Asian neighbours. From 1985 to 2005 annual Foreign Direct Investment in China is reported to have averaged nearly 3 per cent of GDP, a fairly large figure, whereas during their high-growth eras Taiwan and Korea each had FDI inflows of only about 0.5 per cent of GDP, and Japan less than 0.1 per cent.[25] Whereas almost all exports from Korea, Taiwan, and Japan were accounted for by domestic firms, in the case of China, since the early 1990s, foreign firms have accounted for a third or more of all exports.[26] When it comes to high-tech products the situation is even more lopsided, with foreign firms accounting for around three quarters of exports, and the figure reaching 90 per cent of the exports of computers, components, and peripherals.[27]

Not surprisingly, US big business soon became China's closest foreign ally. During the Clinton administration, its lobbying overcame a powerful array of motley forces composed of traditional right-wing elements linked to Taiwan, human rights advocates in the Democratic Party, and a Pentagon that was increasingly convinced that China would be the US's principal strategic competitor. As one of the most authoritative accounts of the development of US-China economic relations described the situation,

> The Clinton team was prodded by business lobbyists who had long been pressing the administration and Congress to help China with its WTO bid. In the mid-1990s, Boeing formed what it called 'the Rump Group' of ten major US exporters, including AT&T, AIG, Chrysler, and General Electric to push a 'normalization initiative' for improved economic relations between the United States and China. Boeing would put up $2 million in seed money for a lobbying campaign that would spend far more in the years ahead. The group flooded US negotiators with information about Chinese markets and the trade barriers they wanted dismantled as part of a 'commercially meaningful' agreement for China's entry into the WTO.[28]

The corporate lobby not only secured the passage of the Permanent Normal Trading Relations (PNTR) Act, 'normalizing' relations with China under Clinton; it was also able to muster Washington's strong support for China's entry into the World Trade Organization in 2001.

China fulfilled most of its WTO commitments on time, and foreign businesses immediately benefited from the measures that followed China's accession,[29] so that by 2003, 'roughly 70 per cent of US firms surveyed in China reported that Chinese domestic reforms had improved their business climate "to a great extent" or "to a very great extent".'[30] Corporate America's support for strong trade and investment ties with China would remain firm through succeeding administrations until the Trump presidency, when some actors would start peeling off, owing to fears of China's stealing a march on them in advanced technologies.

While the China-US TNC alliance was based on mutual interest, their strategic goals were different. The TNCs were out to exploit Chinese labour for super-profits. China offered its manufacturing labour force for exploitation, but its goal was to gain the investment and technology needed to comprehensively develop the economy. As Leo Panitch and Sam Gindin pointed out, in pursuit of its strategic goal the Chinese leadership used foreign investment as a substitute for a domestic capitalist class. Indeed, in the halcyon years of the first decade of the twentieth century, they favoured foreign over domestic capital, this preference being 'expressed in various ways, including the tax system, subsidies, trade regulations, and access to finance'.[31]

At some point in the future, however, when China would have built up its industries and begun a self-sustaining process of developing advanced technology, the common interest that originally propped up the alliance would be superseded. Beijing, however, had seen this divergence from the very beginning, and was confident of being able to manage foreign capital precisely because it was, to a degree not paralleled by any other country, largely independent of foreign capital and its main protector, the US government.

What the TNCs and Washington failed to appreciate at the outset, blinded as they were by the prospects of super-cheap labour, was that the Chinese state was not like previous client regimes that had been integrated by force into global capitalism. The Chinese state was the product of a nearly three decade long successful popular national revolution and had gone on to stop US forces in Korea in the 1950s, and to play a decisive role in assisting the Vietnamese to win their war against Washington in the 1960s. The Chinese state was far stronger than even the South Korean and Japanese states, whose capacity to resist Washington's economic and political demands was limited by their structural subordination to the US state, as a protectorate in the case of South Korea, and a defeated and occupied rival state in the case of Japan.

The cost of China's willingness to have its workers exploited was considerable. A recent estimate shows that for the period 1960-2018, among countries of the global South, China suffered the greatest loss in terms of value transfer – or unequal exchange – to the global North, some $19 trillion.[32] But from the Communist Party's perspective, the cost in the short- and medium-term of allowing global capital to exploit China's labour in return for comprehensive development of the economy – and securing its own legitimacy in the process – was a devil's bargain that had been worth making. By the end of the second decade of the twenty-first century, moreover, the relative power of Beijing's foreign corporate allies had been reduced by the combination of a decade-long stagnation in the US market, followed by a Covid-19 recession, and by China's technological advances, although there are sectors where American high-tech companies remain important.

THE CHINESE MOMENT AND WHAT PRODUCED IT

In the interval, the alliance between corporate America and China's communist party elite made possible the swiftest rise in history of a nation state from a marginal status in the global capitalist economy to its very summit

– the latter moment marked by President Xi Jinping's appearance in Davos in January 2017 to claim the mantle of being the leader of globalization.

Several conditions external to China facilitated this phenomenal ascent. First was the fact that China appeared on the scene as the provider of the cheapest accessible labour in the world at a time when the US corporate elite was tearing up their informal social contract with labour that had prevailed during the so-called 'thirty golden years' from the late forties to the late seventies.

Second, China's emergence as an export-led industrial power coincided with the TNCs perfection of a revolutionary way of dispersing the different phases of production according to the complementary logics of labour cost reduction, locational advantage, and fiscal advantage, to gain maximum profitability, a process that came to be known as 'global value chains'. A key innovation here was the development of containerized shipping:

> Prepacking goods at the factory into standardized metal containers revolutionized [the shipping] process. The same box could be used interchangeably across all modes of transportation. Trucks and trains could arrive at a port, drop off their cargo, get new containers, and roll off to their next destination in a matter of minutes. Even heavy containers could be moved quickly and safely by a handful of people using cranes. The hard work of packing and unpacking would only be done at the beginning and end of the entire trip, rather than at the beginning and end of each leg.[33]

Third, China benefited from the reduction of tariffs and elimination of quotas that came with the establishment of the World Trade Organization, which China joined, with the US virtually acting as wedding sponsor, in 2001. While US free trade ideologues and trade technocrats had promoted the WTO in the belief that the US, being the 'most competitive' economy in the world, would gain most, it was actually China that proved to be its greatest beneficiary. Among other things, it meant that China did not have to struggle for markets with the force of arms or coercion, which all other previous rising capitalist powers had had to employ.

A CAPITALIST POWER *SUI GENERIS*

There was no doubt that even as Chinese leaders continued to describe China's political economy with variants of Deng Xiaoping's 'Socialism with Chinese Characteristics', by the end of the second decade of the twenty-first century China was a capitalist country.[34] The market relations that had been experimentally initiated in the countryside in the late 1970s, and spread to the cities in the 1980s, had become the dominant economic relations. Non-strategic sectors of the economy, which meant most of the economy, had been privatized and were marked by intense competition.

While market signals stemming from local consumer demand and global demand became the dominant determinant of resource allocation, the visible hand of the state did not disappear, although it became, as some analysts put it, 'smarter'. While departing from central planning, the Chinese state did not follow the Northeast Asian developmental state model that restricted, if not banned, foreign investment in the domestic market. Most economic sectors were opened up to competition among state-owned enterprises, private businesses, and foreign investors, with regulation devolved to local authorities. In contrast, in sectors considered strategic from the point of view of national security, national interest, or overall 'national competitiveness', large-scale foreign investment was managed in ways that enabled the state 'to transfer foreign technology, increase the national technology base, encourage indigenous technology and production capacity, and promote domestic business'.[35] In other words, China allowed foreign investors to come in and exploit its labour and its market, and permitted market forces to reign in most sectors of the economy, but made sure that when it came to strategic, cutting-edge technologies, the TNCs would turn these over. That was the quid pro quo, and most TNCs agreed, if reluctantly, allowing the prospects of profits in the short term to distract them from the risk that they were agreeing to terms that could make them unnecessary to China in the long term.

Given the massive pullback of the state from large swathes of the economy, it is understandable that China's political economy has been described by David Harvey as 'neoliberal with Chinese characteristics'.[36] But this obscures the essence of the Chinese strategy: allowing short-term exploitation of its labour and domestic market in return for rapid, comprehensive development and technology transfers, the terms of which were enforced by a strong state beholden to no imperial power or foreign corporate class, developments that would serve as the foundation of its long-term legitimacy.

CHINA'S RULING CLASS AND ITS FACTIONAL STRUGGLES

This brings us to the question of who rules China? Privatization and the opening to the world have made many Chinese rich. Forbes, for instance, lists 399 billionaires, number one being Jack Ma, founder of the online e-commerce giant Ali Baba.[37] But one can hardly characterize these capitalists as constituting a ruling class. They may individually be exceptional, but their political power and even economic weight is extremely limited, a reality underlined by President Xi Jinpng's scuttling of Ma's Ant Group's initial public offering of $37 billion in November 2020, after Ma made a speech critical of China's economic authorities.[38] The truth is that China's capitalists live with constant apprehension of what the real bosses might do to them should they incur their displeasure, as Ma did.

China's real boss, its ruling class, is the Chinese Communist Party (though this is far from being the dictatorship of the proletariat that Lenin envisioned as the role to be played by a Communist party in the construction of socialism). Rather than engage in theoretical debates revolving around an ideal-typical capitalist ruling class, one should begin with the concrete facts about the CCP.

First, the basic fact is that its situation is not that of a political elite responding to a national capitalist class that has led the way in creating a capitalist economy. Rather, it is a political elite that has led the development of a capitalist economy in partnership with foreign capital, creating, as a by-product, a national capitalist class dependent for its survival on the elite's power to protect and advance its interests on the global stage.

Second, this elite had a strong material presence in the productive process via its control of some 150,000 state-owned central and provincial enterprises that competed and checked the private sector domestically, some of which were in the vanguard of the economy's global expansion.[39]

Third, the state elite controlled instruments which were as powerful as market forces in guiding the development of the economy: the array of technocratic fiscal, monetary, and trade policy tools that it had adopted from the west but joined to a mercantilist, nation state-centred perspective. The CCP was not, in this sense, qualitatively different from the Japanese, Korean, and Taiwanese developmental states. They were all examples of bureaucratic elites that spawned their capitalist classes. The difference lies in the degree of autonomy it had from the capitalist classes it created, and one might say that among its neighbouring Asian states the CCP elite's autonomy was the greatest. Indeed, perhaps the better formulation is that China's nascent private capitalists have little autonomy from the CCP ruling class.

While ascendant over society and any class, the CCP is not monolithic. It is perhaps best to describe the party as the canopy within which different party factions, or coalitions, associated with certain policies, ministries, regions, and enterprises struggle for dominance, though within limits imposed by the party structure, traditions, informal understandings, and the internal power equation. The dominant coalition may be termed the 'power bloc', by which is meant the group or coalition of groups whose interests the country's political economic configuration primarily serves. To determine which is the reigning power bloc, it is useful to look at the struggle over economic policy over the last three decades.

One identifiable faction consisted of the liberalizers, who were committed to transforming the economy into a more full-fledged capitalist economy, marked by a stronger role for market forces, which they believed would promote a more efficient allocation of resources. This faction, led by President Jiang Zemin and, in particular, Prime Minister Zhu Rongji in the 1990s, was dominant until the mid-2000s, when more statist forces in the central bureaucracy and provinces pushed back, limiting any further comprehensive liberalization that would endanger the activist developmental role of the state.[40]

This second faction was the set of interests that had developed and congealed around the export-oriented strategy that had made China the 'world's manufacturer'. This coalition of elites, whose geographical base was the coastal provinces of southeastern China, writes Hung, 'had germinated after China's initial opening to the world ... grew in financial resources and political influence with the export boom and became increasingly adept at shaping the central government's policy in their favour. Their growing leverage in the central government's policy-making process secured the priority given to enhancing China's export competitiveness and the country's attraction to foreign investment.'[41] The posture of this group was to embrace the opening of foreign markets made possible by the WTO agreement, while being more selective or resistant when it came to domestic market liberalization and the dilution of the role of the state it promoted.

A third grouping was made up of party leaders, government officials, and state-owned enterprise (SOE) managers from the western and inland regions that felt that their areas had been left behind by an economic growth process that gave pride of place to the coastal regions, one that had its roots in Deng Xiaoping's policy of letting some regions develop first, instead of always ensuring balanced development. Complex and fluid alliances marked the relations of these groups with one another, though the two main rivals appeared to be the liberalizers and the export lobby.

This is not the place to discuss the evolution of coalition politics.[42] Suffice it to say here that Xi Jinping, who emerged from the coastal export-oriented lobby, has made a determined push to be seen as a unifying leader of all factions since he became president in 2012. There are three major thrusts of this effort. First is a tough campaign against corruption in all quarters of the party, including in the favoured eastern coastal regions, which some say has also been a way to undermine his political rivals. Second is his Belt and Road

Initiative, which has been promoted as a 'win-win' solution for all factions, and one especially gratifying to the relatively underdeveloped western provinces, owing to its Eurasian thrust. Third has been the promotion of his vision of bringing about both the 'Chinese Dream' of higher living standards for all, and 'national rejuvenation'.

UNBALANCED CAPITALIST DEVELOPMENT

Like its East Asian neighbours whose route it followed as a fast-growing export-oriented economy, China's breakneck capitalist development has been marked by severe imbalances. For one, regional disparities have increased, as authorities prioritized the development of the eastern and southeastern coasts in order take advantage of seaborne global trade. Also, China's industrialization became synonymous with environmental degradation, with ecological crises boomeranging on the economy. Economists have estimated that environmental degradation and pollution cost the Chinese economy the equivalent of 3 to 10 per cent of GDP owing to workdays missed, crops lost to pollution and contamination, a decline in tourism, and other problems. A recently published retrospective analysis by the Chinese Academy of Sciences placed the figure higher, at 13.5 per cent of GDP in 2005.[43]

China's breakneck capitalist growth, relying on cheap labour, has had two contradictory effects on the socio-economic conditions of its people. On the one hand, the proportion of people living in extreme poverty declined from 88 per cent in 1988 to 2 per cent at present.[44] On the other hand, it has converted it from one of the world's most egalitarian societies during the Mao period to one of the world's most unequal societies. Research by Branco Milanovic, one of the world's leading experts on inequality, shows that in the period 1988 to 2008, income inequality in China rose far more rapidly than in any other region in the world.[45]

Estimates of China's Gini Index or Gini Coefficient, the most commonly used measure of inequality, range from 0.47, the government's estimate, to 0.55.[46] As Arthur Kroeber notes, 'If we accept the government's figure, China's income inequality is substantially greater than all developed countries. More important, it is much greater than in the successful East Asian economies it emulates (Japan, South Korea, and Taiwan) or even India – a country long infamous for its extremes of wealth and poverty.'[47]

Class-related inequality has recently been joined by gender-related inequality as a great source of concern. Ironically, as China has become more prosperous, the gap between women's incomes and economic status and those of men has increased. With the headlong rush towards capitalism, the earnings of women went down from 80 per cent of those of men at the start of the reform era to 67 per cent in the cities and 56 per cent in the countryside.[48]

China is also burdened with an overcapacity problem, especially in heavy industry and many medium industries. There has been significant overcapacity in the steel, iron, aluminum, and automobile industries, leading to practically flat prices and causing some analysts to say that China is now suffering from 'industrial deflation'.[49] Since China accounts for a great part of global production and trade in heavy goods, its surpluses in these goods have brought down global prices, contributing to global deflationary pressures in the capital goods sector.

Overcapacity is a symptom of overaccumulation, and it is a product of the Chinese way of capitalism. Specifically, it is due to the repression of domestic consumption and excessive investment. Repression of consumption was a policy dictated by the need to channel savings towards the industrial export sector. Excessive investment stemmed from the decentralized economic strategy where local areas were given a great deal of autonomy in investment decisions. Many local authorities, says Hung, perhaps the leading expert in China's overproduction, act 'developmentally', that is, they pick industrial 'winners' and act proactively to set these up at the local level. The totality of these efforts, however, 'creates anarchic competition among localities, resulting in uncoordinated construction of redundant production capacity and infrastructure. Foreign investors, with the expectation that the domestic and world market for Chinese products will grow incessantly, also race with one another to expand their industrial capacity in China.'[50]

Overcapacity is not a problem that has only surfaced recently. As early as the 2000s, in fact, more than 75 per cent of the country's industries were suffering from overcapacity, and fixed asset investment in industries already experiencing overinvestment accounted for 40 to 50 per cent of China's GDP growth.[51] The situation, however, has worsened since then, with state media reporting 21 industries suffering from 'serious' overcapacity, a list that includes cement, aluminum, shipbuilding, steel, power generation, solar panels, wind turbines, construction machinery, chemicals, textiles, paper, glass, shipping, oil refining, and heavy engineering.[52]

To solve the overcapacity problem, China has tried to shut down the less efficient enterprises and 'rationalize' the remainder. This is, however, easier said than done, because officials are scared of provoking worker unrest, since the ability to maintain social stability is one of the key justifications used by the Communist Party for its continued political dominance. Moreover, shutting down enterprises may be demanded from the centre but it is the local authorities that have to deal with the consequences, and so the natural response of the latter is to dig in their heels. Over time, alliances of local officials and enterprise managers have evolved strategies for keeping 'zombies' alive, the key elements of which are subsidizing them, incessantly borrowing from state banks to keep them going while staving off demands for repayment, and engaging in 'internal protectionism', or keeping out competing products from other localities.[53]

The result is that keeping 'zombies', which are mainly SOEs, alive has been extremely costly. Overcapacity brings down prices, bringing down profits throughout an industry. Indebtedness becomes a permanent condition, so that one can speak of a permanent line of credit to banks which is never repaid. Calculations of the levels of debt of the public and private corporate sector in China are not easy to come by, but according to the consulting firm McKinsey, China's companies went from owing $3.4 trillion to $12.5 trillion between 2007 and mid-2014, 'a faster buildup of debt than in any other country in modern times'.[54]

Such massive indebtedness, mainly to Chinese state banks, clearly poses a threat to the economy. But China is no ordinary capitalist economy. Under normal capitalism, when loans are nonperforming, the banks come calling on the debtor and either collect or force them into bankruptcy. But in China, the fact that the state enterprises and the banks are owned by the government places the day of reckoning far into the future. As Dinny McMahon writes: 'The real advantage of China's system of state ownership isn't that the clean-up is easier than in market economies; it's that the clean-up is easier to put off, something that it can do indefinitely but not forever.'[55]

There is, in addition to these problems, China's continued dependence on many advanced technologies from the West, despite the fact that, as Lin Chun observes, the 'government has repeatedly pledged to "rebalance" and "move China up the value chain"'.[56] The technology lag poses a serious threat to Beijing's effort to shake itself free from its dependence on American corporations, despite having successfully pushed many of them to share technology in the past. Indeed, it seems that despite what some have seen as the ascendancy of a more statist orientation under Xi Jinping, regulators are reluctant to 'enforce conditions on foreign investment for technological transfer and diffusion'.[57] The reason may be the government's sense that patience is the better part of wisdom when dealing with TNCs whose technology you need badly.

CRISES OF GROWTH VERSUS CRISES OF DECLINE

China undoubtedly has mounting problems. Perhaps the surplus capacity problem is the most serious. There are also environmental crises and the growing inequality. In fact, dislocations created by breakneck industrialization have triggered mass protests throughout China. Before official media stopped publishing statistics on 'mass incidents' after 2008, such events went from 10,000 in 1994, increasing yearly, with 58,000 in 2003, 74,000 in 2004, and more than 100,000 in 2008.[58]

Protests range from rural actions against land grabs by local authorities in rural areas, to workers' strikes and environment-related mobilizations. While repression appears to be the dominant response to peasant protests, there have also been concessions, such as 'people's centred governance' focused on providing better social welfare benefits and restraining local officials during the Hu Jintao-Wen Jiabao era.

Authorities have been more careful in the cities, where tactical tolerance and concessions have also been part of the government response. In 2018, with the economy slowing down, there were 1,700 workers' actions throughout China, protesting mainly against unpaid wages and factory relocations, up from 1,250 in 2017. While there were reports of protesters and activists being arrested, one analyst monitoring workers' actions said there were 'far too many protests to crack down on' and in most cases the police didn't get involved.[59] Moreover, according to labour researcher Elaine Hui, the Chinese government seems to be aware that union reform could help stabilize labour relations and has made cautious moves to 'strengthen enterprise-level union organizations, along with implementing pilot workplace union elections and collective bargaining'.[60] There has, however, been a pushback under Xi.[61]

Environment-related protests have also been widespread, though most of these apparently take place on the internet. Owing to its large support from the middle class, the government is perhaps more sensitive in the area of the environment than in its handling of labour and peasant protests. Civil society organizations and personalities have been allowed much space to air grievances, although this is narrowing.

The government's oscillation between the iron fist and the velvet glove reflects its nervousness about manifestations of instability. In fact, the Communist Party is obsessed with stability, which is the reason party and government officials often go to great lengths to ensure that worker discontent does not spill out into the streets, by making concessions such as keeping loss-making state enterprises on life support. As McMahon observes, 'one protest above a certain size automatically puts an official's promotion prospects on ice'.[62]

Despite the party's fears, the vast majority of protests are single-issue affairs, motivated by concerns about the welfare of local communities or groups. As a rule, protesters don't reach out across localities to other groups with 'systemic demands'. Some analysts have wondered why there are so few protests calling attention to conditions of great inequality that have become comprehensive and systemic, as in other countries. There is, of course, fear of repression, like the massacre at Tiananmen Square in 1989. But perhaps equally or more important, some point out, is that while inequality has indeed grown, incomes have risen even faster. Average per capita income in China rose between 1988 and 2008 by 229 per cent, ten times the global average of 24 per cent and far ahead of the rates for India (34 per cent) and other developing Asian economies.[63] 'For most of the past three decades, all boats have been rising,' one analyst speculates, 'and most people pay more attention to their own boat than the boats that have risen higher … They may, in short, have bought into Deng Xiaoping's motto early in the reform era that "some people and some regions should be allowed to prosper before others".'[64]

The crises in China might be said to be 'crises of growth' stemming from rapid industrialization. People have responded with protests and mass actions, but few students of China would claim that the ruling regime is undergoing a crisis of legitimacy. There is little challenge to the CCP's political and ideological hegemony, except from democracy and human rights activists who, brave and exemplary though they may be, are few and far between.

The situation is different from the United States, where the crises might be labelled 'crises of decline'. The US's crises are directly related to the rise of China. One of the more solid accounts ties the US's industrial decline directly to China's entry into the World Trade Organization in 2001:

> For American manufacturers, the bad years didn't begin with the banking crisis of 2008. Indeed, the US manufacturing sector never emerged from the 2001 recession, which coincided with China's entry into the World Trade Organization. Since 2001, the country has lost 42,400 factories, including 36 per cent of factories that employ more than 1,000 workers (which declined from 1,479 to 947), and 38 per cent of factories that employ between 500 and 999 employees (from 3,198 to 1,972). An additional 90,000 manufacturing companies are now at risk of going out of business.[65]

Long before the banking collapse of 2008, such key US industries as 'machine tools, consumer electronics, auto parts, appliances, furniture, telecommunications equipment, and many others that had once dominated the global marketplace suffered their own economic collapse'.[66] Employment in manufacturing dropped to 11.7 million in October 2009, a loss of 5.5

million or 32 per cent of all manufacturing jobs since October 2000. The last time fewer than 12 million people worked in the manufacturing sector was right before the beginning of the Second World War, in 1941. In October 2009, there were more people officially unemployed (15.7 million) than were working in manufacturing.[67]

Not all of these cases of deindustrialization were caused directly by relocation to China. And not all the manufacturing jobs lost were lost to China. However, relocating to China was a central contributor. Contrary to neoliberal claims, a landmark study concluded that in the US, 'adjustment in local labor markets is remarkably slow, with wages and labor-force participation rates remaining depressed and unemployment rates remaining elevated for at least a full decade after the China trade shock commences. Exposed workers experience greater job churning and reduced lifetime income. At the national level, employment has fallen in US industries more exposed to import competition, as expected, but offsetting employment gains in other industries have yet to materialize.'[68]

The 'China Shock' is estimated, conservatively, to have led to the loss of 2.4 million American jobs.[69] This, in turn, was one of the triggers of the 'Trump Shock' – Donald Trump's election to the presidency in 2016, owing largely to his winning key deindustrialized mid-western states.

Loss of industries and jobs to China, however, was not the only cause of the United States' troubles. Also important was the redistribution of income to the rich through, among other measures, radical tax reform that brought down the marginal tax rate on the highest incomes from 91 per cent in 1950-63 to 39.6 per cent in 1987-2002.[70] A third key cause was financialization, or the US economic elite's turn to the financial sector as the key driver of its quest for regaining its profitability; and it was the overreach of the speculative economy that triggered the financial implosion of 2008, from which the United States had never really recovered by the time Covid-19 came around. Globalization, income redistribution through fiscal reform, and financialization were the three prongs of the 'neoliberal revolution', the key economic outcome of which, by the middle of the second decade of the twenty-first century, was financial implosion, stagnation, and extreme income inequality. Describing the outcome, Thomas Piketty writes, '[I] want to stress that the word "collapse" [in the case of the US] is no exaggeration. The bottom 50 per cent of the income distribution claimed around 20 per cent of national income from 1950 to 1980; but that share has been divided almost in half, falling to just 12 per cent in 2010-2015. The top centile's share has moved in the opposite direction, from barely 11 per cent to more than 20 per cent.'[71]

IDEOLOGICAL DISILLUSIONMENT IN THE UNITED STATES

Stagnant incomes, worsening income distribution, and a strong sense that Democrats no longer represented their interests, but those of the highly educated and minorities, opened the white middle and working classes to mobilization by the far right.[72] Class anger and racial resentments stoked by dog-whistle or racially-coded rhetoric resulted in the expansion and consolidation of Trumpism, with its informal ideology of white supremacy. The interaction of class anger and racist and nativist resentment greatly contributed to Trump's gaining 11 million more votes in 2020 than he did in 2016, with some 58 per cent of whites voting for him. This was also the volatile formula – the channeling of class resentments into racial anger – that exploded in the 6 January 2021 'insurrection' in Washington. As the philosopher Charles Mills pointed out,

> The psyche of white citizens is foundationally shaped not merely by rational expectations of differential social and material advantage, but also by their status positioning above Blacks. For a significant percentage of white Trump supporters (I don't want to say all), I think the hope was that Trumpism – tapping into their 'white racial resentment' – would address and eliminate both of these dangers, the ending of differential white material advantage and also the threatened equalization of racial status. … What we saw on January 6 was in significant measure the acting out of the rage at this prospect.[73]

For all intents and purposes, the US is today in a state of undeclared civil war, and the reason is not just economic pain caused by neoliberal policies but intense political polarization on racial lines and the loss of the glue provided by a common ideology.

Societies have ideologies that cut across social classes, and when they can no longer do that, that has international implications. In the United States, the ideology that performed that function had two prime manifestations. One was the so-called 'American Dream', or the Horatio Alger myth, that was based on the deeply held belief that the society's class structure was fluid and that if one worked really hard one could rise above the class in which she or he was born. The other was the centrepiece of the US's engagement with the world, the sense that the mission of America was to spread democracy, American-style, around the globe.[74]

By the end of the first decade of the twenty-first century, evoking these two fundamental ideological pillars of domestic solidarity and international hegemony could only evoke great skepticism. Except perhaps for immigrants, the American Dream vanished in the aftermath of the 2008 financial crisis and its terrible toll of millions of house foreclosures. The spreading-democracy myth was dealt a severe blow by the Vietnam War, and an attempt to resurrect it as a justification for the invasion of Iraq in 2003 evoked universal disapproval. By the middle of the second decade of the twenty-first century, the thrust of domestic consciousness was no longer outwards but inwards, and Trump's 'America First' rhetoric fit the mood of much of the country, though the left and the right differed in what the inward turning should focus on.

CRAFTING A NEW IDEOLOGY IN CHINA

In contrast, China, though it had tensions associated with breakneck industrialization, was not suffering from polarization. Partisans of western-style democracy were, as noted above, a very small minority, though spontaneous feelings of alienation against the authorities were expressed widely on the internet. Moreover, the critical importance of ideology was recognized by the astute Xi Jinping, who wrote: 'The disintegration of a regime often starts from the ideological arena, political unrest and regime change may perhaps occur in a night, but ideological evolution is a long-term process. If the ideological defenses are breached, other defenses become very difficult to hold.'[75] The domestic political and ideological unravelling of the United States in the Trump era would probably have been taken by Xi Jinping as a confirmation of his concerns and why he was right to take a pre-emptive strategy when it came to China.

In his landmark speech to the nineteenth Congress of the Chinese Communist Party, Xi delivered his ideological clarion call, laying out the two goals of shared prosperity and revival of the Chinese people:

Never forget why you started, and you can accomplish your mission. The original aspiration and the mission of Chinese Communists is to seek happiness for the Chinese people and rejuvenation for the Chinese nation … In our Party, each and every one of us must always breathe the same breath as the people, share the same future, and stay truly connected to them. The aspirations of the people to live a better life must always be the focus of our efforts. We must keep on striving with endless energy toward the great goal of national rejuvenation.[76]

On the international front, as Trump proclaimed 'America First' and alienated the US's traditional allies with accusations that they were taking advantage of the US, Xi saw an opportunity and dashed off to major international meetings in a bid for global political and ideological leadership.

At Davos, the Mecca of global capitalism, in January 2017, Xi confidently stated that 'the global economy is the big ocean you cannot escape from', and in which China had 'learned to swim'.[77] He called on world political and corporate leaders to 'adapt to and guide globalization, cushion its negative impacts, and deliver its benefits to all countries and all nations'. More importantly, he painted China as the engine of global growth that would counter the secular stagnation gripping the world economy:

> China's development is an opportunity for the world; China has not only benefited from economic globalization but also contributed to it. Rapid growth in China has been a sustained, powerful engine for global economic stability and expansion. The inter-connected development of China and a large number of other countries has made the world economy more balanced. China's remarkable achievement in poverty reduction has contributed to more inclusive global growth. And China's continuous progress in reform and opening-up has lent much momentum to an open world economy.[78]

More than this, Xi offered to back up his words with the $4 trillion Belt and Road Initiative (BRI). Evoking the fabled 'silk routes' through which trade between China and Europe was carried out in early modern times, Xi told his rapt audience of hungry corporate chieftains,

> More than 40 countries and international organizations have signed cooperation agreements with China, and our circle of friends along the 'Belt and Road' is growing bigger. Chinese companies have made over 50 billion US dollars of investment and launched a number of major projects in the countries along the routes, spurring the economic development of these countries and creating many local jobs. The 'Belt and Road' initiative originated in China, but it has delivered benefits well beyond its borders.[79]

The BRI was mainly an effort to solve the pressing problem of overcapacity.[80] But, in a classic case of translating crisis into opportunity, Xi turned it into a beacon in China's push for global political and ideological leadership.

RESHAPING THE MULTILATERAL ORDER

Like the gold standard upheld by Britain in the nineteenth century, the dollar's role as the world's reserve currency was a central mechanism by which the hegemony of the United States has been exercised over the global economy. Unlike in the case of Britain, however, US hegemony has also been mediated by supra-national, 'multilateral' institutions, where Washington has provided political and ideological leadership by virtue of its economic primacy. These institutions might be said to serve as the political canopy of global capitalism, setting the rules of monetary exchange, finance, trade, investment, and development assistance that participants in the system need to conform to on pain of incurring economic and, sometimes political, sanctions. While promoted as beneficial for all, as free trade was by the British in the nineteenth century, these rules respond primarily to the interests of the United States. The three key institutions of what came to be called the 'Bretton Woods system', were the International Monetary Fund (IMF), the World Bank, and the World Trade Organization (WTO). At their zenith in the mid-1990s, when the WTO was established, the role of the IMF was to do away with barriers to capital flows; the World Bank would transform developing countries into free market economies; and the WTO, which a former Director General, Mike Moore, called the 'crown jewel of globalization', would lead in eliminating the remaining barriers to corporate-driven international trade.

Even before Trump came to office, the three institutions were suffering from a crisis of legitimacy. The IMF was associated with the imposition of austerity programmes not only in the global South, but also in Europe following the 2008 global financial crisis. The World Bank had gained the reputation of being the most aggressive institutional advocate of neoliberal policies, and the failure of those policies, as shown by the increase in poverty in parts of the global South and the sharp rise in inequality throughout the South, had so discredited them that even economists who had led in formulating them disowned them.[81]

Perhaps even more consequential, efforts for over 50 years to change the capital allocations and voting power at both the Fund and the Bank in favour of countries of the global South, as well as the so-called emerging economies, had borne little fruit: the United States and Western European countries maintained a tight grip on both institutions. Alienation on the part of the global South was exacerbated by the US and Europe disavowing meritocracy and insisting on what many regarded as the feudal privilege of having the head of the IMF always being a European and that of the World Bank an American.[82]

As for the WTO, owing to its loss of control of decision-making, partly because China added heft to the weight of developing countries, in the mid-2000s the US abandoned it as a means of trade liberalization and the enforcement of intellectual property rights, and brought the organization to a standstill and irrelevance by vetoing appointments to its key dispute settlement mechanism.[83]

As the Bretton Woods system faltered, China was in the process of participating in creating an incipient alternative multilateral system. Four key institutions were set up, with Beijing making a central contribution to each: the Asian Infrastructure Investment Bank (AIIB), the New Development Bank, the Contingent Reserve Arrangement (CRA), and the Regional Comprehensive Economic Partnership (RCEP).

First proposed by President Xi Jinping in 2013 to fund Asia's infrastructure needs, the AIIB currently has fifty-two member states, with eighteen prospective members, and a starting capital of $100 billion. The New Development Bank, also known as the 'BRICS Bank', was set up by China, Brazil, Russia, and South Africa in 2015 to support development projects in the global South. The Contingent Reserve Arrangement, also set up with fellow BRICS, was designed to provide emergency financing, much like the IMF. The RCEP brings together the ten members of the Association of Southeast Asian Nations (ASEAN) with China, Japan, South Korea, Australia, and New Zealand, in the world's biggest free trade bloc. RCEP was seen by many to be the answer from China and its close Asian allies to the aborted Trans-Pacific Partnership (TPP) that had, at US insistence, excluded China.

While some have interpreted these moves as China's effort to supplant the US-dominated multilateral system, Beijing has moved carefully on these initiatives, reflecting the same caution that it has displayed on the matter of promoting the renminbi as a reserve currency. Hung asserts that China's effort to build multilateral banks 'should be seen not as a challenge to the existing system of international finance, but as a way to supplement that system that allows China to sacrifice some of its discretionary power to obtain the cover and legitimacy that other participating countries can provide'.[84] To allay concerns among the Americans and Europeans, Beijing points out that it has relied on the advice and cooperation of the IMF and the World Bank in setting them up.

The Chinese are obviously trying to dampen expectations about these institutions since it does not want to be burdened with responsibilities that would be foisted on it should it be perceived as being out to replace the Bretton Woods institutions. So rather than being displaced or taken over by the Chinese, these organizations are likely to just limp along, providing some ideological competition to the Chinese by promoting a private enterprise-led as opposed to a state-led path of development, but unable to compete with them when it comes to resources. What is clear is that when it comes to borrowing money or seeking development aid, more and more countries in the global South are beating a path to Beijing rather than to the IMF and World Bank headquarters in Washington.

China's ability to maximize its unique position in the international system, of being part of the old order but also subverting it, has been shown in what people have termed its 'Covid 19 vaccine diplomacy'. Not only has Beijing prioritized delivering Chinese-made vaccines to Africa and other regions in the Global South, but its companies have already signed agreements with some countries to manufacture the vaccines.[85] In contrast, US pharmaceutical firms have been busy opposing the so-called TRIPS waiver at the WTO that would suspend their so-called intellectual property rights, giving them the unenviable image of sacrificing public health to corporate profits at a time when the health and lives of millions are at stake.

To be sure, the ability of US imperial power to rejuvenate itself must not be underestimated, as it was in 1980s following the stagflation episode, and in the 1990s in the face of the so-called 'Japanese Challenge'. The global sinews of the US corporate network remain powerful, and the technological edge of American Big Tech remains impressive.[86] Such powers of reinvigoration, however, are greatly dependent on the American state.[87] But it is precisely in the area of the US state's capacity to maintain political and ideological cohesion that the problem lies today. Without decisive leadership at the level of the political and ideological the country's infrastructural resources cannot be fully mobilized, and there is deep political and ideological polarization in the US today, something that was not as serious in the 1980s and 1990s.

STRATEGIC COMPETITION

If there is one area where the United States still enjoys an overwhelming advantage over China, it is on the strategic front. In his speech at the nineteenth National Congress of the Communist Party of China on 18 October 2017 – the famous 'Chinese Dream' speech – Xi Jinping laid out a three-stage schedule for China's military modernization, ending at mid-century with the transformation of the military into 'world class forces' that could 'manage crises, and deter and win wars'.[88] One can read that assertion as Xi's admission that the People's Liberation Army was some thirty years behind the US military, universally regarded as the 'world class standard'.

Since the 1990s, the Pentagon has sounded warnings that China was set to become the US's strategic rival. Its concerns were, however, always placed second to the priority of Washington's political and business elites to integrate China into the global economy. With Trump's accession to power, however, China was defined not only as a competitor but as an antagonistic competitor. As the landmark 2017 National Security Strategy paper put it:

For decades, US policy was rooted in the belief that support for China's rise and for its integration into the post-war international order would liberalize China. Contrary to our hopes, China expanded its power at the expense of the sovereignty of others. China gathers and exploits data on an unrivaled scale and spreads features of its authoritarian system, including corruption and the use of surveillance. It is building the most capable and well-funded military in the world, after our own. Its nuclear arsenal is growing and diversifying. Part of China's military modernization and economic expansion is due to its access to the US innovation economy, including America's world-class universities.[89]

As the US's civilian elites engage in what has become unrestricted political warfare, making even a modicum of consensus impossible in most areas, there is one policy on which both liberal and conservative elites concur, and indeed compete to proclaim their adherence to, and that is to maintain the overwhelming military edge of the US state. Also, it is not impossible that as the civilian elites exhaust themselves in fratricidal strife, the military will take a more and more active role in defining the country's overall direction.

How do the United States and China's armed forces compare today? In 2019, US military expenditures were about three times more than China's, $732 billion to $261 billion. Military spending by the US was 5.3 per cent above its level in 2018, while that of China was up by 5.1 per cent.[90] US officials now routinely describe China as a 'Near Peer Competitor'.[91] This is grossly inaccurate, if we use non-partisan indicators.

First of all, in terms of nuclear weapons, Beijing has a relatively small nuclear force that is guided by a 'No First Use' (NFU) doctrine focused on deterring a potential aggressor via the maintenance of a second-strike retaliatory capability. The US has vastly superior nuclear capabilities and it has not adopted an NFU position. China has only about 260 nuclear warheads while at the end of 2017, the US's nuclear arsenal contains something just under 1,400 deployed, and approximately 4,000 stockpiled, warheads.[92]

Second, China's conventional offensive capabilities are grossly inferior to those of the US. Two key indicators of a country's offensive capability are its overseas bases and its aircraft carriers. China has only one overseas military base, and that is located in Djibouti off the Gulf of Aden, from which it participates in anti-piracy activities. The US has scores of military bases surrounding China, twenty-five major bases and sixty other facilities spread all over Japan; fifteen bases in South Korea; three bases in Guam; and five bases in the Philippines.

In terms of aircraft carriers, China has two operational carriers with an antiquated Soviet-era design, while the US has eleven carrier task forces, one of them, the Seventh Fleet, based in Yokosuka, Japan, which can easily be supplemented by another carrier task force from the Eastern Pacific in the event of conflict. US carriers like the recently commissioned USS Gerald Ford are the state of the art, far in advance of anything China has to offer.[93]

Even the Pentagon does not dispute Beijing's strategic posture as 'strategic defense' which 'is rooted in a commitment not to initiate armed conflict, but to respond robustly if an adversary challenges China's national unity, territorial sovereignty or interests'.[94]

The US strategic posture, on the other hand, is offensive. It has three key components.

One is forward deployment, that is to push the presence of US military power as far as possible from the territorial limits of the US and as near as possible to the borders of a likely enemy.

Second is a war fighting strategy called 'Airsea Doctrine'. A key document explicitly points to China as the enemy, and it calls for 'kinetic and non-kinetic (other words, both explosive and electronic) strikes' against inland command centres, radar systems and intelligence gathering facilities, raids against missile production and storage operations, and 'blinding' operations against Chinese satellites. It also says that China's 'seaborne trade flows would be cut off, with an eye toward exerting major stress on the Chinese economy and, eventually, internal stress'.[95]

Third, the US's long-term strategic perspective is 'Overmatch'. According to noted defense analyst Mike Klare, 'Although reminiscent of containment in some respects, overmatch differs from Cold War strategy not only because it presumes two (and possibly more) major competitors instead of just one, but also because it requires a perpetual struggle for dominance in every realm, including in trade, energy and technology.'[96]

China's strategic dilemma is that large parts of the US military forces in the Western Pacific lie right on its doorstep, entrenched in bases on the so-called 'First Island Chain' or at sea in the forward deployed US Seventh Fleet. Most of China's industrial infrastructure and population are located in the country's southeastern and eastern coasts and thus are very vulnerable to US power in the event of conflict.

China's response to this dilemma has been to push its defenses outwards, placing anti-access, anti-denial weapons (A2AD) in maritime formations it seized in the South China Sea from countries like the Philippines. These moves have been justified unilaterally by saying that 90 per cent of the South China Sea belong to China. China's claim to 90 per cent of the South China Sea is illegal and violates the rights of five other countries that border that body of water, but, from a strategic point of view, Beijing believes it is its only option.[97]

Be that as it may, US-China jockeying for power in the South China Sea is creating a very explosive situation, since there are no rules of the game except an informal balance of power, and resorting to balance of power as a regulator of conflict is quite unreliable, as was seen in the case of the European balance of power that resulted in the First World War. Right now, US and Chinese ships are engaged in provocative games of 'chicken' in which jet fighters buzz 'enemy ships' or warships head for their rivals and then swerve at the last minute.

Clausewitz famously wrote that 'war is the extension of politics by other means'. This gives too much weight to rational calculus as the process of determining when to go to war. It grossly underestimates the role of passion. But what is truly dangerous is when passion is joined to rational calculus, such as when the desire to maintain hegemony is attached to a calculable process of when to go to war. Xi Jinping's estimate at the nineteenth Congress that it will be in mid-century that China will have 'world-class forces' that can match those of the United States has perhaps unwittingly given the Pentagon a sense that it has at most a thirty-year window of opportunity – and most likely less – to do something. Will the Pentagon really allow Beijing to achieve strategic equality, which may well be the last step to America's loss of global hegemony?

Graham Allison, the dean of the American security studies establishment, contends that China and the US are on a 'collision course for war – unless both parties take difficult and painful actions to avert it'.[98] To critical observers, a pre-emptive move on the part of the United States, given its bellicose history, is a possibility that cannot be dismissed.

NOTES

1   John Kemp, 'China Has Replaced the US as Locomotive of the Global Economy', *Reuters*, 5 November 2019.

2   Jonathan Cheng, 'China is the only Major Economy to Register Economic Growth for 2020', *Wall Street Journal*, 18 January 2021.

3   For an extensive discussion of these dimensions of China's rise, see, among others, Walden Bello, *China: An Imperial Power in the Image of the West*, Bangkok: Focus on the Global South, 2019.

4   In the immediate post-war period, according to the overcapacity argument, the United States helped revive the economies of Europe and Japan by providing massive aid as well as serving as a market for their goods. But by the early 1970s, the US, Europe, and Japan built up huge industrial capacity that was not matched by available markets, at a time when many parts of the world were too poor to absorb the output

of the industrialized world. In the late seventies and early eighties, the excess capacity was exacerbated by the massive expansion of industrial and manufacturing plants in the newly industrializing countries of East Asia. Overcapacity led to both a decline in the global growth rate and in an even more drastic decline in profitability. See, among others, Robert Brenner, *The Boom and the Bubble*, London: Verso, 2003, pp. 7–47.

5   Thomas Piketty, *Capital and Ideology*, Cambridge: Harvard University Press, 2020, p. 490.

6   Anwar Shaikh, *Capitalism: Competition Conflict, Crises*, New York: Oxford University Press, 2016, p. 66. Shaikh calculates the rate of profit as the result of the aggregate net operating surplus divided by the net capital stock, both in constant dollars.

7   James Pethokoukis, 'Why We Can't Go Back to Sky-High, 1950s' Tax Rates', *AEIdeas*, 18 April 2012.

8   Shaikh, *Capitalism*, p. 664.

9   'Finance Has Always Been More Profitable', *Noahpinion*, 28 February 2013, available at: noahpinionblog.blogspot.jp.

10   Roderick Macfarquhar and Michael Schoenhals, *Mao's Last Revolution*, Cambridge: Harvard University Press, 2006, p. 2.

11   Macfarquhar and Schoenhals, *Mao's Last Revolution*, p. 2.

12   Rosa Luxemburg, *The Accumulation of Capital*, New York: Monthly Review, 1951, p. 368.

13   Luxemburg, *The Accumulation of Capital,* pp. 362–3.

14   Cited in Minqi Li, *The Rise of China and the Demise of the Capitalist World*, New York: Monthly Review Press, 2008, p. 29.

15   Ho-Fung Hung, *The China Boom: Why China Will Not Rule the World*, New York: Columbia University Press, 2017, p. 50.

16   Hung, *The China Boom*, p. 50.

17   For instance, the much read book by Matthew Klein and Michael Pettis, *Trade Wars are Class Wars*, New Haven: Yale University Press, 2020.

18   Mckinsey Global Institute, *The World at Work: Jobs, Pay, and Skills for 3.5 Billion People*, Washington, DC: McKinsey Global Institute, June 2012, p. 6.

19   McKinsey, *The World at Work*, p. 6.

20   Hung, *The China Boom*, p. 69.

21   Lin Chun, 'China's New Globalism', in *Socialist Register 2019: A World Turned Upside Down?,* Leo Panitch and Gregory Albo, eds., London: Merlin Press, 2018.

22   Lin Chun, 'China's New Globalism', p. 70.

23   Shaikh, *Capitalism*, p. 66.

24   United States Trade Representative, *2019 National Trade Estimate Report on Foreign Trade Barriers*, Washington, DC: USTR, 2019.

25   Arthur Kroeber, *China's Economy*, New York: Oxford University Press, 2016, pp. 52–3.

26   Kroeber, *China's Economy*, p. 53.

27   Krober, *China's Economy*, p. 53; and Leo Panitch and Sam Gindin, *The Making of Global Capitalism: The Political Economy of American Empire*, London: Verso, 2013, p. 297.

28   Bob Davis and Lingling Wei, *Superpower Showdown: How the Battle between Trump and Xi Threatens a New Cold War*, New York: HarperCollins, 2020, p. 70

29   Yeling Tan, 'How the WTO Changed China', *Foreign Affairs*, March–August, 2021.

30   Tan, 'How the WTO Changed China'.

31   Panitch and Gindin, *The Making*, p. 296.

32   Jason Hickel, Dylan Sullivan & Huzaifa Zoomkawala, 'Plunder in the Post-Colonial Era: Quantifying Drain from the Global South Through Unequal Exchange,1960–2018', *New Political Economy*, 30 March 2021.

33   Klein and Pettis, *Trade Wars are Class Wars*, p. 25.

34   The Communist Party's efforts to square the circle ideologically is discussed in Lun Chun, 'China's New Globalism'.

35   Roselyn Hsueh, *China's Regulatory State: A New Strategy for Globalization*, Ithaca: Cornell University Press, 2011, pp. 3-4.

36   David Harvey, *A Brief History of Neoliberalism*, Oxford: Oxford University Press, 2007.

37   'China Rich List', *Forbes*, November 2020,.

38   'Chinese President Xi Personally Halted $37 bn Ant IPO', *Al Jazeera*, 20 November 2020.

39   Kroeber, *China's Economy*, p. 99

40   Tan, 'How the WTO Changed China'.

41   Hung, *The China Boom*, p. 72.

42   See Walden Bello, *China: An Imperial Power in the Image of the West*, Bangkok: Focus on the Global South, 2019, pp. 37-41.

43   Bello, *China: An Imperial Power,* p. 158.

44   Max Roser, 'The global decline of extreme poverty – was it only China?', *Our World in Data*, 7 March 2017.

45   Kroeber, *China's Economy*, p. 197.

46   Kroeber, *China's Economy*, p. 197.

47   Kroeber, *China's Economy*, p. 197.

48   Amy Qin, 'A Prosperous China Says 'Men Preferred,' and Women Lose', *New York Times,* 16 July 2019.

49   Nathaniel Taplin, 'Chinese Overcapacity Returns to Haunt Global Industry', *Wall Street Journal*, 10 January 2019.

50   Hung, *The China Boom*, p. 155.

51   Hung, *The China Boom*, p. 155.

52   McMahon, *China's Great Wall of Debt: Shadow Banks, Ghost Cities, Massive Loans, and the End of The Chinese Miracle*, Boston: Mariner Books, p. 43.

53   McMahon, *China's Great Wall of Debt*, p. 43.

54   McMahon, *China's Great Wall of Debt*, p. 31.

55   McMahon, *China's Great Wall of Debt*, pp. 32-33.

56   Lin Chun, 'China's New Globalism'.

57   Lin Chun, 'China's New Globalism'.

58   'Why Protests Are So Common in China', *Economist*, 4 October 2018,. In the three years before he was seized by police in 2016, the indefatigable chronicler of protests, Lu Yuyu, and his girlfriend, recorded over 70,000 outbreaks of social and political protest. Wu Qiang, 'What Do Lu Yuyu's Statistics of Protest Tell Us About the Chinese Society Today?', *China Change*, 6 July 2016.

59   Terry Shelton and Jason Fang, 'China's economic downturn leads to increased worker protests and strikes across the country', *ABC News*, 16 February 2019.60

60 Elaine Hui and Eli Friedman, 'The Communist Party vs. China's Labor Laws', *Jacobin*, 2 October 2018,.

61 Hui and Friedman, 'The Communist Party'.

62 McMahon, *China's Great Wall of Debt*, p. 36.

63 Kroeber, *China's Economy*, p. 199.

64 Kroeber, *China's Economy*, p. 199.

65 Richard McCormack, 'The Plight of American Manufacturing', *The American Prospect*, 21 December 2009.

66 McCormack, 'The Plight of American Manufacturing'.

67 McCormack, 'The Plight of American Manufacturing'.

68 David H. Autor, David Dorn, Gordon H. Hanson, 'The China Shock: Learning from Labor Market Adjustment to Large Changes in Trade', *National Bureau of Economic Research Working Paper*, No 21906.

69 Eduardo Porter, 'Ross Perot's Warning of a "Giant Sucking Sound" on Nafta Echoes Today', *New York Times,* 9 July 9, 2019.

70 Pethokoukis, 'Why We Can't Go Back to Sky-High, 1950s'.

71 Piketty, *Capital and Ideology*, p. 9.

72 Piketty, *Capital and Ideology*, pp. 812-18.

73 Daniel Steinmetz-Jenkins, 'Charles Mills Thinks Liberalism Still Has A Chance', *The Nation*, 28 January 2021.

74 Frances Fitzgerald, *Fire in the Lake*, New York: Random House, 1973, p. 116.

75 Quoted in Economy, *The Third Revolution*, p. 42.

76 Xi Jinping, 'Secure a Decisive Victory in Building a Moderately Prosperous Society in All Respects and Strive for the Great Success if Socialism with Chinese Characteristics for a New Era', Speech delivered at the 19th Party Congress of the Chinese Communist Party, Beijing, 18 October 2017, p. 1.

77 President Xi's Speech to Davos, Jan 26, 2017.

78 President Xi's Speech to Davos, Jan 26, 2017.

79 President Xi's Speech to Davos, Jan 26, 2017.

80 See the extensive discussion of the BRI in Bello, *China: An Imperial Power*, pp. 54-66.

81 See the mea culpa of the Oxford economic guru Paul Collier, who headed the World Bank's Research Development Department from 1998 to 2003, in his *The Future of Capitalism*, London: Penguin, 2018.

82 See Walden Bello, *The Bretton Woods Twins in the Era of Covid 19*, Bangkok: Focus on the Global South, 2020, pp. 19, 25.

83 See Walden Bello, 'Good Riddance to the WTO', *Foreign Policy in Focus*, 20 December 2019.

84 Ho-Fung Hung, 'China and the Global South', in *Fateful Decisions: Choices that will Shape China's Future*, Thomas Fingar and Jean Oi, eds, Palo Alto: Stanford University Press, forthcoming, p. 31.

85 Abigail Ng, 'Developing Countries Are First in Line for China's Covid Vaccines. Analysts Question Beijing's Intent', *CNBC*, 9 December 2020.

86 See, in this connection, Sean Kenji Starrs, 'Can China Unmake the American Making of Global Capitalism', in *Socialist Register 2019: The World Turned Upside Down?*, Leo Panitch and Greg Albo, eds, London: Merlin Press, 2018, pp. 173-200.

87 Panitch and Gindin, *The Making*, p. 331.

88   Xi Jinping, 'Secure a Decisive Victory in Building a Moderately Prosperous Society in All Respects and Strive for the Great Success if Socialism with Chinese Characteristics for a New Era', Speech delivered at the 19th Party Congress of the Chinese Communist Party, Beijing, 18 October 2017, pp. 48-9.

89   White House, *National Security Strategy of the United States of America*, Washington, DC: White House, 2017, p. 25.

90   Matthew Schwartz, 'Global Military Spending is Up, Driven by Two Stop Spenders – the US and China', *National Public Radio,* 29 April 2019.

91   Dan Grazier, 'The Chinese Threat is Being Inflated to Justify More Spending', *Defense News*, 17 February 2021.

92   Eric Gomez, 'US Missile Defense and the Future of Nuclear Stability with China', Paper presented at the International Studies Association Conference, Toronto, March 2019, p. 20.

93   See tabulation of bases and forces in Walden Bello, *The Persistence of Unilateralism: Trump and the Asia Pacific*, Bangkok: Focus on the Global South, 2020, pp. 16-17.

94   US Department of Defense, *Annual Report to Congress: Military and Security Developments Involving the People's Republic of China 2019*, Washington, DC: Department of Defense, 2019, p. 27.

95   Summed up in Bill Hayton, *The South China Sea: The Struggle for Power*, New Haven: Yale University Press, 2014, p. 218.

96   Mike Klare, 'Why 'Overmatch' is Overkill', *The Nation*, 20 December 2018.

97   The only viable peaceful solution to conflicts in the area lies in multilateral negotiations among China and the Southeast Asian countries towards demilitarizing and denuclearizing the area that would demand compliance from third parties like the United States.

MARKET POLARIZATION MEANS POLITICAL POLARIZATION: LIBERAL DEMOCRACY'S ERODING CENTRE

INGAR SOLTY

In the early 1990s, hardly anyone – at least outside the shrunken socialist circles – would have doubted that liberal market economics was the path towards technological innovation and efficiency, economic welfare, and political stability. According to mainstream opinion, liberal economic policy, based on the liberalization of trade, the deregulation of (labour, housing, money, etc.) markets, and the privatization of public assets would lead to prosperity and even to the democratization of authoritarian regimes, even if neoliberalism had to come into existence by authoritarianism.[1] Liberal economics implied that releasing the forces of the market would not simply benefit capital elites, but also tend towards 'spontaneous orders' (as Friedrich Hayek put it) and the most efficient allocation of resources. And if this does not occur, neo-classical economists tend to blame 'state failure' or unforeseeable things such as natural disaster for it.[2]

Actually-existing neoliberalism, however, understood as the social order we have lived in since the 1980s, has led to quite the opposite. Instead of reducing economic and social imbalances, neoliberalism brought about the highest level of wealth inequality since the 1930s, with all its consequences for democracy.[3] Neoliberalism has created vast geographical divergences: between, on the one hand, the global North and the global South, between a eurozone core and periphery, and between prosperous metropolitan regions adapted to the transnationalized economy like the San Francisco Bay Area, the North Carolina 'Research Triangle' or Germany's Rhein-Main area; and on the other hand, dilapidated and depopulated regions like the US Midwest or Germany's Mecklenburg-Vorpommern. Furthermore, it has created the same spatial divergences between functioning inner-city islands of wealth like central Paris or Brussels, and their dysfunctional banlieues such as Paris' Clichy-sous-Bois or Brussels' Molenbeek. And it is no coincidence that hatred for liberal values builds up among segregated and predominantly immigrant working-class populations, some of whom turn to radical religiosity.

The notion that liberal market economies would lead to innovation, efficiency, and economic as well as political stability has also been shattered. In contrast to what the life stories of Bill Gates, Steve Jobs and other high-tech capitalists suggest, the market is far from innovative in itself. As economists such as Mariana Mazzucato have shown, neoliberalism has been the opposite of innovative, given that so many of the innovations of the digital age – any feature you choose to look at inside an iPhone, for example – came out of publicly-funded research projects that were subsequently patented and plundered by private corporations.[4]

Neoliberalism's market efficiency is quite distinct from social efficiency. Beyond mere profitability, how efficient is it, for example, from a wider societal and planetary perspective, to catch fish in the North Sea, transport it to South Asia for processing, and then resell it in British supermarkets? Beyond the narrow market logic behind global supply chains, one thing seems irrefutable: can the impending – and possibly irreversible – climate catastrophe be anything but the biggest market failure in the history of humankind?[5]

Neoliberalism has not led to *economic* stability either – a fact demonstrated not only by uneven geographical divergences but also by the never-ending cascades of financial crises since the 1980s: New York 1987, Mexico 1994-95, Asia 1997-98, Russia 1998-99, Argentina 1998-2002, the Dot.com bubble crash 2000-01, the global financial meltdown 2007-10, and the current Covid-19 bio-economic pandemic hit. The mathematized and de-historicized economic theory that is the ideological buttress for neoliberal policy is based on the assumption of a 'self-regulating' market in which crises, at least in theory, are simply not supposed to occur.[6]

And, finally, neoliberalism has also led to the opposite of *political* liberalism. This should not come as a surprise. Who would be so foolish as to believe that one could have market polarization without political polarization? The history of the 1920s and 1930s has clearly shown that wealth inequalities and capitalist crises always tend to undermine representative democracy, as democratic theorists have always understood.[7] Neoliberalism's 'free markets' have consistently fostered 'strong states' and authoritarian political, administrative, and constitutional practices.

THE CRISIS OF DEMOCRACY

It should therefore come as no surprise that today liberal democracy is again in retreat and in crisis. The stable party systems of the post-war liberal democracies of the West are falling apart in front of our eyes. Former 'catch-all parties' like the French Socialist Party or Greece's PASOK have collapsed, and electoral systems – particularly those based on proportional representation – are increasingly fragmented ('Italianized'), with five, six, or even seven political parties competing to form stable governments, with increasing difficulty.[8] In 'first-past-the-post' electoral systems like those of the US or the UK, grassroots revolts are more or less successfully challenging the eroding 'centre' from within the traditional, dominant parties. To generalize, the 'crisis of centrism' in the neoliberal – and imperial – heartland has created new political tendencies and poles: a fracturing neoliberal centre that encompassed traditional conservative parties and 'third way' social democracy; a right-wing authoritarian nationalism forming as a faction within traditional conservative parties, and in new hard right political organizations; and a class conflict-oriented new socialist left, found in both older parties of the left and new political organizations. This last political development has been most visibly represented by the ultimately defeated surges of Jeremy Corbyn and Momentum within the British Labour Party, and Bernie Sanders and the 'Sanders Democrats' within the Democratic Party in the United States,[9] as well as by new left-wing party formations such as Die Linke in Germany (whose growth has held the rise of right-wing authoritarian nationalism at bay for a time).[10]

The crisis of representation, which the neoliberal turn has brought about, created right-wing populist forces early on. They have been a feature of some Western political systems since the mid-1970s and surged during and since the 1990s, when former social democratic parties also started to promote neoliberal globalization, adopting Margaret Thatcher's political line that 'there is no alternative'.[11] But since 2016 right-wing authoritarian nationalism has proven increasingly capable of winning political majorities and seizing political power: in the US under Donald Trump; in Great Britain with the right-wing populist government of Boris Johnson, strongly influenced by nationalist forces outside the party; and by a plurality of roads to power in Hungary, Poland, Austria, Italy, Brazil, the Philippines, India, Australia, and other countries.

The emergence of a 'new politics' has several forms: of would-be macho strongmen like Trump, Boris Johnson, Narendra Modi in India, Jair Bolsonaro in Brazil, and Austrian Chancellor Sebastian Kurz;[12] the rise of charismatic leaders seeking direct acclamation from 'the people' and sidelining parliaments and traditional public spheres via Twitter or billionaire-owned TV channels; the transformation of a 'large swath of deputies into herdsmen for one or a few "leaders", who form the cabinet and obey blindly, as long as they are successful'.[13] Such a resurgence of a certain 'Caesarism' in politics represents a crisis of liberal-representative democracy and fragmented political party systems. Today, faith in the healing capacities of liberal-representative democracy has taken a hit, not only among the popular classes but among intellectuals too.[14] As early as the 2007 global financial crisis, even ideological promoters and popularisers of neoliberal economics and politics, such as Francis Fukuyama and Thomas L. Friedman, expressed their open envy of the potent statecraft of the Chinese state and its one-party system.[15] Meanwhile, debates about the 'dysfunctionality' of a 'plutocratic' political system were rampant in the United States, suggesting that 'vested interests' were blocking necessary reforms of capitalism.[16]

THE IMPASSE OF NEOLIBERALISM

Even if one dislikes these global historical trends, if one is honest it is difficult to have faith in the problem-solving capacities of neoliberal policy regimes and liberal-representative democracy. This impasse can be sketched across six dimensions, each mutually reinforcing, and in and of themselves capable of pushing global capitalism into a period of political and economic turbulence: (1) a crisis of an over-accumulating global economy with its speculative bubbles of surplus capital seeking profitable investment outlets in asset bubbles in financial markets and in infrastructure development projects of all kinds; (2) a crisis of social reproduction, due to the feminization of the labour market under neoliberal conditions and the 're-familialization' of social reproductive labour resulting from austerity measures; (3) a crisis of social cohesion resulting from neoliberal policies of flexibilization which produce a precaritization of work, now compounded by the insecurities arising from a capital-driven digitization of work, and the transformation of the welfare state into a workfare state; (4) a crisis of liberal democracy in its representative institutions and proliferating forms of authoritarian policy measures and political movements; (5) a crisis of world order connected to the US unwillingness to concede global primacy to a multi-polar world order, notably by attempting to use military and non-military means to keep China in a subordinate position amongst the major powers and in the international division of labour; and (6) a crisis of ecological sustainability with the inability to meet greenhouse targets to avert a climate catastrophe.

In all of this, it is at once striking yet unsurprising that liberal-democratic capitalism has proven to be unable to plan for the future, underscored by the relative ineptitude of the core capitalist states of the West to administer effective public health measures to deal with the Covid-19 crisis. In a societal crisis as pervasive as a pandemic, political parties with a natural claim to power – such as the German Christian Democrats (CDU – Christlich Demokratische Union Deutschlands, in an alliance with the CSU – Christlich-Soziale Union in Bavaria), who have been governing for most of the period since the end of World War II – could have been expected to formulate a grand vision which addressed all levels of this compound crisis in a coherent political project to reconstruct capitalist institutions on a new foundation while incorporating all members of society, from the exploiters to the exploited. Instead, beyond leftist attempts such the British Labour Party's electoral platform of 2019, the socialist Green New Deal suggested by Bernie Sanders, and similar projects proposed by Germany's Die Linke and various other left parties, the political sphere is largely devoid of big schemes and plans. It appears that the bigger the challenges of the multi-dimensional crisis noted above, and the greater the need for bold, radical reforms, the narrower has become the horizon of political leaders. All visions of a 'better tomorrow' seem to have adopted the various cyber-utopias constructed within a liberal political order, ranging from 'liquid democracy' and 'transhumanism' to the colonization of space.[17] In contrast, the liberal-technocratic parties of the political centre, which pose as the opposition to the authoritarianism consolidating on the conservative right on a corroding electoral base, are increasingly short-term, tactical, parliamentarist machines.

As the global financial crisis showed, and as the climate and Covid-19 crises are illustrating again, the liberal-representative systems in the core capitalist states, thoroughly dominated by corporate and billionaire interests, appear to be incapable of addressing fundamental challenges such as climate change, pervasive economic precarity, or a global pandemic. Why should it be any other way? Elections in liberal democracies take place every four or five years; the average rotation time of management in for-profit capitalist enterprises is four years; the internal economic plans of these enterprises tend to be for five years at best. So, the mentality emerging from both political and corporate organizational structures is – let someone else figure out a solution to the climate apocalypse, we need to be re-elected and we need to make profits today or be gone tomorrow.

The general ineptitude of centre-right political parties at recreating bourgeois hegemony under neoliberalism through big reforms from above, however, has a pedigree. The market polarization which the dominant 'catch-all' parties produced over the course of the past four decades threatens to undermine those parties very existence. Strong parties unifying the bourgeoisie and elements of the working class can hardly exist in an economically polarized society. Insofar as political polarization follows from market polarization, a party like Germany's CDU/CSU tends to undermine its very existence. The German conservatives are increasingly incapable of bridging the gap between a younger, urban, professional, and usually academicized workforce in the metropolitan areas, which are economically and culturally adapted to global capitalism, and the older, non-academic, and more localized populations in the provincial areas bypassed or peripheralized by globalization. As a result, the CDU/CSU is being torn apart by two much more homogenous bourgeois parties, namely the Greens, who more and more represent the urban pro-globalization bourgeoisie, and the far-right party AfD (Alternative für Deutschland), who mobilize against the internationalist and diversity culture spawned by globalized capitalism. This process of being torn apart by these contending forces has shown itself in the infighting and struggles over the party leadership after sixteen years of Angela Merkel's chancellorship. The Merkel wing barely managed to install as the new party leader, and hopefully new chancellor, Armin Laschet, who is expected to continue Merkel's project of modernizing the party in accordance with the culture of global capitalism, against an anti-Merkel right-wing revolt from the ranks of the so called 'Values Union' ('Werte-Union'). Nevertheless, it remains clear that such a shift against Merkel's and Laschet's modernization project would risk ceding even more segments of the bourgeoisie to the Greens, while staying the course will keep shedding votes to the far right and the AfD. In short, there are few less attractive political jobs than being a CDU/CSU strategist today.

The weakening of political parties through the centrifugal tendencies of liberal economics, however, reinforces the exhaustion of neoliberalism's problem-solving capacities. In essence, liberal capitalism is haunted by a paradox that both Nicos Poulantzas and Jürgen Habermas observed as early as the 1970s in different ways. Overcoming crises within advanced capitalism, they argued, necessitates tremendous political-managerial capacities and statecraft, but the crises themselves tend to erode the administrative capacities and state powers needed to respond to them. As Poulantzas wrote, in his 1974 book *Fascism and Dictatorship*, trying to explain the rise and appeal of fascism in the 1930s, 'Throughout the rise of fascism we witness a *proliferation* of the organizations (including the parties) of the dominant classes and fractions. This proliferation is characteristic of the impotence and the instability of hegemony; while a non-fascist solution to the crisis would … require the fusion of these organizations into a single party of the bourgeoisie.'[18] It is this erosion of the political brokering needed to resolve crises which also explains the narrowing and self-serving programmatic horizons of the traditional dominant parties. As the German example of the CDU shows, the traditional parties of conservative governance also can become directly self-serving in the form of corrupt personal enrichment through the government deals made to cope with the pandemic.[19]

Whether the Biden administration's surprisingly bold economic and financial policies might demarcate a break from the lack of vision and leadership among the traditional bourgeois parties in the West, and might even help rebuild US hegemony domestically and abroad, remains to be seen. Clearly, the two-party presidential system and the imperial nature of the US state facilitate bolder politics in comparison to the institutionally fragmented party systems of continental Europe and the fractured European Union. A number of factors determine the relative boldness of Biden's fiscal expansionary politics – especially in comparison to Obama's cautiousness. Bidenomics surely underscores the notion that economic and social reforms from above depend on both social pressure from below, like the Sanders Democrats within the party, and external pressures to modernize. In this sense, the hyper-competitiveness that China has achieved through its state interventionism may now encourage a 'passive revolution' in the US and possibly even in the EU. Insofar as China's planned, expansive, and highly active industrial policy proved superior to the West's austerity course during and after the global financial crisis, the West may now actually be forced into a process of emulation, reinforced by the re-localization of manufacturing which the Covid-19 pandemic necessitated.[20]

FROM ANTI-AUSTERITY POLITICS TO AUTHORITARIAN NATIONALISM

The multi-dimensional form of the crisis has, of course, also led to a resurgence of anti-neoliberal opposition. Since 2011 we have seen the largest cycle of 'contentious politics', to use Charles Tilly and Sydney Tarrow's term, since the period of 1967 to 1973.[21] We have been living in a global 'age of mass protests', as not only in the West but all over the world hundreds of millions of people have protested against the impact of austerity.[22] And when it became clear that no matter how many people poured out into the streets (as with the March 2013 'Screw the Troika' protests in Portugal, which mobilized a quarter of the population), governments still continued with their austerity measures, some of these protests were transformed into political projects aimed at state power, like those of Syriza in Greece, Podemos in Spain, and Bloco in Portugal. It had become clear that taking power is a precondition for actually changing the world.[23] The ruling elites' response to the global financial crisis had been strategies of 'internal devaluation' (of wages and costs) in the name of 'competitiveness',[24] the latest incarnation of 'competitive austerity'.[25] But these new left-wing parties and movements outlined a socially inclusive, ecologically constructive exit strategy from the crisis based on 'up-valuation' (instead of de-valuation), that is, a high-road exit strategy of raising wages and working conditions and extending low-carbon, decommodified public services.[26] This core programme is essentially what the left's 'Green New Deal' for social-ecological transformation, across its many incarnations, pivots around.

These movements have, for the time being, been defeated. The thrashing of the Syriza government by the Troika (comprised of the European Central Bank, the European Commission, and the International Monetary Fund), and the rise of the far right in 2015-16 during the European 'refugee crisis', must be seen as connected. Returning to Poulantzas's analysis of the causes of different forms of authoritarian rule, he contended, against the notion that the fascist parties had come to power in the 1930s because of the *strength* of the parties of the socialist labour movement, that it was actually their *weakness* that enabled the right to take power in conditions of deep social and economic crisis.[27] Poulantzas was arguing against Marx's – and Antonio Gramsci's and August Thalheimer's – notion that 'Bonapartism' was the result of an equilibrium in the relationships of forces between capital and labour. Instead, he was convinced that the far right emerges in a situation of economic, social and political crisis when the ruling consensus is radically fragmented, and the labour movement is ultimately too weak to enforce a socialist solution. Seen in this light, the defeat of the global left in Greece and the succeeding rise of the far right must be analyzed together. When we evaluate the rise of Donald Trump in 2015-16, for example, the US could not have been farther away from any such equilibrium in the balance of forces between capital and labour, given that working-class counter-power measured in terms of strike levels, union density and the wage share was at an all-time low.[28] As a result, Trump was elected, against the expressed preference of the majority of the transnationalized fraction of the capitalist class, through a coalition of energy-intensive extractive capital, nationally-centred capital, and a measure of mass support from the working class. And even if, once in power, Trump's economic nationalism was constrained by transnational capital, which showed in both the forming of his cabinet and his subsequent realpolitik, his administration shifted politics well to the right.[29]

As Poulantzas understood, the far right may seize power in situations when the lower classes do not want to live in the old way and no new way is in sight that would lead to a better life for all. The lack of an exit strategy from the crisis based on hope, self-emancipation, and the idea that there is enough for everyone, created and creates the condition for exit strategies based on despair, passive subordination to charismatic leaders, and the political exclusion and isolation of the 'less deserving'. Subjective social powerlessness is right-wing authoritarian nationalism's kerosene.   When radical change is necessary, but the left is too weak to enact the change, it is the far right with its politics of exclusion that fills the void.[30] The weathered belief in self-organization and self-emancipation of the working classes, reflecting the inability of the left to implement its programme and vision, is the foundation for the resurgence of Caesarism, individual Bonapartist figures, and fascist mass movements. 'No saviour from on high delivers/ No faith have we in prince or peer'?[31] Millions of people today would beg to differ.

Opposition to fascism is helpless and powerless as long as its strategies are restricted to moral finger-pointing and appeals to the corporate media to not feature right-wing demagogues, to conservatives not to leave the 'popular front', or to the state to prosecute and possibly outlaw far right parties. You cannot discredit, silence, or outlaw a strong political force with socio-economic roots in the socially polarized world of neoliberalism. Only a visible third pole, beyond neoliberalism and right-wing authoritarian nationalism, with a real and plausible path to relieving the hardships that liberal economics have caused among the working classes, can banish the threat of fascism. If the left offers no more than protection from the global market and its merciless rules, in the name of anti-discrimination, equity, and 'affirmative action' for a few special groups, without formulating a project to overcome the mercilessness of capitalist society for all workers, the resistance to fascism will be doomed.

What is needed is a politics which links struggles against racism, and for feminist emancipation, with struggles for social justice, and which founds them all on materialist politics. The task is to develop a new class politics which is universalist, benefiting all workers regardless of sex, gender, race, and ethnicity, but which at the same time is feminist and anti-racist in essence because it benefits women and minority workers in particular. For instance, the tremendously popular Berlin rent cap, which was introduced by the left government in Germany's capital on 30 January 2020 and was defeated by a political Federal Constitutional Court order on 25 March 2021, can be considered as a new form of feminist and anti-racist class politics. This is because women and migrants are disproportionately represented in the low-wage sector labour force and were therefore also disproportionately represented among the 1.5 million households whose rents were frozen at 2019 levels, and among the 0.5 million households whose rents were lowered.[32] The rent cap, which Die Linke has now turned into a federal political demand, protected migrants from being pushed further into the peripheral districts such as Marzahn-Hellersdorf. And it would also protect women from sexualized violence because it would enable working-class women, who are paid less and often can only work part-time, due to the patriarchal division of reproductive labour, to find affordable housing and leave abusive husbands. Another example of such a new class politics may be the US$15 minimum wage, which benefits all workers insofar as it creates a limit to wage suppression, but which also benefits women and migrant workers in particular, insofar as they are over-represented in the low-wage sectors such as the health and food industries.

THE REVOLT OF THE 'MIDDLE CLASSES' AND THE 'VÖLKISCH' DREAM

Given the social polarization which neoliberalism has brought about, the rise of the far right during the global financial crisis and the preceding years should not come as a surprise. As in all three previous major crises of capitalism (the Long Depression 1873-1896, the Great Depression 1929-1939 and the crisis of Fordism 1967-1979), the far right has also risen in today's multi-dimensional organic crisis.[33] And as in those earlier organic crises it has done so, initially, through a right-wing radicalization of the 'middle classes'.

The 'middle class', in Poulantzian terms the old and new petty bourgeoisie, is especially vulnerable to the appeal of fascism not only because it seeks upward mobility and because its aspirations are therefore tied to the bourgeoisie. In a situation of crisis which undermines its aspirations and confronts it with status panic, its strong belief in meritocracy, its internalization of market competition as a given, its disdain for the working class and its ultimately social-Darwinist crisis consciousness – according to which there is no longer enough for everyone – means that large middle-class segments will seek to protect their economic status by appealing to Bonapartist individuals and the state to punish and exclude the less deserving: the hungry mouths of the Greeks, the hungry mouths of Syrian refugees, and also the hungry mouths of the domestic poor. When solidarity fails, or rather when it is defeated, it turns exclusive: solidarity with the deserving, solidarity with the in-group, the homogenous 'Volk'.

For this, the ideology of 'producerism posits a noble hard-working middle group constantly in conflict with lazy, malevolent, or sinful parasites at the top and bottom of the social order',[34] and leads to the nation, that is, nationalism, directly functioning as the catalyst for those interests in three ways. First, belonging to 'the nation' (and the rights which it guarantees its citizens vis-à-vis latecomers or outsiders) is supposed to protect the individual from the mercilessness of global market forces. Second, belonging to 'the nation' also provides the individual with a form of solidarity, a sense of identity and community, which relieves him or her of the horror of having to live their life as the monadic market individual, the *homo oeconomicus* of neoliberal theory – nationalism serving, in Adorno's words, as a form of 'collective narcissism'.[35] And third, 'the nation' functions as an idealistic and mythical rebuilding of a homogenous society of social cohesion which counteracts, at least ideologically, the centrifugal forces of neoliberalism and its deconstruction of society. This is what makes the 'völkisch' ideology so dangerous: instead of being brought about by the creation of an egalitarian society, based on the common ownership of the vital means of production and a democratization of all spheres of economic and social life, social cohesion is to be brought about, in voluntaristic ways, by means of a national myth and 'the exclusion and annihilation of the heterogenous', that Carl Schmitt, one of the key intellectuals of German fascism, called for in his 1923 book *The Crisis of Parliamentary Democracy*.[36]

The authoritarian appeal to charismatic leaders to ensure, by whatever illiberal means, that the 'legitimate' members of the nation are protected from the forces of the market, while the undeserving are punished, is reinforced by the fact that many members of the 'middle classes' are structurally or social-psychologically unable to seek class solidarity-based exit strategies. The traditional middle class of the self-employed and small-business owners either cannot unionize, or they depend economically on employing and exploiting non-unionized workers, and thus their class interests conflict directly with strategies of class solidarity. Similarly, members of the 'professional-managerial class' may not only have control over other wage-dependent workers but also have internalized the social-Darwinist logic of market competition – from high school grades to personal looks, status and wealth – to the extent that it leads to individual isolation and an authoritarian, cynical, and often misanthropic outlook on the world. If these middle classes fail in their upwardly mobile aspirations, and cannot admit their subjective failure to themselves, they may seek scapegoats to blame. As psychologists know, narcissism is over-compensation for a sense of low self-esteem; and the 'collective narcissism' of nationalism can alleviate the trauma of individual failure, as belonging to a 'successful nation' enables one to feel superior to the 'others'.[37] For instance, Stephan Balliet, the 27-year old who sought to storm the Synagogue in the East German city of Halle, and Tobias Rathjen, the 43-year old right-wing terrorist, who in February 2020 shot nine 'foreigners' in two shisha bars in the west German town of Hanau, were both college dropouts, unemployed, and still living at home with their respective parents. While Balliet considered the Jews responsible for the presence of Muslim migrants in Germany, Rathjen wrote a manifesto in which he expressed a worldview according to which he belonged to the deserving, successful race, as opposed to the low-performing, predominantly Muslim nations of the global South.[38]

RIGHT-WING AUTHORITARIANISM IS A BLIND REVOLT

Right-wing authoritarian nationalism therefore is not false consciousness, but a particular way of interpreting specific social class locations and experiences. Further, it is wrong to say that capital as such is behind fascism today. Historically, certain sectors of the German capitalist class grouped around the Thyssen steel corporation supported Hitler's Nazi Party early on, and by March 1933 the whole bourgeoisie came out in full support of Hitler.[39] It is also true that today some individual billionaires like Peter Thiel, Sheldon Adelson, Charles Koch and August von Finck, Jr., and fossil-fuel and energy-intensive fractions of capital, and domestically-oriented capitals, may support right-wing authoritarian nationalist forces, because they serve their particular class interests. Nevertheless, while historical fascism was functional for the dominant fractions of then still national bourgeoisies and their interest in imperial expansion, today's authoritarian nationalisms and neo-fascisms are dysfunctional for the interests of the transnational capital dominant in the power blocs of the core capitalist countries. In the United States, Donald Trump was nominated through a far-right grassroots revolt during the Republican primaries and came to power against the will of the Fortune 500 corporations.[40] Trump's policies that went directly against the interests of transnational capital, such as the notorious 'Muslim Ban' or legislation hampering the constant influx of super-exploited farm labourers from Central America, were soon blocked by capitalist elites. And when Trump's supporters attempted an insurrection after his electoral defeat, the American bourgeoisie came out strongly against Trump. The Business Roundtable, for example, a group of CEOs representing two hundred of the largest American corporations, including Walmart, Amazon, Delta Airlines, Pfizer, and PepsiCo, demanded an 'end to the chaos' and a 'peaceful transition of power', emphasizing that 'the country deserves better'. The US Chamber of Commerce declared that 'the attacks on the Capitol of our nation and on our democracy need to end now'. Apple's CEO Tim Cook came out demanding that Trump needed to be held accountable for the attack; and the traditionally Republican-leading National Association of Manufacturers even urged Vice-President Mike Pence to replace Trump until Biden's inauguration. Facebook and Twitter suspended or deleted Trump's accounts, while Google and Apple deleted the far-right twitter alternative 'Parler' from their app stores.[41] In short, the dominant, transnationalized fractions of capital in the US were united against a continuation of Trump as president.

The same shifting alliances of capital on the far right applies to Germany. As long as the German far right party AfD does not embrace the euro (the common currency being integral to German capital's transnationalization), the EU (the political stepping stone for future power projection around the world), and NATO and Atlanticism (preconditions for the protection of private property around the world through the military capacities of the American Empire), it cannot expect to gain the support of transnational corporations like Mercedes, BMW, Bosch, Siemens, or Bayer. Nor can the AfD expect to be in national governing coalitions with the Christian Democrats (as the natural ally of transnationalized capital in Germany).

In other words, the rise of right-wing authoritarian nationalism gains its political space in the economic instabilities and centrifugal tendencies that have been integral features of actually-existing neoliberalism. It is, as I have argued, impossible to have economic polarization without political polarization. Those who say yes to economic liberalism are, however much it may be denied, also saying yes to fascism.

While right-wing authoritarian nationalism may be a fallout from the globalization of capitalism, and while it revolts against the modernity of globalized capitalism, it merely attacks the symptoms and never the root causes, that is, capitalism, imperialism, and patriarchy. Hence, authoritarian nationalist movements will, first of all, mobilize against migrants and refugees, but hardly ever address the causes of immigration and the record numbers of people displaced by neoliberal structural adjustment policies, 'free' trade agreements, state failure, and 'racialized and confessionalized' armed conflicts.[42] Second, authoritarian nationalism always makes crime a major theme of its propaganda (as long as it has been committed by people who do not fit into 'völkisch' ideas of homogeneity). Yet it never addresses rampant wealth and income inequality, even though the most unequal countries such as Brazil also happen to be the most crime-infested and insecure countries in the world. And third, authoritarian nationalism expresses a toxic masculinity which seeks to 'put women (back) into their place', to re-establish patriarchal power over women and limit feminist ambitions to distribute the labour of social reproduction equally. But it never tackles the crisis of social reproduction caused by the dual exploitation of paid work and domestic labour for female workers that is the source of the feminist rebellion.

It can be speculated why right-wing authoritarianism only tackles symptoms instead of root causes. Maybe it has to do with the fact that conservatism and fascism, understood as historical conservatism's radicalized form,[43] are *literally reactionary* ideologies which have historically responded and revolted against egalitarian claims from below by maintaining the unequal worth of individuals and groups.[44] Unlike liberalism and socialism, conservatives have never agreed on a coherent state and social theory and a coherent programme for constructing the economy and society. In fact, ever since conservatism's birth in opposition to the egalitarian ambitions of the French Revolution, it has always defended the status quo by rejecting the very idea of constructing 'ideal' orders, which it deemed to be liberal and socialist in nature.[45] In the late nineteenth century, variants of conservatism – such as the Prussian 'Social-Conservatives' and the left-wing of the 'Verein für Socialpolitik' in Germany or the 'Social Catholics' in France and Austria – were suddenly in favour of relatively strong interventions in the market in order to prevent socialist revolution from below.[46] In the 1970s, conservatism suddenly embraced the free-market ideology of Austrian neoliberalism. In that sense, 'conservatism ought to be understood in terms of what it rejects rather than what it positively represents'.[47] To quote the American neo-conservative David Horowitz, conservatism is 'sui generis – *anti* the left, rather than *for* anything else'.[48]

Today, far-right leaders have learned to use anti-immigration, anti-liberal and anti-elite rhetoric as a highly effective demagogic tool for assuming power. Nonetheless, the far right *as a mass movement* can be understood as a blind revolt against the modernity of globalized capitalism. This modernity has forced people to radically alter their social behaviour, their mentality (to use a foreign language, to accept and embrace other cultures, and so forth), and their skills and attitudes. The traditional, older 'middle class', nationally and locally bound, provincialized by globalization and eroded by global competition, who cannot keep pace, are the key social group behind this revolt. However, a blind revolt of 'returning to the old', of 'making America great again' for such class fractions, is a Sisyphean task. Just as neoliberals can always argue that 'neoliberalism has not failed, it has never been fully implemented and therefore we just have to deepen it', right-wing authoritarian nationalism may continue with its Don Quixote-like struggle against the new economic and cultural order which globalized capitalism has brought about. Still, capitalism is the elephant in the room which right-wing authoritarianism and fascism's supporters either do not see and many of them do not want to see, because they believe in capitalism's key principles and accept the ideological justifications of inequality. The 'völkisch' homogenous society which contemporary right-wing authoritarian nationalism seeks cannot be realized under capitalist conditions. A real meritocratic society would in fact be a post-capitalist society, where not wealth and class origin but socially necessary hard work would decide the fate of aspiring and industrious individuals. After all, in capitalism it is not hard work which makes people rich but the ability to exploit other human beings' labour-power through stock portfolios or real estate property. The subjective hard-working 'top performers' within the so called professional-managerial class – lawyers, doctors, professors, TV anchors, for example – will never make it into the one percent by means of the professional work that they do. In other words, capitalism is the opposite of a society based on merit; socialism would be the precondition to a society in which hard work is actually acknowledged. As Bertolt Brecht noted so poignantly in his 'Meti: Book of Changes', 'only when conditions have been made equal will it be possible to talk about inequality. Only when everyone's feet are standing on the same step will it be possible to judge who ranks higher than others.'[49]

ANTI-FASCISM PRESUPPOSES ANTI-CAPITALISM

To conclude, right-wing authoritarian nationalism and neo-fascism are neoliberalism's immediate relatives, movements emerging from the contradictions of the actual states and policy regimes of neoliberalism today. Yet the far right's practical policies, where it has been able to influence or assume power, simply continue to make the effects of neoliberalism worse. It is not just that these policies are contrary to their populist 'Honest Joe' rhetoric, but also that far-right leaders like Trump, Bolsonaro and Modi have implemented radically pro-capitalist measures, such as financial and environmental deregulations, or gross tax cuts for the wealthy and billionaire class (income stratums which many of them belong to personally). Furthermore, like a self-fulfilling prophecy, the far right's racist rhetoric and policies create the conditions of a global civil war which it keeps warning about in ever more extreme ways, justifying its own violence against Muslims, migrants, and refugees, including pogroms like the March 2020 one in New Delhi, which it called 'self-defence' against 'Islamization'. Instead of creating a society of common ownership and common work for a greater whole and for a greater purpose, as an alternative to the social and political polarization that neoliberalism has caused, right-wing authoritarianism merely seeks to paint over social heterogeneity and the class divergences of 'life-chances' with a mythical notion of the 'Volk'.

Neoliberalism and fascism thus are like dangerous siblings: the ruthless behaviour of the older creates the blind rage of the younger. Neoliberalism thus breeds authoritarianism and fascism. Still, neoliberalism and the far right are more siblings than parent and child, because despite the older's optimism and individualism, and the younger's pessimism and 'völkisch' dreams of homogeneity, they have more in common than either would like to admit. For instance, the older sibling was always open to the authoritarian ruthlessness of the younger, as was shown by the political embrace of authoritarianism and fascism by neoliberalism's forefathers (notably by von Mises), as well as neoliberalism's birth through dictatorship (as in Chile), and the amalgamations of right-wing populist rhetoric (against too much equality and the cultural liberalism of the New Left) with Thatcherism and Reaganism.

The younger sibling, observing and fearing the destruction that the older sibling produced, negates neoliberalism and its modern values of tolerance and diversity with vehement rhetoric and polarizing politics. And yet its revolt is a pseudo-revolt. It is futile, because the younger sibling was also brought up with the same bourgeois and 'middle-class' values of competition, and because it often cannot escape market forces due to its class location. As its revolt is blind, purely negative and 'un-civilized' in manner, the far right simply produces more destruction, barbarism. The two siblings, who seem to be at each other's throat, embody no alternatives. A new family of socialist values of equality, commonality, humanity and universal solidarity is needed. If, however, no new political family is founded, and undoes the market polarization the two siblings uphold and replaces it with a democratically planned, eco-socialist society, together the two siblings are bound to move the world further and further down the slippery slope of liberalism into fascism.

NOTES

1   To enforce this path towards general prosperity and stability even collaboration with some of the most ruthless fascist dictatorships, like Mussolini's Italy in the 1930s and General Pinochet's in Chile after 1973, seemed acceptable to many liberals like Ludwig von Mises and the Nobel laureates Friedrich August Hayek and Milton Friedman. Von Mises had praised fascism for its role in eliminating the organizations of the labour movement (trade unions and socialist parties) and its leaders, writing that: 'It cannot be denied that Fascism and similar movements aiming at the establishment of dictatorships are full of the best intentions and that their interventions have … saved European civilization. The merit that Fascism has thereby won for itself will live on eternally in history.' See Ludwig von Mises, *Liberalism. The Classical Tradition*, translated by Ralph Raico, Indianapolis: Liberty Fund, 2005, p. 30. Forty-five years later, even after fascism had resulted in the most horrific barbarization of capitalist society, Friedman's 'Chicago

Boys' collaborated with the Pinochet dictatorship in the 1970s. See: Naomi Klein, *The Shock Doctrine. The Rise of Disaster Capitalism*, New York: Metropolitan, 2007. Hayek defended the neoliberals' inclination to authoritarianism even after criticism had been levelled against this historic legacy when he wrote in 1981: 'Competition is, after all, always a process in which a small number makes it necessary for larger numbers to do what they do not like, be it to work harder, to change habits, or to devote a degree of attention, continuous application, or regularity to their work which without competition would not be needed. If in a society in which the spirit of enterprise has not yet spread, the majority has power to prohibit whatever it dislikes, it is most unlikely that it will allow competition to arise. I doubt whether a functioning democracy has ever newly arisen under an unlimited democracy, and it seems least likely that unlimited democracy will destroy it where it has grown up ...' See: F. A. Hayek, *Law, Legislation and Liberty, Vol. 3: The Political Order of a Free People*, Chicago: University of Chicago Press, 1981, p. 77.

2   David Harvey, *A Brief History of Neoliberalism*, Oxford: Oxford University Press, 2007, pp. 67-70.

3   See Thomas Piketty, *Capital in the Twenty-First Century*, translated by Arthur Goldhammer, Cambridge, MA: Harvard University Press, 2014.

4   Mariana Mazzucato, *The Entrepreneurial State*, New York: Anthem Press, 2013.

5   Elmar Altvater, *Das Ende des Kapitalismus wie wir ihn kennen*, Münster: Westf. Dampfboot Verlag, 2005; and Naomi Klein, *This Changes Everything: Capitalism vs. the climate*, New York: Simon & Schuster, 2015.

6   Dimitris Milonakis and Ben Fine, *From Political Economy to Economics: Method, the social and the historical in the evolution of economic theory*, New York: Routledge, 2009, pp. 279-85.

7   Reinhard Kühnl, *Formen bürgerlicher Herrschaft: Liberalismus – Faschismus*, Reinbek: Rowohlt, pp. 99-117.

8   Ingar Solty and Stephen Gill, 'Krise, Legitimität und die Zukunft Europas', *Das Argument: Zeitschrift für Philisophie und Sozialwissenschaften*, 301, 2013, pp. 82-94.

9   Ingar Solty, 'Die politische Artikulation der globalen Krise heute: Politische Polarisierung, 'dritter Pol', Sanderismus und Corbynismus', *Z. Zeitschrift Marxistische Erneuerung*, 107, 2016, pp. 8-18.

10   Ingar Solty, 'The Significance of the New German Left Party', *Socialism and Democracy*, 46, 2008, pp. 1-34.

11   Oliver Nachtwey, *Marktsozialdemokratie: Die Transformation von SPD und Labour Party*, Wiesbaden: VS Verlag für Sozialwissenschaften, 2009.

12   Rainer Rilling, 'Strongmen, politische Krieger und Empire', in B. Fried, ed., *Weltordnungskonflikte*, Berlin: Rosa-Luxemburg-Stiftung, 2017, pp. 16-23.

13   Max Weber, *Wirtschaft und Gesellschaft: Grundriss der verstehenden Soziologie*, 5th revised edition, Tübingen: Mohr Siebeck, 1980, p. 853.

14   Joshua Kurlantzick, *Democracy in Retreat: The Revolt of the Middle Class and the Worldwide Decline of Representative Government*, New Haven: Yale University Press, 2014.

15   Compare, for example, Francis Fukuyama, 'U.S. democracy has little to teach China', *Financial Times*, 17 January 2011, and the concluding chapter in Thomas L. Friedman, *Hot, Flat, and Crowded: Why We Need a Green Revolution – and How It Can Renew America*, New York: Farrar, Straus and Giroux, 2008.

16   See Paul Krugman, 'A Dangerous Dysfunction', *New York Times*, 20 December 2009.

17   Thomas Wagner, *Robokratie: Google, das Silicon Valley und der Mensch als Auslaufmodell*, Cologne: Papy Rossa, 2015. See also: Leo Panitch and Greg Albo, eds, *Socialist Register 2021: Beyond Digital Capitalism*, London: Merlin Press, 2020.

18   Nicos Poulantzas, *Fascism and Dictatorship*, London: New Left Books, 1974, p. 75.

19   Jens Thurau, 'COVID corruption scandal hounds Angela Merkel's CDU/CSU', *Deutsche Welle*, 9 March 2021.

20   Ingar Solty, *Der kommende Krieg: Der USA-China-Konflikt und seine industrie- und klimapolitischen Konsequenzen*, Berlin: RLS, 2020.

21   Stefan Schmalz and Nico Weinmann, 'Zwei Krisen, zwei Kampfzyklen: Gewerkschaftsproteste in Europa im Vergleich', in S. Schmalz and K. Dörre, eds, *Comeback der Gewerkschaften? Machtressourcen, innovative Praktiken, internationale Perspektiven*, Frankfurt: Campus, 2013, pp. 76-98; and Charles Tilly and Sydney Tarrow, *Contentious Politics*, Second edition, Oxford: Oxford University Press, 2015.

22   Paul Mason, *Why It's Still Kicking Off Everywhere*, London: Verso, 2013; Samuel J. Brannen, Christian S. Haig and Katherine Schmidt, *The Age of Mass Protests: Understanding an Escalating Global Trend*, Washington: The Center for Strategic & International Studies, March 2020.

23   Ingar Solty, 'Is the Global Crisis Ending the Marriage of Capitalism and Liberal Democracy? (Il-)Legitimate Political Power and the New Global Anti-Capitalist Mass Movements in the Context of the Internationalization of the State', in M. Lakitsch, ed., *Political Power Reconsidered: State Power and Civic Activism between Legitimacy and Violence*, Zürich: LIT, 2014, pp. 161-204.

24   For the US example see Ingar Solty, *Die USA unter Obama: Charismatische Herrschaft, soziale Bewegungen und imperiale Politik in der globalen Krise*, Hamburg: Argument, 2013, pp. 15-71.

25   Greg Albo, '"Competitive Austerity" and the Impasse of Capitalist Employment Policy' in Ralph Miliband and Leo Panitch, eds, *Socialist Register 1994: Between Globalism and Nationalism*, London: Merlin, 1994.

26   Christoph Hermann, *The Critique of Commodification: Contours of a Post-Capitalist Society*, Oxford: Oxford University Press, 2021.

27   Nicos Poulantzas, *Faschismus und Diktatur*, München: Trikont, 1973, p. 63.

28   Ingar Solty, 'Der 18. Brumaire des Donald J. Trump? Überlegungen zum Sieg des Autoritarismus in den USA', in Martin Beck and Ingo Stützle, eds, *Die neuen Bonapartisten: Mit Marx den Aufstieg von Trump und Co. verstehen*, Berlin: Dietz, 2018, pp. 74-92.

29   Ingar Solty, 'What Do "Unruly" Right-Wing Authoritarian Nationalists Do When They Rule? The United States under Donald Trump', in Vishwas Satgar and Michelle Williams, eds, *Destroying Democracy: Neoliberal Capitalism and the Rise of Authoritarian Politics*, Johannesburg: Wits University Press, forthcoming.

30   Ingar Solty, 'Links/rechts', in W.F. Haug, et al., eds, *Historisch-kritisches Wörterbuch des Marxismus*, Vol. 8/II, Hamburg: Argument, 2015, pp. 1153-68.

31   Eugène Pottier, *The International*, available at www.marxists.org.

32   Henning Jauernig, 'Vermieter verlieren pro Monat 21 Millionen Euro', *Spiegel*, 23 November 2020.

33   Stephen Gill and Ingar Solty, 'Die organischen Krisen des Kapitalismus und die Demokratiefrage', *Juridikum – Zeitschrift für Kritik/Recht/Gesellschaft*, No. 1, 2013, pp. 51-65.

34   Chip Berlet and Matthew N. Lyons, *Right-Wing Populism in America*, New York: The Guilford Press, 2000, pp. 348-49.

35   Adorno writes: 'Collective narcissism ultimately amounts to the fact that people ... compensate for their awareness of their own powerlessness as well as the guilt that they are not what they think they should be and do through turning themselves, in reality or in their imagination, into limbs of a Higher Power, of something bigger. To it they will attribute everything that they are missing in themselves and through it some of these qualities will be passed on to them in return.' See Theodor W. Adorno, 'Theorie der Halb-Bildung' in Th. W. Adorno, *Gesammelte Schriften*, Vol. 8, Darmstadt: Wissenschaftliche Buchgesellschaft, 1998, p. 114, my translation.

36   Carl Schmitt, *Die geistesgeschichtliche Lage des heutigen Parlamentarismus*, 8th edition, Berlin: Duncker & Humblot, 1996, p. 14.

37   See Robert Altemeyer, *Enemies of Freedom: Understanding Right-Wing Authoritarianism*, San Francisco: Jossey-Bass, 1988, pp. 105-35; Karen Stenner, *The Authoritarian Dynamic*, Cambridge: Cambridge University Press, 2005, pp. 239-68; and Chris Hedges, *American Fascists: The Christian Right and the War on America*, New York: Free Press, 2008, pp. 40-52.

38   Frank Jansen and Sven Lemkemeyer, 'Was über den Täter von Hanau bekannt ist', *Tagesspiegel*, 21 February 2020, available at: www.tagesspiegel.de.

39   Henry Ashby Turner, *German Big Business and the Rise of Hitler*, Oxford: Oxford University Press, 1985.

40   Also see: Ingar Solty, 'Rechtsautoritärer Nationalismus oder autoritär-imperialer Neoliberalismus? Die USA unter Donald Trump im globalen Beggar-thy-neighbor-Kapitalismus', *Zeitschrift für Internationale Beziehungen*, 2 December 2018, pp. 199-223.

41   Phil Wahba and Katherine Dunn, 'Business leaders decry "disgusting" storming of Capitol by rioters, urge Trump to end chaos', *Fortune*, 6 January 2021; Shana Lebowitz, '23 memos from CEOs responding to the US Capitol riot', *Business Insider*, 8 January 2021; and Max Muth, 'Ein Rückzugsort für Trump wird unerreichbar', *Süddeutsche*, 10 January 2021, available at www.sueddeutsche.de.

42   One exception is the fascist leader Björn Höcke within the German AfD who, in an eclectic way and with very little political economy understanding, draws on left-wing analyses of globalization in order to reintroduce early-twentieth century fascist concepts of the autarkic economy as a path to the racially homogenous society he seeks to re-establish. His plan of a 'great re-migration' of first, second, and third-generation immigrants to the countries of their ancestors amounts to nothing less than the open declaration of a future civil war and genocide. See: Björn Höcke, *Nie zweimal in denselben Fluss*, Lüdinghausen: Manuscriptum, 2018.

43   Corey Robin, *The Reactionary Mind*, Oxford: Oxford University Press, 2011.

44   Solty, 'Links/rechts'.

45   Kurt Lenk, *Deutscher Konservatismus*, New York: Campus, 1989.

46   Johann Baptist Müller, *Konservatismus – Konturen einer Ordnungsvorstellung*, Berlin: Duncker & Humblot, 2007, pp. 134-40.

47   Ted Honderich, *Das Elend des Konservatismus: Eine Kritik*, Hamburg: Rotbuch, 1994, p. 9.

48   David Horowitz, *Radical Son: A Generational Odyssey*, New York: Touchstone, 1998, p. 392.

49   Bertolt Brecht, *Gesammelte Werke*, Vol. 12, Frankfurt/Main: Suhrkamp, 1967, p. 488.

THE RATTLE ON THE TAIL OF THE RATTLESNAKE: TRUMP AND THE DANGER OF RIGHT-WING POPULISM IN THE US

BILL FLETCHER JR.

For much of 2020, the US left vacillated as to what approach to take towards the national election. For many, including most of the Democratic Socialists of America (DSA), there was the continuation of the 'Bernie or Bust' approach that focused exclusively on securing the Democratic Party nomination for Senator Bernie Sanders.[1] This orientation, not limited to DSA, largely ignored state and local office elections and the possibility for united action by the left and, just as importantly, limited its view of the electoral scene to the presidential choice of Joe Biden versus Donald Trump.

The left and progressive movements also tended to downplay Trump's authoritarian threat – despite the experience of his authoritarian behaviour since his 2016 election – which became very pronounced in the spring of 2020, when Trump suggested that the only way that he could lose the election was through fraud. He went further, as time progressed, avoiding answering the question – or being coy about – whether he would respect the election results.[2]

With few exceptions, this was not taken seriously. The threat of Trump remaining in office, should he lose the election, or the staging of a coup, was met with silence in many left and progressive circles.[3] In my personal experience, attempting to get organizations focused on the danger of electoral shenanigans was met with either silence or, in some cases, the suggestion that discussions about the electoral threat were a distraction from the issues being raised by the Black Lives Matter protests and rebellions.[4]

And then something happened in late August/early September. It remains unclear what that 'something' was, but almost suddenly, anxiety and fear spread throughout the left: there was a new and growing awareness of not only the stakes involved in the election but the possibility that, yes, there could be a Trump-sponsored coup. At that point there was a demonstrable shift of gears as greater numbers of left and progressive activists engaged in the electoral battle, which included a minority in the DSA that argued more vocally for the need to mobilize for Biden against Trump, and the circulation of major pieces by individuals such as Noam Chomsky arguing that it was essential that Trump be defeated.

What accounts for this shift? The first and most important reason was a belated recognition that the 2020 election was not a contest between two individuals but a clash between a right-wing populist movement – led by Trump – and a broad 'pro-democracy multitude' to a great extent backing Biden. The mistake of looking at the electoral contest as being between two reprehensible individuals had misread the moment and failed to recognize that something entirely different was unfolding. It appears that over the summer, greater numbers of progressives, as well as liberals and even many Republicans, became convinced that Trump just might try to stage a coup, or take some other anti-democratic action.[5]

Following the 3 November defeat of Trump, and certainly by the time of the 6 January coup attempt,[6] some on the left wanted to turn their attention to attacking Biden who, it was believed, portended a warmed-over neoliberal administration. In so doing, these comrades again misread the moment in which we are operating, and in which we will be operating for the foreseeable future.

TRUMP DID NOT APPEAR OUT OF NOWHERE

It is difficult for the US left to recognize that there are a lot of *very bad* people in the US. Too many of us operate as if the 'bad people' are only a small number of individuals ensconced within the ruling class. Mass right-wing movements, as a result, are treated as if they are artificial operations, 'Astro Turf movements,' as the Tea Party was frequently described in 2009-10. The idea that a right-wing *mass movement* could emerge in the post-1965 US was not factored in by much of the left, even though all the evidence indicated that not only could such a movement emerge, but that over the course of several decades such a movement *had* indeed emerged.

Trump surfaced as one of a series of leaders of a right-wing populist movement. This movement's origins could be traced back to the nineteenth century but most recently to the post-1964 era among veterans of the Barry Goldwater campaign.[7] This project, which came to fruition as the so-called New Right, involved a conscious effort to eliminate the liberal wing of the Republican Party; to make it the 'non-black party'; and to mount a counteroffensive against the progressive victories of the twentieth century. This project, strategically directed and coordinated through a proliferation of right-wing think-tanks and other political organizations, included litigation, legislative/political work, and the creation and seeding of specific mass movements (such as the anti-busing, anti-abortion and anti-tax campaigns).[8]

The conservative segments of capital backing this effort, particularly the extractive industries, along with the organized small business sector, sought to 'overthrow' the twentieth century and return to a pre-New Deal moment.[9] The success of this effort was to depend on the building of a new ruling consensus, which did partially arise in the 1970s and crystallized as neoliberalism in the 1980s.[10] But the counter-revolution was not purely economic. It was a movement that also opposed the great democratic victories of the twentieth century, including the advances made by workers, people of colour, and women. It was also a reaction against growing concern about the state of the environment and the shifting role of the US in world affairs.

DR. FRANKENSTEIN AND THE MONSTER

The evolution of the right-wing of the Republican Party is a fascinating example of alliances between different segments of the right, managed to some degree by what is often called the 'Republican Establishment'. The first battle was within the Republican Establishment, supplemented by both religious and secular movements on the ground. This multi-decade battle has resulted in the chasing out of Republican Party leaders and voters who were inclined towards a politically liberal or semi-liberal approach to politics. The famous label for them was 'social liberal/fiscal conservatives', although this sometimes meant Democrats too. In either case, this element was chased out of the Republican Establishment (with a few exceptions, a prominent one being actor-turned-California politician Arnold Schwarzenegger).

The aim of the Republican Establishment, once it had been captured by Ronald Reagan's allies in the 1980s, was to be the voice of a white and male backlash against political liberalism and progressivism. This movement of white and male resentment was driven by multiple factors, including a revolt against globalization (which has roots in a deep hatred by the far right of global agreements of any sort); the role of government in introducing progressive change; evolving demographics; and a revolt against aspects of neoliberalism. There was not one coherent ideological orientation, but there were various tendencies that gravitated in this direction. The aim, at least at that point, however, was not the complete destabilization of democratic capitalism and constitutional rule.

But advancing the agenda of this Republican-neoliberal alliance necessitated shifting the 'common sense' of the US, which could not be done by communications strategies alone. Mass movements were necessary in order to mobilize the anger of the so-called 'silent majority' (later the so-called 'moral majority'). Religious and secular forces needed to be tapped, even forces which sometimes despised one another. The religious right initially tended to focus on domestic issues and then, interestingly, turned to international concerns, with faltering efforts in support of apartheid South Africa and Angola's UNITA counter-revolutionary formation;[11] but more successfully against women's rights, and in support of Israel against the Palestinians (the rise of so-called Christian Zionism).

The Republican Establishment was successful in thus cultivating its mass base. During the 1980s, neo-fascist groupings – including instances of armed action – also emerged around the country, but this was not the major characteristic of the rising right-wing mass movement. The leaders of the right-wing mass movements were largely held in check by the Republican Establishment, a job made easier as the Republican Establishment itself shifted more and more to the right.

Every indication, then, was that the Republican Establishment saw in these mass movements what Dr. Frankenstein saw in his monster – a mechanism which it could control and which would do its bidding. As with the mythical Dr Frankenstein, there was little thought that the monster might become self-aware and pursue its own agenda.

THE REPUBLICAN APPROACH TOWARD MINORITY RULE

Newt Gingrich and his *Contract with America* movement,[12] which resulted in the 1994 mid-term disaster for the Democrats, was Act III of a drama that had started in the late 1960s with the New Right and Richard Nixon's 'Southern Strategy', followed by the 'Reagan Revolution'. It was not just the content of the proposals advanced by Gingrich and his faction of the New Right, but the entire tone of the movement's discourse that represented a declaration of war on the remnants of the New Deal and the Democratic Party.

Although there is a long history of subversion within mainstream politics – including armed coups, such as the 1898 coup in Wilmington, North Carolina – in the more recent period there have been generally accepted parameters for disagreement between the parties. When these have been challenged, such as the plotting of a coup against Franklin Roosevelt in the 1930s[13] or even Nixon's Watergate antics in the early 1970s, the combined political establishment has in the past always moved quickly to get 'the house' back in order and to neutralize the threat and downplay its significance.

The 1980s, however, saw a new combination of insurgent right-wing, populist, authoritarian movements with the spread of more openly fascist and fascistic groups. By the early 1990s, amid a growing disappointment with the first two years of the Clinton administration (and particularly its continued embrace of economic neoliberalism, despite his campaign promises), the Republican Establishment struck back with a vengeance. This was when it issued a clear signal that so-called 'bipartisanship' was a dead letter, though it took time for this to sink in, as the older members of the Democratic Party and, especially, the Republican Establishment gradually retired or died.

The end of bipartisanship must be understood in the context of demographic and political changes that were under way in the US, and the growing awareness within the Republican Party that something needed to be done to block a political transformation of the country.[14] The leadership had limited options. They could diversify the Republican Party and reach out to not only disillusioned white Democrats but also specific racialized minority populations, such as Latinos. Or they could become the party of the White Republic and advance a strategy that could, in a peculiar fashion, include racialized minorities but in a clearly subordinate role. In either case, at least before 2016, the party would also be the party of neoliberalism and neoliberal globalization. The battle between these two directions could be seen, on the one hand, in the politics of the Bush family, representing the effort at some level of inclusion, mixed with neoliberalism and global unilateralism; and, on the other, in the politics that came to be associated with Donald Trump, and that had previously been represented by individuals such as Pat Buchanan.

For both tendencies, the question of the nature of the dominant bloc in the US was critical. In some respects, one could say that for the Bush wing, there was a conferring of 'white-hood' on additional populations, such as some Latinos and Asians. For the proponents of the White Republic, it was strengthening the hierarchy. In both cases, these forces were trying to come to grips with the possibility that the changing face of the US could result in permanently weakening the Republican Party and its capacity for dominance. Thus, at the end of the day they were grappling with what could be the character of white *minority* rule in the US when, since its inception, the notion of white hegemony has been hardwired into the soul of the country.[15]

The fight to establish numerical (white) minority rule also helps one understand the configuration of male supremacist politics within the Republican establishment, especially when it is even articulated by women. The move, which had a strong appeal within the burgeoning right-wing populist movement, was not only a challenge to the victories of the women's movement in general, but a challenge to changing gender roles. The anti-abortion/anti-choice movement was about a specific role for women, even when articulated in religious or pseudo-religious terms. But it was also an explicit appeal to white women to see their interests as aligned with the 'white republic' as opposed to being aligned with emancipatory feminism.

THE MONSTER GROWS

It is critical to appreciate that the right-wing populist movement was not a simple puppet of the Republican Establishment. It was a movement that was consciously advanced by far-right political forces which sought to alter the Republican Party and beat back the advances of the twentieth century. That said, the Republican Establishment appears to have believed that they were in the driver's seat and could manipulate this movement to serve their electoral aims. Two developments indicated that the relationship between this developing movement and the Republican Establishment was complicated, both emerging at roughly the same time – the 'Birther Movement' and the Tea Party.

The election of Barack Obama as president in 2008 was not only historic, but, for the right, it was more than frightening. His victory upset the way they saw the US.[16] Obama could have done nothing but sat in the West Wing and there would have been a right-wing counteroffensive. Instead, he was under assault for both being black and for introducing even modest reforms that challenged Republican views on the economy and whom it should serve.

The Birther Movement, ultimately led by Donald Trump, tapped into the White Republic sentiment within much of the Republican base, a sentiment suggesting that Obama was an interloper and that there was no conceivable way that an African American could have been legitimately elected president of the US. In that sense, in addition to being racist, it was very much the precursor of the attempts by 'Trumpsters' to create a legitimacy crisis in the aftermath of the November 2020 elections. Put bluntly, if someone Republicans do not like is elected, they cannot have been legitimately elected.[17]

The Birther movement grew substantially and, unfortunately but predictably, liberals wrote it off. Instead of Obama providing his birth records, he could have gone on the offensive about the nature of the attacks. But then, of course, he would have been described as an 'angry Black man', which appears to have been his greatest fear.

The Tea Party movement, a direct response to a Black president of the

US and to efforts to pass both an economic stimulus package and national healthcare reform, was bound together by a common message. In doing so, the Tea Party implied an open racism, but it also offered a deeper challenge to the role of government, even in times of crisis. Had the Obama administration, along with forces on the left, taken a more offensive posture in early 2009, it is quite possible that the appeal of the Tea Party would have been diminished. In either case, with the open backing of politically conservative sectors of capital and small business, it became a right-wing mass movement. It was commonplace for liberal and left pundits to classify the Tea Party as a so-called 'Astro Turf movement', that is, not a legitimate mass movement but simply a creature of capitalists. This analysis was one-sided and did not see in both the Birther Movement and the Tea Party an energizing of the monster.[18]

It was with Donald Trump's announcement of his 2016 candidacy that the monster arose from the operating table fully formed and filled with energy and anger. Trump tapped into this but did not create it. He became the voice, the *rattle*, to use the metaphor from our title, for this movement. And the movement now began challenging the Republican Establishment, even while it advanced many of the Establishment's aims.[19]

Trump's alleged protectionism and 'America First' rhetoric resembled the language of the Polish right-wing populists who articulate a peculiar form of 'welfare statism', but one that only benefits 'legitimate' Poles.[20] The sometimes open and often subtle racism of Trump combined a race-neutral appeal to 'unite around a right-wing platform', with a demonization of select racial minorities, usually at specific moments, as with 'Mexicans' in 2015; African Americans responding to police brutality; and, later in his administration, Asians.[21] Thus Trump could, ironically, appeal to the growing dissatisfaction with neoliberalism – as practised by both Republicans and Democrats – while arguing, explicitly and implicitly, that he was the person who would look out for the genuine 'American'. This was very similar to the approach of the Polish right-wing populists. Neoliberalism comes to be described as an attack on the genuine 'American' and blamed on racial minorities, Jews, so-called Eastern elites, and so forth.

The right-wing populist movement saw itself as taking on the establishment even when, after Trump's election, it had become a movement to advance interests of the Republican Establishment, such as the 2017 so-called tax reform which overwhelmingly benefited the elite. The right-wing populist base heard what it wanted to hear and simply felt empowered that someone as racist, sexist, and crude as Trump could now hold national office.

In reviewing the Trump administration's legacy and the November 2020 election, it is worth asking how is it that Trump did not lose the vote of every person of 'colour'. Racism, after all, seemed to be dripping from the White House.[22]

The answer needs to be understood in the context of what Frantz Fanon might have characterized as a 'colonial mentality'.[23] While it was certainly the case that specific émigré populations saw in the rise of Bernie Sanders the danger of socialism, its importance was limited. What was not limited was the particular racial message and configuration of the White Republic symbolism offered by Trump (and something that can be seen in many right-wing populist and fascist groupings). Let us explain.

In understanding the 'racial system' of the United States it is important to appreciate that the forms racism takes and has taken are specific to particular racialized minorities. Jim Crow segregation, for instance, was aimed at African Americans. Open genocide and reservations were perpetrated against Native Americans. People of Mexican descent have suffered under a regional variant of what might be referenced as de facto Jim Crow legalised discrimination. Asians – particularly those who arrived prior to 1965 (when immigration laws changed dramatically) – were and are the subjects of specific forms of anti-Asian racism, including ghettoization, job segregation, and violence, as well as an odd form of sexualization and exaggeration, the latter paralleling the anti-semitic aggrandizement of Jews. The totality of the system, however, has no name other than 'racism' or 'racist oppression'.[24]

The Trump-led right-wing populist movement has incorporated a form of *neo-apartheid* vision for the future of the US and a way of ensuring white minority rule. It allows a place for those individuals and groups of colour who accept white hegemony and who will refuse to challenge the racial system. These are groupings that have a 'colonial mentality' reminiscent of Malcolm X's famous line where he spoke of Blacks who so identified with their oppressors that when the slave owners were sick, the slave would offer, '… are WE sick boss?'

Thus, Trump's anti-Latino racism could be written off by some Latinos as supposedly not applying to Latinos already living in the US. Trump's anti-Black racism could be written off by some US African Americans as supposedly not applying to African American right-wing evangelists and hard workers. The beat goes on. This has become so intense that there are some from within these demographics who will not identify as being of colour.

The colonial mentality makes various assumptions. One, that the target of the racist assault is someone other than them. Two, that there is a way that they – as a member of a racialized population – can achieve a modus vivendi with the larger system. Supreme Court Justice Clarence Thomas, for instance, began as a revolutionary nationalist but evolved into his current state in part, apparently, based on an assumption that white folks will be what white folks will be, and that there is little that we, people of colour, can do about it other than find a place within this system.

THE MONSTER IS DELUSIONAL

No slogan could be better associated with today's right-wing populist movement generally, and 'Trumpsters' in particular, than that from the iconic television show *The X-Files*: 'I want to believe.' One can argue that the right-wing is always delusional, but there is a specific aspect to what we are witnessing in the context of the rise of Trump and today's right-wing populist movement: its unprecedented scale. The size of Trump's 2020 vote of 74 million, along with the vitality of the right-wing populist movement and its allies amongst the so-called mainstream media and social media, has resulted in a relatively successful delusional bubble within which this movement exists. One can operate within such a bubble and never come up for air, and rarely face the facts about anything. This is very different from the pre-social media era, when there might be a reliance on local news outlets and/or targeted rightwing media. With the emergence of cable outlets such as Fox, as well as the explosion in social media, people can encase themselves in a world that is completely out of touch with reality.

As noted earlier, the Birther Movement was the epitome of irrationalism. The web woven by Trump and others around it was comedic in content and thoroughly reactionary. It assumed that there had to have been a conspiracy since the birth of Obama to keep his origins secret and that there was no institution in the US capable of discovering the truth.[25]

The importance of understanding the delusions is not just their irrational content but the purpose that they serve. In each case, whether it was the Birthers or, more recently, the response to the Covid-19 pandemic, these delusional narratives reinforce preexisting biases, worries, suspicions, and so on. They also help to explain the sorry condition of so many white people as being the result of a massive ethno-nationalist and gender-based offensive against them. Thus, people of colour have agency, but not whites: if whites are failing, whether working class or small business, it cannot possibly be the result of the individual's failure to act, and it cannot be the result of a larger capitalist system. Instead, it must be the result of the just described conspiracy which is displacing them in the interests of an undeserving population that, metaphorically, has jumped ahead in the line.

The advent of social media has made it possible for this mass base to find one another and develop a collective voice. Contrary to even twenty years ago, one need not rely on stumbling across a newspaper from a particular sect or movement; the answers are now literally at one's fingertips.

The challenge for the left in such a situation is particularly profound. In November 2020 *74 million people voted against reality*. While one can convincingly argue that many Trump voters were not out of touch with reality but voted for Trump (and other Republicans) for very particular reasons, the truth is that they were throwing their support to someone who, in addition to being racist and sexist, openly denies the environmental catastrophe and missed the reality and significance of the Covid-19 pandemic. Whether or not all Trump voters agreed with his fantasies is irrelevant. They were prepared to tolerate and, thereby, be complicit with them. This situation was capped off by Trump's unsubstantiated challenge to the November 2020 election results as allegedly being flawed. Despite repeated court decisions and investigations, millions of people were prepared to accept Trump's diagnosis of the situation rather than the facts.

ELECTION AFTERMATH AND THE 6 JANUARY COUP ATTEMPT

Trump's challenge to the November 2020 election results recalled the infamous 1876 presidential election, the latter only settled via a compromise ending Reconstruction. The big difference, of course, is that the November 2020 election was not close and there was little documentation of any significant fraud (it was also not settled via a compromise). The allegations, despite the vociferous language of Trump (and his many allies within and outside the Republican Party) could not be substantiated.

The delusional attacks on the election results were aimed at destabilizing the political system.[26] One can speculate as to whether Trump intended on using the chaos that unfolded as a means for declaring martial law. What is clear is that he was able to convince most of his followers that the results were tainted. Implied in his criticism of the election results was a commentary regarding the racial character of the core of his opposition, especially among African Americans and Latinos. Each suggestion of fraud was lined with the implication that *certain people* either should not be voting or voted fraudulently. This was, as we were to see, accompanied by a call to his followers to converge on Washington, DC on 6 January in order to demonstrate their displeasure with the election process and results. His call, of course, was about much more than that: *a call to insurrection*.

It is worth noting that this coup attempt was not that of disenfranchised and impoverished white people moving against the 'Establishment', although a central feature for the crowds that marched on the Capitol was the belief that white people are being displaced.[27] We shall not explore the details of 6 January, but a few points are worth noting.

First, the US has experience of similar such insurrections, with the Civil War being an obvious example. In addition to thousands of lynchings of African Americans, Chicanos, Native Americans, Asians, as well as Jews and Sicilians, open insurrections have unfolded, including but not limited to the Hamburg (South Carolina) massacre of 1876, and the Wilmington, North Carolina coup of 1898, the latter overthrowing a duly elected progressive populist administration.

Second, the *coup attempt* was inspired by Trump, irrespective of whether he coordinated it. His speech at the rally instructed his supporters to converge on the Capitol (though he did not); he refused to deploy the National Guard; he refused to acknowledge what was happening at the Capitol. All these actions point, at a minimum, to Trump's complicity in the chaos that ensued.

Third, 6 January was not an operation mounted by one tendency on the far right alone. It was a manifestation of the fascists within the right-wing populist movement who, apparently, believed that they could create sufficient confusion and turmoil to overturn the election. That is called a coup: it was no dustup or demonstration suddenly turned into rioting.

Fourth, the willingness of the fascists to engage in open violence at the Capitol was indicative of two things: (a) that because it was a largely white protest, the expectation was that they would not be repressed; and (b) the fascists had concluded that peaceful and judicial means of addressing their concerns were no longer effective.

Fifth, it is worth noting that the coup attempt did not receive the support of any major segment of the capitalist class. It did receive, however, both open and closed support by Republican elected officials. This has led to a very curious situation whereby the Republican Party has begun attacking major corporations that have reacted against Republican policies pursuing various forms of authoritarianism, as with voter suppression laws being passed in many states, positioning themselves as allegedly the 'working class party'. There are multiple examples, with one of the most public being the response of the Republican Party to Major League Baseball moving the July 2021 All-Star Game away from Atlanta (and to Denver, Colorado) in protest against the draconian voter suppression statute passed by the Republicans. Congressional Republicans then threatened to remove MLB's anti-trust exemption as punishment. Progressives have, for years, been attempting to eliminate the anti-trust exemption – always facing Republican opposition

– but now the Republicans chose to claim the banner of going against so-called 'woke' corporations.

To be clear, the Republicans continue to receive huge corporate contributions, but there are divisions among the capitalists as to how to relate to the increasingly authoritarian Republican Party and what all this means for the legitimacy of the system.

We now have a situation where most Republicans and approximately 40 per cent of independent voters believe that Biden was elected illegitimately. Whether that view stands will be an open question. What is likely is that a very divided right-wing populist movement nevertheless feels empowered. Why? Because the Republican establishment has continued to provide cover and support for them. Though many in the Republican establishment, such as Minority Leader Kevin McCarthy, were clearly panicked by the coup attempt, they soon withdrew this concern and ran rapidly to rebuild ties with Trump. In some cases, as with Wisconsin Senator Ron Johnson, they have even attempted to argue that what people witnessed on television had not happened: it was either nothing more than a minor conflict or a false flag operation called by the Black Lives Matter and Antifa networks.[28]

Moreover, the former President has not disavowed them. Though Trump gave a disingenuous condemnation of violence, he reaffirmed that the coup people had been on the right side.[29] He has not backed away from that. He continued, despite the advice of his advisers, to insist that the election was stolen, and he has taken a threatening posture towards Republicans who challenged him. Thus, the base believes that they remain on the right course.

And they have not felt the full brunt of prosecution, at least as of now. The authorities have moved steadily on prosecutions against the coup participants.[30] Yet the attitudes in the courts have been uneven, one of the more outrageous examples being a judge permitting an arrested real estate agent – who had pictures of herself at the coup attempt – to leave the country and go to Mexico![31] There have been other such examples, but there have also been some strong stands taken against many of the coup people. For this reason, the perpetrators of the coup seem to have arrived at different conclusions about how bad the situation was and is. A contributing factor to their confusion has been the revelation of police infiltration in their groups, notably within the Proud Boys.

An additional factor about 6 January is something that I would refer to as 'anarcho-fascism' in the US. The fascist tendencies within the US are very divided and tend to be quite sectarian. They are not united in one national fascist organization or party. The Republicans have consolidated as a hard, right-wing party that tolerates and, to some degree is complicit with, fascists, but it would be quite misleading to call it a fascist party.[32] Moreover a significant current among US fascists downplays national organization and leadership and adheres to decentralized networks and alliances, all of which aim to bring about the great conflagration that will end the current status quo.[33]

The far right comprises, to borrow from theorist Matthew Lyons, more than the fascists, and this is the reason to refer to it as a *right-wing populist mass movement*. Within the wider right-wing populist movement, there are those who actively oppose the existing democratic capitalist constitutional state, while others believe that they are operating in the name of the state. This plurality of hard right movements is a source of contradictions within the US right.

Right-wing terror can be expected to continue and escalate because it is supported by wide swaths of the Republican Party, with Senator Johnson's obscene denial of reality being only one example. The question is whether terrorism and other disruptions become a more concerted plan for the elimination of constitutional rule.

THE CHOICE OF THE FAR RIGHT

Fascism is a choice, but, metaphorically, it is a shifting current within a larger 'river' of right-wing populism. The river of right-wing populism contains multiple currents, the character of which I have defined as 'neo-Confederate'.[34]

The fascists do not seek to put more conservative Republicans in office. They seek to eliminate 'office' altogether, in the sense of eliminating constitutionally limited democratic capitalism. Their alignment with Trump is one of convenience but also strategy in the effort to build a broader front. But it is also tactical in that they do not necessarily trust that Trump will follow through on his rhetoric. Such disillusionment could be perceived in the aftermath of 6 January, when many of the coup people were dismayed that Trump had not pardoned them. It can be argued that Trump has evolved into something of a 'crypto-fascist'. But even with his authoritarian instincts, Trump is not one of 'them', at least as far as the fascists themselves are concerned.

Thus, one should anticipate several potential scenarios. The Republican Party will continue to lose so-called moderates who became disgusted with Trump and with the thuggishness of his rule and the flagrant abuse of power in government (and perhaps also disgusted with the Republican elected officials and operatives who have enabled Trump). More than likely, such moderates will shift toward the 'Independent' non-aligned category in US electoral politics.

The Republican Party may well come to rely more on voter suppression and parliamentary disruption over the coming years (perhaps even reminiscent of some of the disruptive activities of the Nazis in the Reichstag pre-1933). This sort of disruption always carries with it the potential to escalate into various forms of threatening behaviour. Such a scenario can only be blocked by a massive electoral realignment shattering the confidence of the neo-Confederates and disorganizing their forces.

An additional feature of such an escalation in the use of force and threatening behavior is that the the armed right will aim some of its violence at liberal, progressive, and left targets. This would be a version of what was witnessed in the 1980s in the Midwest farm crisis, with the rise of grassroots fascist formations such as Posse Comitatus. This could include assassinations and provocations, few of which will receive condemnation from an increasingly complicit Republican Party.[35]

Finally, we can expect demographic groups of colour to be targeted with misogyny, xenophobia, and rightwing religious fundamentalism as a means of peeling off segments of them and winning them to neo-Confederate politics. In this, misogyny and right-wing religious fundamentalism are deeply intertwined with growing attacks from the right on the politics of gender liberation, such as on the transgendered community regarding participation in school sports.

But what of Trump? That remains a key question. His impact on the Republican Party remains quite strong, though his impact on the larger electorate is increasingly questionable. Trump has positioned himself so that he can be the 2024 Republican nominee, but it is quite plausible that there will be another right-wing populist opponent who will be smoother and will present as being the one who can be a uniter.

Yet, even having lost access to much of the media, Trump remains the orator of irrationalism and a threat to those who contemplate challenging him, a fact seen in the reversals carried out by various Republican officials who contemplate running for office. Trump is very unforgiving and demands obedience.

IMPLICATIONS FOR THE LEFT

Despite the unsettling prospects, this is not a gloom and doom scenario. That said, the coming years will necessitate a level of sophistication that has often eluded the US left. In that regard, there are several things to consider.

First, the current moment is *not* one in which to downplay the threat from the far right and turn our attention towards making centrist Democrats the *main* enemy. The Trump years, if they demonstrate nothing more, show us the fragility of the US political system. A less narcissistic and more strategic autocrat could very well have pulled off an electoral crisis, resulting in a declaration of martial law. Still, a socio-political atmosphere formed that normalized the authoritarianism and irrationalism spreading throughout the US during the years of the Trump administration. This normalization was abetted by much of the mainstream media and even seeped into left and progressive circles. The outrages of Trump – and those of his supporters – became so common that nothing seemed shocking.

If the right is reorganizing, arming, and becoming increasingly disruptive, the approach of the left must change too. Whether the right-wing populist movement seeks to directly terminate constitutional democratic capitalism or simply to block progressive change, does not fundamentally matter in terms of the tasks of the left (except and insofar as the right is prepared to engage in armed violence). The left cannot avoid, in such a context, thinking through the politics and reality of popular self-defence.

Second, this is a time for intense and sincere united front work. The actual level of organization of the left in the US means that it cannot defeat the right-wing populists by itself. We will need allies, and the basis for alliances – as uneven as these will be – must be the questions of justice and democracy. The left must be proponents of *consistent democracy* and *consistent justice*. This means going beyond a defence of the status quo. In fact, it means critiquing and challenging the status quo, including the neoliberal regime that, along with white and male supremacy, has contributed to the rise of today's right-wing populist movements.

United front work must appreciate that some forces with which we shall need to make alliances will have a quite different vision of the future. They may not be progressive at all. They may, however, have contradictions with the right-wing populists that can be exploited to the advantage of progressive forces. This may involve tactical alliances, in the case of specific campaigns or around very specific issues. In other cases, the alliances may be longer term. To borrow from the words of an Iraqi trade unionist I once saw reported, he said 'we walk together as long as we can'. We should not romanticize tactical alliances, but we should not deprecate them either. Tactical alliances can be invaluable in particular battles.

Third, our united front work must be consistent with forward-focused efforts at securing political power, including the fight for 'governing power' – within the context of democratic capitalism – and ultimately the fight for state power and the goal of fundamental social transformation. The political polarization of the US necessitates that the left is organized around an *alternative* set of politics and an *alternative* practice. The Trump legacy, in the form of a rabid right-wing populist movement, cannot be fought by attempting to stop time or turn the clock back to a more comfortable era. It must be fought through the destruction of the right-wing populist movement and the ideological undercurrents that support its existence. This approach distinguishes what I believe the left should advance versus the more defensive coalitions of which most of us have been part. Defeating the right will, obviously, include substantive defensive work, but we must always be looking towards laying the foundation for a counter-offensive, and that necessitates the alternative politics and practice noted earlier.

What might this all look like? There is a desperate need for left organization. Objective blocs and united fronts can form around any number of issues – even strategic – but in the absence of a left core, such blocs will tend to unravel. One can see in the period of Reconstruction (1865-1877) the impact of the absence of such a consistent core. One can also see how the era of the late 1960s, which brought together multiple social movements, was unable to cohere into a full-fledged popular democratic bloc.[36] Left organization can be decisive in building the bloc that is necessary.

The immediate aim of defeating the 'New Confederacy' necessitates a very broad front that unites around the defence of democracy. For the left, however, there must be more than that, as I have noted. Thus, forces on the left must be willing to unite with those in the Democratic Party who are strategically our opponents but who, at this moment, are in opposition – hostile opposition – to forces on the right who are advancing authoritarianism. Unity around matters such as voting rights, women's rights and, in many cases, workers' rights are quite possible.

Further, the left must be at the core of building left/progressive organizations that are advancing the fight – mentioned above – for governing power. This means being prepared to challenge so-called centrist Democrats where the left is building base areas. It means advancing programs that push the boundaries of democratic capitalism. Fights on matters such as the Green New Deal (including pro-people, pro-environment economic development), repairing the results of racism and national oppression within the US, the financing of elections, opposition to gender oppression, workers' rights, and a reformed foreign policy need to be central components.

But the left must appreciate that the electoral battle is not mainly about exposing the system through the electoral process – it is a battle to win. And in winning we must be prepared to engage in class struggle within the political system and not just against the political system. This will mean new forms of organization that tap into and engage masses of people in their own liberation. This will mean creating new organizations of governance and oversight, among other things.

Finally, there is a need for an uptick in social movement organizing in traditionally conservative states and regions. Environmental and union organizing immediately come to mind, both of which can be utilized to raise questions of environmental justice and economic justice. Gerrymandering will, in many states, make it increasingly difficult for Democrats in general, and progressives in particular, to win certain elections. But that should not mean that the mass base for progressive organizing has disappeared. Years of union organizing, for instance, have demonstrated that the existence of a unionized workforce can not only influence the politics of union members (and their families) but can also influence the broader community.

The forward-facing politics of the left must create fronts of struggle around the environment, gender, race and national oppression, the economy, and international relations. This is far removed from a purely electoral battle with the right, but a process of engaging in struggles for power and a remaking of a popular common sense. Our battles, for instance, around economic justice have no alternative but to be linked to the environment, insofar as we are advancing ideas about what needs to be produced and how. Our battles around gender are not limited to abortion rights, but include self-definition, wealth disparities, and opportunities for self-expression. The list goes on and on. The politics to challenge right-wing populism and neo-fascism, then, are the politics of optimism and liberation, rather than the politics of retreat, nostalgia, and hierarchy.

NOTES

I wish to thank Hannah Levine for the research assistance which made this essay possible.

1   I hasten to add that, particularly late in the year, segments of DSA which had been relatively silent, moved towards a position of 'critical support' of Biden.

2   This included Trump's narrative as told through Twitter: Trump suggested on Twitter in spring 2020 that the election would be rigged. Marianna Spring, '"Stop the steal": The deep roots of Trump's "voter fraud" strategy', *BBC News*, 23 November 2020. Trump reiterated his message regarding the only circumstances under which he could lose. See Steve Inskeep, 'Timeline: What Trump Told Supporters for Months Before They Attacked', *NPR*, 8 February 2021.

3   But there were warning bells. See David Graham, 'Trump Is Brazenly Interfering With the 2020 Election', *The Atlantic*, 20 May 2020.

4   This issue of alleged distraction from the Black Lives Matter protests following the murder of George Floyd was particularly curious. It was raised directly with me by several white colleagues who were trying to figure out how best to respond to such a line of argument.

5   There were clearly those who recognized the danger. See, for instance, Panayota Gounari, 'Authoritarianism, Discourse and Social Media: Trump as the "American

Agitator'", in Jeremiah Morelock, ed., *Critical Theory and Authoritarian Populism*, London: University of Westminster Press, 2018.

6   There is some dispute as to whether the 6 January events constituted a 'coup'. We are using that term as, literally, a 'quick blow'. A coup is usually associated with the military, but this need not be the case. It is a form of insurrection, and frequently associated with a segment of the ruling class moving against another segment. In this case, there is sufficient evidence to suggest that Trump either approved or tolerated this attempt to destabilize the federal government and alter the election results. It was also clear that the 'coup people' believed that they had the support of Trump and, in many cases, were stunned that they were not all pardoned after the coup failed. For a discussion on the meaning of coup in similar ways see: David Runciman, *How Democracy Ends*, New York: Basic Books, 2018.

7   Two of the best sources of information on right-wing populist is Chip Berlet and Matthew Lyons, *Right-wing Populism in America*, New York: The Guilford Press, 2000; and Michael Kazin, *The Populist Persuasion*, Ithaca, NY: Cornell University Press, 1998.

8   Steve Coll, in *The New Yorker*, offers the argument that George Wallace was the most important predecessor of Donald Trump. See Steve Coll, 'Donald Trump, George Wallace, and the Influence of Losers', *The New Yorker*, 4 December 2020. See also Alan Crawford, *Thunder on the Right: The New Right and the Politics of Resentment*, New York: Pantheon, 1980; Daniel Schlozman, '"We Are Different from Previous Generations of Conservatives": The New Right and the Mobilization of Evangelicals,' in *When Movements Anchor Parties: Electoral Alignments in American History*, Princeton: Princeton University Press, 2015; and Alf Tomas Tønnessen, *How Two Political Entrepreneurs Helped Create the American Conservative Movement, 1973-1981: The Ideas of Richard Viguerie and Paul Weyrich*. Lewiston, NY: Edwin Mellen Press, 2009.

9   Kazin notes that the anti-New Deal movement championed white men who ran small businesses. Over the course of time, the right wing within the Republican Party was able to assemble an alliance that included so-called Sun Belt corporations that opposed federal regulation and taxes, along with ideological forces, such as right-wing ministries. See *Populist Persuasion*, pp. 222 and 239.

10   The new ruling consensus was built not only on the attack on the New Deal, but also on the crisis of Keynesian capitalism and the desertion of capitalist support from that form of accumulation.

11   The National Union for the Total Independence of Angola (UNITA) was an organization that originally arose in opposition to Portuguese colonial domination of Angola. But it joined hands with the apartheid South African regime in order to undertake efforts to crush the Popular Movement for the Liberation of Angola (MPLA), which had control of the capital and significant portions of the country.

12   The *Contract with America* was the platform upon which Republicans ran during the mid-term elections of 1994. They were committing to cutting taxes and regulations, among other things. It was an open declaration of a brutal neoliberal agenda, and an implied attack on the gains won by the progressive social movements.

13   The plot has been documented over time, but also faced strange attempts to debunk it as fact. Sally Denton addresses this in her book, *The Plots Against the President: FDR, a Nation in Crisis, and the Rise of the American Right*, New York: Bloomsbury Press, 2012. See also Michael Donnelly, '"Wall Street" Failed 1934 Coup', *CounterPunch*, 2 December 2011.

14   See: American National Election Studies, 'Race: 1948-2016', *The ANES Guide to Public Opinion and Electoral Behaviour*, available at: electionstudies.org.

15   The Republican Party has become the party of voter suppression and foregoing any efforts to be a truly majoritarian party. See Ezra Klein, 'The crisis isn't too much polarization. It's too little democracy', *Vox*, 12 November 2020.

16   This cannot be overemphasized. There are many on the left who see in the growth of the political right a disenchantment with the neoliberal turn of the Democrats. The problem with this analysis is that the racial shift of whites from the Democratic Party and to the Republican Party began years before the economic downturn of the mid-1970s, and the growing sway of neoliberalism within the Democratic Party. This is what Richard Nixon understood so well with his Southern Strategy. The Obama victory showed, in the eyes of white America, that the country was undergoing a change that many whites saw as illustrating so-called white replacement or white genocide.

17   Alana Abramson, 'How Donald Trump Perpetuated the "Birther" Movement for Years', *ABC News*, 16 September. Significant percentages of the US population continue to believe this myth.

18   Which is not to say that there was no evidence of corporate manipulation. What is missing is the assumption that this was all a shell game and that there was no mass base. See: Eric Zuesse, 'Final Proof the Tea Party was founded as a Bogus Astro Turf Movement', *Huffington Post*, 22 October 2013.

19   Tim Alberta argues that Trump capitalized on the Republican Party's lack of cohesion in the aftermath of Bush. This would help to explain his ability to use unorthodox politics to challenge the Republican Establishment. *American Carnage: on the Front Lines of the Republican Civil War and the Rise of President Trump*, New York: HarperCollins, 2019.

20   On Poland see Artur Lipinski and Agnieszka Stepinska, 'Polish Right-Wing Populism', in Jo Harper, ed., *Poland's Memory Wars: Essays on Illiberalism*, Budapest: Central European University Press, 2018, pp. 80-95.

21   One example, with which we are familiar, has been the anti-Asian racism associated with Covid-19. Dylan Scott, 'Trump's new fixation on using a racist name for the Coronavirus is dangerous', *Vox*, 18 March 2020.

22   It is truly remarkable to read or hear the words of people of colour who supported/support Trump. Though it is important to keep in mind that the percentages were limited, they had an importance in that these populations were either prepared to disregard Trump's racism or assume that he was talking about someone else. See: Ashitha Nagesh, 'US Election 2020: Why Trump gained support among Minorities', *BBC*, 22 November 2020.

23   The mentality of those who are colonized.

24   This system contrasts with the colonial and apartheid system in pre-1994 South Africa. That system allowed for a *specific* hierarchy of oppression in which various populations were subordinated to the White Republic. *Apartheid* created an order for everything, and everything had an order.

25   A conspiracy akin to that from the famous Alexander Dumas novel, *The Man in the Iron Mask*, London: Penguin Classics, 2003.

26   Inskeep, 'Timeline'.

27   Sections of the left repeatedly attempt to find an economic 'cushion' or explanation in white right-wing populist risings, or some other form of indignation against the

system which might contain some legitimacy. Reality has demonstrated that it is more complicated. Regarding the 6 January coup attempt, see Dartagnan, 'Study Indicates the Jan. 6 Riots were motivated by Racism and White Resentment, not "Election Theft"', *Portside*, 17 April 2021.

28   Chris Cillizza, 'Ron Johnson just dropped a ridiculous conspiracy theory at the Senate Capitol attack hearing', *CNN*, 23 February 2021.

29   Inskeep, 'Timeline'.

30   Josh Gerstein and Kyle Cheney, 'Capitol riot cases strain court system', *Politico*, 10 March 2021.

31   'Judge: Texan charged in Capitol riot can go on Mexico trip', *AP*, 5 February 2021.

32   It would not be inaccurate, however, to identify the Republican Party as being the 'party-for-dictatorship' as demonstrated by the consistent failure to place restraints on the fascists, and more importantly, by their embrace of voter suppression as a key strategy (reminding one of the Democratic Party of the US South from the end of the Civil War through the 1960s).

33   It is important to qualify that there were various tendencies among the people involved in the right-wing coup on 6 January. I would characterize most as 'fascists' but that did not necessarily mean that they were part of existing organizations. Robert Pape and Keven Ruby, 'The Capitol Rioters aren't like other Extremists', *The Atlantic*, 2 February 2021.

34   In my article in *Socialist Register 2016: The Politics of the Right*, 'Stars and Bars', I argue that the nationally-specific character of right-wing populism in the US is 'neo-Confederate'. This does not mean only those who dress in Confederate uniforms or celebrate Confederate heroes. It means that their critical image, for lack of a better term, is linked to the Confederate States of America and its repressive, white supremacist state. Right-wing populism develops nationally-specific forms and is not a cookie-cutter. Thus, the right-wing populism of France is not the same as in Italy, though right-wing populism has certain common characteristics which I address in the *Register* article. The 'Neo-Confederacy' is being used as a more generic term to identify the nature of the reactionary bloc that has become hegemonic in the Republican Party, and which seeks to impose a dictatorship. As raised earlier in this essay, I would amend that to argue that the right-wing populists are uniting around a neo-apartheid vision for the future of the US.

35   A debate exists as to the connections or not between economic distress and right-wing terrorist activity. There appears to be a strong linkage between economic distress and right-wing populism, but that connection is not necessarily about the actual experience as opposed to the anticipation of economic distress (and in that regard is frequently linked with a fear of white replacement). In either case, we should anticipate a growth of right-wing extremism (including but not limited to rightwing terrorism). See Robert O'Harrow, Jr, Andrew Ba Tran, and Derek Hawkins, 'The Rise of Domestic Terrorism: Data shows surge in incident of homegrown terrorism not seen in 25 years', *The Washington Post*, 13 April 2021, and Abigail Hauslohner, 'Right-wing group says its membership is up after Jan. 6', *The Washington Post*, 14 April 2021.

36   I addressed a number of these issues in a lengthy essay for Monthly Review: 'The Modern Tecumseh and the Future of the US Left', *MRonline*, 17 June 2021, available at: https://mronline.org.

WHAT IS WRONG WITH SOCIAL MEDIA? AN ANTI-CAPITALIST CRITIQUE

MARCUS GILROY-WARE

The most revolutionary thing one can do is always to proclaim loudly what is happening.

Rosa Luxemburg

As the liberal fantasy of a stable 'capitalist democracy' has steadily dis-integrated in the last few years, the digital giants – Google, Apple, Twitter, and in particular, Facebook Inc. – have provided some of the most conspicuous evidence of the increasingly bitter and polarized nature of political discourse, having been amongst the main arenas in which many of these discursive conflicts have been played out.

This staging has led many people to draw an association between social media and the broader political moment, and often to suggest that there might be causation between the two. There are good reasons to talk about social media together with polarization and other social and political problems. There are also many urgent criticisms of digital platforms that are much deserved, both in connection with these political circumstances and in broader political-economic terms. Unfortunately, however, many of the most frequently cited critiques of social media giants are not only inaccurate, but harmful, because of the ways in which they obscure our understanding of the threats that social media *do* represent, and the other more immediate causes of this political turbulence; the relative ease with which these erroneous charges can be rebutted; and the missed opportunities they amount to for understanding and protecting ourselves from social media apps appropriately, and responding to reactionary politics more effectively.

To resist these criticisms can sometimes appear, to a superficial reader, to be defensive of social media corporations, but the opposite is true: in order to mobilize against the forms of capital that social media corporations represent, the world needs to stop repeating unsustainable arguments that rely on unsubstantiated claims, and that exceptionalize and isolate the pathologies of social media corporations as though they were some kind of unprecedented surprise; and to focus instead on the material and structural factors that are so commonly ignored by liberal and conservative commentaries alike. This essay will offer a summary and critique of these flawed arguments, suggest some alternative critical approaches, and then discuss some broader strategies for addressing the pathologies that social media *do* represent.

ARE SOCIAL MEDIA A PRIMARY CAUSE OF HARM?

At the risk of repeating some of what I have written elsewhere about the relationship between various forms of digital and social media, misinformation, and reactionary politics, it may be helpful at the outset to summarise some of the ways that the critiques of social media and their relationship to reactionary politics have tended to be oversimplified and stripped of their political sting.[1]

These arguments appear in a number of different forms, but generally their thrust is that social media cause large numbers of people to be exposed to inaccurate, subtly manipulative or deliberately misleading messaging originating from hostile foreign governments, 'populist' figures, or ruthlessly commercial bloggers and tricksters. Because the platforms where this occurs fail to challenge or rein in these malicious acts, and leave it to the users to challenge and contest each other, this exposure results in behavioural modifications on a scale significant enough that electoral outcomes can be changed and political movements formed or directed.

One notable version of this argument is that social media platforms, and in particular Facebook, Twitter, and Whatsapp, are responsible for the phenomenon of 'fake news', which is in turn responsible for reactionary political movements such as the Trump campaign and subsequent administration. In early December 2016, as the world was attempting to make sense of Trump's victory, his losing opponent Hillary Clinton told the world that there was 'one threat in particular that should concern all Americans – Democrats, Republicans, and independents alike, especially those who serve in our Congress: the epidemic of malicious fake news and false propaganda that flooded social media over the past year. It's now clear that so-called fake news can have real-world consequences.'[2]

According to this view, not only were social media apparently fine until the year Clinton lost the election, but these 'real world' consequences of 'fake news' included her defeat – an idea she repeated and developed in her subsequent book about her 2016 loss, *What Happened?*[3] Only a fortnight before she made this statement, an editorial in the *New York Times* had excoriated Facebook for the 'fake news' appearing there that had supposedly facilitated Trump's victory.[4]

It is fair to interpret these rather superficial analyses in the context of liberal America's acute trauma at that moment, but this narrative has been repeated many times since then by numerous pundits and journalists. In 2018, a study reported by the *Washington Post* suggested a link between exposure to 'fake news' and defection from the Democratic Party between Obama's 2012 victory and Hillary Clinton's 2016 defeat.[5] We should always be happy to be corrected by a reliable set of research findings, but the study is instructive in ways other than those its authors hoped. Based on a single internet-based survey that asked roughly 1,600 participants to remember what they had been exposed to, it primarily focused on the 585 respondents who reported that they had voted for Obama in 2012 but not for Clinton in 2016. It did not account for the 32 per cent of US adults not using Facebook at all.[6] It also did not feature any reference to the by then plentiful work of scholars in the social sciences to understand why people *had* been motivated to defect from the Democrats to support Trump nor any analysis of the political developments of the preceding decades; nor did it mention the location of the participants, or whether they were located in swing states or not.[7] No wonder it was not peer-reviewed. While of course it is only one study, it is illustrative of precisely the fantasy that the Trump movement and the politics it represents could be explained away by reference to a small number of technology corporations, because of their large scale and lax regulation, without the need to look any deeper. In short, it was another iteration of the same banal technological exceptionalism that had led US liberals to believe that Twitter and Facebook alone could bring about the fall of repressive governments in the Middle East a decade earlier.[8] Technology, in the liberal story, is often either the main problem or the main solution, while structural factors are obscured or minimized. Another example of this tendency appeared when the UK riots occurred in 2011, and the encrypted messaging service BBM was blamed in the pages of *The Guardian*.[9]

Only a month after the above-described study was published in the United States, in April 2018, the Cambridge Analytica scandal broke as a result of a year of tenacious and exhaustive research by the investigative journalist Carole Cadwalladr and a couple key whistleblowers. In the months leading up to the 2016 US election, the company, which was funded by hedge-fund philanthropist Robert Mercer and initially directed by Trump strategist Steve Bannon, had exploited a major loophole in Facebook's lax data policy and negligent enforcement strategy in order to build voter profiles which were used to determine what messaging would be most influential with individual Facebook users.[10] Not only had Cambridge Analytica also been used by some of the unofficial Brexit campaign groups, such as Leave.EU, but another linked company known as AggregateIQ, based in Canada and outside British jurisdiction, whose proprietary technology was also owned by Robert Mercer, had been used by the official Vote Leave campaign, accounting for 40 per cent of its campaign spending.[11]

This was undoubtedly an extremely important story for our understanding of the triple-helix of politics, the internet, and capitalism. Any attempt to undermine democratic processes should be taken seriously, and it is perfectly fair to say that Facebook bore *some* culpability for what had happened. But what *had* happened? Once again, the reaction to this story was plagued by false causation, oversimplification, baseless assumptions, and a stubborn insistence on missing the point. That there was so much indignation about political interference when the scandal broke, including a call for people to delete their Facebook accounts entirely,[12] and that so much money had been given to Cambridge Analytica and its network of companies offering election outcomes to their clients using social media, underscored the irresistible appeal of the basic assumption that messaging on social media platforms is not only automatically and powerfully influential, but more so than the many other forms of political messaging that co-exist with social media – particularly television and mass print media. The long history of potent political interference by other means had seemingly been dwarfed, replaced, or long forgotten.

In the context of societies on both sides of the Atlantic that were already amnesic about their long history of political meddling, internal and external, there was perhaps something superficially understandable about this emphasis. The scale, accessibility, and emotion-driven nature of social media platforms makes them *seem* like they *might* be effective in swaying public opinion, and it is obviously essential to discover as much as possible about the extent to which this is true. But it was and remains a monumentally foolish approach to reach this conclusion based on assumption alone, because the results of an election were unexpected, and thereby choose to remain blind to the many other factors that ultimately determine the winner of an election – not least the steady degradation of democratic processes and institutions of the market-driven world of the last few decades.

Indeed, there were many good reasons to delete a Facebook account before this scandal ever broke, and this momentary outrage appeared to ignore the fact that when the exact same techniques had been mobilized by the digital marketing sector to convince people to buy products they didn't need, destroy the environment, undermine their mental health, and waste hours of time, very few people had been interested. Perhaps some exceptionalism around the importance of democratic process was a good sign, but while the outrage was fair enough, the naivety was embarrassing.[13]

Amongst the manifold attacks on the democratic process that a political scientist or sociologist might point out, this particular way of eroding it – by subjecting it to the same data-driven advertising techniques that are central to all other forms of mass-persuasion common to contemporary capitalism – represented some kind of excess in the minds of an outraged public. In hindsight, putting this exceptionalism in the context of that familiar liberal tendency towards techno-centrism makes visible what may well have been an element of wishful thinking: please can we blame social media for Trump and Brexit, so that we can 'fix' those problems by fixing or punishing social media, and avoid our own complicity in the process?

Another area where superficial, selective arguments are offered about social media is in relation to political polarization itself. We have been reminded about the scourge of 'filter bubbles' and 'echo chambers' on numerous occasions. Barack Obama said they were bad, David Letterman nodded, and the administrator of the Office of Information and Regulatory Affairs, the legal scholar Cass Sunstein, wrote a book on why filter bubbles led to division, replete with standard enlightenment-derived liberal reasoning and John Stuart Mill quotations.[14] Strangely however, somewhere along the way, the original meaning of filter bubble had changed from being a way of talking about the automated personalization features that Google and other corporations had been developing a decade earlier, which meant that different users would see different content – as per the original coinage from the writer Eli Parisier[15] – to being a way of mystifying the issue of political polarization such that technology was assumed (with almost no proof) to be its cause.

Here too, scholars from diverse fields including sociology, anthropology, political science and economics have offered other, much more convincing and thorough explanations for the sharply polarized political rupture we have experienced,[16] while studies show that we are often exposed to a *greater* range of political opinions on social media than via other forms of social contact,[17] that most people's primary motivations for using social media are not political,[18] and that other forms of social contact and media may have more influence on our political opinions than social media platforms. Despite all of this, the belief that 'filter bubbles' and 'echo chambers' on social media are the driving cause of political polarization remains remarkably persistent.

As indicated above, this is not to say that there is no issue at all. Facebook's own internal research showed in 2020 that the company's products did have a tendency to make an already-polarized society more polarized, before that research was later shelved by the company's executives.[19] Furthermore, one area where a filter bubble-like pattern can be observed is in the facilitation of already-extreme groups, such as Alternative für Deutschland (AfD) in Germany.[20] Indeed, the storming of the US Capitol in January 2021 in support of Donald Trump's false claims that the 2020 US election was rigged was largely blamed on digital platforms more friendly to the far-right, such as Gab and Parler, but the statistics showed that there was far more activity on Facebook groups than on those platforms. Probably the clearest example is one from 2016, in which Russian technicians working at the Internet Research Agency in St Petersburg are known to have organized two opposing protests – in defence of, and against, Islam – on different sides of the same Texas street simultaneously.[21]

This is of course irresponsible and stupid at best, and the issue is precisely that, as with disinformation and propaganda, more complex factors originating beyond social media are regularly ignored, despite being hugely interesting and of crucial importance. Why have societies as diverse as Brazil, Hungary, the United Kingdom, the United States, France, Turkey, and the Philippines become so polarized? Is it because the Russians have successfully used Facebook to turn them all against one another? The more that we centre the answers on social media, particularly on the popular debates that are widely circulated, the more other questions and answers are obscured and neglected, just at a moment when the public's literacy around political economy seems to be so in need of development and reinforcement.

Even if we are to focus on the media ecosystem, a narrow, almost surgical isolation of social media seems bizarre. As Natalie Fenton and Des Freedman argued brilliantly in the 2018 volume of the *Socialist Register*, the mainstream media, whether commercial or state-supported, have played an extremely important role in the degradation of Western democracy.[22] If an incendiary and misleading Fox News article is shared widely on Facebook's platform, it makes sense that we should ask questions of Facebook about the extent to which that is appropriate, but we should also be asking about Fox News and the general climate of right-wing media in the United States, not only on social media but on cable TV, radio, and in print. Why choose one and not the other? In fact, we could go further and ask about the US as a media ecosystem, and why, far more than in the UK or other jurisdictions, it allows a purist and historically inaccurate interpretation of the principle of freedom of speech to prevent sensible media regulation that might mitigate some of these harms. A certain amount of culpability can and should be laid at Mark Zuckerberg's and Facebook's doors, but where, for example, is Rupert

Murdoch's name in the debate about polarization and political extremism? We could ask the same about the efforts of the Internet Research Agency to use Facebook to stoke up US Americans' political disagreements. The truth is that while social media are technologically unique, and historically specific, they are not politically exceptional.

The idea that exposure to social media content that is mendacious, manipulative, or of poor quality may lead to forms of political influence, conflict, or violence need not be discounted in order to avoid using simplistic or selective arguments peppered with untestable assumptions, fallacious reasoning, and downright ignorance. The issue is precisely that in a world so often unwilling to do the work of engaging with nuance and complexity, to facilitate liberal social media-blaming arguments whilst ignoring the bigger picture is not a tenable position, especially for the left, however much we may loathe what social media corporations represent.

Moving away from the myths outlined above is motivated neither by pedantry nor a wish to defend social media corporations. On the contrary, just as with any apparent solution that is not really a solution, the greatest problem we face in our fight against the threats that social media corporations do pose is precisely that ineffective critiques *strengthen* the very system they appear to attack. Making Facebook and its executives primarily responsible for the rise of reactionary politics, for misinformation and disinformation, for unexpected election outcomes, or for polarization, or for articulating critiques that *appear* to offer this simplified causation and selective reasoning, makes it harder, not easier, to fight against social media corporations, the reactionary politics for which they are blamed, and the ruthless forms of capitalism that they epitomise. It gives the ruthless public relations teams these companies employ an opportunity to easily and correctly respond: 'we are not the ones who caused these problems.' This makes it *more* likely, not less, that social media giants will be able to pass without meaningful challenge or consequence, and extend their reach into ever more intimate quadrants of our lives.

WHAT IS WRONG WITH SOCIAL MEDIA?

Attention and Human Vulnerability

There comes a point in the dystopia of late capitalism at which all principles and values other than the perfect functioning of the market, the maintenance of the status quo, or some ambivalent and inconsistent combination of the two, seem to have largely been forgotten, and need to be reinserted into the conversation. Accordingly, the first critique to be articulated here is based on a relatively straightforward moral objection: quite simply, the engineered exploitation of human frailty is something that we should always condemn.

This exploitation is precisely what social media corporations do on an unimaginable scale, however, and it is the guiding principle in their design. But there are misconceptions here, too. Social media platforms do not normally 'sell your data' as is often alleged. Rather, they are built on a ruthless commodification of human attention, demanded and extracted by any means their engineers and designers can think of, and then sold to advertisers. Data do play an important role, however. In order to sell our attention in a way that is effective, digital platforms need to know as much about our interests as possible and take every possible liberty in order to find it out. Thus, the capturing of data is essential to the 'platform capitalism' model that this process represents, because those data enable users to be understood, and the likelihood of our attention and engagement predicted.[23] This means tracking every click and tap, keeping a record of everything you have 'liked', including on third-party websites, and every message, comment, or other interaction that you have typed on the site, even if you thought better of it and deleted before posting. It means crunching all these data and applying sophisticated analysis to them, even holding information about users that the users themselves cannot access. If private citizens did to each other what Facebook and Google do, we would call it stalking. When the state does it, we rightly call it intrusion and overreach. When Facebook or Google does it, it is mostly greeted with a shrug, which in itself is instructive as to users' stoic acceptance of their relative disempowerment; but it also tells us that social media companies have nothing but contempt for the privacy of their users – a protected human right in much of the world.

Privacy can seem like something of an abstract, distant issue compared to the affectively laden micro-proximity of the content and social relations mediated by social media platforms in their attempt to gain our attention, which perhaps also explains the shrug; so it is worth going a bit deeper to explore the ways that the attention economy has been built into social media platforms. Mark Zuckerberg, the founder of Facebook, was a *psychology* and computer science double-major before dropping out of Harvard, but it does not take a genius of psychology to understand that the things that most effectively command our attention are not the banalities of life, though these have been enclosed by digital giants as well – particularly Google – but the most salient topics and media: cute animals, highly palatable foods, sociality, sex, politics, conspiracy theories, and various other forms of controversy and intrigue. And for all the hedonism of watching a 45-second tutorial on a smartphone on how to make cheesy noodles at 3 a.m. in an attempt to calm one's anxiety, let us remember that we do not need to enjoy media for it to command our attention. Sometimes we simply cannot look away from the very worst of sights. As Richard Seymour has noted, through the same attention-centric model, 'we can become attached to the *miseries* of online life, a state of perpetual outrage and antagonism'.[24] Sometimes it is precisely our anger, fear or indignation that makes it impossible to disengage.

In other words, the most potent reinforcers of the underlying business model that drives social networking platforms are many of the very same things that are said to be harmful about them. Particularly cruel is the fact that the *purpose* of social media is so utterly disguised. Users are lulled into the belief that they have been offered a free set of tools with which to build a profile and thus to present themselves, to socialize, and to discuss and learn about their shared world together. But nothing could be further from the truth. Every feature of social networks is rolled out with at least a tacit knowledge that many of the things that are best able to command our attention are also those things that have the greatest potential to mislead us, inflame latent social and political tensions that are already in the culture, and exacerbate insecurities and mental health issues that we may otherwise have been able to manage more easily. The intention may never be to harm users but there is a sinister calculation that the potential for harm is a risk worth taking if it means more of our attention can be commanded and sold.

When fighting an adversary who often resorts to a language of false empiricism in self-defence, where possible we must try to be genuinely empirical about the impacts of the negative impacts we allege. The usage of social media is at the very least correlated with a wide array of psychological issues, such as depression, life dissatisfaction, body image dissatisfaction and eating disorders, and bullying, as well as being riven with the misinformation, rumour, and bigotry that have heralded the general deterioration of capitalist market-driven societies in the last few years. The *timing* of their arrival also coincides with a steady increase in a number of the above issues. This is still correlation, however. Actual causation is very difficult to establish because of the intrinsic limitations on observation and measurement of social media users – data that only Facebook and its friends hold – and because most studies tend to rely on self-reporting questionnaires, which have severe limitations. However, some studies do claim to show direct causation. A major study from the University of Michigan found that the use of Facebook directly led to a decline in the 'subjective wellbeing' and life satisfaction of participants in the hours and days that followed.[25]

But even if the data can't always reveal an unambiguous causation of depression, misinformation, or loneliness, social media certainly do feed off them and exploit them.[26] Is that so much better? As far as causation is concerned, the most likely scenario is a circularity in which the use of social media leads to a decline in our wellbeing by worsening the severity of the very conditions that capitalism as a whole tends to produce, and that in turn drives further social media usage: poor mental health, social isolation, and alienation. For example, we can feel lonelier because of using social media and seeing what a great time everyone else appears to be having, but also use them because we feel lonely – the two are not mutually exclusive.

In the last few years, a number of what are essentially confessions as to the sinister nature of these technologies have surfaced from various co-founders and senior engineers who were key to Facebook's early development, clarifying in some cases that Facebook's plan was always to exploit key psychological vulnerabilities. In fact, these were the exact words used by Facebook's founding president Sean Parker, in a 2017 speech in which he reflected on Facebook's early aims.[27] Others, such as Justin Rosenstein, the inventor of the 'like' button, and Asa Raskin, the inventor of infinite scrolling, have similarly expressed regret for their role in developing these platforms, with Raskin confessing to the BBC that 'Behind every screen on your phone, there are generally like literally a thousand engineers that have worked on this thing to try to make it maximally addicting'.[28]

One does not need to allege calculated malice or assume reliable psychological impact or wholesale behavioural influence to observe that building a business that exploits poor mental health, poor literacy, and misinformation, and is correlated with a deterioration in all three, is utterly indefensible. Every time that we insist that Facebook simply needs to change its algorithm or add clear labels to address 'fake news', to moderate its content better, or introduce safety checks on certain Instagram posts, even if we mean well and are trying to ameliorate these harms, we are calling for a technological or operational fix in order to redeem a business platform that ultimately is built on the systematic exploitation of vulnerabilities in both universal and individual human experience on an unprecedented scale. These are approaches that, to use the words of Rosa Luxemburg, offer little more than the reform of capitalism and the 'the suppression of the abuses of capitalism instead of the suppression of capitalism itself'.[29]

Performative Censorship and Control

In recent years, in response to the perceived problem of misinformation and disinformation on their platforms, both Facebook and Twitter have refused to be held accountable for disinformation in political ads, or to take any action in respect of those ads. Users, they said, could decide for themselves what was true and what was not, which was another implicit articulation of the rudimentary John Stuart Mill-informed understanding of politics and public debate that has so often coloured conversations on these topics.[30]

Though large numbers of people may have been happy that Donald Trump was removed from social platforms, the elation at seeing him silenced should have been followed by a sense of dread at the sinister precedent this represented. One of the world's loudest and most dangerous reactionary voices had been sideswiped by the awesome power of surveillance capital. In January 2021, the same month that the United States Capitol building was attacked by Trump supporters who believed that the election had been rigged, Twitter was busy suspending a significant number of left-leaning anti-fascist accounts which had never spread any misinformation, or advocated for any violence whatsoever.[31] This type of shutdown was by no means new. It has happened to similar targets for years: content drawing attention to the occupation of Palestine, the Black Lives Matter movement, and many other progressive causes has been regularly censored or removed with little explanation or warning.[32]

In practice, it is not that Facebook, its subsidiary Instagram, or Twitter are deliberately or consciously hostile to left-leaning views specifically, although Instagram did implement a change to its algorithm in order *not* to remove content about Palestine quite so readily during the 2021 bombing of Gaza – in response to public outcry.[33] It is more that they are inconsistent: laissez-faire to the point of recklessness about what is on their platforms when it suits them, while being regularly overzealous about removing content that is too prominent in the 'wrong' ways. YouTube has deployed a similarly unpredictable approach. While the platform is generally rife with disinformation, conspiracy theories, and other questionable content, the company has also been inconsistent and seemingly unsure about what should be allowed on its platform, and what should be removed or have its advertising disabled – known as demonetization.[34]

By contrast, the social media platform TikTok, owned by the Chinese multinational firm ByteDance, has happily embraced a more classic censorship model, according to moderation guidelines that were leaked to *The Guardian*. Not only are videos that contain swearing or sexual themes (even in text alone) at risk of deletion, or of being made 'visible to self', which renders them invisible to TikTok's discovery algorithm, but content that mentions sensitive aspects of Chinese history such as Tiananmen Square, or controversial foreign policy, religious groups, or ethnic conflicts is also grounds for removal.[35]

Rather than simply calling for better systems of moderation, we need to ask some bigger questions. The first, as the companies themselves often disingenuously ask regulators in their bid to escape responsibility, is whether we really want large private interests to be responsible for deciding which ideas and what content are permissible. As Derek Hrynyshyn wrote in the 2020 volume of the *Socialist Register*, 'the decision of where to draw the line [about what to remove] is an inherently political one, and leaving this judgment up to the owners of the platforms is not a democratic way to ensure communication serves the public'.[36] Often however, it is not their encroachment into the political so much as their cynical and selective retreat from it that betrays their real motives. Opaque procedures and inaccurate algorithms mean that the content control mechanisms of these platforms are open to serious abuse. In August 2021, *VICE News* broke the story that mercenary scammers had been manipulating Instagram's automated content control mechanisms, as a client-facing service, in order to have users suspended on demand.[37] The coordinated abuse of reporting features that allow users to flag offending users and content is a common tactic of military campaigns, and was used by Israel's 'Cyber Unit' in May 2021 to remove hundreds of posts and accounts advocating support for Palestine.[38]

This leads to the second question. Is 'censorship' in the normative sense really the best way to characterize what we see here, on the part of the platforms themselves? While the kind of 'classic' censorship utilized by TikTok is undeniably disturbing, and amounts to ideological intervention in a way that befits the label of 'censorship', as does that of the Cyber Unit, a narrow rhetorical focus on this kind of censorship provides an element of deniability for platforms that are more motivated by profits than by the desire to suppress messages on the basis of ideology. It thus obscures another element in the content control and moderation approach used by Facebook, Twitter, and YouTube: a prioritization of surplus value over any control of political speech. For example, the harsh reality is that in suspending Donald Trump's account, Twitter actually eliminated a valuable asset for their enduring relevance and visibility as a platform under *popular* pressure. Executives did not want to 'censor' him, and it was pressure from the public and from rank-and-file employees that brought about his removal.[39] More than anything else, this should illustrate how truly flawed the model that social media platforms embody really is. Until five minutes before Twitter and Facebook removed Trump's accounts, they were benefiting from his presence there. YouTube even allowed the Trump 2020 campaign to plaster its front page with ads on election day.[40] For those in the business of attention, any proposal to limit the salience or appeal of content exerts a downwards pressure on revenues that is likely to be met with the aloof reluctance that the executives of Facebook, Twitter, and other social networks have shown over and over again.

The third question, given this realization, is whether there really is any version of this model that would actually be acceptable. Is the contradiction between needing Trump and deleting him; between enclosing and then intensifying public spheres for private gain, and taking responsibility for the problems that this business invites, something that can be fixed with a bit of tweaking? Ultimately, this does not seem to be a matter of 'getting the balance right' between freedom of expression and enforcing 'community standards'. The functional, inclusive, pluralistic public spheres that Facebook's proponents are always so quick to tell us they want is and has always been an illusory construct that meaningfully benefits only Facebook's and Twitter's shareholders. No amount of technical adjustment by California's scores of twenty-something techno-utopians, or policy updates from its cold-hearted middle management, will ever get around the fact that the company does not really care about what actually appears on its platforms, so long as it gets our attention – it only cares about how much it *appears* to care. Content removal occurs largely at the performative level in order to preserve an air of legitimacy for an otherwise irredeemably flawed model and keep regulators from closing in. No surprise, then, that we see here too a familiar disregard for the quality of those public spheres that have arisen on social media – the same contemptuous, reckless lack of interest as the one with which social platforms address the psychological impacts of their products, or the privacy of their users.

GREED AND CAPITALISM

Looking at all these issues with social media together provides insight of its own, and so it is perhaps helpful to summarize them here. Even if they do not cause it, social media *do* lubricate and amplify the spread of harmful misinformation – for example, disinformation about Covid, or bigoted or dangerous conspiracy theories. And in so doing, their platforms *do* cause further harms in terms of the public spheres that they host. Whereas some media do this with licensed broadcasting from the 'top down', social networks dredge from the bottom up, their greed for our attention encouraging us to attempt to mislead and influence *one another* with little restriction or regulation. Likewise, social media do erode our privacy and exacerbate poor mental health for the sake of gaining and then targeting our attention. In so doing, they exacerbate a mental health crisis that, even prior to the pandemic, was one of the most serious public health crises in Britain, the US, and other countries.

Ultimately, however, the issue is not whether these or any harms flow from social media, but whether it is appropriate to respond as though these harms flow *largely* or *only* from social media. Simplistic causation and pure exceptionalism must give way to the certainty that social media platforms are proliferated by their owners and creators in reckless indifference as to whether they cause any harm or not. The truth is that they are quite prepared to tolerate the harms that their platforms may produce if these are offset by the value created for shareholders. They *know* that they may do harm – they just don't care. This inhumane, nihilistic, reckless, greedy disregard for the human beings on which their businesses are founded – those that tend to be called 'users' – reveals a character of Facebook and other digital platforms' development over the last decade and a half that is both familiar and predictable. It is the same one that is destroying our planet. Marx and Engels themselves wrote that the bourgeoisie had 'left remaining no other nexus between man and man than naked self-interest, callous "cash payment"' and had 'resolved personal worth into exchange value, and in place of the numberless indefeasible chartered freedoms, has set up that single, unconscionable freedom—Free Trade'.[41] The aspects of social media that I have critiqued above can be seen as a development and intensification of exactly those tendencies within capitalism, despite the huge interval in time between Marx and Engels' critique and the arrival of today's 'social' media. The point is precisely that to make sense of social media properly, the meaningful picture we must grasp is one of global and transhistorical scope that cannot be isolated to a handful of technology companies in the twenty-first century. A narrow and selective focus on certain misdeeds of tech companies, however grave, only serves as a way of *not* having to critique or even discuss the capitalist system more generally, which reproduces the self-obfuscation that benefits the capitalism system – and is at best is a missed opportunity and precious time wasted, at worst abject disingenuity. If we are to have any chance of redressing these harms, we need to see them in the context of, and as a predictable extension of, the detrimental commercial imperatives, social expectations, and cultural and political pathologies in capitalism that the globalized market-driven world has only intensified in the last few decades. The social media platforms have brought enclosure, commodification, and the pointless cycle of sublimated demand and unsatisfying supply further and more intimately into human life than any prior form of capitalism. It is our responsibility to criticize them for *that*, as well as the specific damage that their products do.

LOOKING AHEAD

The question of what is to be done, or where we can go from here, is always the most challenging and controversial within the left, and could be an entire essay by itself. There are both practical and philosophical ideas to be considered, and having argued against social media exceptionalism makes it necessary to address capitalism more broadly as well as offering ideas specific to social media.

Firstly, on a more practical note, as with so many pathologies of capitalism, the place where conversations usually start about how the harmful effects of social media may be addressed is with regulation. Even in light of the hollowing out of the state, and the 'fake democracy' that has slowly arisen in recent years, there are undoubtedly legislative challenges to be undertaken.[42] One key aspect of this is that in fighting back against a problem of global significance and impact, we can and must be ready to call for *international* regulation, as more than just a backstop for national government initiatives. Binding international treaties, including incentives and peaceful sanctions, even with all their complications, represent a means by which meaningful long-term change can be brought about in respect of anything that happens via the internet. But even the most comprehensive international regulation is not a magic bullet. There will probably always be some place where the instruments of global capital can hide. In the context of social media specifically, as Derek Hrynyshyn has noted, the combination of complexity, opacity, and the business model of targeted attention limits the realistic prospects of regulation: 'Capitalist platforms … inevitably require the hidden operation of algorithms in ways that enable the social harms that regulation is intended to counter. Platforms would have every incentive to not co-operate with regulators, and regulators would have little ability to ensure compliance'.[43]

Another practical approach is the possibility that the left might learn better how to produce technology, rather than to leave it to predatory entrepreneurs and libertarian hackers. Indeed, free and open-source technology continues both to set a precedent and to provide an opportunity for meaningful agency that, all too often, the left has ignored. As Hrynyshyn has also explored, with better government support and alternative funding models, open-source alternatives to social media and their ruthless business models may become more feasible than at present. Here too, however, there are some important caveats. First, it is vital to remember that technology fixes practical problems, not political problems, and that attempts to produce political solutions using code are generally doomed to failure, or even to cause further harm. Second, building one small means of production will not immediately guarantee independence from all the others that are part of the problem. If someone were to build an app tomorrow that proved to be a useful tool for organizing political movements, for example, it would still rely on hardware developed by the merciless logics and supply chains of Apple, Samsung, or Huawei – not necessarily an insurmountable obstacle in the long term, but an important consideration nonetheless. Third, it is intrinsic to the user experience of timeline media as we know them that they are sorted and curated by algorithms. A 'pure', un-curated timeline that simply shows you everything your connections have posted would be unfeasible for most users, so our demands need to be for better, and radically transparent, algorithms, rather than for their elimination altogether. Finally, social media usage is motivated partly by the need for compensatory media experiences that are necessitated by the affective maladies of capitalist life, and a public, open version with anything like the same levels of engagement would not escape this reality.[44]

Besides exploring these practical possibilities, however – especially given their limited prospects – there are some tactical and discursive avenues to consider. If the conversations we have about the digital giants and their pathologies require that we engage with the fundamental qualities of capitalism, and capitalism systematically manufactures obfuscation about its own processes and pathologies, part of how we challenge these social media corporations must be to make explicit what has been obscured about capitalism itself.

Virtually all of the major global challenges we currently face – our inability to get to grips with the Covid-19 pandemic on a global scale, the turn to nationalism and reactionary libertarianism, the decline of public literacy that leaves us vulnerable to disinformation and conspiracy theory, and most of all, the existential global threat of the climate catastrophe – are all products of the same capitalist system that has also given us Facebook, Google, and the monstrous edifice of 'surveillance capitalism'; consequently our conversations must have an equally broad scope. Despite the electoral failures of left-wing leaders such as Jeremy Corbyn and Bernie Sanders for the time being, the crises their projects responded to represent an opportunity to break with the discursive and dogmatic associations with which positive left-wing political articulations have been unfairly laden for so long, and to make mainstream the importance of frank conversations about the realities of capitalism. Indeed, historically speaking there has not been a more important moment, or a better opportunity, to have critical conversations about capitalism for a very long time, and it is a moment that should be seized. From there, there is a further opportunity to outline bold, ambitious, positive visions of the world that needs to be built.

Crucial to these processes will be media, both conventional and emergent, but since the focus of this essay has been social media, and there are other writers more qualified to discuss conventional media, let us consider two things. First is the question of *whether* these same platforms, accepting all the limitations outlined above, can be put to use in the service of left policies and agendas. Although this essay has taken issue with the self-defeating, oversimplified ways in which the critique of social media is too often formulated, and argued that the model these platforms represent is flawed beyond redemption, it does not follow that they offer no short- to medium-term practical benefits for progressive politics. Indeed, left-aligned political movements in several countries have already made use of social media in ways that provoked a regulatory response from right-wing governments, including Donald Trump when he was president.[45] As long as the trap is avoided of assuming that such content automatically makes a meaningful difference, and the nature of platform capitalism is not forgotten, these media may still be helpful as part of a broader communicative pivot towards more affective and creative advocacy for left-wing causes, and there are some cautiously encouraging examples. For example, even allowing for intergenerational and other sociological factors, it is hard to look at the way that May 2021 escalation in aggression towards the Palestinians was covered on TikTok or Instagram, for example, and not wonder if those representations might have played a role in raising awareness of the occupation and its brutality, particularly for younger audiences and those who did not already have strong views on the subject. Indeed, even despite the censorship described above, and often in defiance of it, TikTok in particular contains a lot of political, economic, and scientific content that is sympathetic to progressive and socialist politics.

Despite the obvious caveats, Tanner Mirrlees, writing in the 2020 volume of the *Socialist Register*, has called for cautious participation on existing platforms in order to help catalyze support for socialist politics.[46] In the short term, this is the right approach. Natalie Fenton and Des Freedman are absolutely correct to say that 'we need to figure out how best to build a radical political project in which truth-telling and communicative capacity emerge from the bottom up and not through paternalistic diktat or pure market exchange'. They rightly argue that we need 'a democratic communications system genuinely in the hands of its users as opposed to controlled by billionaires and bureaucrats'.[47] This is surely a longer-term goal, however. In the short term we need to cultivate forms of communicative capacity and bottom-up truth-telling that complement the conversations already taking place on the platforms people currently use, exploitative and flawed though they are. This may amount to 'dancing with the devil', since, as Mirrlees puts it, 'the relationship between platform owners and users is authoritarian, not democratic'. But for now, we do not have the luxury of considering ourselves above a participative approach, at least while we do what we can to erode the power of these platforms and build something better.

Secondly there is the question of *how*. Crucial to this process are sources from which those conversations and interventions can draw, and so a key part of the escape from a market-driven world is the construction of new networks, institutions, and organizations. This is not for one second to overlook the work of those successful collective structures we have built, particularly some of the smaller, newer trade unions that remain untainted by corruption, or networks such as NEON, Acorn, or Progressive International. Rather, it is precisely that we need to build many more of these, both to act as collective repositories for sharing all the creativity and talent we already possess, and to develop our movements and causes further. In fact, besides the synergic benefits of working together, collective action is *itself* an important ingredient of political freedom. Received wisdom is generally that the left is collectivist while the free-marketeers, libertarians, and the right are individualist and distrust any notion of the common good; but this conflates intention with method. As any recent history of right-wing media and institutions will show, the neoliberals and the right are adept at collective action so long as it is in service of an ideal which enshrines individual freedoms and protects private property.[48] By contrast, especially without the financial backing that the right and the market fundamentalists enjoy, and possessed only of the abundant intellectual and cultural strengths we have, the question posed so often by those motivated to ameliorate the crises we face is an individualist 'what can I do?'; but there are better places to start. As Byung-Chul Han has written, riffing on Marx, 'being free means nothing other than self-realization with others. Freedom is synonymous with a working community.'[49] If there is an escape from the power of social media corporations, the market-driven society that facilitates them, or capitalism itself, it is almost certainly one that is collective, creative and collaborative.

NOTES

1   See Marcus Gilroy-Ware, *Filling the Void: Emotion, Capitalism & Social Media*, London: Repeater Books, 2017; and Marcus Gilroy-Ware, *After the Fact? The Truth about Fake News*, London: Repeater Books, 2020.

2   Callum Borchers, 'How Hillary Clinton might have inspired Trump's "fake news" attacks', *The Washington Post*, 3 January 2018.

3   Hillary Clinton, *What happened*, New York: Simon & Schuster, 2017.

4   'Facebook and the Digital Virus Called Fake News', *New York Times*, 20 November 2016.

5   Richard Gunther, Paul Beck and Erik Nisbet, 'Fake News May Have Contributed to Trump's 2016 Victory', *Ohio State University*, 2018, available at: www.documentcloud. org.

6   Shannon Greenwood, Andrew Perrin, and Maeve Duggan, *Demographics of Social Media Users in 2016*, Pew Research Center: Internet, Science & Tech.

7   Sephen Morgan, and Jiwon Lee, 'Economic Populism and Bandwagon Bigotry: Obama-to-Trump Voters and the Cross Pressures of the 2016 Election', *Socius: Sociological Research for a Dynamic World*, 5, 2019.

8   Evegeny Morozov, *The Net Delusion: The Dark Side of Internet Freedom*, New York, NY: Allen Lane, 2011.

9   Josh Halliday, 'London riots: how BlackBerry Messenger played a key role', *The Guardian*, 8 August 2011,.

10   Carole Cadwalladr, 'The great British Brexit robbery: how our democracy was hijacked', *The Guardian*, 7 May 2017.

11   Carole Cadwalladr and Mark Townsend, 'Revealed: the ties that bind Vote Leave's data firm to controversial Cambridge Analytica', *The Guardian*, 24 March 2018.

12   Tom Gerken, 'WhatsApp co-founder says it is time to delete Facebook', *BBC News*, 21 March 2018.

13   Marcus Gilroy-Ware, 'Cambridge Analytica: the outrage is the real story', *openDemocracy*, 29 March 2018.

14   Cass Sunstein, *#Republic: Divided Democracy in The Age Of Social Media*, Princeton: Princeton University Press, 2018.

15   Eli Pariser, *The Filter Bubble*, London: Penguin, 2011.

16   See for examples: Sivamohan Valluvan, *The Clamour Of Nationalism*, Manchester: Manchester University Press, 2019 for a sociological approach; Arile Russell Hochschild, *Strangers in Their Own Land: Anger and Mourning on the American Right*, United States: The New Press, 2019, for a social-anthropology approach; Wendy Brown, *In the Ruins of Neoliberalism*, New York: Columbia University Press, 2019, for a political science analysis; and Mark Blyth, *Austerity: The History of a Dangerous Idea*, Oxford: Oxford University Press, 2013, for an economist's view.

17   Frederik Zuiderveen Borgesius, Damian Trilling, Judith Möller et al., 'Should we worry about filter bubbles?', *Internet Policy Review*, 5(1), 2016.

18   Axel Bruns, *Are Filter Bubbles Real?*, Cambridge: Polity Press, 2019.

19   Jeff Horwitz and Deepa Seetharaman, 'Facebook Executives Shut Down Efforts To Make The Site Less Divisive', *Wall Street Journal*, 26 May 2020.

20   See Bruns, *Are Filter Bubbles Real?*

21   Lorenzo Franceschi-Bicchierai, 'Russian Facebook Trolls Got Two Groups of People to Protest Each Other In Texas', *Vice*, 2017.

22   Natalie Fenton and Des Freedman, 'Fake Democracy, Bad News', in Leo Panitch and Greg Albo, eds., *Socialist Register 2018: Rethinking Democracy*, London: Merlin Press, 2017.

23   Nick Srnicek, *Platform Capitalism*, Cambridge: Polity Books, 2017.

24   Richard Seymour, *The Twittering Machine,* London: The Indigo Press, 2019.

25   Ethan Kross, Phillipe Verduyn, Emre Demiralp, et al., 'Facebook use predicts declines in subjective well-being in young adults', *PLoS ONE*, 8(8), 2013.

26   See Gilroy-Ware, *Filling the Void.*

27   Olivia Solon, 'Ex-Facebook president Sean Parker: site made to exploit human "vulnerability"', *The Guardian*, 9 November 2017.

28   Hilary Andersson, 'Social media apps are 'deliberately' addictive to users', *BBC News*, 2018.

29   Rosa Luxemburg, *Social Reform or Revolution?*, 1900, Chapter 8, available at: www. marxists.org.

30   Emily Stewart, 'Watch AOC ask Mark Zuckerberg if she can run fake Facebook ads, too.', *Vox*, 23 October 2019.

31   'Twitter Suspends Antifa-Linked Accounts Following Inauguration Day Riots', *CBNC*, 22 January 2021.

32   See Gilroy-Ware, *Filling the Void*, pp. 158-67.

33   Kim Lyons, 'Instagram making changes to its algorithm after it was accused of censoring pro-Palestinian content', *The Verge*, 2021.

34   Matthew Gault, 'Infowars Returns To Youtube After CEO Said It Will Allow 'Offensive' Content [Updated]', *Vice News*, 2019.

35   Alex Hern, 'Revealed: how TikTok censors videos that do not please Beijing', *The Guardian*, 25 September 2019.

36   Derek Hrynyshyn, 'Imagining Platform Socialism', in Leo Panitch and Greg Albo, eds, *Socialist Register 2021: Beyond Digital Capitalism: New Ways of Living*, London: Merlin Press, 2020.

37   Joseph Cox, 'Scammer Service Will Ban Anyone From Instagram for $60', *Vice News*, 5 August 2021.

38   Nadim Nashif, 'Israel's digital apartheid is silencing Palestinians', *OpenDemocracy*, 20 May 2021.

39   Jacob Kastrenakes, 'Hundreds of Twitter employees call for Trump to be banned', *The Verge* 8 January 2021.

40   Isobel Asher Hamilton, 'Trump's campaign booked out YouTube's homepage for Election Day. YouTube won't let that happen again – but insists it's nothing to do with Trump', *Business Insider*, 3 November 2020.

41   Karl Marx and Friedrich Engels, *Manifesto of the Communist Party*, 1848.

42   For explorations of 'fake democracy' see: Fenton and Freedman, 'Fake Democracy, Bad News', and Gilroy-Ware, *After the Fact?*, pp. 6-63.

43   See Hrynyshyn, 'Imagining Platform Socialism'.

44   See Gilroy-Ware, *Filling the Void*.

45   Maggie Haberman, and Kate Conger, 'Trump Prepares Order to Limit Social Media Companies' Protection', *New York Times*, 28 May 2020.

46   Tanner Mirrlees, 'Socialists on Social Media Platforms', in Leo Panitch and Greg Albo, eds, *Socialist Register 2021: Beyond Digital Capitalism: New Ways of Living*, London: Merlin Press, 2020.

47   Fenton and Freedman, 'Fake Democracy, Bad News'.

48   Jane Mayer, *Dark Money*. London: Scribe, 2016.

49   Byung-Chul Han, *Psychopolitics: Neoliberalism and New Technologies of Power*, London: Verso, 2017.

THE EVOLUTION OF 'RACE' AND RACIAL JUSTICE UNDER NEOLIBERALISM

ADOLPH REED JR. AND TOURÉ F. REED

[The] Civil Rights Revolution is not confined to the Negro; nor is it confined to civil rights, for our white allies know that they cannot be free while we are not, and we know that we have no future in a society in which six million black and white people are unemployed and millions more live in poverty ... Yes, we want a Fair Employment Practices Act, but what good will it do if profit-geared automation destroys the jobs of millions of workers, black and white? We want integrated public schools, but that means we also want federal aid to education — all forms of education.

A. Philip Randolph
Speech at the 1963 March on Washington for Jobs & Freedom

One of the most consequential, but seldom discussed, features of post-World War II black American politics and political discourse is a steadily increasing disconnection of programmes of racial justice from political economy. The orientation Randolph expressed in his speech at the March on Washington was already in retreat. Tellingly, the 1963 March has gone down in history not as an initiative of Randolph's labour-based Negro American Labor Council (NALC), or as, initially, a march to demand a federal jobs programme, but as the showcase for Martin Luther King, Jr.'s 'I Have a Dream' speech.[1] Three years later, the AFL-CIO's[2] A. Philip Randolph Institute (APRI), led by Randolph himself and long-time civil rights and labour activist Bayard Rustin, released *A 'Freedom Budget' for All Americans,* which laid out a pragmatic agenda for realizing a full-employment economy, from which, they insisted, black Americans would benefit disproportionately.[3]

APRI and allies distributed the document to a variety of liberals and progressives, which further broadened its reach. The League for Industrial Democracy, through Michael Harrington's and fellow Socialist Tom Kahn's efforts, published and distributed its own edition, as did Americans for Democratic Action. The AFL–CIO's Industrial Union Department published and distributed two editions – one for union leaders that by 1968 totalled 85,000 copies and a shorter twenty-page version that eventually totalled 100,000. Union magazines and other publications touted and excerpted the document, and Rustin and allies discussed a public education campaign, including speaking tours and other forms of outreach.[4]

Despite endorsements from prominent individuals and civil rights, labour, liberal, and religious organizations, Randolph and Rustin failed to mobilize a national movement in support of their programme. Several factors combined to pre-empt the effort to generate a national campaign around the Freedom Budget. Most immediately, President Lyndon Johnson's opposition to the idea stayed active involvement from labour, civil rights, and liberal groups that depended on his administration's support for other initiatives that were important to them. Randolph, Rustin, and former New Dealer and Chair of President Harry Truman's Council of Economic Advisors, Leon Keyserling, the document's principal architect, anticipated arguments that the programme was fiscally infeasible, because of the escalating cost of the Vietnam War. They, therefore, sought to demonstrate that the federal government could pursue both 'guns and butter' without generating unacceptable deficits or inflation. While the antiwar movement interpreted these concessions as an endorsement of the war, Randolph et al. were responding to the limitations imposed on them by the Johnson administration's commitment to Commercial Keynesianism. By the mid-1960s, the Kennedy and Johnson administrations had resolved a decade or more of contestation – in effect deflected class struggle – over whether national economic policy should prioritize the pursuit of full employment or the maintenance of currency stability.[5] A weakening US balance of payments situation at the end of the 1950s strengthened the hand of conservatives who pressed the incoming Kennedy administration to give priority to minimizing deficit spending and controlling inflation.

At the same time, chronically high unemployment called for federal intervention, as did increasing concern to address racial inequality. Two developments would help harmonize calls for state remedies for inequality with the comparative economic conservatism of the 1950s and 1960s. First, postwar liberals' invention of 'poverty' as an essentially cultural phenomenon rather than an economic one – a formulation that revealed the impact of the McCarthyite evisceration of the American left – and the related tendency to reduce racial inequality to a problem of individual discrimination and prejudice, appeared to offer a way to address structural unemployment and racialized economic inequality without requiring large-scale public spending or a systemic critique of the postwar pro-growth consensus. Second, the Kennedy administration committed to a 'commercial Keynesian' strategy that promised to reduce unemployment to acceptable levels via a combination of stimulating aggregate demand by means of a large tax cut, and targeting remedial interventions at populations whose location in economically depressed regions, or low skills or education, placed them beyond the reach of growth-driven employment resulting from the tax cut. But elite support for the tax cut, which was not realized until the Johnson administration, required a pledge pre-empting new large federal spending initiatives.

Randolph had conceived the 1963 March as a popular intervention into debates over poverty, structural unemployment, and equal employment for black Americans, as well as a demonstration pressing the generic civil rights agenda. The full employment versus currency stability dichotomy paralleled a contemporaneous debate over the scope of the landmark Civil Rights bill that would establish the institutional foundation for federal civil rights enforcement. In 1964, the *Economic Opportunity Act* – which authorized the War on Poverty – and the *Civil Rights Act* would definitively separate black economic inequality from political economy. Adopting an approach to black economic inequality centred narrowly on employment discrimination, the Civil Rights Act would affect black politics in subtle but significant ways.

As Judith Stein argues, in the early 1960s most of the prominent civil rights leadership preferred an approach that tied fair employment policy to pursuit of a full employment agenda. The passage of Title VII of the 1964 *Civil Rights Act,* however, softened their commitment, as the law established new opportunity structures. Title VII, which represented the successful culmination of a twenty-year struggle for a permanent Fair Employment Practices Committee (FEPC), attributed disproportionately high black rates of unemployment to racial discrimination and did not take into account the role of structural economic transformation – or 'automation', as Randolph et al. commonly summarized it. To be sure, the deep roots of black workers' disadvantage in confronting changing labour market dynamics lay in the material consequences of a history of racial discrimination – for example being concentrated in deindustrializing cities, and having been denied access to training for more highly skilled jobs through structural inequalities that did not derive directly from racial discrimination. Anti-discrimination enforcement was, therefore, incapable of remedying these ills.[6]

The civil rights establishment embraced Title VII as the mechanism for attacking employment inequality rather than the more expansive Humphrey Bill, S. 1937, which would have located the FEPC in the US Department of

Labor and linked its anti-discrimination provisions to manpower planning and active federal intervention in labour market dynamics. Alive to the impact of structural unemployment on blacks, many key black policy elites preferred the Humphrey bill. But few were so deeply committed to S. 1937 that they would focus attention on fighting for it as a preferable alternative to Title VII. In part, that lack of follow-through reflected a judgment that, as NAACP lobbyist Clarence Mitchell opined, pushing through two major civil rights initiatives in 1964 would be nearly impossible, and for most people the Civil Rights Act took priority. At the same time it is not unreasonable to wonder whether this assessment may have derived in addition from a class-inflected calculation that subordinated working-class employment needs to other items on the civil rights agenda.[7] The National Urban League's Whitney Young, for instance, while indicating his support for S. 1937, also expressed a reservation that linking fair employment legislation to the pursuit of full employment implied that federal anti-discrimination efforts should await full employment – a position which no one advocated. The burden of Young's concern was that fair employment enforcement should take precedence over the pursuit of full employment, and that view fitted comfortably with his commitment to liberal equality of opportunity as the baseline principle of social justice. 'I want to see qualified workers,' he declared, 'who are working, and I want to see the people who are not qualified fall into that 3 percent [unemployed].'[8] In positing a false dichotomy between enforcement of equal employment opportunity for blacks and pursuit of full employment, Young articulated just the view that Randolph et al. rejected.

Regardless, as Stein points out, once Title VII passed, black interest-group leadership took a proprietary interest in it and preferred to 'strengthen it rather than replace it'. That change in orientation underscores the fact that politics is 'processual'. Stances, commitments, interests and alliances, group agendas, and even the publicly recognized and understood nature of groups themselves evolve within, and partly constitute, a matrix of dynamic and changing political opportunity structures. This mundane truth of political life has seldom been recognized with respect to black Americans' political activity because of the dominance of an interpretive orientation that reifies black people as a singular entity and de-historicizes black political practice through unitary and ahistorical abstractions like the 'black freedom movement' or 'black liberation struggle'. This perspective is inadequate intellectually and politically for making sense of political developments, because it fails to register the impact of changing institutional relations and contexts of interest formation, and cannot conceptualize black political interests and aspirations as an evolving, historically specific product of generative processes. In particular, it cannot apprehend the significance of the sea change for black politics that occurred in the mid-1960s.[9]

It is possible to see in retrospect, as the dust settled around the biggest civil rights and anti-poverty legislative accomplishments, the outline of the terms on which black systemic incorporation would proceed, and how poverty and inequality would increasingly be understood. As Stein describes the moment, 'the critical edge of 1963 was blunted in the legislation of 1964, as the causes of both poverty and black unemployment were separated from the workings of the economy … Manpower policies would focus on the bottom end of the labor market',[10] addressing soft and hard skill deficits while growing the economy as an alternative to direct job creation.

One irony in these developments is that in multiple domains the retreat from social democracy and the effacement of political economy took the form of an activism that set out to connect with the 'grassroots', or to attend to those worst-off, or both. This was consistent with both interest-group pluralism and commercial Keynesian understandings of the causes of poverty and inequality in culturalist and individualist terms. It coincided with subordination of full employment to a social and economic policy approach that identified minimizing inflation as a guiding principle. This moment witnessed the birth of a new policy regime, and a new liberal-leftism, in which representation supplanted redistribution and public social wage policy interventions increasingly targeted specific populations held to have particular needs and 'disadvantages'. Moralistic rhetoric would license liberal policymakers' tendency toward triage and patchwork remedies that failed, by design, to address the root causes of racial inequalities. In the long arc of postwar American capitalism, moralism would ultimately help to legitimize retrenchment and means-testing as restrictive cornerstones of social policy.

These shifts articulated with tensions internal to black American politics. They enabled and reinforced the resolution of a core contradiction within the popular-front style black political alliance that had driven, or been a central force in, the struggle for racial justice and equality, from roughly the mid-1930s until well into the 1950s.[11] This is the contradiction that the political scientist Preston H. Smith II has characterized as the tension between racial-democratic and social-democratic imperatives in black politics.[12] By the late 1940s, several factors began to shift the energetic centre of black popular front politics toward the racial-democratic tendency. Between the mid-1930s and the mid-1940s, civil rights litigation strategy centred largely on labour rights arguments rooted in the Thirteenth Amendment's prohibition of involuntary servitude, including debt peonage, and on minority rights arguments emanating from the Fourteenth Amendment's equal protection mandate. As legal historian Risa Goluboff points out, civil rights litigation as a systematic practice was in its infancy, and the climate of the courts in general was in a state of flux after the end of the anti-labour, anti-regulatory state Lochner era.[13] The Fourteenth Amendment equal protection approach gained momentum in part because, in line with the leftward shift in national political discourse, and the Roosevelt administration's pattern of judicial appointments and pressure on the Supreme Court, the federal judiciary began responding favourably to such arguments. In 1944, the Supreme Court outlawed white primaries, the legality of which the Court had upheld only nine years earlier.[14] The Court overturned racially restrictive real estate covenants in 1948, and a series of education cases chipped away at state-enforced segregation between 1938 and *Brown v. Board of Education,* which in 1954 found state-enforced segregation unconstitutional by definition. The shift toward grounding racial justice arguments on the Fourteenth Amendment's equal protection clause fuelled a common-sense understanding of the pursuit of racial democracy – anti-discrimination and equality of opportunity – as the basic norm of racial justice.[15]

Parallel developments in postwar academic life and liberal commentary also separated racial inequality from political economy. Psychology's success as an academic discipline encouraged the embrace of methodological individualism and pluralism across the social sciences and fuelled liberal tendencies to formulate racial inequality as a problem rooted most significantly in individual attitudes or dispositions, such as prejudice or intolerance. Perhaps even more significant was the emergence of Cold War anti-communism, which had a chilling effect on arguments linking racial inequality to capitalist political economy and its class dynamics, to the extent that, as historian Leah Gordon demonstrates, even racial justice advocates who, as late as the mid-1940s, had been prominent voices advancing political-economic arguments regarding the roots of racial inequality, by the end of the decade had retreated entirely into the prejudice/intolerance frame of reference. No doubt such shifts from political-economic to individualist views of the nature and sources of racial inequality were influenced by increasing opportunities in the one direction as well as increased risk or danger in the other. The pertinent point, however, is that by the end of the 1940s, the social-democratic tendency in black American political life was beginning its retreat.[16]

The crucial tension between the political goals of racial and social democracy had been, and largely remains, submerged in unitary formulations such as 'the Negro's struggle for freedom', 'the black liberation movement', and others. Its resolution in favour of the racial-democratic imperative, and the political forces advancing it, has been the most important and least recognized feature of what we think of as 'black politics' since the mid-1960s. The triumph of the racial-democratic tendency was the triumph of a particular professional-managerial, petit bourgeois orientation that both reflected and propelled the primacy of those strata in determining what would be known as 'the black agenda', and its increasingly smooth articulation and integration with the institutional and ideological complex that would be characterized as neoliberalism.

BLACK POWER, THE VOTING RIGHTS ACT, AND CONSOLIDATION OF A NEW BLACK CLASS POLITICS

An ample literature, some of which has appeared in the *Socialist Register,* exists on the consolidation of post-1965 black politics as a class politics.[17] In a controversial essay that appeared in February of that year – in the wake of Lyndon Johnson's inauguration after his landslide victory against the reactionary Republican Barry Goldwater, and between the passage of the 1964 *Civil Rights Act* and that of the 1965 *Voting Rights Act* – Bayard Rustin identified a fundamental challenge that faced the movement for racial justice. He argued that,

> [t]he civil rights movement is evolving from a protest movement to a full-fledged *social movement* – an evolution calling its very name into question. It is now concerned not merely with removing the barriers to full *opportunity* but with achieving the fact of *equality*. From sit-ins and freedom rides we have gone into rent strikes, boycotts, community organization, and political action. As a consequence of this natural evolution, the Negro today finds himself stymied by obstacles of far greater magnitude than the legal barriers he was attacking before: automation, urban decay, *de facto* school segregation. These are problems which, while conditioned by Jim Crow, do not vanish upon its demise. They are more deeply rooted in our socio-economic order; they are the result of the total society's failure to meet not only the Negro's needs, but human needs generally.[18]

Rustin articulated the perspective of the movement's social-democratic tendency and its vision of the way forward from the victories of the mid-1960s. The developing Black Power tendency took shape as a militant racial-democratic alternative, on the strength of a discourse and ostensible programme of racial self-determination.[19] Roughly a year and a half later Rustin confronted the Black Power alternative directly. While empathetically cataloguing the variety of frustrations that undergirded the Black Power turn, he observed that in contrast to Randolph's *Freedom Budget*, Black Power advocates had no programmes 'aimed at the reconstruction of American society in the interests of greater social justice'. He concluded, 'what they are in fact arguing for (perhaps unconsciously) is the creation of a *new black establishment*'.[20]

Rustin's observation was prescient. Over the next decade or so, new opportunity structures created in part by civil rights legislation provided for the expansion and institutional solidification of the black political class of functionaries, officials, and contractors that had emerged over the postwar years. Although early association with a militant populist rhetoric, and identification with Third World anti-colonial struggles, gave Black Power politics a radical appearance as a political programme it was, as we have argued elsewhere, consistent with ethnic politics in general, insofar as it was a class-based affair that harnessed 'an abstract and symbolic racial populism to an agenda that centred concretely on advancing the interests and aspirations' of the new political and entrepreneurial strata.[21] Moreover, rather than having been pressured or co-opted as dependent partners in a regime of market-driven social policy and retrenchment, as scholars and critics commonly assert, the post-*Voting Rights Act* black political class was, and remains, an active agent at both national and local levels in the constitution and legitimation of the political order, based on limited racial redistribution within overall retrenchment, that eventually became what we know as neoliberalism. At the local level in particular, the emerging black political class often aligned with modernizing, redevelopment-oriented elites to displace entrenched, patronage-driven regimes that resisted both publicly subsidized downtown growth strategies and the full incorporation of blacks into their governing coalitions. Over time, the insurgent alliance, notwithstanding occasional frictions around issues related to racial redistribution, evolved from an uneasy bi-racial governing arrangement to approximate a more coherent interracial governing class.[22]

Arguments that black officials have been purely passive or dependent actors evade the black political class's embeddedness within the processes that shaped the Democratic Party's commitment to a programme of retrenchment. That evasion hinges on the imputation of an abstract racial interest that both obscures concrete class interests and, ironically, deprives black actors of agency. That view, which yields inadequate critical categories like 'mis-leadership' or 'sellout', also impedes recognition that the formation of a racially integrated governing class-for-itself is a predictable outcome of straightforward sociological processes. As one of us previously argued,

As the dominant metaphor of class hierarchy has shifted away from race and as black and white elites increasingly live in the same neighbourhoods, interact socially as individuals and families, attend the same schools and functions, consume the same class-defining commodities and pastimes, and participate in the same civic and voluntary associations, they increasingly share a common sense not only about frameworks of public policy but also about the proper order of things in general. They share a sensibility and worldview and a reservoir of their class's cultural experiences, aspirations, quotidian habits and values, as well as the material interests that unite them as a stratum. Despite the fact that grievances or competition within the consensual framework of governance still may be expressed in more or less muted racial terms, perception that deep racial cleavage remains the key fault line around which elites align is a badly out of date vestige of the tense politics and structural conflict that were especially salient during the period of racial transition.[23]

Of course, it is not only the black political class that has expanded and become entrenched institutionally. Class differentiation among black Americans has increased generally since the late 1960s,[24] which sheds light on the curious development that within the last two decades concern with racial disparity has come entirely to displace concern with broad inequality as the default indicator of racial justice. Moreover, while parity has always been the racial-democratic ideal, the 'racial wealth gap' has become the iconic measure of racial justice.[25] And that fact underscores the degree to which what we think of as black politics has become a very particular class politics. Matt Bruenig found that 'the overall racial wealth disparity is driven almost entirely by the disparity between the wealthiest 10 per cent of white people and the wealthiest 10 per cent of black people' and that eliminating the gap between the bottom 90 per cent of each group would leave 77.5 per cent of the gap intact. He found as well that eliminating the gap between the bottom 50 per cent of the two populations would eliminate only 3 per cent of the 'racial' gap.[26] Therefore, beneath the counterfactual, and largely ahistorical, statistical calculations of black wealth foregone or pre-empted by racial injustice that so appeal to academics and pundits, the reality is that the focus on the racial wealth gap is a politics that expresses only the interests of the rich and comfortably well-off. (Another tip-off regarding the class character of the disparitarian focus is its proponents' frequent resort to the trope of the white co-worker whose parents provide down payment on an expensive condo. That story is not a working-class lament.)

ANTIRACISM:
FROM CHALLENGE TO CAPITALIST INEQUALITY
TO WEAPON OF IT

By 2008, in an essay attempting to delineate what he presumed to be a generational divide in black politics, the journalist Matt Bai described a new cohort which included Obama thus: 'Comfortable inside the establishment, bred at universities rather than seminaries, they are just as likely to see themselves as ambassadors *to* the black community as they are to see themselves as spokesmen for it'.[27] Bai did not suggest where Obama et al. were ambassadors *from,* but the substantive explanation would be forthcoming before long. If Obama's presidency did not make the answer clear – and, to be sure, he still has no shortage of 'the devil made him do it' defenders – the 2016 and 2020 campaigns for the Democratic presidential nomination left little room for doubt. In 2016 prominent members of the Congressional Black Caucus (CBC), most aggressively former civil rights icon John Lewis (D-Georgia), another former civil rights activist James Clyburn (D-South Carolina), and CBC chair Cedric Richmond (D-Louisiana), viciously attacked Bernie Sanders and his leftist political programme, to the extent of denouncing his calls for de-commodified health care and higher education as 'irresponsible'.[28] In 2020, Clyburn was widely credited with having played a crucial role in securing Joe Biden the nomination against another challenge from the left by Sanders.

Donald Trump's election only strengthened centrist Democrats' commit-ment to racialist frameworks, which helped obscure the role played in the predictable rise of Trumpism by the Clintons' and Obama's commitment to neoliberal orthodoxies. Specifically, the Democratic National Committee (DNC), the corporate media, and many left-identitarians took Trump's surprise win over Secretary Hillary Clinton as evidence of working-class whites' pathological commitment to white-skin privilege, despite the fact that Trump's victory over Secretary Clinton resulted from a combination of depressed Democratic turnout and the celebrity gameshow host's having flipped a substantial number of white voters who had voted for the nation's first black president once or even twice before, and often for Bernie Sanders in the 2016 primaries (2008/2012).[29] Liberal commentators – including such well-known figures such as Ta-Nehisi Coates, Ezra Klein, and Joy-Ann Reid – have insisted that the Trump victory made plain the futility of class-based political coalitions, as working-class and middle-class whites rejected Barack Obama's and Hillary Clinton's alleged progressive economic agenda in favour of Trump's hateful, racist, xenophobic, homophobic, and transphobic politics of resentment.[30]

This perspective, of course, imputed an economic progressivism to the Clintons and Obama that was absent from their brand of Democratic politics. Indeed, few trade unionists would perceive the North American Free Trade Act (NAFTA) or their proposed Trans-Pacific Partnership (TPP) as evidence of a worker-friendly agenda. And Obama's signal supposedly progressive accomplishment was the means-tested, Heritage Foundation-inspired Affordable Care Act (ACA).[31] To be sure, these policies were less transparently harmful to working people than President Jimmy Carter's and Federal Reserve Chair Paul Volcker's efforts to curb inflation by – to paraphrase Volcker – reducing the living standards of the average American.[32] Still, it is no coincidence that the Carter, Clinton, and Obama administrations pursued policy agendas that undercut the livelihoods of a substantial stratum of working people and were then voted out or succeeded by right-wingers who advanced a disingenuous populist pitch.

Social or cultural resentments – including racism, sexism, xenophobia, and homophobia – certainly played a role in the rise of Ronald Reagan, George W. Bush, and Donald J. Trump. But to acknowledge the important influence of race in American political and social life is not to insist that it operates independently of evolving political and economic relations of power. The problem is that the discourse of social justice now dominant presumes, even demands, an either/or construction of the relationship between inequalities rooted in capitalist class dynamics and those attributable to ascriptively-based ideologies of hierarchy such as race or gender. Postwar racial liberalism generated a moralistic discourse that seems rhetorically powerful. However, because it is devoid of meaningful content, moralism – affirming, though it may be – offers neither useful interpretive frameworks nor practical remedies capable of redressing the social, historical, and political-economic dynamics that reproduce inequalities of all sorts in US capitalism. High-minded idealist constructs such as 'racism is our nation's Original Sin' or 'our national disease' or, more recently, that 'racism is in our DNA', are evasions that deflect attention from the historical and material sources of racial inequality past and present.

Many self-identified liberals and far too many leftists continue to embrace these evasive metaphors that treat ideological or cultural attachments as if they can, in fact, 'take on a life of their own'. Such constructs have become especially appealing in recent years because, much like underclass ideology, they allow one to sidestep the proximate material and cultural processes that inform the constitution of racial ideology and its evolution. Ironically, this ostensibly antiracist view, in asserting that race/racism transcends specific historical and social contexts, is itself quintessentially racist.

If race is a social construct, racists are not born, as is implied by the Original Sin and DNA metaphors, they are nurtured. Conservatives – in both the old Democratic party and the new Republican party—have long ginned up racial resentment for political gain. Likewise, prior to the enactment of antidiscrimination laws, employers, and real estate investors alike fostered resentment toward racial/ethnic groups via racially tiered labour and housing markets – which explicitly pitted racial and ethnic group members against each other.

Today, putatively liberal constructs like 'structural racism' along with the dominant understandings of 'diversity', and even 'intersectionality', presume the existence of discrete racial group interests, owed to shared group identity. While equity and inclusion are often the formal aims of these constructs, since 2016 they have been deployed against egalitarian political projects that would benefit poor and working-class Americans. The fact that black and brown Americans are disproportionately represented among the ranks of the poor and working class is an irony that underscores contemporary antiracism's class character. We saw Hillary Clinton, for example, use the language of 'structural racism' and implicit bias to attack Senator Sanders's calls for banking regulation and tuition-free higher education,[33] while deflecting attention from her complicity in Clinton-era tough-on-crime policies ('super-predators') and Bill Clinton's contribution to the subprime mortgage crisis – which did, indeed, impact blacks disproportionately. Following the brutal murder of George Floyd by Officer Derek Chauvin in May 2020 we witnessed multinational corporations embrace intersectionality and structural racism as frameworks that provided corporate executives (like Jamie Dimon) with a way to treat racial disparities as if they were owed to primordial or epigenetic 'identities' or attachments instead of capitalist processes that may impact blacks disproportionately but not exclusively.[34]

Corporate-friendly visions of social justice that insist that 'representation matters' while identifying the racial wealth gap as the main barrier to racial progress ultimately offer poor and working-class blacks little more than vicarious wins. Predictably, the centrality of the racial wealth gap – which, again, exists mainly between the richest 10 per cent of blacks and whites – to the dominant reparations discourse has led some policymakers and corporations, as with Goldman Sachs, J. P. Morgan, and Uber, to propose policies or programmes that seek to foster *wealth-parity* by promoting black entrepreneurship, encouraging homeownership, and, of course, diversifying the ranks of corporate and government leaders. Instead of much-needed structural change, the current racial justice discourse lends itself to modest reforms to a system that is less and less capable of distributing its rewards to a growing swath of working people across racial lines.

Race-centred perspectives, or others based on ascriptive identities, cannot address the fifty-year regime of regressive redistribution marked by the downward slide of real wages caused by automation, deindustrialization, the decline of the union movement, public sector retrenchment, and a depressed minimum wage. Indeed, those perspectives call for changing the subject. They accept the givenness of inequalities produced by capitalist market dynamics and insist that we focus on what might be considered the 'excess' inequalities that appear as disparate outcomes between groups. The disjunction between popular understandings of 'gentrification' as a phenomenon driven by a logic of racial or cultural displacement, and the realities of the material and institutional foundations of neighbourhood transition, illustrates how identitarian political perspectives obscure the class dynamics that generate even what can appear superficially as racially invidious outcomes.

The natural history of the 'gentrification' idea shows clearly how politics centred on ascriptive identities can obscure capitalist class dynamics and thereby undermine resistance to displacement and regressive redistribution. The gentrification notion entered Anglo-American intellectual and political life in the late 1970s and early 1980s, advanced principally by left-oriented theorists of urban political economy to characterize the spreading phenomenon of neighbourhood 'upgrading' in which a relatively affluent new 'urban gentry' displaced working-class residents and neighbourhoods, in the US often racial minorities. Gentrification discourse emerged as an element in what would become the critique of neoliberalism.[35] It drew attention to a practice of accommodation in urban governments to unfettered capital mobility and retrenchment in the Thatcher-Reagan era, which increased the pressure on municipalities to shift tax burdens from businesses to workers. Concentration of capitalist class power reinforced cities' incentives to subsidize privately-generated redevelopment projects intended to intensify rent extraction for developers, and to court upscale residents capable of paying the taxes necessary to support urban infrastructures.[36] Thus 'gentrification' was from the first bound up with diverting public resources from the provision of social goods to subsidizing privately generated and appropriated rent-intensifying redevelopment.

Yet popular political criticism of gentrification has focused much more on displacement as a cultural injustice than on the programme of regressive redistribution that reproduces it. Desperation is one factor impelling toward a superficial, moralistic focus. The culturalist presumptions that inform the dominant discourse on gentrification help to obscure the full implications of these generally 'de-democratized'[37] redevelopment initiatives, which are shielded from public oversight behind special authorities, commissions, and public-private entities. Consequently, those likely to be adversely affected by such projects do not even learn of their existence until the public-private coalitions backing them are too powerful to be stopped. The deck is stacked so heavily in favour of the rent-intensification process that resistance takes on a scattershot character in which activists grab at whatever arguments and practices – typically pro forma protests (that do not reflect mobilization of a popular base) combined with moral appeals on behalf of an abstract notion of justice for the actual and potential victims of displacement – are handy and might generate enough public support to help wrest the best possible terms of defeat.[38]

Defining gentrification as a project of displacement of populations depicted as indigenous can seem pragmatically useful for activists, partly because it comports with a liberal-paternalist sensibility of the same ideological genus as 'noble savage' imagery. Thus, debates over gentrification commonly pit clichés of cultural preservation and progress against each other. This obscures the source of gentrification in market-driven policy and government support for upward redistribution, which undercuts serious efforts to challenge the dynamic. That mystification of political-economic forces also sustains another significant and anti-popular evasion. As the primacy of market-forces disappears into moralistic and racialized debate, the inclusion of nominal representatives of the groups held to be adversely affected appears as a satisfactory compromise. Those representatives' racial or cultural status provides a halo that obscures the material dynamics driving the process and provides them with a form of capital – race as capital rather than 'racial capitalism' – facilitating market entry and penetration in the name of the group.[39]

CONCLUSION: SOLIDARISTIC AGENDAS

How the critique of gentrification has evolved from marking a new current in capitalist political economy to being an instrument for making it invisible illustrates in a thumbnail the role of antiracist politics within the reproduction of contemporary neoliberalism. Race-reductionist politics depends on an alchemy that turns economic inequality into group disparities, and presents 'inclusion' or representation in 'groupist' terms as an alternative to redistribution. That is, it takes the inequality produced by capitalism as legitimate and considers injustice only as the relative inability of members of pertinent ascriptively-defined groups to participate fully in the dominant regime of exploitation.

It is significant that the racial interest-group politics that displaced the social-democratic trend embraced by Randolph and others in the years following the civil rights successes of the 1960s is what is now understood to be black politics. That shift coincided with and reflects the emergence of a new black political class embedded in a political economy of racial representation. It is also striking that race-reductionism became dominant precisely as specifically racial strictures on black Americans have receded in importance as direct determinants of blacks' life chances and economic circumstances, which result most proximately from political-economic drivers of inequality. The race-reductionist agenda is not actually concerned with winning reforms that would improve even black Americans' circumstances; such demands as reparations and defunding the police have no chance of being met or implemented, certainly not on a broad scale. Their real purpose is to insist that race, and only race, is the framework within which any and all political questions concerning black Americans be discussed. That motive is what lies beneath such tortured and ultimately useless constructions as the assertion that mass incarceration be recognized as the 'New Jim Crow', a formulation that does not help us understand the complex, historically specific origins of the massive carceral apparatus in the United States or point to strategies for dismantling it.

From that perspective, race-reductionism, no matter how militant or radical its rhetoric and public performance may seem, is not an alternative expression of left politics; it is an alternative *to* left politics. As we have seen, in keeping with its fundamental embrace of racial democracy as its guiding norm, this politics is much more in line with growing the ranks of black millionaires and billionaires than with eliminating black poverty and ensuring that black children and adults have access to quality education, quality housing, well-paying jobs, and health care. It is also intrinsically polarizing, and antagonistic to pursuit of solidaristic agendas and organizing. It is incapable of contributing to generating the sort of popularly-grounded left movement we need if we are to hope ever to challenge capital's unrestrained power.

As Samir Sonti points out in this volume of the *Register*, even prominent neoliberal economists have come around to acknowledging a chronic problem of secular stagnation in the US economy and have begun to consider measures, an active industrial policy for example, that for decades have been anathema to neoliberal ideology and practice. We would add that, especially in light of the rising tide of authoritarian governments, parties and movements across the capitalist world, neoliberalism may be exhausting its capacities for delivering enough benefits and security to enough people to maintain legitimacy as a nominally democratic order. If so, that means that we may be living in a moment of the greatest polarization we have seen since the Great Depression, a moment in which there could be only two ways forward: toward authoritarianism or socialism. In the United States, the forces of what Colin Crouch describes as a 'politicized pessimistic nostalgia'[40] have condensed around Trumpism as a militant, potentially putschist insurgency that, as we write, poses a potentially dire, perhaps terminal threat to liberal democracy, and as early as 2024, if not 2022.

We believe that the only hope for defeating that tendency is to concentrate our efforts on formulating, organizing around, and agitating for an ensemble of policies that reinvigorate the notion of government in the public good, which has been a casualty of more than four decades of bipartisan neoliberalism. The 'pessimistic nostalgia' that Trumpists and other authoritarians propagate and mobilize around is most consequentially the result of decades of bipartisan failure to provide concrete remedies that address the steadily intensifying economic inequality and insecurity that have driven so much of the working class to the wall. We need to provide an alternative vision that proceeds unabashedly from the question: What would be the thrust and content of public policy if the country were governed by and for the working-class majority?

Through the administration's first six months, Bidenism has turned out to be more attentive to addressing the legitimation problems than most leftists expected. Biden has committed to restoring labour rights and has openly encouraged unionization. That is already an improvement on the record of the three previous Democratic administrations – of Carter, Clinton, and Obama – that promised pro-labour reform and reneged. Biden has also expressed commitment to a public good approach to government, as is indicated in his infrastructure plans. We agree also with Sonti's caution that what the administration does on this front is most likely to be considerably less than is needed. Moreover, the infrastructure spending is unlikely to result in an expanded public sector, as Biden and his Wall Street Keynesian advisors see the warrant of the stagnation diagnosis as engaging government spending to help 'escort' private capital to investment opportunities. To that extent even triumphant Bidenism would likely reset the political-economic moment to a contemporary equivalent of US state-market relations in 1950.

Nevertheless, despite the likelihood that Biden feels comfortable with pushing in this direction because of the centrist Democrats' sound defeat of the party's left wing in 2020, the fissures in Democratic neoliberal politics have created space for serious left organizing, inside and outside of organized labour. But all the possibilities Biden might open hinge on holding and increasing the Democratic congressional majorities in the 2022 mid-term elections. And the right is laser-focused on taking majorities in both houses. All their efforts at state and national levels, including coordinated voter suppression campaigns in forty-three states, and for that matter the apparent insanity of their efforts to undermine public health enforcement during the pandemic, are directed toward that end. Many in top party leadership have made clear that their intention is to perpetrate a coup against liberal democratic institutions, and, as their actions in this moment indicate, that threat is one for which we must prepare as much as possible. The US left has to get past 2022 if we are to try to articulate and organize popularly around an agenda, and vision, that speak to addressing the needs, concerns, fears, and anxieties of the working class. Building a broad working-class based movement is the only way we might successfully defeat the reactionary right wing, and that sort of popular movement needs to be built between now and 2024.

To return to our starting point, bluntly, the time is too perilous to give the benefit of the doubt regarding those opposed to pursuit of working-class solidarities. There is no doubt that racism is real and has negative consequences for people's lives. This is why we have consistently argued for the continued value of anti-discrimination policies. But race reductionism's insistence on uncoupling disparities from political economy lends itself to individualist reforms (anti-racism training and swelling the ranks of black capitalists) as responses to structural ailments. We must reject race-reductionist analyses and refuse to accommodate charges that a left focused first and foremost on critique of and challenge to capitalist political economy as such, with its corrosive human consequences, is unacceptably 'class reductionist'. To summon an old Maoist slogan, at a time such as this, it is imperative that we clarify who are our friends and who are our enemies.

Finally, the emergence of the sort of neoliberal left we have described here is not only a problem for an anti-capitalist, working-class based left in the United States. It is also a component of the counter-solidaristic exports of American imperialism intended to undermine working-class politics globally – in Cuba, Brazil, elsewhere in Latin America, Europe, and other destinations.[41]

NOTES

1   William P. Jones, *The March on Washington: Jobs, Freedom, and the Forgotten History of Civil Rights,* New York: W.W. Norton & Co., 2014.

2   The American Federation of Labor, founded in 1886 and largely comprised of craft unions, and the rival Congress of Industrial Organizations, an offshoot founded in 1935,

focused on organizing industrial workers in the US and Canada, merged in 1955 to create the American Federation of Labor-Congress of Industrial Organizations, known more popularly as the AFL-CIO.

3   A 'Freedom Budget' for All Americans: Budgeting Our Resources 1965-1975 to Achieve 'Freedom from Want', New York: A. Philip Randolph Institute, 1966. See also Paul Le Blanc and Michael D. Yates, A Freedom Budget for All Americans, New York: Monthly Review Press, 2013; Adolph Reed, Jr., 'Revolution as "National Liberation" and the Origins of Neoliberal Antiracism', in Leo Panitch and Greg Albo eds, Socialist Register 2017: Rethinking Revolution, London: Merlin Press, 2016, esp. pp. 315-16; and Adolph Reed, Jr. 'The Black-Labour-Left Alliance in the Neoliberal Age', New Labor Forum, 25 (Spring), 2016, pp. 28-34.

4   Le Blanc and Yates, A Freedom Budget for All Americans, p. 97.

5   Samir Sonti, 'The Strange Career of Institutional Keynesianism', in R. Huret, N. Lichtenstein, and J-C. Vinel, eds, Capitalism Contested: The New Deal and Its Legacies, Philadelphia: University of Pennsylvania Press, 2020, pp. 75-93; Leo Panitch and Sam Gindin, The Making of Global Capitalism: The Political Economy of American Empire, New York & London, Verso, 2012, p. 125; and Hobart Rowen, The Free Enterprisers: Kennedy, Johnson and the Business Establishment, New York: G. P. Putnam's Sons, 1964, pp. 31-33.

6   Judith Stein, Running Steel, Running America, Chapel Hill: University of North Carolina Press, 1998, p. 76; Touré F. Reed, 'Title VII, the Rise of Workplace Fairness, and the Decline of Economic Justice, 1964-2013', Labour: Studies of Working-Class History of the Americas, 11 (Fall) 2014, pp. 31-36; and Touré F. Reed, 'Why Liberals Separate Race from Class', Jacobin, 22 August 2015.

7   Stein's discussion of Title VII and Humphrey's S. 1937 specifies the politically significant differences between the two approaches and situates them clearly in within that key political moment. See: Running Steel, pp. 70-88.

8   Equal Employment Opportunity: Hearings before the Subcommittee on Employment and Manpower of the Committee on Labor and Public Welfare, United States Senate, Eighty-eighth Congress, First Session on S. 773, S. 1210, S. 1211; and S. 1937, Bills Relating to Equal Employment Opportunities, July 24, 25, 26, 29, 31; August 2 and 20, 1963, Whitney Young, Jr., testimony, July 25, 1963, 178.

9   As one augury of how black politics would evolve over the next half century, at a Congressional hearing on the War on Poverty, Whitney Young urged that the legislation provide as many opportunities as possible for outsourcing administration of initiatives to community groups and entrepreneurs. See Economic Opportunity Act of 1964: Hearings before the Subcommittee on the War on Poverty Program of the Committee on Education and Labour, House of Representatives, Eighty-Eighth Congress, a second session on H. R. 10440 and 10459, part 1, Hearings Held in Washington, DC, March 17, 18, 19, 20; April 7, 8, 9, 10, 13, and 14, 1964, Whitney Young, Jr. Testimony, pp. 637-38.

10   Stein, Running Steel, p. 87.

11   Touré F. Reed, Toward Freedom: The Case Against Race Reductionism, New York: Verso Books, 2020, pp. 15-47. A good illustration of how broad support for social-democratic interventions was among black civic elites at the end of World War II is Rayford W. Logan, ed., What the Negro Wants, Chapel Hill: University of North Carolina Press, 1944.

12 Preston H. Smith II, *Racial Democracy and the Black Metropolis: Housing Policy in Postwar Chicago,* Minneapolis: University of Minnesota Press, pp. 4-6, 252. Smith contends that regarding housing politics in Chicago at least the social-democratic ideal in black politics was 'no longer considered a viable approach' already by 1954. See also: Reed, 'Revolution as "National Liberation"', pp. 310-12.

13 Risa Goluboff, 'The Thirteenth Amendment and the Lost Origins of Civil Rights', *Duke Law Journal,* 50 (April), 2001, pp. 1609-85.

14 The white primary was an instrument of late-nineteenth-century racial disfranchisement in de facto one-party Democrat-dominated southern states. State Democratic parties defined themselves as private entities that could determine their own criteria for membership. Excluding blacks from membership prohibited them from voting in the party's primary elections, which in such states were in effect the general election. *Smith v. Allwright,* the case that eliminated the white primary, had an almost instantaneous impact on blacks' voting, particularly in the region's larger cities. In New Orleans, for example, where only 400 blacks were registered voters in 1940, more than 28,000 were registered by 1952. See Arnold R. Hirsch, 'Simply a Matter of Black and White: The Transformation of Race and Politics in Twentieth-Century New Orleans', in Arnold R. Hirsch and Joseph Logsdon, eds, *Creole New Orleans: Race and Americanization,* Baton Rouge, LA, 1992, p. 273.

15 Risa Goluboff, *The Lost Promise of Civil Rights,* Cambridge, MA: Harvard University Press, 2010.

16 Leah N. Gordon, *From Power to Prejudice: The Rise of Racial Individualism in Midcentury America,* Chicago: University of Chicago Press, 2015; John P. Jackson, Jr., *Social Science for Social Justice: Making the Case Against Segregation,* New York: NYU Press, 2001; and Landon R. Y. Storrs, *The Second Red Scare and the Unmaking of the New Deal Left,* Princeton: Princeton University Press, 2015.

17 Adolph Reed, Jr.: 'The Post-1965 Trajectory of Race, Class, and Urban Politics in the United States Reconsidered', *Labour Studies Journal,* 41(3), 2016, pp. 260-91; 'Revolution as "National Liberation"', pp. 314-17; *Stirrings in the Jug: Black Politics in the Post-Segregation Era,* Minneapolis: University of Minnesota Press, 1999, pp. 79-178; Touré F. Reed, *Toward Freedom,* pp. 69-100; Cedric Johnson: *Revolutionaries to Race Leaders: Black Power and the Making of African American Politics,* Minneapolis: University of Minnesota Press, 2007; Cedric Johnson, 'The Half-Life of the Black Urban Regime: Adolph Reed, Jr. on Race, Capitalism, and Urban Governance', *Labor Studies Journal* 41(3), 2016, pp. 248-55; Cedric Johnson, 'The Black Panthers Can't Save Us Now', *Catalyst* 1(Spring), 2017, pp. 57-85; Dean E. Robinson, 'Black Power Nationalism as Ethnic Pluralism: Postwar Liberalism's Ethnic Paradigm in Black Nationalism', in Adolph Reed and Kenneth Warren, eds, in *Renewing Black Intellectual History: The Ideological and Material Foundations of African American Thought,* Boulder, CO: Paradigm Press, 2010, pp. 184-214; and Preston H. Smith II, 'How *New* is New Urban Renewal? Class, Redevelopment, and Black Politics', *nonsite.org,* 9 September 2019, available at: nonsite.org; Karen Ferguson, *Top Down: The Ford Foundation, Black Power, and the Reinvention of Racial Liberalism,* Philadelphia: University of Pennsylvania Press, 2013; and John David Arena, *Driven from New Orleans: How Nonprofits Betray Public Housing and Promote Privatization,* Minneapolis: University of Minnesota Press, 2012.

18 Bayard Rustin, 'From Protest to Politics: The Future of the Civil Rights Movement', *Commentary,* February 1965, p. 27.

19   Reed, 'Revolution as "National Liberation"', pp. 314-17.

20   Bayard Rustin, '"Black Power" and Coalition Politics', *Commentary,* September 1966, p. 36. He also remarked on the class-skewed character of the Great Society's actual distribution of benefits: 'Because there has been a lack of necessary funds, the programme has in many cases been reduced to wrangling for positions on boards or for lucrative staff jobs. Negro professionals working for the programme have earned lucrative salaries … while young boys have been asked to plant trees at $1.25 an hour. Nor have the Job Corps camps made a significant dent in unemployment among Negro youths; indeed the main beneficiaries of this programme seem to be the private companies who are contracted to set up the camps.' "Black Power", p. 38.

21   Reed, 'Revolution as "National Liberation"', p. 315.

22   Reed, 'Post-1965 Trajectory', p. 271.

23   Reed, 'Post-1965 Trajectory', p. 271; and Arena, *Driven from New Orleans.* The racial transition from white to black (and where pertinent Hispanic)-led local governments resulted from postwar demographic shifts in many substantial metropolitan areas, driven by deindustrialization of the urban core and racially skewed suburbanization. By the end of the 1960s, populations of many large cities had become majority or near-majority black. That straightforward demographic shift in concert with consolidation of the civil rights victories of the period enabled election of black mayors and black city council majorities, which fuelled consolidation of a stratum of officials, functionaries, contractors, and aspirants grounded in what might be described as a political economy of racial representation.

24   Adolph Reed, Jr., 'The Surprising Cross-Racial Saga of Modern Wealth Inequality', *The New Republic,* 29 June 2020. Income differentiation among blacks also has increased significantly, which should not be surprising as a testament to the legislative and cultural victories of the 1960s. In 1967, the percentage of blacks with annual income (in 2018 dollars) of $150,000 or more was negligible; in 2018, four per cent of blacks reported annual income between $150,000 and $200,000. An additional three per cent reported 2018 income of over $200,000. And the percentage reporting incomes between $100,000 and $200,000 quadrupled, from three to twelve per cent, between 1967 and 2016. See blackdemographics.com. In 2019 nearly a third of employed blacks were in management, professional, or related occupational categories (see www.bls.gov/opub/reports/race-and-ethnicity/2019/home.htm; that compares with just over 10 per cent in 1970 (see: stats.bls.gov/opub/mlr/1982/06/art5full.pdf). Moreover, 'the richest 10 per cent of African Americans ended up in the small portion of the distribution in which incomes rose relative to the national mean over the last 50 years. The poorest 70 per cent were in portions of the distribution in which income shares contracted substantially'. Robert Manduca, 'Income Inequalities and the Persistence of Racial Economic Disparities', *Sociological Science,* 5 (March) 2018, p. 193.

25   Adolph Reed, Jr. and Merlin Chowkwanyun, 'Race, Class, Crisis: The Discourse of Racial Disparity and Its Analytical Discontents', in Leo Panitch, Greg Albo, and Vivek Chibber, eds, *Socialist Register 2012: The Crisis and the Left,* London: Merlin Press, 2011, pp. 149-75; and Walter Benn Michaels and Adolph Reed, Jr., 'The Trouble with Disparity', *nonsite.org.,* 10 September 2020, available at: nonsite.org. The literature on the racial wealth gap is voluminous; the ur-text is: Melvin Oliver and Thomas Shapiro, *Black Wealth/White Wealth: A New Perspective on Racial Inequality,* New York: Routledge, 1995.

26   Matt Bruenig, 'The Racial Wealth Gap Is About the Upper Classes', *Jacobin*, 5 July 2020.

27   Matt Bai, 'Is Obama the End of Black Politics?', *New York Times Magazine*, 6 August 2008.

28   Adolph Reed, Jr., 'The Trouble With Uplift', *The Baffler* #41, September 2018; and Bradford Richardson, 'Clyburn: Sanders's Plan Would Kill Black Colleges', *The Hill*, 21 February 2016; and Aaron Gould Sheinin, 'John Lewis on Bernie Sanders: 'There's Not Anything Free in America'', *Atlanta Journal-Constitution*, 17 February 2016.

29   Adolph Reed, Jr., 'Black Politics After 2016', *nonsite.org*, 11 February 2018, available at: nonsite.org; Geoffrey Skelley, 'Just How Many Obama 2012-Trump 2016 Voters Were There?', *Sabato's Crystal Ball*, 1 June 2017, available at: centerforpolitics.org; Leslie Lopez, '"I Believe Trump Like I Believed Obama": A Case Study of Two Working-Class "Latino" Voters, My Parents', *nonsite.org*, 28 November 2016, available at: nonsite.org; Christian Parenti, 'Listening to Trump', *nonsite.org*, 17 November 2016, available at: nonsite.org; and Mark Dudzic, 'The Origin of the Species', *nonsite.org*, 25 January 2017, available at: nonsite.org.

30   Reed, *Toward Freedom*, pp. 131-32, 149, 162-63.

31   Unionists had lobbied President Obama to strike the offending 'Cadillac tax', which would impose penalties on employer-provided benefits deemed under the ACA to be too generous. See: Avik Roy, 'Labor Unions' Latest Problem: Obamacare's 'Cadillac Tax' Harms Their Gold-Plated Health Insurance Plans', *Forbes*, 6 August 2013.

32   Doug Henwood, 'Paul Volcker Was a Hero to the Ruling Class', *Jacobin*, 9 December 2019.

33   David Weigel, 'Clinton in Nevada: "Not Everything Is About an Economic Theory"', *Washington Post*, 13 February 2016.

34   The phrase 'structural racism' has only recently made its way into popular discourse, but the construct has been around for several decades. In the late-1990s, sociologist Eduardo Bonilla-Silva would attribute lingering racial disparities following the Civil Rights Movement not to public sector retrenchment or deindustrialization, but to 'structural racism.' Rejecting the view that racism was merely prejudice, Bonilla-Silva described racism as the practice of group domination 'in which economic, political, and ideological levels are partially structured by the placement of actors into racial categories or races'. According to Bonilla-Silva, socially constructed racial categories ultimately fostered discrete racial group interests, as whites fought to maintain their domination over blacks and other people of colour. Whites' commitment to their structural dominance over blacks did not recede following the Civil Rights Movement; instead, it had morphed into the 'colour-blind racism', which Bonilla-Silva believed was at the heart of contemporary inequalities. In a moment characterized by widespread disillusionment in the abilities of neoliberal regimes to meet the material needs of their citizens, the vision of 'structural racism' laid out by Bonilla-Silva and others offers an attractive alternative to public goods-oriented governance. First, the construct's insistence on the existence of discrete racial group interests shifts the focus on inequality away from political economy toward tribalism. Second, the essentialist presumptions driving the framework lend themselves to modest, targeted reforms – centred largely on anti-discrimination policies and cultural tutelage – that pose no threat to capitalist power. Finally, a project that insists that all whites are members of a privileged group while all blacks are members of a disadvantaged group is transparently counter-solidaristic.

35   See: Timothy P. R. Weaver, *Blazing the Neoliberal Trail: Urban Political Development in the United States and the United Kingdom,* Philadelphia: University of Pennsylvania Press, 2016.

36   In the US at least, this turn was an organic outgrowth of the dominant postwar regime of local and metropolitan pro-growth politics that centred on governing coalitions held together by mobilization of public resources to stimulate economic growth, the proceeds of which were disproportionately appropriated by private interests. For careful examinations of this growth politics and its coalitional processes, see, in addition to Weaver: John Logan and Harvey Molotch, *Urban Fortunes: The Political Economy of Place,* Los Angeles: University of California Press, 1987; and the studies by Clarence N. Stone, 'Systemic Power in Community Decision Making: A Restatement of Stratification Theory', *American Political Science Review,* 74 (December) 1980, pp. 978-90; 'Social Stratification, Nondecision-Making, and the Study of Community Power', *American Politics Research,* 10 (July) 1982, pp. 275-302; and *Regime Politics: Governing Atlanta, 1946-1988,* Lawrence, KS: University of Kansas Press, 1989.

37   Damien Cahill, *The End of Laissez-Faire? On the Durability of Embedded Neoliberalism,* Cheltenham: Edward Elgar, 2014, p. 106. The political scientist Paul Peterson, in his *City Limits,* Chicago: University of Chicago Press, 1981, was an early apologist for removal of development policy from public oversight, advancing the sophistry that doing so did not violate democratic norms because development was a universally shared interest and that the only decisions likely to produce controversy were technical issues best left to experts.

38   Larry Bennett and Adolph Reed, Jr., 'The New Face of Urban Renewal: The Near North Redevelopment Initiative and the Cabrini-Green Neighborhood', in Adolph Reed, Jr., ed., *Without Justice for All: The New Liberalism and Our Retreat from Racial Equality,* Boulder, CO: Westview Press, 1999, pp. 175-211.

39   Adolph Reed, Jr., 'Response to Backer and Singh', *Verso Blog,* 10 October 2018, available at: www.versobooks.com.

40   Colin Crouch, *Post-Democracy after the Crisis,* Cambridge, MA: Polity Press, 2020, pp. 91-117.

41   Marci Smith examines a similar arrow in the quiver of American imperialism's pursuit of 'regime change' elsewhere in her critique of Cold War defence intellectual Gene Sharp's lengthy career in utilizing a disruptive 'revolutionary non-violence' and Potemkin popular insurgency to subvert governments and movements the US opposed. See: 'Change Agent: Gene Sharp's Neoliberal Nonviolence, Part 1', *nonsite.org,* 10 May 2019, available at: nonsite.org; and 'Change Agent: Gene Sharp's Neoliberal Nonviolence, Part 2', *nonsite.org,* 29 December 2019, available at: nonsite.org.

THE CRISIS OF US LABOUR, PAST AND PRESENT

SAMIR SONTI

Towards the end of his first one hundred days in office, Joe Biden signed an Executive Order establishing a White House Task Force on Worker Organizing and Empowerment. The group, to be led by Vice President Kamala Harris and Secretary of Labor Marty Walsh, was charged with identifying tools the executive branch has at its disposal to facilitate union organizing. Among other things, that could include establishing a condition that all contractors retained through the federal government's $600 billion procurement budget must accept neutrality agreements and expedited unionization processes, a step that would immediately benefit hundreds of thousands of workers. Whatever the details, Biden's statement held that the goal was to return to the original spirit of the National Labor Relations Act of 1935 (NLRA) – as his administration read that statute, 'to _encourage_ worker organizing and collective bargaining, not merely to allow or tolerate them' (emphasis in original).[1]

White House task forces, it has been said, are where big ideas go to die, and it remains to be seen whether and to what extent the recommendations issuing from this one will translate into substantive policy. Nevertheless, the executive order capped what those on the labour-left were forced to admit had been a pleasantly surprising start to the new administration. Within hours of taking the oath of office, Biden terminated the ghoul whom Donald Trump had appointed as General Counsel of the National Labor Relations Board (NLRB), and he followed that action by staffing the Department of Labor with personnel possessing strong labour movement credentials. Walsh became the first former union official to lead the department in a generation, and his deputy, Julie Su, has been a long-time a favourite of worker advocates in California. Likewise, those tapped for senior posts at the Occupational Safety and Health Administration and the influential Wage and Hour Division came straight from organized labour.

Garnering the most applause, however, were Biden's pro-union public statements, above all his intervention into the widely-watched Retail, Wholesale, and Department Store Union (RWDSU) organizing drive at an Amazon warehouse in Bessemer, Alabama. Without mentioning the company by name, Biden denounced the vicious anti-union tactics Amazon had employed, and all but encouraged the workers to vote 'yes'. As many observers noted, not since Franklin D. Roosevelt has a president taken so strong a position in support of unionization. Nonetheless, the Amazon drive was defeated, a stark reminder that the drubbing the US labour movement has received in recent decades will not be ended by mere well-wishes from Washington.[2]

At this point, organized labour has been in decline for a period longer than its mid-twentieth century heyday itself lasted, a sobering fact which raises questions about how usable that past remains. After a period of rapid growth during the New Deal and World War II, union membership peaked at one-third of the workforce in the mid-1950s. While capital flight and automation began to erode the manufacturing core by the early 1960s, increasing Cold War expenditures and the scaling up of military production in service of the carnage in Southeast Asia stabilized industrial employment for a bit longer. The swift expansion of public sector unionism around that time added much-needed – and, as time would tell, more durable – reinforcements to the movement's ranks.[3]

But the onset of stagflation in the 1970s and its brutal resolution by the Volcker Shock at the end of the decade exposed how precarious that regime had been. By 1980, the industrial unions found themselves deep in a crisis from which they have still not recovered, and Ronald Reagan's smashing of the air traffic controllers' strike two years later only gave further sanction to the broader corporate war on workers that was already underway. For nearly a half-century now, private sector union density has been in freefall, and attacks on public sector unions have intensified in the years since the financial crisis as well – most infamously in Wisconsin in 2011 and through the Supreme Court's *Janus* decision some years later. Today, just 6 per cent of private sector employees, and 10 per cent of the total workforce, enjoy union representation on the job.[4]

What are the prospects for a reversal of this trend in the post–Trump and post-pandemic period? How can we make sense of the Biden administration's agenda, both the opportunities and obstacles it presents? In what ways do changing structural conditions bear on those opportunities and obstacles? My objective in this essay is to begin thinking through these questions and reflecting on their strategic implications. The sociopolitical and class polarizations produced by neoliberalism, and the spectacular crises they set in motion, have over the years spurred discussion about the future of neoliberalism itself, with some asserting that it is near its end and others concluding that it is stronger than ever.[5] As the Biden administration attempts to make its mark on the political economy, this debate is likely to continue. Neither perspective, however, allows for a complete assessment of the particularities of the current conjuncture. What may be more useful is an interpretation of the specific ways in which the forces driving those polarizations have set the stage for what comes next. History is processual, and the range of possibilities and constraints in the present must be understood in relation to the contradictions of the recent past.

In this vein, my point of departure is a brief review of the evolution of American finance, the central driver of neoliberal accumulation, and the political entailments of post-2008 dynamics on Wall Street. The active monetary policy implemented in the wake of the crash has reconfigured the financial landscape, enabling an incredible asset price boom that has accrued most of all to the wealthy. Yet the low interest rates that prevail also provide the space for an ambitious fiscal policy that could facilitate productive investment, solidify employment, and create the conditions for a revitalization of the labour movement. Historically, the barrier to an expansionary program of this sort has been inflation – or more precisely, the independent central bank's refusal to allow it – but for now moderate increases in the consumer price level do not conflict with the imperatives of asset price appreciation. In a sense, then, the political economic logic of the Biden administration may express the coalescence of a liberal financial bloc, one seeking to address the structural decay that nurtured Trumpism with an economic program capable of providing real relief to working people. But this coalition is not without contradictions of its own. For one, there is by no means consensus across the ruling class on the tolerability of inflation, even in small doses, and it is not clear how much the administration will be able to resist demands from more hawkish forces. More importantly, this general economic policy vision is only conceivable within the context of the sustained low inflation of the past few decades. This, in turn, has been the product of the profound weakness of the organized working class during that time. To the extent, if any, that 'Bidenomics' succeeds in empowering American workers, it may undermine an important condition of its own existence: the tremendous class polarization of our times. The question then is how exactly the labour-left should relate to it in the first place.

THE EVOLUTION OF AMERICAN FINANCE

American finance has undergone an important evolution in the years since 2008, one obscured by the extent to which wages and working-class living conditions remained stagnant during the years that followed. At the same time, the cultural standing of Wall Street has been challenged, and it no longer shines as bright as it once did. Politically, these shifts carry significant implications. Indeed, if the logic animating the Obama administration's response to the financial crisis was a holdover from the 1990s and early 2000s, the Biden administration's sensibilities have been shaped by everything that unfolded over the subsequent decade. Neither arguments emphasizing the Democratic Party's enduring captivity to the financial sector, nor those celebrating its newfound reformist impulses, provide a sufficient explanation of the ways in which the landscape continues to change. There is a bit of both at play, but the current blend is specific to the context made by the last crisis and the response to it.

The most commented upon development has been that within the Federal Reserve and global central banking circles. After a generation during which the spectre of inflation haunted every economic policy decision, the rolling crises of the past dozen years have led the leaders of the Fed to reconsider basic principles.[6] Even after their unprecedented 'quantitative easing' interventions in the immediate aftermath of 2008, the rate of inflation stubbornly refused to budge through the 2010s. In response, in August 2020 the Fed issued a revision to its long-term goals on monetary policy strategy to allow inflation to run above its 2 per cent target until such time as labour market conditions have improved.[7] The technical aspects of their statement mask the underlying political rationale: chronic economic slackness and the resulting employment insecurity, deriving from decades of underinvestment and union decline, had produced what they saw as powerful deflationary headwinds. And 'Hitler,' as the economist George Warren once said to Franklin Roosevelt, 'is the product of deflation'.[8]

Related to that Fed response has been an important reorganization within the broader financial sector – the rise of what Benjamin Braun has called 'asset manager capitalism'.[9] Since the financial crisis, colossal firms like BlackRock, Vanguard, and State Street Global Advisors – often referred to as the 'Big Three' – have begun to displace investment banks as the principal power centre in global finance. The Big Three alone now have $15.5 trillion in assets under management (compared to $500 billion at the turn of the century) and together hold more than 20 per cent of the shares of the average S&P 500 company, with little intention of ever selling them. Indeed, given their reach and their mandate to act in the fiduciary interest of their investors, they are effectively prevented from exiting the companies in which they have positions due to the adverse ripples such actions would have.[10] Whereas in 2007, the major investment banks managed twice as much as the largest asset management firms, by 2017 the latter oversaw half again as much as those older powerhouses. In 2006, investment banks earned half of all financial sector revenues. A little over a decade later, that was down to a third, while the asset managers saw their take rise by a quarter, from 40 to 50 per cent. BlackRock alone has grown seven-fold since 2009, with $9 trillion under management as of early 2021. In fact, the banks themselves are starting to emulate the business model pioneered by the Big Three: Goldman Sachs's asset management arm, for example, now accounts for 20 per cent of firm revenues, twice its level before the crash.[11]

What is going on here and why does it matter? To start, this development represents the rise of passive investing over and above the active investing characteristic of Wall Street in the years prior to 2008. Through their sweeping index and exchange traded funds, asset management firms enable their clients to gain exposure to the entire market at once, a strategy that ostensibly smooths out risk and minimizes investment fees, both of which appealed to institutional investors and households after the tumult of the housing crisis. But it is a story of public policy as well. Financial regulations implemented in the wake of the crash, namely capital requirements on systemically important financial institutions (SIFIs), forced the investment banks to pare back operations. Yet the asset management firms were spared designation as SIFIs, an exclusion that has since allowed them to balloon in size and scope. Finally, and perhaps most important, has been the role of the Fed. The reliably expansive monetary policy of the past decade has had the effect of moderating those swings that banks' trading desks had in the past exploited while at the same time enabling the steady sort of asset appreciation that benefits passive investment strategies. In short, although its roots do extend further back, the explosion of asset manager capitalism is the outcome of the state's response to the last crisis, and the dynamics it has set in motion have their own political consequences.[12]

One can hope that this deepening concentration and centralization of ownership – some observers expect the Big Three to control 40 per cent of the S&P 500 within 20 years – may increase the financial sector's preference for stability and predictability.[13] To that end, advocates of responsible stewardship place much faith in the Environmental, Social, and Governance (ESG) framework that organizations of institutional investors have developed. More significant in the near term, however, is how this development may feed back into the politics of economic policy – especially as it pertains to monetary management and inflation. As Braun has argued, whereas the 'financial sector has long been treated as the most powerful "hard money" constituency, because inflation devalues banks' nominal claims against borrowers', the vast asset management industry is concerned with the risk of the devaluation of their asset base more than inflation, making them a powerful "easy money" constituency.'[14] To be sure, a financial sector preference for the sort of monetary policy that provides a lift to asset prices is hardly unprecedented; markets can only turn bullish if central bankers permit it. But if Braun's provocative formulation may overstate the point, there does appear to be a shift in strategic interest at play. The profound price stability experienced during the post-crash recovery forced a reconsideration of the relationship between monetary policy and inflation, reducing at least one of the perceived risks associated with sustained ease. And this may create a new set of opportunities for economic policy.

The financial sector is, as always, well positioned to influence which of those opportunities the federal government pursues, and at present the asset manager bloc is playing a key role. BlackRock has enmeshed itself at the commanding heights of the American state. Brian Deese, formerly BlackRock's Global Head of Sustainable Investing, now serves as Director of the National Economic Council, the nerve centre of economic policymaking in the executive branch. His colleague at BlackRock, Adewale 'Wally' Adeymo, is Janet Yellen's deputy at the Department of Treasury, and the firm's former Global Chief Investment Strategist, Mike Pyle, is chief economist to Vice President Kamala Harris. BlackRock founder and chief executive, Larry Fink, was reportedly on the shortlist of candidates for Secretary of Treasury. During the pandemic market frenzy in March 2020, no one spoke to Federal Reserve Chair Jerome Powell and Treasury Secretary Steven Mnuchin more frequently than Fink.[15] BlackRock has cultivated an especially close relationship with the Fed, which retained the firm's consulting arm to assist in executing their emergency corporate bond buying program early in the pandemic.[16] That decision raised red flags about potential conflicts of interest, but BlackRock's designs at the central bank run deeper than the transactional. Given their stake in just about every public company in the US, they do not bother much with picking favourites.[17] The basis for their collaboration is rather more mundane: their unsurpassed market expertise and concern with macroeconomic stability compelled them to play a role in managing the crisis.

A 2019 BlackRock report anticipating the challenges that 'the next downturn' would present provides a window into what they feel is to be done. The experience of the post-crisis decade, the authors observed, threw into relief a dilemma facing most advanced capitalist states: monetary policy had reached the limits of what it alone could accomplish, as interest rates can only be pushed down so far; yet fiscal policy is 'typically not nimble enough' to rise to the occasion. To overcome this predicament, the BlackRock economists proposed a program of monetary and fiscal coordination whereby the central bank and fiscal authorities would together ensure the availability of adequate financing for stimulative public and private investment. In other words, the central bank should 'go direct' by finding ways to get capital into the hands of public and private sector actors ready to spend. Theoretically, they acknowledged, there is not much separating this idea from what proponents of Modern Monetary Theory (MMT) have advocated – that is, 'monetary financing of fiscal expansion'. But in practice they believe they would be more responsible, managing it through 'a pre-defined exit point and an explicit inflation objective'. Its association with MMT notwithstanding, the report stressed that this principle is neither radical nor new. Indeed, it was once the norm, and it only 'came to an end when central banks got serious about controlling inflation' in the 1970s. That constraint is long since gone, enabling them to try it once more. In the United States, the most useful precedent for such an approach was the monetary-fiscal agenda maintained during the New Deal and World War II. That program was only ended by the momentous Federal Reserve-Treasury Accord of 1951, widely understood as a watershed moment in the history of central bank independence.[18]

Something like what the BlackRock report proposed took shape early in the pandemic and appears to be continuing through the collaboration between Jerome Powell and Janet Yellen, herself previously the head of the central bank. On the one hand, this approach may allow for a substantial degree of economic policy experimentation, a kind of pump priming that would have been unimaginable during the days of the 'deflationary bloc' that had been dominant since the stagflation of the 1970s.[19] And indeed, Biden's ambitions have been dependent upon Powell's insistence that hysteria about inflation should not pre-empt such expansionary measures. While Larry Summers – Treasury Secretary under Clinton and National Economic Council Director under Obama – has publicly criticized the administration for what he sees as a reckless disregard for inflationary risks, the White House has for the most part been able to ignore him.[20] Even as certain price pressures built up in the spring of 2021, with commodities like lumber spiking, Biden resisted calls to dial back his spending ambitions on account of inflation prevention.

Still, it should be clear that this approach is only conceivable within the context of the balance of class power that has resulted from the corporate onslaught of the past half century and the state institutions that enabled it. The Federal Reserve remains an independent actor, one as insulated from democratic pressure as any 'public' authority. It is notable that as soon as reports of 'shortages' of low wage workers began to appear, the central bank adjusted its policy forecast, suggesting that a tapering of asset purchases or an interest rate hike may come sooner than had been anticipated.[21] Similarly, the Biden administration had to concede on its initial request that the states provide the federally funded unemployment insurance supplement through September 2021 in the face of strong right-wing opposition.[22] Every Republican controlled state promptly opted out of the program months before its expiration. To be sure, this is still far from an austerity agenda. But it does suggest that the fate of expansionary policy will be contingent on how inflation, as an index of working-class power, develops.

On the other hand, if the kind of wage militancy that could propel sustained inflation were to manifest, might it correlate with a shift in the balance of class forces favourable enough to foreclose the option of returning to straightforward neoliberal austerity? In theory, perhaps. More to the point, given that an expansionary policy is for now on offer, what opportunities are there for building and institutionalizing the kind of working-class power that could push it further? That depends on how one interprets what has come to be celebrated as 'Bidenomics'. After a generation of relentless assault on the idea that government can or should do anything to improve economic conditions for working people, even the sharpest and most acute critics have found a great deal about which to be optimistic in the Biden administration. Cedric Durand, for instance, went so far as to characterize it as representing a 'structural break in the regulation of capitalism, the shockwaves of which will reverberate in the global political economy for years to come'.[23] One certainly hopes. But the break that Bidenomics is said to represent comes with its own set of contradictions that, though somewhat different from those which preceded it, continue to present significant challenges for a transformational class politics.

THE CHARACTER OF BIDENOMICS

After the passage in March 2021 of the pandemic emergency relief package, the $1.9 trillion American Rescue Plan – which together with *CARES Act* for Covid-19 assistance signed by Trump amounted to an annual expenditure of fully 20 per cent of US GDP – Biden outlined his longer-term program in two instalments: the American Jobs Plan (AJP) and the American Families Plan (AFP). As proposed, the measures sought to address what the administration had identified, no doubt in response to sustained movement pressure, as the most urgent crises they confront: climate change and the issue of care. A proposal, of course, is not a policy, and especially given the Democrats' exceedingly narrow margin in the Senate (they cannot afford to lose a single member's vote) the range of possible outcomes is considerable. Already by mid-2021, the administration had indicated a willingness to accept substantial concessions in pursuit of an initial bipartisan agreement while continuing to pursue the rest the agenda in subsequent legislation. How this will play out is an open question, and therefore my purpose here is not to forecast congressional dynamics but rather to reflect on how the coalition around Biden has made sense of the conjuncture they confront. To that end, the original blueprint the administration laid out is taken here as a statement of guiding principles.[24]

In total, the AJP and AFP called for $4 trillion – the equivalent of the amount deployed between March 2020 and 2021 – to be spent over eight to ten years on a range of physical and social infrastructure projects: upgrading the national transportation system, in part through a substantial expansion of electric vehicles; improving water and power systems; modernizing housing as well as public and commercial buildings; establishing universal pre-kindergarten and providing direct aid to millions of parents; enhancing the quality of care for the elderly and those with disabilities; making higher education more affordable; and more. Laced through both plans were emphases on the centrality of union labour and commitments to leverage federal expenditures in support of workplace organizing. Finally, to finance it all, Biden proposed a suite of tax increases on the wealthy, on corporate profits, and on capital gains that – though modest in comparison to the mid-twentieth century tax rate structure – were intended to pay for it all within some fifteen years. Accompanying these were diplomatic efforts by Treasury Secretary Yellen to reach an agreement among the G7 on a Global Minimum Corporate Tax.[25]

The design of the administration's proposals reflects a structural interpretation of the current crisis, one that has been gaining ground within Democratic policymaking circles for some time. As early as 2013, Larry Summers warned the IMF that the US economy had become mired in a 'secular stagnation', invoking a term coined by the country's first famous Keynesian, Alvin Hansen, in the late-1930s.[26] It was quite an admission from one of the architects of modern economic policy. But while Summers intended to draw attention to the poor recovery from the financial crisis alone, Biden's team, like Hansen during the Depression, appears to find the concept useful for explaining a deeper kind of political economic rot.

Their orientation has been informed by a growing body of academic research on the historical aspects of economic underperformance. As the economist Robert Gordon has demonstrated, after the conclusion of a 'special century' of US capitalism around 1970, domestic growth has been sluggish, and slowing. At the heart of this weakness has been inadequate investment. Apart from a short burst around the dot.com boom in the latter-1990s, the rate of private business investment has steadily fallen in the US, and indeed across the advanced capitalist world since the late-1960s – dropping by almost two-thirds since then. At the same time, US public physical capital investment has shriveled, settling some 70 per cent below its mid-1950s level. The consequences of these trends on employment have been profound. Although the official unemployment rate was quite low by late 2019, labour force participation, which had risen through the latter half of the twentieth century, in large part due to the entry of women into the formal workforce, peaked around 2000 and has since been in steady decline.[27]

Figure 1. Five-Year Moving Average Ratio of Net Private Business Investment to Private Business Capital Stock, 1966-2016

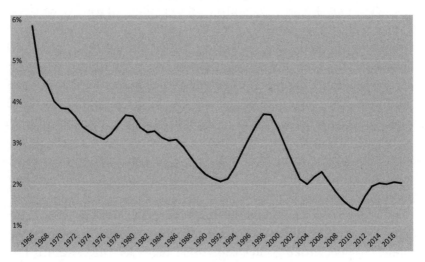

Source: Bureau of Economic Analysis Fixed Assets Accounts, Tables 4.1, 4.4, and 4.7. Adapted from Robert Gordon, *The Rise and Fall of American Growth*, 587.

Figure 2 Major Public Physical Capital Investment Outlays
as a Share of GDP, 1954-2020

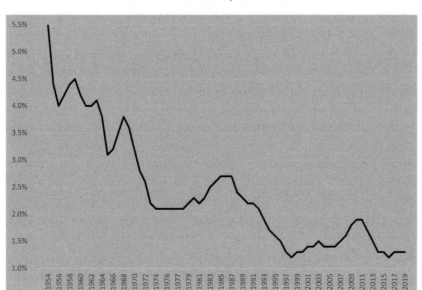

Source: Office of Management and Budget, *Historical Tables*, Table 9.3, 'Major Public
Physical Capital Investment Outlays in Percentage Terms: 1940-2021'.

This is not to say that US has been stuck in a 'long downturn'.[28] Rather,
it may be understood as another expression of the combined and uneven
character of capitalist development. As Leo Panitch and Sam Gindin
established in *The Making of Global Capitalism*, the extraordinary capacities
of the financial sector to facilitate the internationalization of production
and to absorb and expand global savings drove the renewed dynamism
of accumulation in the years after stagflation.[29] The mid-1980s through
mid-2000s were, after all, a great time to be on Wall Street. But if finance
played a role in allocating capital for productive investment in parts of the
Global South, within the US its effect was to draw corporate profits away
from reinvestment and towards the acquisition of those assets promising to
appreciate rather than produce value anew. The increasing volume of share
buybacks, corporate takeovers, and speculative trading, that is, have been the
flip side of the declining rate of fixed investment.[30]

Reflection upon these conditions warmed Biden and his team to the
idea of an 'industrial policy', something that had not received a hearing
inside the beltway in at least a generation. Prior to the pandemic, Jake
Sullivan, who now serves as Biden's National Security Advisor, argued in
a co-authored piece with the security analyst Jennifer Harris that 'secular

stagnation, not debt, is far and away the more pressing national security concern' and called for an industrial policy of 'deliberate and directed public investment that underwrites a shift to a post-carbon U.S. economy'.[31] Another senior administration official, Jared Bernstein of the Council of Economic Advisors, who served as chief economist to Biden during his time as Vice President and directed the labour-sympathetic Economic Policy Institute, has advanced similar arguments for some time.[32] And Brian Deese of the National Economic Council proclaimed to the audience of a popular *New York Times* podcast his commitment to 'the things that people in prior eras would demean or mock as industrial policy'.[33] According to reports on internal discussions during the transition period, the document that most influenced Biden himself as well as members of his inner circle was a UAW report stressing the need for such an industrial policy designed to enhance US productive capacity, above all in the area of electric vehicles (EVs).[34] The union position, however, is not far from that of management, as GM has also called for a national EV policy for some time.[35]

Viewed historically, this emphasis on public investment and industrial policy is the feature of the Biden vision that most distinguishes it from the recent past.[36] To their credit, the administration is correct both in seeing the secular decline in the rate of investment as the material driver of many of our social, economic, and environmental challenges, and in believing that the private sector is on its own incapable of reversing it. Nevertheless, both the details of the proposals as well as their overall conceptualization also reveal the limits of 'Bidenomics'. Consider, for instance, the obsession with EVs. As Sean Sweeney and John Treat have argued in the *Socialist Register*, EVs are no substitute for an expanded and improved mass transit system. For the foreseeable future, they will likely remain too expensive for poor and working-class people to afford, and in any case technological challenges around battery manufacturing and electricity generation continue to raise questions about sustainability.[37] Moreover, as Adam Tooze has observed, while the scale of Biden's plan may have sounded significant, in the scheme of things it was not. At most $1.5 trillion of the *proposed* expenditures could be considered as directly bearing on carbon emissions – spread out over eight years, this would amount to some 0.5 per cent of GDP per year, a fraction of what most experts believe is necessary to save the planet. Senator Bernie Sanders, by contrast, has called for about ten times as much.[38]

Likewise, the proposals in the American Family Plan appeared grand only relative to their starting point – the minimal nature of social infrastructure in the US. Among advanced capitalist states, the US spends far less, as a share of GDP, on family policy, and it is the only one that has historically offered *zero* paid family medical leave. The Biden administration's effort to rectify this rests upon means-testing, tax credit frameworks, and cooperation from the states, a degree of Rube Goldberg complexity that stands in sharp contrast to the uniform and universally accessible programs found elsewhere in the world. Some parts would expire in five years, a risky bet given the volatility of recent US politics, while others, like paid family leave, would only be implemented over the course of a decade. Finally, Tooze's point about the size of the climate plan applies here as well. Spread over its entire lifespan, the care provisions as proposed would amount to an annual expenditure of 1 per cent of GDP – just enough to catch the US up to Italy, the laggard of European social policy.[39]

To be sure, basic political calculations played no small role in the shaping the size of the package. Although the surprise victory of two Democratic Senators in the January 2021 Georgia run-off elections clinched a congressional majority for Biden, his margin is razor thin. The most conservative Democrats, like Joe Manchin of West Virginia and Kyrsten Sinema of Arizona, therefore, retain veto power over all legislation, and they have been resistant to just about everything demanded by the left wing of the party – from a $15 minimum wage to an end to the filibuster. Moreover, they have refused to part with that old obsession with the federal debt. As a result, 'pay-fors' and other wonkish revenue-speak have loomed large in the early discussions, tax politics that only further complicates the path forward in such a deadlocked Senate.[40] These are the very fiscal constraints that the BlackRock report lamented.

Perhaps with greater legislative room to manoeuvre, Biden would have pressed for a bit more – but orders of magnitude more, like what Sanders and Alexandria Ocasio Cortez have called for? Probably not. The Biden administration's theory of public investment, Keynesian pathbreaking as it may seem after decades of neoliberalism, is decidedly not one of expanding and making more durable the public sector, much less pursuing public ownership of key sectors. Instead, it stems from a conventional liberal conclusion that the inadequate business response to the crises of climate and care reflect specific kinds of market failure for which neoliberal principles cannot account. The goal, then, as Deese has put it, is to identify areas where 'public investment or the public sector can play a catalytic role'. In short, they hope to use public investment to 'unlock private investment' or to 'escort private capital' to otherwise un-investible ends. The idea is to leverage what they see as a once-in-a-generation public investment program to kickstart a new phase of capital accumulation, but this time on a foundation that is, to some degree, decarbonized.[41] To repurpose a framework that Daniela

Gabor has used to explain the financial sector's recent position on economic development in the Global South, Biden's plan is in essence about 'de-risking' those investments that the private sector has thus far judged too risky to undertake.[42]

Whether a program of one-time public expenditure intended to entice and leverage private investment will prove sufficient to meet the scale of the climate crisis is, to say the least, not the kind of vision socialists should find satisfactory. Most alarming, however, is the frame through which the entire economic policy has been expounded: the intensifying great power struggle with China. From the first paragraph of the American Jobs Plan – stressing that it will 'position the United States to out-compete China' – onwards, the economic program has been cast as an imperial one. 'They are,' Deese said of China, 'the ascendant economic and military power in the world,' and 'as we think about the competitive dynamics' that result, 'we need to ask ourselves a more serious set of questions about our own vulnerability.' This perceived vulnerability is the ultimate rationale for the program of public investment and industrial policy, a national security Keynesianism that should make anyone with internationalist sensibilities uneasy.[43]

On its own, then, perhaps the best that can be concluded about the Biden program is that it may provide some breathing room from Trumpism. That alone is not nothing given the threat the American right presents to basic democratic principles, but the window of opportunity may not last for very long. In any case, even if it is effective on its own terms, Bidenomics is designed to provide public stimulus for a new wave of accumulation controlled by private actors. It is hard to imagine how such a terrain would be more favourable for working-class struggle than any other. To be sure, to the degree that the renewed accumulation comes with a burst of productive investment and employment growth, it would be beneficial for a time. A tightening labour market is rarely a bad thing. But the monetary policy foundation on which Bidenomics rests was itself built for conditions of stagnation, not growth. The potential contradiction there is a familiar one, a variety of what Michal Kalecki famously described as the 'political business cycle', with central bankers now representing the capitalist class as a whole. Breaking that cycle would require nothing less than moving from a one-time stimulus to longer-term democratic planning and disarmament of the financial sector through public control if not outright socialization of the investment function. And it will take a vastly greater level of working-class organization and power than the labour movement currently wields, and perhaps has ever possessed, to stand any chance at pulling that off.

ROADS TO UNION RENEWAL?

Debates about union renewal are as old as the decline of organized labour itself. A natural starting point may be to consider what many union officials see as the biggest problem: the dismal state of federal labour law, which has been turned on its head through anti-union amendments to the NLRA, like the Taft-Hartley Act of 1947, and a steady stream of negative NLRB precedents. In contrast to Democratic candidates since at least Jimmy Carter, who made a habit of mentioning labour law reform on the campaign trail and abandoning it after election day, Biden has maintained his public support for the AFL-CIO's reform proposal, the Protect the Right to Organize (PRO) Act. The various components of the PRO Act are together intended to address a principal reason why union membership has fallen so steeply over the past few decades: the inability to achieve private sector union growth due to the extraordinary hostility of employers and right-wing state governments. Deindustrialization and the resultant hollowing out of manufacturing unionism has been only one part of the story; the other has been the failure to organize large numbers of new workers, especially those in expanding sectors like services and logistics. The unions that have mounted some of the more successful organizing drives in those areas have done so outside of the formal NLRA process; that is, they have prevailed despite, not thanks to, labour law. But such efforts – for instance, SEIU's celebrated Justice for Janitors campaign – have required a substantial investment of resources, a reality that makes such a strategy difficult to replicate.

The experience of Amazon workers in Alabama was only the most recent and high-profile illustration of what those trying to organize under the NLRA are up against. The law permits a wide range of intimidation tactics, refined by a multi-billion-dollar anti-union industry, and imposes few penalties on employers for violations, effectively incentivizing illegal behaviour. What is more, because the NLRA only covers direct employees, employers can rely on misclassification and all manner of contracting arrangements to foreclose organizing avenues from the outset. Meanwhile, workers and unions are highly constrained in the actions they can take with legal protection – solidarity strikes and secondary boycotts, for instance, have been prohibited since 1947. Finally, even when a union does succeed in overcoming every obstacle and winning an election conducted by the NLRB, employers have several means of delaying bargaining, stalling which can sometimes obstruct settlement of a contract for years.

The PRO Act would do much to change this playing field by streamlining and expediting union election and first-contract bargaining processes; restricting employers' ability to intimidate workers and establishing meaningful penalties when they do so; allowing solidarity actions between unions; revising the definition of employee to encompass a broader scope of coverage by the law; and effectively abolishing state right-to-work statues. In short, it is a wish-list for organizers, providing an immediate policy fix for many of the intractable obstacles union drives have encountered over the years. But there is a reason nothing like it has passed for so long: the Democratic Party has historically refused to go all-in on the issue. In 2009, when Barack Obama enjoyed supermajorities in both chambers of congress, his administration declined to pursue an earlier version of labour law reform, the Employee Free Choice Act. Thus, the fate of the PRO Act may end up reflecting where the centre of gravity within the Democratic Party is today. Republicans have vowed to filibuster the measure, along with every other progressive proposal, and the only question that remains is how far a handful of powerful Senate Democrats are willing to go. Will they reform or abolish the filibuster? If not, can they manage to incorporate elements of labour law reform into an infrastructure bill that they hope to pass through the fifty-vote shortcut of budget 'reconciliation'? Perhaps, but this is far from certain. In any case, the fact that it all rests on obscure parliamentary procedures underscores the fragility of the Biden coalition.

This uncertainty is a reason why the administration established its Task Force on Worker Organizing and Empowerment. While some observers have worried that the task force is likely to distract attention from the more consequential legislative struggle, others see real potential in executive action. To be sure, the White House is not without power, especially when it comes to decisions over how to leverage the federal government's substantial procurement budget. By favouring union firms in the selection of suppliers, evaluating bids based on a capacious definition of 'value' rather than price alone, and conditioning contracts on 'labor peace agreements', Biden may be able to support organizing and bargaining for some share of the hundreds of thousands of private sector workers who indirectly serve the federal government. Indeed, one of his early executive orders raised the minimum wage for federal contractors to $15 per hour, a sign that the administration sees procurement as a laboratory for broader labour policy goals. But even under the best of circumstances, executive action alone is unlikely to have much structural effect in a private sector labour market of roughly 110 million people.[44]

The incredible difficulty of finding ways to grow traditional unions has led some strategists to ask whether the new challenges confronting workers under twenty-first century capitalism demand new solutions entirely. Even if passed, the PRO Act, like the NLRA on which it builds, is premised upon the idea of organizing and bargaining at the level of the employer. Such a framework, they hold, was perhaps sensible in the days when masses of workers assembled in the mills and factories of giant corporations. But today, as the economist David Weil has put it, increasing numbers of people labour in a 'fissured workplace' where they, and those with whom they interact daily, may be employed by different corporate entities.[45] Millions more, including many of those in the rapidly growing care workforce and almost the entire 'gig economy', work on their own, often in private residences. Ensuring that workers are properly classified and covered under the law would no doubt address a part of this problem. But the deepening concentration of both ownership and control levels above the 'worksite', a result of the financialization driven by predatory investors like private equity firms as well as the broader dynamics of asset manager capitalism, has done much to blur the lines between employers and ultimate decision makers across much of the economy.[46]

From this perspective, improving the conditions of work requires going beyond the firm and bargaining at the sectoral level. Precedents for such an approach exist in the tripartite arrangements briefly established during the New Deal and World War II, or the co-determination schemes that still exist in Western Europe, and in certain jurisdictions unions have sought to rehabilitate those models. For instance, in response to the SEIU-backed Fight for $15 campaign, the New York State Labor Commissioner established a Fast-Food Wage Board that in 2015 voted to raise the industry minimum wage to $15 an hour. This success demonstrated the concrete ways in which workplace struggle can today be politicized even for those without a union. And none of this, proponents of sectoral bargaining note, is mutually exclusive with firm-centred organizing – it is simply a different approach for those situations where a traditional union may not be viable in the near term.[47]

It goes without saying that any of these reforms would be beneficial, and insofar as even parts of such measures are winnable at the national, state, or local levels, they are worthy of support. But as Jane McAlevey has put it, there are 'no shortcuts' to building the kind of power capable of contending with ruling-class authority.[48] Indeed, sectoral bargaining could be of material benefit to workers, but only if unions possess sufficient political muscle to make it so, and such strength is not mechanically related to union density or any other metric. What is more, in the absence of real organization within democratically accountable bodies, policies passing as sectoral bargaining can be imposed upon workers and thereby serve to undercut any promise of self-activity. In New York, a cynical attempt by Uber and certain unions to pass legislation granting ride–share workers a minimal degree of representation and wage standardization in exchange for permanent misclassification as contractors was only narrowly defeated after strenuous efforts by the NY Taxi Workers' Alliance and intervention by the AFL–CIO.[49] In the US and around the world, sectoral bargaining-type schemes have proved effective when they were implemented in response to struggles waged by a powerful and militant labour movement. They alone cannot create those conditions.

The recent New York experience might be read as confirmation of the arguments long advanced by Kim Moody and others associated with the publication *Labor Notes* that the only road to union renewal is through the unions themselves. In this view, bureaucratization, the suppression of internal democracy and militancy, and short-sighted or opportunistic political alliances with the Democratic Party have prevented unions from rising to the historic challenge presented by the onslaught of the past few decades. Nothing less than a long-term rank-and-file strategy can breathe life into these essential yet decaying institutions, a conclusion that since the 1970s has led many radicals to enter strategic sectors in pursuit of just that. At this point, Moody considers logistics to be the most strategic, as the sprawling supply chains managed by juggernauts like Amazon, with their insatiable demand for labour, provide workers across the country with immense leverage.[50] Few would argue with the wisdom of targeting one of capital's critical choke points, and one hopes to see more organizing drives at Amazon in the future. But it would be a mistake to draw the lesson that the defeat in Bessemer was due principally to the RWDSU's failures, not least because there would not have been a campaign in the first place were it not for the RWDSU. Whatever one feels about the 'union bureaucracies' denounced by Moody and others, they also happen to be at this point the principal organizational infrastructure available to support working-class struggle. Moreover, there is no guarantee that a successful rank-and-file strategy will prevent the kind of 'business unionism' that these critics describe. The president of the Transport Workers Union, John Samuelson, which collaborated with Uber on that New York measure, initially won office through just such a program. To adequately understand the compromises all union officials are forced to make requires a deeper and more textured analysis than any single framework can provide.

Jane McAlevey's analysis of the distinction between organizing and mobilizing presents a more nuanced perspective on the same set of questions. Organizing, she stresses, is about one thing: building power, both inside and outside the workplace. Like Moody, McAlevey understands the strategic significance of certain industries, and the central ones in her account are those of social reproduction: care and education, where the providers and the beneficiaries of public goods share a mutual interest and therefore have the basis for a broad and durable solidarity.[51] This insight is valuable not only for union organizing but also for thinking about a broader class politics in our time. If nothing else, the pandemic has demonstrated the importance of public health and the inadequacies of a private healthcare system, something already well understood by millions of uninsured and underinsured people. The devastating impact of the virus on residents of long-term care facilities shed light on the unconscionable working and living conditions endemic to for-profit nursing homes. With an aging population and increasing elder care needs, this disaster is sure to worsen. And as more and more people experience the intensification of climate change with each passing year, the scale of the emergency is being thrown into ever sharper relief. Accompanying these crises, however, is an opportunity. In the near term, the sectors in which employment will grow the most, in part due to Bidenomics, happen also to be those in which workers daily address these most urgent social needs. It is a context in which the potential for an independent working–class politics for the public good is tremendous.

A POLITICS FOR THE PUBLIC GOOD

Decades of neoliberalism have not just decimated union membership, but also overhauled the composition of the labour movement itself. Half of all union members in the US now work for government at the local, state, and national levels (See Table 1). An additional 20 per cent are employed in education and health services or utilities and transportation, occupations made possible by significant public subsidy.[52] Still more, like many building trades, are tied to the state in complex ways, whether through government procurement or private contractors in jurisdictions where project labour agreements are a political necessity. In other words, discussions about the labour movement are at this point already inseparable from discussions about the public good.

This could, as has been the case in the past, produce a politics of resentment, with the unorganized many pitted against the organized few. But it could just as well be pushed in the other direction, through intentional efforts to align the interests of workers who provide vital public services with those of communities that depend upon them. Indeed, the most successful campaigns in recent years have started from this premise. The group of educators that more than a decade ago won power in the Chicago Teachers Union turned their fight against the savage attacks waged by that city's neoliberal elite into, as the late Karen Lewis put it, a 'struggle for the soul of public education'. Since then, educators elsewhere in the country have followed suit, in conservative states like West Virginia, Oklahoma, and Arizona as well as traditional labour strongholds.[53]

Table 1. Union Membership by Sector, 2019

Sector	Union Members (000s)	% of Labour Mvmt.
Local Government	4,050	27.8
State Government	2,043	14.0
Education and Health Services	1,885	12.9
Manufacturing	1,291	8.9
Transport and Utilities	1,166	8.0
Construction	1,055	7.2
Federal Government	974	6.7
Wholesale/Retail	741	5.1
Business and Other Services	511	3.5
Leisure and Hospitality	384	2.6
Other	475	3.3
TOTAL	14,575	100.0

This principle has been the inspiration for a national campaign of Bargaining for the Common Good (BCG), which seeks to use contract fights to link workplace issues with broader public needs and thereby to lay the foundation for durable labour-community coalitions.[54] In Los Angeles, for instance, demands around class size and the number of school nurses and social workers enabled educators and school employees to cultivate meaningful relationships with parents and students in advance of their 2019 strike. The United Teachers Los Angeles (UTLA) also conducted extensive popular education programming to drive home how the same private equity firms bankrolling the charter school industry, with its agenda of privatization, owned a growing share of the city's housing stock and contributed to the crisis of rent intensification. And they showed how these predatory firms also benefited from a state tax policy that privileges global investors and commercial real estate owners, even as schools and other vital public services suffered chronic funding shortages.[55] BCG coalitions in California and elsewhere have since begun building on this kind of groundwork to wage electoral and legislative 'Tax the Rich' campaigns that have the potential to at last shift the debate around public goods away from the expenditure and towards the revenue side of the ledger.

Although the most high-profile BCG campaigns have occurred within the public sector, this need not always be the case. Again, even within the private sector, increasing numbers of workers and much of the labour movement does work directly bearing on the public. Among the first unions to endorse the Green New Deal, for instance, was the Association of Flight Attendants-CWA, an encouraging echo of the environmental leadership demonstrated by the Oil, Chemical, and Atomic Workers a generation prior. The militant 1199 New England, which represents nearly 30,000 mostly private sector long-term care workers in Connecticut and Rhode Island, have long linked worker and patient conditions to state-level struggles over Medicaid funding. In the irrationally privatized US healthcare system, they are one of several unions that have played a leadership role in highlighting the importance of staffing levels to the quality of patient care. Others, like the National Nurses United, have served as the face of the struggle for Medicare-for-All, and still more private sector unions, including those outside of healthcare, have long provided crucial support for the Labor Campaign for Single Payer. Insofar as Bidenomics succeeds in pumping money into climate related infrastructure, it is not impossible to imagine parallel developments by transport, industrial, and even building trades unions around widely felt environmental issues.

None of this is bound to happen, of course, and to the extent that it does it will be shaped by struggles both inside and outside of the labour movement. As usual, we are likely to lose at least as many of these fights as we win, and even victory will often involve the kinds of compromises that many on the left will find unsatisfactory. This is not, on its own, socialist struggle. But it may represent the beginnings of *our* working-class movement, one that we build in the context created by our predecessors' defeat. The contradictions of four decades of neoliberalism have delivered to us an opportunity – perhaps not what we would have chosen, but the one with which we will have to make our own history. Already, the legacy of the Sanders insurgency, the great educator strike wave of 2017-2019, the growth of DSA, the shock of the pandemic, and the deepening climate crisis have created the space to expand the terrain of social struggle considerably. Moreover, the present fiscal-monetary arrangement at least ensured that the immediate aftermath of the COVID emergency would not bring the kind of crushing austerity that many had expected prior to Trump's defeat. But accompanying this opportunity is a very grave threat. The declining capacity of neoliberalism as we have known it to reproduce an electoral constituency also has given way to the most dangerous threat to stability the advanced capitalist world has seen since the interwar period: a violent right wing that is now willing and perhaps eager to overthrow constitutional democracy itself. Trump is for the moment out of office, but Trumpism is alive and well. If that current manages to gain institutional power once more, it may well be the end not just of the left but of liberalism for the foreseeable future, to whatever extent there is one. The only option, it thus seems, is to go all in on this opportunity before it passes, and hope for the best.

NOTES

1   White House Fact Sheet, 'Executive Order Establishing the White House Task Force on Worker Organizing and Empowerment', 26 April 2021.

2   Astead W. Herndon, 'How Biden Is Trying to Help Working-Class Voters in Red-State Alabama', *New York Times,* 9 March 2021.

3   See Nelson Lichtenstein, *State of the Union: A Century of American Labor*, New York: Princeton University Press, 2002.

4   Bureau of Labor Statistics, 'Union Members Summary', 22 January 2021.

5   For a sharp critique of the premature assertions that the financial crisis marked the end of neoliberalism, see Merlin Chowkwanyun, 'The Crisis in Thinking About the Crisis', *Renewal,* 17, 2009, pp. 57-66.

6   See for example, Adam Tooze, 'The Death of the Central Bank Myth', *Foreign Policy*, 13 May 2020.

7   Board of Governors of the Federal Reserve System, 'Guide to Changes in the 2020 Statement on Longer-Run Goals and Monetary Policy Strategy', 27 August 2020.

8   Quoted in Zachary Carter, *The Price of Peace: Money, Democracy, and the Life of John Maynard Keynes*, New York: Random House, 2020, pp. 233-34.

9   Benjamin Braun, 'Asset Manager Capitalism as a Corporate Governance Regime,' in Jacob Hacker, Alex Hertel Fernandez, Paul Pierson, and Kathleen Thelen, eds, *American Political Economy: Politics, Markets, and Power*, New York: Cambridge University Press, 2021.

10   David McLaughlin and Annie Massa, 'The Hidden Dangers of the Great Index Fund Takeover', *Bloomberg*, 9 January 2021; Braun, 'Asset Manager Capitalism'; Johannes Petry, Jan Fichtner, and Eelke Heemskerk, 'Steering Capital: The Growing Private Authority of Index Providers in the Age of Passive Asset Management', *Review of International Political Economy*, 28:1, 2021, pp. 152-76; Anusar Faruqi aka Policy Tensor, 'Seeing Like BlackRock', *Substack*, July 9, 2021.

11   Liz Hoffman, 'How Banks Lost the Battle for Power on Wall Street,' *Wall Street Journal*, 7 September 2018; and Jeanna Smialek, 'Top U.S. Officials Consulted with BlackRock as Markets Melted Down', *New York Times*, 24 June 2021.

12   Hoffman, 'How Banks Lost.'

13   Lucian Bebchuk and Scott Hirst, 'The Specter of the Giant Three', *Boston University Law Review*, 99, 2019, pp. 721-40.

14   Braun, 'Asset Manager Capitalism.'

15   Jeanna Smialek, 'Top U.S. Officials Consulted with BlackRock as Markets Melted Down', *New York Times*, 24 June 2021; and Dawn Lim and Gregory Zuckerman, 'BlackRock Emerges as Wall Street Player in Biden Administration', *Wall Street Journal*, 1 December 2020.

16   BlackRock also assisted the Fed in its crisis response in 2008. See Jeanna Smialek, 'Top U.S. Officials Consulted with BlackRock as Markets Melted Down', *New York Times*,

24 June 2021; and Cezary Podkul and Dawn Lim, 'Fed Hires BlackRock to Help Calm Markets. Its ETF Business Wins Big,' *Wall Street Journal*, 18 September 2020.

17   BlackRock does have an $80 billion 'alternative investments' arm that engages in private markets, but that amounts to just one per cent of the firm's assets under management. There, too, however, BlackRock has demonstrated an interest in longer-term private investment, so much so that they have struggled to raise funds from institutional investors eager for quicker returns. See Dawn Lim, 'BlackRock Scales Back Private-Equity Fund Ambitions', *Wall Street Journal*, 1 January 2021.

18   Elga Bartsch, Jean Bovin, Stanley Fischer, and Philipp Hildebrand, 'Dealing with the Next Downturn: From Unconventional Monetary Policy to Unprecedented Policy Coordination', *Black Rock Investment Institute*, August 2019.

19   Yakov Feygin, 'The Deflationary Bloc', *Phenomenal World*, 9 January 2021.

20   Lawrence H. Summers, 'The Biden Stimulus is Admirably Ambitious. But It Brings Some Big Risks, Too', *Washington Post,* 4 February 2021.

21   James Politi and Colby Smith, 'Fed Signals First Rate Rise Will Come In 2023,' *Financial Times*, 16 June 2021.

22   Jeff Stein, 'Biden Says It "Makes Sense" for Enhanced Jobless Aid to End in September', *Washington Post*, 4 June 2021.

23   Cedric Durand, '1979 in Reverse', *New Left Review Sidecar,* 1 June 2021.

24   White House Fact Sheet, 'The American Jobs Plan,' 31 March 2021; and White House Fact Sheet, 'The American Family Plan', 28 April 2021.

25   Alan Rappeport, 'Finance Leaders Reach Global Tax Deal Aimed at Ending Profit Sharing', *New York Times*, 5 June 2021.

26   Lawrence H. Summers, 'Demand Side Secular Stagnation', *American Economic Review*, 105 (May) 2015, pp. 60-65.

27   Robert J. Gordon, *The Rise and Fall of American Growth: The U.S. Standard of Living Since the Civil War,* New York: Princeton University Press, 2017, esp. pp. 566-604. The decline in the rate of labour force participation is not attributable to the aging of the US population as the trend is visible in all age cohorts with the exception of those older than 60, who are working more than in the past. See: Lauren Bauer, Patrick Liu, and Jay Shambaugh, 'Is the Continued Rise of Older Americans in the Workforce Necessary for Future Growth', Brookings, 4 April 2019; Katharine G. Abraham and Melissa S. Kearney, 'Explaining the Decline in the U.S. Employment-to-Population Ratio: A Review of the Evidence', *Journal of Economic Literature,* 58 (September), 2020, pp. 585-643.

28   Robert Brenner, *The Economics of Global Turbulence: The Advanced Capitalist Economies from Long Boom to Long Downturn, 1945-2005*, London: Verso, 2006.

29   Leo Panitch and Sam Gindin, *The Making of Global Capitalism: The Political Economy of American Empire*, London: Verso, 2012.

30   William Lazonick, 'The Financialization of the U.S. Corporation: What Has Been Lost, and How It Can Be Regained', *Seattle University Law Review,* 36, 2012-13, pp. 857-909.

31   Jennifer Harris and Jake Sullivan, 'America Needs a New Economic Philosophy. Foreign Policy Experts Can Help', *Foreign Policy*, 7 February 2020.

32   Jared Bernstein, 'The Time for America to Embrace Industrial Policy Has Arrived', *Foreign Policy*, 22 July 2020.

33   Ezra Klein, 'The Best Explanation of Biden's Thinking I've Heard', *New York Times*, 9 April 2021.

34   Noam Schreiber, 'The Biden Team Wants to Transform the Economy. Really', *New York Times,* 11 February 2021.

35   Sebastian Blanco, 'GM Calls for National Electric Vehicle Policy', *Forbes*, 26 October 2018.

36   See, for historical context, Judith Stein, *Pivotal Decade: How the U.S. Traded Factories for Finance in the 1970s*, New Haven: Yale University Press, 2010.

37   Sean Sweeney and John Treat, 'Shifting Gears: Labour Strategies for Low-Carbon Public Transit Mobility', in Leo Panitch and Greg Albo, eds, *Socialist Register 2021: Beyond Digital Capitalism*, London: Merlin Press, 2020.

38   Adam Tooze, 'America's Race to Net Zero,' *New Statesman,* 21 April 2021.

39   Adam Tooze, 'American Family Values and Biden's Families Plan', *Substack*, 8 May 2021; and Matt Bruenig, 'Problem's with Biden's American Family Plan', *People's Policy Project*, 28 April 2021.

40   See, for example, Andy Kroll, 'What Joe Manchin Wants', *Rolling Stone*, 10 May 2021.

41   Klein, 'The Best Explanation of Biden's Thinking'.

42   Daniela Gabor, 'The Wall Street Consensus', *Development and Change*, 52, Summer 2021; Anusar Faruqi aka Policy Tensor, 'Is it Feasible to Publicly Fund the Global Energy Transition?' *Substack*, 14 April 2021.

43   Tobita Chow and Jake Werner, 'U.S.-China: Progressive Internationalist Strategy Under Biden', Rosa Luxemburg Stiftung, 19 January 2021.

44   White House Fact Sheet, 'Biden-Harris Administration Issues Executive Order to Raise the Minimum Wage to $15 for Federal Contractors', 27 April 2021. For an insightful perspective on the potential of executive action to encourage labour organizing, see Brandon Magner, 'Using Executive Authority to Incentivize Employer Neutrality', *Labor Law Lite – Substack*, 26 April 2021.

45   David Weil, *The Fissured Workplace: Why Work Became So Bad for So Many and What Can Be Done to Improve It*, Cambridge, Massachussetts: Harvard University Press, 2014.

46   Eileen Appelbaum and Rosemary Batt, *Private Equity at Work: When Wall Street Manages Main Street,* New York: Russell Sage, 2014.

47   Kate Andrias, 'The New Labor Law', *Yale Law Journal*, 126, October 2016, pp. 46-100.

48   Jane McAlevey, *No Shortcuts: Organizing for Power*, New York: Oxford University Press, 2016.

49   Steven Greenhouse, 'Unionized but Impotent? Row Erupts Over Gig Workers' Labor Proposal', *Guardian*, 27 May 2021.

50   Kim Moody, *On New Terrain: How Capital is Reshaping the Battleground of Class War,* New York: Haymarket Books, 2017.

51   See Jane McAlevey, *No Shortcuts: Organizing for Power,* New York: Oxford University Press, 2016.

52   Bureau of Labor Statistics, 'Union Affiliation of Employed Wage and Salary Workers by Occupation and Industry', 22 January 2021.

53   Eric Blanc, *Red State Revolt: The Teachers' Strike Wave and Working-Class Politics,* New York: Verso, 2019.

54   For more information visit: www.bargainingforthecommongood.org.

55   Sarah Jaffe, 'The Radical Organizing that Paved the Way for the LA Teachers' Strike', *The Nation*, 19 January 2019.

AMERICAN WORKERS AND THE LEFT AFTER TRUMP: POLARIZED OPTIONS

SAM GINDIN

The widespread alienation of Americans from politics, which Donald Trump so handily exploited in his 2016 presidential election run, arose out of the uneven class and regional impacts of neoliberal globalization in the previous three to four decades. By the 2020 election, his success in polarizing the country through a politics of hate had reversed falling electoral engagement and brought record voter turnout, a majority of whom showed up at the polls to vote Trump out. Does the arrival of Joe Biden to the presidency signal the restoration of the legitimacy of American institutions? Does it even, as some on the left hope, suggest that the US is on the verge of a historic turn in the left's favour? Or will we see a further resurgence of the right as voters become disillusioned with Biden?

There is ample space for reform in American capitalism given high profits, the stunning scale that inequalities have reached, the comparatively modest levels of social provisioning, and the massive military budgets. But a radical turn to the left is quite another thing. Its likelihood doesn't rest on Biden, but on organized pressures from below, and here it is the labour movement – or rather the possibilities for a new kind of labour movement – that is pivotal. What scope is there for socialists to directly engage workers and contribute to the birth of a coherent working class with the vision, confidence, and strategic and organizational capacities to lead a struggle for social transformation?

I

Neoliberalism established, Adolph Reed Jr has tersely noted, a 'capitalism without an effective working-class opposition'.[1] And class was a discourse that conservative, liberal, and social democratic politicians were all too anxious happy to marginalize. Globalization, though no less a class project, allowed elites to respond to discontent on the more comfortable terrain of national unfairness, tending to normalize the neoliberal policy regime.

Globalization could, more readily than neoliberalism, either be blamed – 'globalization made us do it', 'cheap labour abroad is taking our jobs' – or identified as an opportunity for domestic prosperity through 'meeting the competitive challenge'. A left nationalism emerged, in the US and elsewhere, as the critical voice of dissent. But its emphasis on the loss of 'state sovereignty' as a unifying democratic principle likewise tended to obscure the salience of class. The new trade agreements were rather attacks on *popular* sovereignty, and were essentially global economic constitutions protecting property rights through each national state.

The key contradiction of globalization lay in the unevenness of its impact on different countries, and in the case of the US imposed the burden of 'superintending globalization' upon the American state.[2] This unevenness – not just between countries but especially within them – generated resentments among those who lost out, tending to undercut for many the appeal of globalization and the legitimacy of the governments and political parties which had sold globalization by making grandiose promises.[3] Immigration flows, which were so often the direct or indirect consequences of global restructuring, fuelled further domestic social antagonisms, especially when they occurred in a context of austerity, aggravating angst over jobs and concern over the 'diversion' of social benefits.

For the US, globalization seemed to have provided unequivocal gains. Americans got access to cheap consumer goods and business inputs produced by low-cost labour, with the international status of the dollar sidelining any concerns about trade deficits. The role of the dollar also gave the US singular access to global savings, which helped finance US fiscal deficits, corporate investments, and consumer debt. Yet overseeing the making of global capitalism also had its burdens. US multinational corporations increasingly located their investments abroad, steadily eroding millions of relatively high-paying jobs. In maintaining and extending its global empire, the US spent astronomical sums on its military in defence of global supply chains and in securing global resources and the world market for the international capital of all 'legitimate' states.

That both the benefits and burdens of globalization were so unequally distributed across class and regional divides in the US provided Trump with potent rhetorical ammunition for pitting globalization against a nostalgic nationalist appeal to pre-globalization days. The solutions Trump offered were contradictory and confused – partly performative, partly a deliberate heightening of regional geopolitical rivalry, and partly a concern to protect and restore US dominance in high tech. At the same time, Trump studiously avoided dealing with the underlying class dynamics that allowed – or drove – capital to 'nestle everywhere, settle everywhere, establish connections everywhere', in the enduring phrase of Marx and Engels in *The Communist Manifesto*. Nonetheless, Trump's non-solutions performed their rallying function to perfection. Trump, as one commentator put it, 'fed the richest in society in the currency they prefer – dollars – and he fed his fans lower down with a temporarily effective substitute – recognition'.[4]

II

The American working class made major gains in the period after the Second World War, a result of both its relative strength and capitalism's ability at the time to deliver. But the policy reforms of the so-called 'welfare state' left the power structures of capitalism untouched, and thus working-class gains vulnerable to reversal as political circumstances shifted.

In the 1970s, as the Bretton Woods framework unravelled in the face of global competition and political unrest, the US faced a fall of confidence in the dollar, stagnating productivity, and a squeeze on profits. The state's response to this crisis in capitalism, which came to be summarized as 'neoliberalism', was in essence a turn to *more* capitalism. It included the acceleration of globalization, liberalization of finance, a dramatic rise in interest rates to compel a restructuring of American industry, and an undisguised attack on the labour movement intended to lower working-class expectations and undermine resistance to these changes.

Capitalist elites and states had essentially concluded they could no longer afford to buy off workers with steady material progress. The working-class gains earlier characterized as indicators of capitalism's successes were now redefined as barriers to American competitiveness and global leadership. Working-class resistance was significant enough to frighten elites, and it took time, state coercion, and bitter conflicts to contain the militancy of the times. But even if the militancy revealed working-class potential, it was not enough. Without the political capacity to force some democratization of investment, even in the modest form of some workplace and community controls over capital investments, scattered skirmishes dissipated. Workers, weakened and divided by the intensified competitive pressures and permanent insecurity, gave in to a soul-destroying fatalism.

Working-class resignation has made the task of legitimizing capitalism through steady popular gains in wages and social provisioning less pressing for capital and the state. Absent movements, practices of resistance and working-class institutions equal to the task of challenging this turn in capitalism, workers have generally channelled their response into personal and family adaptations to sustain livelihoods. An exhausted labour movement has come to accept collective bargaining 'concessions' as the only way to protect the greatest portion of what was previously won. Consumption levels have been maintained by families increasing their collective hours of work and increasing their debt loads. Young people have stayed at home longer. Tax cuts are viewed as wage increases. Over time, neoliberalism's ethos of individualism has replaced collective visions of progress.

Much of the left insisted that the economic shift that defined the end of the twentieth century, particularly the turn toward the greater weight of financial markets, was unsustainable. Strong economic growth, they were certain, could not be revived, and sooner or later workers would rebel against the diminished life that came along with neoliberalism. Both predictions were categorically wrong (though this didn't stop their repetition). Given time to adjust, and with steady – even enhanced – state support, the scope for capitalists to redeploy their investments, remake labour processes, and solve their problems on the backs of workers proved greater than expected.

Individual companies did fail as a result of the restructuring, and some industries were wiped out or dramatically downsized, but capital came out of the intensified competition more powerful *as a class*, with stronger and more productive firms replacing the weaker. New and dynamic sectors emerged, corporate profits were restored, the dollar continued to rule, and the US retained its position as superintendent of global capitalism. In contrast, competition undermined workers' main weapon – their solidarity – and weakened workers as a class force. Fading worker engagement, together with a relentless corporate assault, saw falling union density and union participation. Involvement in an increasingly impervious electoral politics also fell. Amidst a booming economy that brought few benefits for most and heavy losses to others, popular alienation spread and trust in state and party institutions withered.

The 2008-09 financial crisis seemed to mark the end of the neoliberal era. The gargantuan efforts by the US Treasury and Federal Reserve to rescue the banks and the wider financial sector was interpreted by some to mark, at long last, a swing away from 'leaving it to the market' and a 'return of the state'. More than a decade later, however, it's clear that pronouncements of the demise of neoliberalism – or of financialization, or the marketization of the state – were premature. The reasons for these misreadings lie, at least in part, in the fact that neoliberalism has *never* revolved around a 'markets versus states' axis; capitalist markets and capitalist states are inherently symbiotic, mutually dependent on the other for their reproduction. For example, the 'liberalization' of finance in the sense of less regulations of a certain kind came with a level of volatility that demanded state regulations of a new kind. Trade agreements could not be negotiated without the state determining the trade-offs to be made among various economic sectors, and mediating disputes. Economic restructuring occurred via markets, but, as with the imposition of record interest rates in the early 1980s, the markets were shaped by the state.

The significance of the 2008-09 bank bailout didn't therefore lie in the intervention of the state per se, but on *whose behalf it was acting*. Faced with the choice between saving finance and getting capitalism back on its feet, or saving the people most impacted, the American state didn't hesitate to support the investors who speculated on mortgages rather than the millions who were losing their homes. Neoliberalism did not die with the crisis of 2008. Rather, the interventions of the American state served to end the crisis in a way that re-established the neoliberal functioning of the economy.

III

The Trump presidency advanced a politics of extremism in discourse, attitude, and identity on a series of issues – the border, race, trade, tax cuts, the pandemic – that empowered right-wing populists. Recycling xenophobic and nationalist tropes, Trump rallied regional and class anger against the Democratic Party, economic elites, and globalization. More ominously, he perverted the already compromised practices of liberal democratic politics, including rejecting broadly held norms regarding the sanctity of elections.

Significantly, however, the polarization around these issues in the US wasn't limited to partisan party clashes; the battles were also fought within both major parties. In both cases it was party outsiders who were the key voices calling for the disruption of the status quo, and in both cases, the leading role of outsiders highlighted a brewing legitimacy crisis confronting each of the major parties. On the Republican side, Trump challenged the GOP establishment not only by mobilizing a coalition around social conservatism, white nationalism, and hostility to immigrants, but also by offering a rhetorical opposition to free trade and globalization, even though both were firmly supported by economic elites, including business leaders allied to the Republicans.

For the Democrats, the problem lay in having to defend an economic path, long fostered by the party, which had disillusioned its working-class base. The Sanders alternative, concerned to address those disappointments, was rejected by the Democratic Party establishment – most vocally in questioning the electability of Bernie Sanders, but just as much because of the dangers Sanders posed to their control over the nature and direction of 'their' party. Most of the senior Democratic leadership had little interest in supporting programmes such as Medicare for All, having gone all-in for the compromise of Obama's Affordable Care Act, and were keen to protect their relationships with corporate donors.

Yet, beneath these sharp divisions between and within the major parties, there lay an elite consensus on the policy parameters framing key issues. The priority of maintaining US geopolitical leadership, for example, was hardly debated, and enjoyed an implicit bipartisan concurrence. Similarly, globalization might be tweaked but not rejected, basic corporate property rights were not to be breached, and – less explicitly – US international competitiveness had priority over social needs. Any improvements in labour conditions, or any measures to address the looming environmental catastrophe, were to be contained within that framework.

The gap between the discordant rhetoric and the cross-party shared commitment to the status quo was clear in the disjuncture between Trump belligerently blaming Mexico for 'stealing' US manufacturing jobs, and the limited scale of his response. For all of Trump's harangues on returning automotive jobs to the US Midwest, the 'new' US–Mexico–Canada Trade Agreement was hard to distinguish from its NAFTA predecessor signed off by Bill Clinton: the US automotive majors and the Mexican state were both quick to express their great relief, and the impact on the Midwest manufacturing jobs that Trump had made so much of was minimal.[5]

Despite Trump's bombastic positioning of himself as the defender of the abandoned American working class, he uttered not a word of criticism of his allies in various state jurisdictions who had wreaked havoc on union rights. His signature policy was a massive tax gift to corporations, introduced early in his administration, following a trend of tax cuts the Democrats had also adhered to. It is true that unemployment rates fell under Trump's watch, but this was part of a post-financial crisis trend that began under Obama. In any case, the jobs boom involved many former manufacturing workers moving into more precarious jobs, in particular in the service sector and the gig economy. And for many rural communities, the 2008–09 crisis in fact never ended. These communities didn't just suffer unemployment, but *depopulation,* as young people moved to employment – or unemployment – elsewhere.

As for the negotiations with China, when the dust cleared it turned out that here too, the Trump administration's concern with manufacturing jobs was largely performative. The negotiations focused instead on further opening China to US financial firms and high-tech companies – that is, to advancing, not eroding, international economic liberalization. In China's case, however, the tensions went deeper. Trump was expressing broad concerns within the American state over China's rapidly rising geopolitical role and its threat to US technological supremacy. The trick was to challenge this advance without risking continued access to the Chinese market, cheap goods for consumers and supply chains, and the flow of capital from Chinese trade surpluses back to the US (China's central bank remains the largest foreign buyer of American Treasuries). In this regard, Trump's ill-thought-out bluster proved ineffective and even counterproductive, leaving business leaders nervous about the long-term economic disruptions. Biden's style was more cautious and deliberate, but no less concerned to 'contain' China.

The elephant in the political room, the topic neither the Democratic or Republican party establishments broached in their increasingly loud clashes, was the half century of cross-party consensus on continuing with the neoliberal policy regime and its associated inequalities and lopsided class power.

IV

What then of Trump's defeat and Biden's promise to 'heal the nation'? Will Biden reverse the damage done by Trump, contain the growth of right-wing populism, or perhaps even author a post-neoliberal, social-democratic turn?

Biden's election as the non-Trump removed what for many was the ugliest of American presidencies. Yet as was commonly warned, it did not represent the end of Trumpism – a political expression of deep-rooted discontent and alienation. Trump nurtured a growing right-wing presence in the country, giving the presidential stamp of approval to the hard right, from anti-state right-wing nationalists to militias and white supremacists.

This danger cannot be ignored, but neither should progressives panic; the extremists have their own limiting contradictions. They are fragmented, suspicious of national organization, generally opposed by both US economic elites and the American security apparatus, and have no alternative economic programmes of substance. Fascism must obviously be fought, and it remains to be seen how far Biden's policies will reduce the threat, but the primary role of the socialist left remains to understand and react to the Biden turn, and above all to work toward transforming the working class – currently a marginal social force – into a coherent and radical social actor.

President Biden's early months in office have, in some respects, been auspicious. He entered office free of the Clinton-era Third Way baggage of balanced budgets. Jerome Powell, the chair of the Federal Reserve and a Republican, has been ready to print as much money as needed, with the support of Secretary of the Treasury Janet Yellen. Biden has called for massive public investments that extend the meaning of 'infrastructure' to include 'soft' infrastructure such as childcare and long-term residential care. He has appointed Lina Khan, an anti-monopoly champion, to lead the Federal Trade Commission, and Toby Merrill, the founder of Harvard Law School's Project on Predatory Student Lending as Deputy General Counsel in the Department of Education. And Biden's statements on the labour movement have been unabashedly pro-worker.

It is, however, far too early to declare Biden's appointments and policy directions a sign that the Democrats are significantly shifting their orientation.[6] Though Biden may have surprised with his ambitious opening moves, many of his actions were conjunctural – pragmatic responses to unique events that, for the most part, had little dissent from the US corporate sector. In this regard, politicians everywhere have accepted the need for exceptional expenditures during the pandemic and its still uncertain aftermath; the disputes are over how high deficits should be, and what the monies should be spent on. Conjunctural too was Biden's desire to distinguish his administration from Trump's and – looking ahead to the 2022 mid-terms – to distance himself from the Democratic Party policies and tactics that made Trumpism possible.

Moreover, in the face of Republican intransigence and minimal pressure from below, the compromises and indeed the erosion of Biden's ambitious plans has already begun. Universal healthcare is not on the table, with the Affordable Care Act gaining new life. The card check (automatic recognition of a union if a majority of workers have signed authorization cards), which is a key to facilitating union organizing and which Biden strongly supported during the Obama administration, has been dropped. And the proposed corporate tax increases fall well short of returning to where they were when Trump entered office and radically cut taxes. The Biden backsliding has occurred with rather minimal objections from the left, the union movement, or anyone else.

Projections of Biden's environmental expenditures look impressive, but the programmes Biden advocates convey neither the urgency, nor the requisite degree of planning and challenges to corporate power, that addressing the environmental crisis demands. Similarly, Biden's initial support for a $15 minimum wage was an important gesture, but hardly radical. With minimum wages having fallen so far behind the wage norm for half a century, higher-waged companies are less concerned that raising the floor would affect the broader labour market and, in any case, wage pressures in the low-paid segments of the labour force are already being signalled by market forces.[7] Still, Republican obstinacy has led Biden to retreat here as well.

Similarly, while the proposal of Treasury Secretary Janet Yellen for a global minimum tax on corporations of 15 per cent is worthy of support, it highlights the contradictions involved in changing a specific policy without changing the larger context. Even if this rather modest tax were implemented, the competitive conditions under which corporations operate, and the freedom this entails, will simply trigger a shift in tactics, including even greater pressure on workers' wages and conditions.

Foundational to Biden's new direction has been his industrial strategy, enthusiastically described by the head of the National Economic Council (an advisory group to the president) as 'a vision for a twenty-first century American industrial strategy'.[8] That the state may improve its capacity to do some modest planning of infrastructure and high-tech development is welcome. But what stands out about Biden's industrial vision is its focus on 'incentivizing' and strengthening corporations, not unlike the move to neoliberalism at the end of the 1970s, while workers are at most an afterthought, presumably content with vague promises of jobs as competitiveness improves.

Still, with profits not under pressure, and even elites recognizing that inequality has gone so far that *some* correction is inevitable, there is space for reforms that break with fiscal austerity. Biden's rhetoric and actions, however qualified, have reinforced these sentiments toward fiscal activism. But what can be expected once the mid-terms are over, and the pendulum shifts once again towards anxieties over deficits and inflation? It's a stretch to expect that Biden, the Democratic Party point-man charged with defeating Sanders, and now also facing a hostile Senate, will take on board significant parts of the Sanders programme and mission.

At that point the left, justifiably relieved at Trump's departure, will be back facing the conundrum that has, through the decades of neoliberalism, bedevilled social democrats everywhere, including those with a much stronger base than Biden: beyond a certain range of reforms, left governments face the polarized choice between lowering expectations and accepting their social democratization, and pursuing a riskier, more radical strategy for advance.

V

For American socialists, the indispensable project at this moment is not electoral, but to contribute to the formation, at long last, of a working class with a growing capacity to challenge the status-quo and lead a struggle for social transformation. Essential to the making of such a class is an organization of committed and developed activist-leaders. Absent a coherent working class with an independent vision, coalitions or common fronts will leave workers as subordinate participants, and electoral victories will be little more than brief interludes in capitalism's overriding neoliberal trajectory of social polarization and gross inequalities.

The special place of workers as potential agents of social transformation doesn't lie in their being inherently revolutionary, but in the organizational and strategic place they occupy in capitalism. Forming unions based on shared daily experience in workplaces brings structured access to resources to support struggles, institutional continuity and capacities, and the potential to disrupt the workings of the economic system in ways that organizations that rely on symbolic protest actions or periodic mass mobilizations cannot match or sustain. And critically, in the context of any future socialist government confronting a hostile capitalist class (or just in working-class struggles to win structural reforms), workers have the potentially decisive role of intervening to keep production and services flowing.

Yet, despite the pivotal place that workers occupy in the relations of production, the complex realities of working-class life in capitalism militate against their spontaneous development into the required militant social force. People may hate their boss, but their everyday experience is a constant reminder of their dependence on their employer. They may daydream about a different world, but immediate survival pushes them to focus on the short term and the pragmatic, limiting an active contemplation of alternatives. They share the oppressive experience of work with workers in other regions, sectors and occupations, yet are divided from them not only by race, gender, and age, but also, as Howard Botwinick has emphasized, by 'persistent inequalities' across workplaces in wages, working conditions, degree of control over work, status as full-time or part-time workers, and so on.[9] The point is that the formation of a class *for* itself doesn't just 'happen', and never has, at least not to the extent necessary: it must be consciously and laboriously *made and remade*.

Unions overcome some of the isolation and alienation of individual workers in capitalism, but they do not resolve this dilemma. Unions tend to be particularistic, not class organizations: that is, they represent specific groups of workers in certain workplaces or sectors. The weakness of unions across the period of neoliberalism is often blamed on antagonistic external factors – bad corporations, hostile governments, globalization, free trade. True enough. But it also bears noting that a major reason that such 'external' factors have become so damaging is because unions, even in their most powerful periods, did not develop the capacity to effectively respond to such attacks.

The 'internal' factors explaining the weakness of labour unions are typically summed up as the conservatism of labour bureaucrats and/or a lack of internal union democracy. This explanation is partially correct. Bureaucratization is indeed a problem; there are no doubt many leaders and staff who are comfortable with blaming inaction on external constraints. But this critique passes too quickly over the limits of the rank-and-file, and their deference to union leadership. If workers have become reluctant to challenge their own elected leaders, it's hard to imagine them spontaneously taking on the far greater challenge of seizing control of their workplaces and offering alternate workplans, let alone building an entirely new society. And while union democracy is essential to developing a true working-class opposition, it alone will not necessarily overcome the particularism that capitalism embeds in unions. Only a far broader working-class organization, one committed to explicitly focus on class formation, could break this impasse.

Throughout the decades of neoliberalism, many new social movements sprang up to fill the vacuum left by the political dormancy of the union movement in the US as elsewhere. Some showed flashes of vibrancy and added to critiques of capitalism. But they have nevertheless fallen short of their goals, and while the left is often eager to discuss the failures of unions, it has been much less ready to raise the weaknesses of recent activist mobilizations outside the labour movement. Occupy Wall Street is a clear example of the political and strategic challenges raised by new left social movements. Occupy garnered strong public sympathy, and its highlighting of the '1%' placed class (if somewhat crudely) on the public agenda. But its demise left behind progressive sensibilities around inequality, rather than organizational structures that could be used to build a working-class opposition. It also exposed the limits of symbolic takeovers, as opposed to the involvement of workers and working-class communities seizing factories, schools, or government offices.

The Black Lives Matter protests have raised similar issues. Since the murder of Trayvon Martin nearly a decade ago, the dramatic series of mass protests that erupted brought new people into politics and catalyzed a sympathetic shift in popular narratives against racism and oppressive policing. Yet Black Lives Matter has only made limited strides in reforming the carceral state or in addressing the poverty and inequality suffered disproportionately by Black Americans. The durability and strategic direction of Black Lives Matter is also unclear. Its orienting vision is quite distinct from, say, the ambitions of the 1963 March on Washington. In that moment, civil rights leaders grasped that in fighting for the rights of black workers, they could lead the labour movement in a fight for decent jobs, expansive universal social programmes, and security for *all* workers.[10] The current struggle to unionize workers in the logistics and caring sectors, both of which disproportionately involve black workers (and workers of colour more generally), and which hold out the promise of reviving the labour movement with young militant workers, new leadership, and new confidence, seems an opportune and long overdue opportunity to revive the promising connection made in the 1963 March on Washington between race and class.

All of this is to say that the progressive social movements that have emerged over the past decade, while clearly significant, are not likely to fill the void left by the diminishment of organized labour – they remain unlikely to be the vehicle for a reconfiguration of class forces. But as vital as it is to expand unionization, reviving unions in their current form is clearly not enough. Nothing demonstrates this more forcefully than the failure of the labour movement to come out of the Covid-19 pandemic stronger. The pandemic has exposed capitalism's gross inequalities and lack of preparation for catastrophic events (further highlighting capitalism's still-cavalier response to climate change) and has generated widespread sympathy for front-line workers in all kinds of neglected and often poorly paid occupations. Yet unions are failing to use the crisis to both expose the iniquities of neoliberal capitalism – and indeed capitalism itself – and to develop a strong oppositional movement. As in the 1930s, the transformations required to amplify the power of the working class today will only happen in conjunction with, and the general intervention and concrete support of, organized socialists with one foot inside the unions and one outside.

VI

The Sanders' presidential campaigns created precious political space for the US left and radical policies to get a mass public hearing. The 'working class' and 'socialism' re-entered the political lexicon in the US as it seldom has; a new generation shifted from protest to politics, evidenced in the explosion of the Democratic Socialists of America's membership base (from 8,000 circa 2016 to over 90,000 in 2021); and some high-profile candidates, standing as socialists, subsequently won local election battles. India Walton, for example, won the Democratic mayoral primary in Buffalo, New York, in June 2021. A Walton victory in November 2021 would be the first time a socialist has sat in the mayor's office of a major US city since 1961.

Walton's campaign demonstrates a heartening tenaciousness among young socialists to keep building after Sanders's loss. But the electoral victories of the past few years also raise questions about how to build the political infrastructure necessary for a lasting movement for radical change. Elections, while sometimes electrifying and even life-changing for participants, can facilitate an over-dependence on candidates, leaving socialists uncertain about how to move beyond the electoral terrain.

A few clear directions seem pertinent. Developing socialist leadership and doing popular education must be the priority, and the enthusiasm Sanders generated in every major city suggests that it isn't too ambitious to imagine the creation of a series of socialist leadership schools spread across the country. It also seems worthwhile to experiment with new kinds of working-class organizations – what Bill Fletcher and Fernando Gapasin term regional 'worker assemblies' – that extend beyond labour councils by including the unemployed, workers in workplaces without unions, and movement activists of all kinds.[11]

Especially important, at its current size and level of organizational development, the movement needs to identify a small number of focused national campaigns which could give the socialist schools, popular education, and new institutions a foundation in struggle. As well, without campaigns to bring the infrastructure that emerged with Sanders back to life, the communication networks, publications, up-to-date contact lists, regular forums and so forth will atrophy. With socialists scattered across Congress in Washington, and concentrated in a few cities like Seattle and New York, and many activists across the country returning to local campaigning, it is even more important to have national campaigns that situate individual socialists and local activity within a larger frame, averting the fragmentation that has plagued socialist politics in the US.

National campaigns could also alleviate the potentially divisive split between those 'going into' the Democratic Party and those 'staying outside'. Many socialists will, given existing options, set their reservations aside and participate in the Democratic Party. Though this tactic should be part of an ongoing debate about building a socialist movement, and a constant discussion of how to build working-class capacities and develop a programme independent of the limits of existing electoral politics, those going in must not be written off as 'sell-outs'. It is important instead to engage them in working together on common campaigns independent of the Democratic Party.[12] As working within the Democratic Party poses the constant hazard of a political drift toward centrism, and the 'social democratization' of even committed socialists, common national campaigns could serve as a constant challenge to Democratic Party policies and orientations, and provide the 'protection' of constant reminders of the limits of the Democrats.

If the well-founded expectation on the part of socialists working within the Democratic Party is that they will either be thrown out at some point or leave (the former being more likely, and probably coming sooner rather than later), then joint campaigns are especially vital. It not only keeps the door open to unity among socialists in or out of the Democratic Party once the expected occurs, but also moves from the very start to developing an independent working-class base. So that if a 'dirty break' with the Democrats does occur, it doesn't end in isolation and demoralization (a problem common to entryism in all its variations).[13]

VII

The choice of which national campaigns socialists should pursue necessitates the widest discussion on the left, and will differ across countries and time. The point here is not to lay out policies for a newly elected government of the left, but to identify issues that, in the context of the US, might be taken on *now*. The criterion is that these struggles be strategic in the sense of directly engaging workers and their communities around immediate needs in a way that builds capacities, poses larger questions, and raises larger possibilities. Their full implementation would of course depend on eventually taking state power, but the current key task is to start building the kind of base that might later make the carrying out of radical policies an actual possibility.

An issue the left gives far too little attention to is the disciplining power of 'competitiveness'. The importance of class power is generally raised, but far less attention is given to the *context* of that power. As a result, discussions around democratizing the economy tend to settle on solutions such as putting workers on boards of directors, forming worker co-ops, or pursuing anti-trust legislation. But if the political context retains the market authoritarianism of competition (or, as with anti-trust policy, *increased* competition), the pressure on workers as board or co-op members to behave like capitalists tends to undermine the point of worker participation. Is it possible to carve out spaces within capitalism that are liberated from the pressures of profits and competitiveness – spaces that can conform to different social relations and values?

Three such possibilities, each potentially involving major sections of the economy and key sectors of the working class, are the environment, public services, and finance. These spheres are, to varying degrees, currently the subject of progressive reform campaigns, but they have the potential to be much more ambitious.

Environment: moving beyond techno-fixes

Some progress can be made on the environment through market mechanisms, opportunistic capitalists, and states concerned with the security risks associated with climate change. But if 'fixing' the environment means overturning rapacious systems of production, distribution, and disposal – that is, transforming how we work, consume, travel, and live – then something far more fundamental is necessary.

The scale of such transformations will, as struggles over industrial conversion and factory takeovers have always shown, demand productive and administrative capacities.[14] Since plant shutdowns and public sector sell-offs are a daily occurrence in communities across the country, robbing us of the needed capacities, this makes them potential sites for organizing workers and their communities around jobs, restructuring, and the environment. In this framing, the otherwise abstract slogan of a 'just transition' emerges as a concrete series of local working-class struggles linking jobs, conversion, and the environment. This demands not only planning capacities, but control over what is to be planned, organically leading to pressure to expand public ownership and challenge corporate property rights.[15]

To support local struggles for conversion, a national campaign could mobilize around the establishment of a National Conversion Agency to supply expertise, funds, and planned government procurement. The campaign could include supplementing this with, for example, demands for regional environmental-technological research hubs, each populated by hundreds of young, enthusiastic engineers, skilled trades, researchers, and community activists studying social needs and applying and developing the kinds of skills needed to make conversion projects feasible.

Decommodifying public services

Public services are supposed to be *for* the public, yet ensconced as they are in the hegemony of the private sector, elected officials and public servants face constant pressure to commodify them – to run them as businesses, or prepare them to be outsourced, and to make sure that public sector workers don't have the kind of benefits that push private sector workers to demand more. Historically, moves to challenge this market logic have been immediately attacked, with public sector workers isolated from the public by framing their compensation demands as taxes on the rest of the working class.

Transforming public services could run the gamut from blocking their further commodification to expanding the services provided (e.g., universal health care and pharma care, the production of vaccines and medical equipment), extending public ownership into new spheres, and improving the quality of public services.[16] Another goal should be to democratize public services, making them exemplary in their responsiveness to those receiving the service, which could legitimate and protect the services. State workers collaborating with the people they are hired to serve, for example, could dramatically influence and improve the direction and administration of public services, as was done with notable success in London in the 1970s before the Thatcher government stopped it, and more recently in the demands raised by the radical cities movement in Spain.[17]

As with policies on the environment, insulating the public sector from the pressures coming from the private sector would place a very significant part of the economy on a different plane, engendering values and considerations other than competition and profitmaking. It would also place public sector workers in a position to set higher standards and demands for all workers, thus contributing to broader social goals and overcoming costly divisions between public and private sector workers.

Public banks

Any move to introduce a democratic element into a capitalist economy requires control of the social surplus and how it is allocated. Since we already treat financial institutions as 'public utilities' that must be preserved at all costs, we should make them into publicly-owned institutions. The left is, however, in no position yet – either politically or in having the requisite technical skills – to take on and radically transform finance.

The interim solution often voiced by progressives, of breaking up finance through anti-trust policies in the name of stimulating competition, is, however, no solution at all: the consequent restructuring and intensified competition would do nothing for workers. It wouldn't block capital from developing new financial instruments to serve business purposes rather than consumer needs. Nor would it prevent the eventual restoration of financial concentration.

An alternative is to campaign for publicly owned green or infrastructure banks that aren't forced to compete for funds with private banks, and thereby end up differing little from current ones. The capitalization of such banks could emerge from community trusts, crowd-funding, issuing bonds tied to green objectives, and more, but it would also need, and organically pose, to go further and push for capturing a share of the sums held by big finance.[18] A levy on all private financial institutions and perhaps on financial transactions could, for example, be fought for, with the funds generated then passed on to the public banks to allocate according to democratically determined priorities.[19] Campaigning for the democratic mechanisms to carry out those priorities would be a step towards winning public recognition of the need to eventually place all finance in the public domain.

VIII

The question for socialists, as André Gorz and the New Left argued in the late 1960s, is not reform or revolution, nor whether to make compromises; partial steps are the messy but concrete stuff of any grounded politics. The challenge rather is to conceive of reforms that change the terrain of the struggle, contribute to working-class formation, educate and – through their own contradictions – raise larger questions and possibilities.[20] Gorz also warned that there is no silver bullet, no abstract set of 'non-reformist reforms' that exist outside a particular political or economic context. Moreover, it is not just the demand that matters, but how it is framed and fought for. Specific reforms and how they are addressed may be radical in one setting and moment, but vulnerable to cooptation in another.

The American left often considers universal health care, and a doubling or tripling of union density, as structural reforms. That is, they rupture the logic of commodification, challenge bureaucratic controls over social provisions, and shift the balance of class power towards workers. Yet the Canadian working class already has these advances (not only universal health care but a unionization rate near 30 per cent against the US rate of a little over 10 per cent), but as much as they have contributed to Canada being a better place, they do not necessarily signal a definitive breakthrough. The Canadian labour movement remains mired in its own stagnation, and many of the more creative and militant struggles in North America are occurring on the US side of the border.

But the process of getting there matters a great deal. Might the struggle for winning a health care system in the US, fought on the principle of 'to each according to their needs, from each according to their ability to pay', encourage a cultural change affecting other social needs? And might the project of unionizing Amazon, if approached through the systematic cooperation of unions, as opposed to competition for dues or ad-hoc casual support, facilitate new class solidarities, a new confidence within the labour movement, and the emergence of new, more ambitious leaders?

Underlying the emphasis on structural reforms lies a more basic question: how and by whom is such an orientation to 'non-reformist reforms' decided and carried out? Raising this question shifts us to the terrain of socialist parties – that is, the creation of institutions whose prime focus would be on constructing spaces for posing and debating strategic interventions, and doing so not in the abstract, but in struggles that are rooted in the working class. The New Left was disillusioned with existing social democratic and communist parties, and with unions that, even when militant – which they often were – nevertheless had limited objectives. But that generation of socialists failed, not always for want of trying, to remake existing socialist organizations, foster new kinds of socialist parties, contribute to a more creative trade union movement, and block the aggressive advance of neoliberalism.

The current left is saddled with the costs of that failure. It is no exaggeration to say that, despite real progress in tackling issues of race, ethnicity, and gender, in terms of ending capitalism we are more or less 'starting over'. Yet we should not romanticize earlier eras; the socialist left was never close to winning. As intimidating and overwhelming as this may be, we cannot accept that the cold immorality of capitalism, its stubborn drift toward environmental catastrophe, its anti-social rhythms and outcomes, and its thin veneer of democracy vulnerable to dangerous authoritarian impulses, is all that humanity can strive for. 'There is,' to rework Thatcher's contribution to capitalism everywhere, *'no alternative but to resist'*, and to do so on a scale that matches what we are up against. The times cry out for a new kind of labour movement. The openings are there. Is the nascent American socialist movement up to the challenge of building it?

NOTES

1   Adolph Reed, Jr., 'Marx, Race, and Neoliberalism', *New Labour Forum,* (20:1), 2013, p. 65.
2   Leo Panitch and Sam Gindin, *The Making of Global Capitalism: The Political Economy of American Empire,* London, New York: Verso, 2012.
3   Dani Rodrik, 'Populism and the Economics of Globalization', *Journal of International Business Policy*, (1:1), 2018.
4   Thomas Meaney, 'Trumpism After Trump', *Harpers*, February 2020.
5   See transcript of Sandra Polaski and David Dollar, 'How have Trump's trade wars affected rust belt jobs?', Brookings Institute, 19 October 2020, available at: www.brookings.edu.
6   As Samir Sonti notes in this volume in 'The Crisis of US Labour, Past and Present'.
7   Eric Morath, 'Lower-Wage Workers See Biggest Gains from Easing of Covid-19 Pandemic', *Wall Street Journal,* 4 July 2021.
8   Brian Deese, National Economic Council Director, 'The Biden White House Plan for a new US Industrial Policy', *Atlantic Council*, 23 June 2021, available at: www.atlanticcouncil.org.
9   Howard Botwinick, *Persistent Inequalities,* Chicago: Haymarket, 2017.
10 See Adolph Reed, Jr. and Touré Reed in this volume; and Tim Schermerhorn, 'The 1963 March on Washington: Reclaiming Labor History', *Labor Notes*, 29 October 2013.

11   Bill Fletcher, Jr and Fernando Gapasin, *Solidarity Divided,* Berkeley: California University Press, 2014.

12   A similar case is being made for Britain in the interview with James Schneider published in this volume.

13   The 'dirty break' is a strategy of running socialists on the Democratic Party ballot line with the aim of consolidating sufficient forces to break off and eventually form a democratic socialist party. See Eric Blanc, 'The Ballot and the Break', *Jacobin,* December 2017.

14   For such conversion struggles, see the case of Green Jobs Oshawa: *Take the Plant, Save the Planet: The Struggle for Community Control and Plant Conversion at GM Oshawa,* Socialist Interventions Pamphlets, Toronto: Socialist Project, 2020, available at: www.socialistproject.ca/pamphlets.

15   Sean Sweeney and John Treat, 'Shifting gears: Labour Strategies for Low-Carbon Public Transit Mobility', in Leo Panitch and Greg Albo, eds, *Socialist Register 2021: Beyond Digital Capitalism: New Ways of Living,* London: Merlin Press, 2020.

16   Christoph Hermann, *The Critique of Commodification: Contours of a Post-Capitalist Society,* New York: Oxford University Press, 2021.

17   Maureen Mackintosh and Hilary Wainwright, *A Taste of Power,* London: Verso, 1987; and Ramon Fumaz and Greig Charnock, 'Barcelona en comu: Urban Democracy and the Common Good', in Leo Panitch and Greg Albo, eds, *Socialist Register 2018: Rethinking Democracy*, London: Merlin Press, 2017.

18   Tom Marois, *Public Banks*, Cambridge: Cambridge University Press, 2021.

19   Scott Aquanno, 'The Bank of Canada: In Crisis and Beyond', *The Bullet,* 2 June 2020, available at: www.socialistproject.ca.

20   Andre Gorz, *Strategy for Labour,* Boston: Beacon Press, 1968. Also see: Mark Engler and Paul Englert, 'André Gorz's Non-Reformist Reforms Show How We Can Transform the World Today', *Jacobin,* 22 July 2021.

PANDEMIC POLARIZATIONS AND THE CONTRADICTIONS OF INDIAN CAPITALISM

JAYATI GHOSH

For some time now India has been viewed by the western powers as an important ally in the fight against 'the other' – now perceived to be an authoritarian China.[1] The growing neoliberal bent of successive governments in power in India has generated further enthusiasm in western capitals, especially in global financial markets. India is important both economically as a potential 'rising power', with its vast and predominantly young population, and in geostrategic terms as a bulwark against China. To that end, especially over the past decade, mainstream western observers ignored various flaws and inadequacies in the pattern of capitalist development in India, such as sharply increasing inequalities, the continuing poverty and insecurity of the vast majority of Indians, and poor improvement and even slippage in basic human development indicators;[2] relatively high GDP rates were celebrated, irrespective of their lack of plausibility. The fascist tendencies of the ruling party and growing signs of intolerance and authoritarianism on the part of the central government were met with only mild admonishments by the self-appointed rulers of the world, such as the G7.[3] This inconsistent stance would in any case have been hard to sustain over time. But the Covid-19 pandemic may turn out to be a watershed in revealing the extent to which the vision of India competing with China on even somewhat equal terms – a vision which academics have long shown to be a fantasy – will finally have to be abandoned.

The Covid-19 pandemic has revealed much about the nature and contradictions of Indian capitalism and its social context. The still ongoing pandemic is clearly the worst health calamity in India for at least a century. But the economic and social devastation experienced by the country during the pandemic may prove so severe as to merit the description 'catastrophe'. This is not due only to the disease. Rather, much of the damage has resulted from government action and inaction, in a context of an extremely frail and inadequate public health infrastructure created by decades of underspending.[4] Very significant policy failures – acts of both commission and omission – have been responsible for the widespread and pronounced decline in people's livelihoods and in many of the basic indicators of well-being among the population. The almost violent increases in inequality and extreme destitution are not just terrible in themselves: they also point to major setbacks to the trajectory of capitalist accumulation and the broader development project in India.

At the same time, the pandemic has accentuated some key polarizations that were already evident but have become much sharper and more intense. Thus, there is the economic polarization reflected in growing asset and income inequality, increased power imbalance between capital and labour, and between 'modern' industry and services and agriculture and low-value services that account for the bulk of the Indian labour force. Within that, there is even an economic polarization within private capital, with a few crony capitalists benefiting even in a period of economic crisis, while other businesses stagnate or decline, and the majority of medium and small enterprises struggle and fail. There is the polarization reflected in access to health infrastructure, health services, and amenities like housing conditions and water. There is the social polarization that has led to already marginalized groups like Dalits, tribals, and Muslims – and women across all social groups – being disproportionately affected by both the pandemic and the inadequate policy responses. There is the polarization between central and state governments, putting significant strains on India's federal polity. There is the political polarization between supporters of the ruling BJP and those who explicitly oppose it politically as well as other dissenters, made worse by the regime's blatant focus on pushing a Hindu nationalist agenda rather than on what are usually seen as essential tasks of governance. Finally, all of these have also brought to the fore an inherent tension: the contradiction between neoliberalism and democracy.

The damage to living and working conditions in India resulted principally from the way the central government first attempted to control the disease through a brutal national lockdown, which also impacted other essential public services, and then did next to nothing to ensure basic protection for the hundreds of millions of people who were denied any income for several months. Since more than 90 per cent of all workers in India are informal,[5] with no legal or social protection, and many already functioned at the margin of subsistence,[6] this had devastating consequences.

These consequences were so severe that they could not simply be forgotten with the receding of the successive waves of the pandemic.

Similarly, the pandemic and the policy response to it did not create the many fissures, vulnerabilities, and fault lines in Indian society and economy; but they exposed them, brought them to the surface, and made them even more significant. Inequalities of incomes, assets, and opportunities, which were already very severe in India before the pandemic, reached previously unimaginable extremes. In this period of crisis, as elaborated in what follows, money and resources defied gravity to flow from the poor and middle classes to the richest corporations and high net-worth individuals, who became richer than ever even as working people faced hunger, destitution, and ever-greater material insecurity. And the intersecting inequalities – India's chronic polarizations – of caste, gender, religion, and migration status became even more marked and oppressive.

While the rise in inequalities has been a global phenomenon, expressed most sharply in vaccine distribution and differential fiscal responses, the Indian experience still stands out because of the extent of the economic collapse and the massive impact it has had on the lives of people, bringing possibly hundreds of millions of people to the point of absolute destitution and creating much greater economic insecurity for the majority of workers,[7] which is likely to persist for several years. This in turn has serious implications for the proposed path of capitalist accumulation in the medium term, such that the pandemic could become a watershed of directional change for the Indian economy: no longer necessarily one of the 'emerging markets' so attractive to global investors, but a potential drag, even within the Asian region.

THE VULNERABILITIES OF THE PANDEMIC

India was poorly placed to deal with a health calamity on the scale of the Covid-19 pandemic, because of the vulnerabilities of the economy and the health system. Even before 2020, the economy was already fragile and on the verge of crisis, with decelerating output, falling employment, consumption, and investment. As well, there was mounting evidence of increased material distress among the poorest groups, alongside indications of significantly increasing wealth among the tiny handful of extremely wealthy individuals.[8] Health conditions were also dire on the whole: successive Indian governments have ignored public health concerns and provided very little money for it, such that government health spending per capita and as a share of national income have been among the lowest in the world, and people have been forced to engage in what are among the highest proportions of out-of-pocket healthcare spending in the world (of around 65 per cent),[9] making access to decent health services unaffordable for most. Household spending for health emergencies has been one of the most significant causes for descent into extreme poverty.[10] Nutrition indicators have remained poor, especially for women and children, adding to health vulnerabilities. There were substantial differences across states. While some states like Kerala had much better health indicators, and others like Tamil Nadu showed improvement, in most of the country health indicators showed the effect of continuous official neglect and inadequate public funding. The Narendra Modi government, led by the right-wing Hindu nationalist BJP (Bharatiya Janata Party), effectively aggravated the commercialization of healthcare by introducing a publicly-funded healthcare insurance scheme, the 'Ayushman Bharat' programme, for poor households, adding another layer of profit-oriented intermediaries, insurance companies, into a broken and unequal system.[11] The underfunded and fragile public health system and its consequences in turn meant that the disruptions brought about by the disease and the lockdowns had even worse impacts than they would have had on a more buoyant economy and a population in better health overall.

In the first wave of the pandemic from March 2020, India was possibly the only country where the virus was given religious overtones, with government officials, ruling party members, and pliant media attempting to link the initial spread of the infection to a particular religious gathering organized by Muslims. Thereafter, the lockdown and subsequent policies perversely operated to spread the infection across the country as migrant workers deprived of incomes were forced to go back to their homes in whatever way they could. However, the incidence of infection and fatality from Covid-19 was relatively low by international standards (though not in comparison to other Asian countries), and appeared to have peaked in September 2020, creating a sense of complacency in the central government that inevitably had an impact on people's behaviour. The second wave was both more infectious and more lethal, associated with the emergence of mutant variants, such as Delta and Delta Plus, that then spread to other countries. Health systems throughout India completely collapsed in this onslaught, with major shortages of hospital beds, emergency facilities, oxygen, and therapeutic drugs – all of which added to the severity and fatality of the disease, and created much greater and more widespread social and economic devastation.

At the peak of the second wave, in early May 2021, the average seven-day rate of new infections, at 283 per million per day, was nearly three times the global and Asian averages.[12] Even this was clearly an underestimate, as was the estimate of deaths, because of insufficient testing, tracking, and reporting of both cases and deaths. In rural areas, it is likely that many if not most cases have simply gone unrecognized and unreported. Serosurveys suggest that more than one-third of Indians had been infected with Covid-19 even before the peak of the second wave,[13] which still points to a lower case-fatality rate than in western countries, but the possibly massive under-reporting of death remains a very significant concern. New estimates based on excess deaths using the data from Sample Registration Surveys suggest that total Covid-19 deaths in the country in the year from the start of the pandemic in March 2020 have been as many as 2.5 million (rather than the officially reported 407,000), with 1.5 million due to the second wave.[14]

At the time of writing, in July 2021, the second wave also appeared to have receded, but with fears of a third wave emerging. Such a fatalistic expectation that presumed little agency on the part of government or society was all the more remarkable because vaccines that can be used to prevent infection exist, and two such vaccines are even produced in India. The terrible mistakes made by the Modi government's vaccine policy, undoing decades of a successful universal immunization programme, are outlined in the next section, but they have meant that India is now globally a laggard in terms of Covid-19 vaccination, with less than 20 per cent of the population receiving even one dose[15] and fewer than 7 per cent fully vaccinated (as of 23 July 2021), thereby leaving most of the country still vulnerable.

THE POLICY RESPONSE AND THE ECONOMIC IMPACT

Several aspects of the Indian government's policy have been responsible for this combination of adverse outcomes. To begin with, the unplanned and brutal lockdown and the unthinking adoption of containment strategies not suited to the Indian context, had immediate and direct effects on employment and livelihoods. The most stringent lockdown in the world was imposed across the nation, without notice or consultation even with state governments, at a time when it was not needed because there were very few cases, and those limited to some pockets. The more expensive (but more effective) strategy of testing, tracing, isolating, and treating those infected was not implemented as a national strategy, although some states such as Kerala did do so in the initial phases. Instead, the onus was put on the population to restrict their own activity, even at the cost of losing whatever little income they had, and with no compensation. The restrictions also assumed that people could obey instructions for 'social distancing' (more accurately physical distancing) and hygiene, when this was not really possible for around half of the population who live in crowded and congested conditions and do not have access to piped running water. The government did not use the breathing space provided by the lockdown to prepare health systems, leaving state governments to manage as best they could with very limited and inadequate resources, as described below.

When the economic disaster became too extreme in terms of collapsing economic activity (which declined by nearly a quarter in the period April–June 2021 compared to the previous year) and employment (with more than 100 million workers losing their jobs and others facing drastic income falls),[16] the central government proceeded to 'unlock' the economy, even as cases mounted and infections spread more rapidly, thereby putting more people at risk. The most irresponsible moment came in late January 2021, when Prime Minister Modi proudly declared to a meeting of the World Economic Forum that India had succeeded in defeating the coronavirus, and that its success would now help the entire world, not only by providing an example and unleashing 'the largest vaccination programme in the entire world', but also by fulfilling the country's 'responsibility towards the global community by sending vaccines and training people'.[17] The hubris proved to be short-lived; the second wave was already under way at that time in Mumbai and other cities, and the government's Covid-19 task force had already warned about the dangers inherent in a second wave. They were ignored; the central government was apparently so self-confident in its own rhetoric that it had not even ordered more than 30 million doses of vaccines from the two companies before March 2021. Not only were most lockdown restrictions eased or removed (other than in some states which had rising case numbers), but in early 2021 the prime minister and other central government ministers actively encouraged massive public gatherings in the run-up to state assembly elections in West Bengal and some other states. In a remarkably obtuse move, the huge religious festival, the Mahakumbh Mela, held every twelve years on the banks of the Ganga River, was actually brought forward by a full year, apparently on astrological advice.[18] This had more than nine million attendees over the month of April 2021 concentrated in the relatively small town of Haridwar, despite the ongoing Covid-19 surge, thereby creating a potent super-spreader event that allowed the disease to proliferate across rural and urban areas of large parts of north and central India.

The centralization of power by the Modi government during the pandemic was rapid. The lockdown was imposed by invoking the Disaster Management Act 2005, which allows the central government and the National Disaster Management Authority to override any other law in force and issue directions to any authority in India, and requires all such directions to be followed. However, the Centre did not use these additional powers to increase coordination; rather, it imposed often changing and sometimes contradictory decisions upon state governments – including the national lockdown, which they got no time to prepare for. Subsequently, specific requests and concerns were ignored or brushed aside, leading to avoidable delays and shortages.[19] Centralization, followed by the central government reneging on its basic responsibility, was even more evident in the matter of vaccine production and distribution (discussed below).

Fiscal centralization had even worse consequences. While the initial lockdown was imposed without any consultation, state governments were made responsible for implementing it, as well as for essential public health measures and all the measures required to deal with the economic effects of the lockdown – but they were completely strapped for cash. The central government provided almost nothing by way of additional resources, and avoided its constitutionally mandated requirement to share tax revenues with state governments by classifying new taxes as cesses and surcharges on existing tax rates and central fuel taxes, none of which needed to be shared with the states. After invoking the centralizing National Disaster Management Act to declare a national lockdown, the Centre then proceeded to avoid any fiscal or other obligation to deal with the pandemic or with the consequences of its own actions. Instead, it left the state governments to deal with the additional health spending and the measures required to deal with the increased economic distress as best they could. Not only did the central government refuse to spend more itself; it also forced the state governments to base their additional required spending on borrowing that will be difficult to repay. The Centre even refused to pay dues that it owed to the states resulting from a prior agreement negotiated in 2017 when the introduction of a national Goods and Services Tax deprived state governments of their own revenue-raising powers. When it became evident in late July 2020 that all this was completely unfeasible and would lead to major humanitarian crises, state governments were allowed to borrow more – but knowing that they would have to repay later with little or no help from the Centre. This created a peculiar combination, whereby state governments had to adjust to often arbitrary decisions by the Modi government (including with regard to the purchase of testing kits and, later, vaccine distribution) on which they were not consulted, while receiving only the most minimal financial assistance.

At a time when governments across the world were significantly increasing public spending to respond to the twin crises of pandemic and the collapse of livelihoods, the Indian government barely increased its own spending, with additional spending coming to only 1.8 per cent more than it had budgeted for, while revenues declined due to the lockdown and the subsequent decline in economic activity. This compared poorly with other governments across the world: not only compared with advanced country governments which provided additional government spending of as much as 5 to 25 per cent of GDP,[20] but even when compared with other emerging market economies. This extremely conservative fiscal stance added to the shock of the lockdown, which had already affected economic activity, prevented wage incomes from increasing, and set in motion additional contractionary tendencies that would inevitably damage economic prospects in the medium term. In macroeconomic terms, this meant that the collapse in demand, from both consumption and private investment, due to the lockdowns and the spread of the disease was not countered significantly by increased public spending, and so the initial contraction led to negative multiplier effects over time.

This curtailment of public spending, at a time when it should have been massively increased, had disastrous effects. Of course, it affected public services, including health services that were already overstretched due to the pandemic. But it also meant that several hundred million people were not afforded any compensation for the loss of incomes during the lockdown, or any significant social protection, and did not recover their incomes even when the economy was allowed to reopen. It generated a shocking humanitarian crisis that was most starkly evident in the desperate conditions faced by migrant workers but extended to the majority of the population to varying degrees. This was astounding in a country where around 95 per cent of all workers are in the informal sector, and around half of those are self-employed; where median wages provide only the most basic subsistence; and where loss of income beyond even a week can lead to absolute starvation for millions who are already at the margin of survival. Even before the pandemic hit, average calorie consumption in India was significantly lower than the EAT-Lancet norms, with only the richest 5 per cent of the population achieving at least that norm;[21] for the majority of the population nutritious diets were unaffordable.[22] There was some distribution of free food grain for some months to those holding ration cards, but this excluded at least 100 million of the needy, and the amounts distributed were inadequate for the need. Astonishingly, the government continued to hold excess food stocks, adding to stock levels through more procurement but releasing only small amounts, even as absolute hunger among the people increased massively, and stopping the distribution of some free food grain even as employment continued to slump and millions faced much worsening nutrition and even starvation. Meanwhile, numerous surveys pointed to massive increases in hunger and destitution among people who had been deprived of livelihoods and exhausted their meagre savings after more than a year of lockdowns and pandemic-driven disruption.[23] The denial of basic food items to hundreds of millions of people is more than a human tragedy in the present: it will be reflected in maternal, infant, and child undernutrition with terrible consequences for the future.

A distinctive policy failure on the part of the central government concerns vaccination. India is one of the world's leading producers of vaccines (if seldom a developer of new vaccines) and had a long and relatively successful history of universal, free immunization. There was significant expectation that as vaccines were developed, tested, and got regulatory approval, vaccine production in India would be ramped up to enable rapid inoculation. Of course, there were several constraints on this, including the advanced countries' continued support of intellectual property rights of the multinational pharma companies that held the vaccine patents, and their attempts to grab the initial production of approved vaccines for their own populations. Nevertheless, since an Indian company (the Serum Institute of India) had the licence to produce the AstraZeneca vaccine (marketed in India as Covishield), and since an indigenously developed vaccine, Covaxin, was also being produced by the Indian company Bharat Biotech, it was presumed that at least these would be available to meet the needs of the Indian population.

However, the Modi government's extraordinary approach to vaccine production and distribution managed to make a mess of even this aspect of pandemic management. To begin with, even though the Covaxin vaccine had been produced under the aegis of a public institution, the Indian Council of Medical Research, the Covaxin company was allowed to hold the patent and have sole production rights. Licenses for its production were not issued compulsorily to other companies, not even to several public sector enterprises with acknowledged vaccine production capacity. The central government also initially promised to provide vaccines only for the initial rollout to health and frontline workers, covering 30 million people, and then for those aged over 55. It did not even order additional vaccines from the two Indian producers until March 2021. Despite formally allocating nearly Rs 3.5 trillion ($5 billion) for vaccination in the Union Budget of 2021-22, the central government then announced that state governments could purchase vaccines at their own cost, forcing them to compete in a hugely supply-constrained global market. Private healthcare providers were then allowed to procure and provide vaccine doses for people aged 18-45 years, to be paid for by the recipients! The vaccine producers started charging much higher rates to private agents and to state governments, coming to as much as $20 per dose for individuals, while global producers simply refused to supply the vaccines without a legal indemnity for the emergency use of their vaccines that other governments were providing. In India, only the central government could provide this, but it did not do so for the states. This was neoliberalism in the extreme, and it made no sense even in a supposedly free market world, which is why no other country adopted it. The absurdity – and fruitlessness – of differential markets and separate 'private' commercial sales for vaccines to deal with a public health crisis, in fact a pandemic, seemed to be lost on both the Indian government and the pharma companies. Such a contradictory policy had to be abandoned relatively quickly, but only after creating avoidable confusion and inexcusable delays in vaccine distribution. Moreover, the government's insistence on the use of an online CoWin platform for accessing vaccines, in a country with huge digital disparities and connectivity problems, further restricted access.

The economic strategies adopted to deal with the pandemic and their outcomes also pointed to the incompetent economic management of the Modi government, an outlier even among other neoliberal governments. In the first instance, the lockdown affected supply, and then, by impacting on employment and incomes, it affected demand, creating a wide range of anticipated and unanticipated effects that were aggravated by the nature of the government response. Immediately, the economy fell off a cliff, with a precipitous decline in GDP in the period April–June 2020 by at least one-fourth compared to the previous year according to official data, and possibly more in actuality. The 'recovery' thereafter was concentrated in some segments of the organized sector and in the stock market, which appeared to move in the opposite direction from indicators like consumption and employment, which continued to decline or stagnate. This was reflected in two striking outcomes: significant increases in economic inequality in an already very unequal society; and a generalized collapse in mass demand that was already depressed before the pandemic. Agriculture benefited from good weather conditions, but farmers were impacted by distribution and marketing problems, as well as other concerns, such as the enactment of controversial farm laws, whose implementation has been delayed by the ongoing farmers' protests.

The dramatic falls in aggregate employment were followed by only partial recovery, while wage incomes remained well below pre-pandemic levels (and in some cases even below the levels of several years earlier, before the 2016 de-monetization). The particularly extreme plight of migrant workers went beyond being a major failure of governance, especially at the central government level, to reveal a gross absence of social cohesion, a breakdown of the social contract, on a hitherto unimaginable scale. Food insecurity and absolute hunger increased sharply, with both immediate and possibly far-reaching adverse consequences. Certain categories of workers, like the self-employed, women, youth, and workers belonging to disadvantaged social groups (especially Dalits, tribals, and Muslims), were particularly badly affected. Women faced multiple disadvantages, as both paid and unpaid workers, and because of relational inequalities that spilled over into domestic violence; these issues were made worse by the gender-blindness of official policies. Education – so critical for India's future – was effectively subverted by the hasty and ill-planned attempt to shift entirely to online learning without reckoning on the country's immense digital divide, which not only excluded most students but did not really enable genuine instruction for those with internet access. In this generally dark scene, a crucial role was played by the rural employment guarantee programme as a cushion for household survival and as an automatic stabilizer for the economy, despite still-inadequate budgetary allocations.

By the time the more devastating second wave of the pandemic swept across the country from early March 2021, it hit a health system that was more strained than ever before, state governments that had exhausted their capacity for additional spending and a population already hugely debilitated by declining incomes and livelihood, eroded savings and increased household debt taken on for sheer survival, inability to access basic needs like food, and coping with other illness and health concerns (especially reproductive health) that had simply been ignored for a year. At the same time, the second wave saw even less in terms of relief measures than the first wave. Most of the so-called 'relief measures' were designed to enable the poor to take on more debt (by providing government support to banks for the issue of such loans), which they would clearly be unable to repay, while minimum compensation, such as enhanced free food rations, remained limited, and cash transfers were not even considered. So the immediate and even medium-term future remains bleak for the bulk of the Indian population.

INTENSIFICATION OF INEQUALITIES

A deep and pervasive inequality was embedded in both official and societal responses to the pandemic and the lockdown. These inequalities operated on many different levels. India was never known for valuing and respecting ordinary workers and the poor; nevertheless, the extent to which leaders and the elite and middle classes abandoned the poor and inflicted immense suffering upon them, while seeking to protect themselves, was startling. The disease was brought into the country by the relatively better off who could travel abroad. But to stop its proliferation, the most extreme containment policies were visited upon those less fortunate, with little thought for their well-being or even survival; and with an almost vicious implementation of rules that were eventually abandoned at a time when the spread of the pandemic, and the potential risks of infection, were actually much greater than before.

The class divide was most evident in the fiscal response: in the previous year, the central government had lost more than Rs 2 trillion ($28 billion) in revenue after bringing in corporate tax cuts that essentially benefited a few large companies and pushed up their retained profits. By contrast, during the pandemic, increased government spending on social services that would directly affect the poor came to less than half that amount. The disease prevention measures that were imposed on the population, like physical distancing and frequent handwashing, presumed living conditions that were available only to the middle classes and elites, and could not be implemented among the urban poor and many rural dwellers. The denial of livelihood to informal workers without providing compensatory social protection was another indication of the class orientation of policy. The refusal to release food grains for the hungry even as grains accumulated in public storage facilities was compounded by the travesty of allowing open market sales of some food stocks to convert into ethanol for making hand sanitizers.

Another stark example of unequal treatment came from controls on mobility and the subsequent provision of transport to migrants. Throughout the period of lockdown, special evacuation flights were arranged for Indian citizens stranded abroad, who are typically among the better off. However, stranded workers within India got little or no assistance. At first movement was completely prohibited, and those who desperately attempted to walk hundreds of kilometres to their homes were detained, attacked, and humiliated in various ways for 'breaking the curfew'. When some trains for internal migrants were finally arranged, impoverished workers were made to pay full fares, and conditions on these trains were often appalling, with prolonged and delayed journeys in intense heat during which food and water were not provided, adding to distress, ill health, and the spread of Covid-19 infections to far-flung and less developed parts of the country.

The still pervasive caste system in India justifies hierarchies and discrimination, and also relies on 'social distancing', which became a natural fit in the current pandemic for those at the top of the socio-economic hierarchy. This added further layers to the impact of pervasive patriarchy. Many of the frontline workers in the fight against Covid-19, especially basic health workers and sanitation workers, come from lower castes, and more of them tend to be women. They are poorly remunerated, most not even receiving minimum wages. During the pandemic, they typically had to work without adequate protection (with a disproportionate number getting infected),[24] faced social discrimination and physical threats, and in many cases did not receive their full pay. Meanwhile, among other workers, the impact of job losses and food insecurity was significantly higher for women, as well as for Muslims, Dalits, and tribal people. As in many other countries, the lockdown was also associated with significant increases in complaints of domestic violence against women, yet there was no administrative effort to ensure that affected women had access to support. Gender blindness was also evident in many official decisions during the pandemic, such as the initial exclusion of sanitary napkins from the original list of essential items whose production and distribution was permitted during the lockdown.

The health, nutrition, and economic consequences of this strategy have been devastating, and have very adverse implications for the future. Nutrition and hunger affect people's lives today, but they also impact on children particularly badly, creating conditions for inadequate development. The digital divide, more pronounced than ever, now extends into all aspects of life, including education and ability to participate as citizens. A particular betrayal has been that of the youth, whose dreams and aspirations to somehow achieve a middle-class existence were among the factors propelling Modi to his first national electoral victory. Their hopes had already been battered by the fall in total employment and worsening labour market conditions for educated youth over the previous six years, but the pandemic's impact was even more direct and brutal, decimating productive income opportunities.

HINDUTVA AUTHORITARIANISM

Instead of providing some support to the population during this terrible period, the central government used the pandemic to advance its agenda of centralizing power and suppressing dissent. Just before the lockdown, there were many peaceful protests across the country against the new citizenship law that effectively gave lower status to Muslims. Some of these peaceful gatherings had been met with violence on the part of police and armed supporters of the BJP. The central government used the opportunity presented by the lockdown not just to prohibit any kind of public protest but also to arrest several of those who had participated in the non-violent protests, while protecting supporters of the ruling party. The crackdown on dissent has affected students, lawyers, human rights activists, journalists, and academics, many of whom have been forced into prisons infected with Covid-19. For example, the noted human rights activist and Jesuit priest Father Stan Swamy, known for his selfless work for decades among impoverished tribal people in rural Jharkhand, was jailed on extreme and completely implausible charges, and denied bail despite being 82 years old and suffering from Parkinson's disease. He was even denied a straw and sipper in jail, contracted Covid-19 in prison, and ultimately died on 5 July 2021.[25] There are hundreds of other cases of innocent people being jailed without trial, sometimes even without charges being framed, and denied bail. The complicity of the judiciary (with a few brave exceptions) speaks to the ability of the ruling government to suborn and subjugate the various institutions necessary for democracy to survive. The purpose of such continued repression during a period of national calamity appears to be to teach a lesson to those who interrogate the government's intentions and actions, and to intimidate others. Unfortunately, this has also meant that the government's own ability to create a widespread social consensus and atmosphere of trust in which to combat the pandemic is correspondingly reduced.

Meanwhile, it became apparent that the government would use the lockdown not only to crack down on dissenters and increase its surveillance of all actual and potential dissenters, but also to suppress the existing institutional checks and balances on its own functioning. Covid-19 was used as the excuse to truncate both the Budget and Monsoon sessions of both houses of Parliament, which in 2020 had the fewest sittings in its history – only 33 days for the entire year. Demands by opposition parties to convene virtual sessions of Parliament, or at least allow online meetings of the various parliamentary panels that are supposed to monitor the executive and consider specific proposed legislation, were ignored or rejected. The refusal to convene Parliament was particularly egregious as the central government progressively eased lockdown restrictions through the course of the year, forcing people (especially the poor) to put themselves at risk at a time of high spread of the disease, because of the need to earn their livelihood; while elected representatives were not enabled or required to attend Parliament, even with appropriate restrictions and distancing norms put in place. And the truncated sessions were used to rush through controversial and strongly pro-private corporate legislation, like the farm bills[26] and labour codes,[27] without any consultation, discussion, or consideration by the appropriate parliamentary committees. Not surprisingly, these moves subsequently generated massive public protests, which the government has sought to suppress with a heavy hand.

What explains the ability of the Indian state to be so remarkably unconcerned about people's needs, when it is apparently operating within a broadly democratic and electoral context? At one level it appears inexplicable, especially given the history of Indian democracy, which has had central and state governments routinely dismissed by the electorate for various reasons, including lack of performance. In the current situation, however, the BJP and Prime Minister Modi have managed to sustain a fundamental popularity despite all the failures of governance. In particular, they have carefully presented Modi's public image, through extremely tight control of mainstream media and attempts to dominate social media, and by maintaining a single-minded focus on winning elections using all possible techniques such as utilizing caste equations, dividing the opposition parties, encouraging elected legislators to change parties, and terrorizing the opposition by using various organs of the state.

To this must be added the essential point that the ultimate aim of the central government is the promotion of 'Hindutva' and the realization of 'Hindu Rashtra', a state ruled by and for Hindus that would subsume all other socio-economic differentiation. In this, a significant role is played by grassroots organizations like the Rashtriya Swayamsevak Sangh (RSS), a 'voluntary' nationalistic group whose founder was a big fan of Hitler,[28] has deep roots in much of the country, and now effectively exercises political control at the national level through the ruling BJP, together with other mass organizations of the Sangh Parivar[29] which share this basic goal.

On the face of it, this project of the BJP may seem antithetical to the neoliberal globalization process that has been at work since the early 1990s, which places markets and the rule of capital above any social norms that divide people according to other criteria. But the Modi government is unabashedly neoliberal and pro-big capital, including global capital. There are some obvious contradictions in this. For example, *Gau Raksha* (or protecting the cow, since this animal is worshipped as being holy by some Hindus) as recently popularized, encouraged, and enabled by some leaders of the ruling party at the central and state government levels, has turned out to be an unmitigated economic disaster. It has attacked the livelihoods (and in some cases the lives) of livestock traders (who tend to be disproportionately Muslim or from lower castes) and destroyed India's once flourishing beef export industry, and the leather industry, which alone employed around 4.5 million people.[30] Meanwhile, it has made it uneconomic to hold cattle after they stop being useful for milking, which has led to farmers simply releasing cows to forage on their own. The abandoned cattle have thus become a threat to farming itself, as they seek to survive by foraging on cultivated fields. Similarly, the tendency of many proponents of Hindutva to glorify and exaggerate claims of scientific knowledge in ancient (supposedly

'Hindu') India may appear laughable, but it has serious consequences in terms of undermining both scientific training and the use of scientific knowledge in all aspects of life, from medicine and health to agricultural practices to industrial innovation. During the Covid-19 pandemic, for example, even official health ministries and institutions have issued problematic statements about the preventive or curative properties of particular diets, of imbibing cow urine, and other ideas that ought to be recognized as wacky rather than scientific. This represents not only an immediate cost: the associated lack of development of science and technology in the country could lead to a setback that would last for many years and have a generational impact.

There are many other ways in which Hindutva actively acts against economic activity, but some have more complex distributional effects. Communal riots are dreadful and ghastly events that bring out the worst in people and cause untold harm to lives, property, and daily life. They can lead to physical displacement as well as a climate of fear and suppression that can hardly be conducive to economic activity. Riots, often instigated cynically by proponents of Hindutva for political and other purposes, are clearly not economically beneficial in the aggregate. However, they can sometimes lead to benefits for particular communities if they succeed in displacing others from lands, assets, livelihoods. This is known to have happened in Gujarat after the 2002 riots, when Muslim entrepreneurs and traders were forcibly displaced or left of their own accord because of fear of further violence, and their assets and income opportunities were taken over by Hindus. Similar processes have occurred elsewhere, for example after the Muzaffarnagar riots in 2013, and are now being openly encouraged in Uttar Pradesh.

This complexity provides an inkling of how Hindutva might actually fit in with a neoliberal capitalist economic agenda, despite the other contradictions noted earlier. It is worth noting that the ideologues of Hindutva rarely if ever refer to distributional justice or improving the lot of the poor. The focus is aspirational, even while seeking to disguise the facts that the poor exist because of the rich and their actions, and that all economic policies have distributive results. The aim of Hindu nationalism is to unify one group (which happens to be in the majority) and exclude, marginalize, or even persecute and oppress those who are not members of this group, even those who are sometimes seen as within the broader 'Hindu' religious fold like Sikhs and Buddhists. This unification occurs on the basis of notions of national pride centred around a powerful leader, who can then set goals that may be vacuous (such as Prime Minister Modi's declared goal of reaching $5 trillion GDP by 2025, which made little sense even when it was announced in 2019, and is now in any case unachievable), but somehow give psychological satisfaction.

Meanwhile big capital within India, especially some of the most important crony capitalists, have greatly benefited individually from this combination of circumstances, despite overall economic decline. The wealth of a relatively small number of super-rich individuals skyrocketed by an estimated 35 per cent during the pandemic;[31] the number of Indian dollar billionaires increased from 102 to 140 in 2020, with just three people adding a further $100 billion to their individual wealth;[32] the profits of listed companies increased by 58 per cent,[33] with the most favoured companies showing even greater gains, even as overall corporate sales declined. Such capital – which now has extensive and deep networks among the political leadership and the bureaucracy and is therefore able to influence policies in its favour no matter what happens – is still firmly with the Modi government.

Of course, all this is deeply undemocratic, but it has become clear – and not only in India – that neoliberal financial globalization is incompatible with democracy, essentially because it undermines living standards of the bulk of the people and therefore requires that they be controlled politically. As a result, in a peculiar way, while the ideology of Hindutva seems to be contradictory to a modern economy, it actually fits in quite well with the functioning of neoliberal capitalism. As the country and its polity move rapidly towards the goal of Hindu Rashtra (a polity that privileges and protects Hindus rather than those professing other beliefs, as well as some idealized notion of Hindu culture), the oppressive embrace of economic neoliberalism directed by global capitalism also persists.

In this scheme of things, even as people grow poorer and more insecure, they can persist in some belief that the economy is doing very well, even if it is not; and that their own poor condition is the result of their own shortcomings or bad karma rather than because of the failure of public policy. Propagation of such beliefs serves neoliberalism very well. Even as income and asset distribution get worse, even as poor people face displacement, material insecurity, and terrible conditions without social protection, they can be diverted to thinking about other things and thereby allow this state of affairs to continue. Their economic concerns can be subordinated to 'national pride' and 'Hindu pride'. Meanwhile those who protest or seek to mobilize against this can be conveniently labelled as 'terrorists' and 'anti-nationals' and locked up under various laws – victims of the new polarizations on which authoritarianism thrives.

However, this also requires that the majority of the affected population be kept unaware that the deterioration of their individual material circumstances is not unusual, that it is not the fault of their personal circumstances or bad karma. In other words, the true state of the economy and of people's livelihoods within them must be disguised, to prevent a more widespread understanding of the extent of economic calamity or the role of public policies in creating or adding to it, or the growing inequalities that are being allowed to fester. In this regard, the manipulation and/or destruction of the Indian statistical system (once a shining example to the world) can be decisive, which is why an aggressive attitude to suppressing or distorting economic statistics has become one of the defining features of the government.[34]

OLD CONTRADICTIONS, EMERGING FORCES

The combination of forces that have brought the Indian economy to this sorry pass could easily inculcate despair. Yet even these apparently entrenched tendencies are subject to change. The continuing vitality of the farmers' movement, despite all attempts to control it, dismiss it, or simply wipe it out, is one sign of the resilience of some forms of protest. The category of agriculturalists is obviously highly internally differentiated, but the unity displayed in the opposition to the new farm laws (themselves a blatant attempt to change power balances in the countryside in favour of large private corporations) has persisted. The caving in of India's other institutions – most notably the judiciary – has been a major part of the democratic decline in recent years, yet a few recent High Court judgments in some states[35] still provide the faint hope that justice has not completely died. Students and other activists across the country, whose attempts at voicing dissent have been suppressed and brutally punished, still remain committed and determined.

Most of all, the political stranglehold of the BJP does not appear to be as complete and inexorable as it was even a few months before the pandemic struck. The results of the April 2021 elections to the state assembly in West Bengal could become a watershed moment in that regard,[36] because the regional opposition party, the Trinamool Congress, was able to retain the state decisively. This came as a blow to the BJP and its most important national leaders, including the Prime Minister, who had invested hugely in terms of time and resources, campaigning to the point of even encouraging massive public gatherings during a resurgent second wave of the pandemic. It also pointed to the potential limits of relying on Hindu nationalism as the driving force for electoral gain. The disastrous second wave, with its devastating impact not just on the poor but also on the middle classes that typically have more political voice in India, is also likely to have dented the BJP's popularity and reduced people's trust in the ruling regime.

Finally, but potentially significantly: despite the recent escalation of private corporate profits amidst the pandemic, there are limits to the ability of large capital to profit in absolute terms as long as the economy continues its current decline. Since the existing economic policies offer little in terms of future likely rises in economic activity, and instead will further suppress domestic demand, even the most favoured corporations may wish for a change of course. Even for purely profit-oriented concerns accustomed to using political access and monopoly power to strengthen their economic power, getting larger and larger shares of a shrinking pie also yields diminishing returns beyond a point. Since big capital, even crony capital, has less commitment to political programmes than to its own self-interest, at some point the poor management of the economy may become a concern even for them.

These processes suggest that the polarizations noted at the start of this chapter are creating political–economic contradictions that will become ever more difficult to resolve. All this points to a renewed period of churning in Indian politics. It is obviously difficult to predict the outcomes of such a process. Yet even recent history in India suggests that political and policy changes can come from unanticipated directions.

NOTES

1   The issues discussed in this essay are considered in more detail in my book, *The Making of a Catastrophe: Covid-19 and the Indian economy*, New Delhi: Aleph Books, 2021.

2   Prashant K. Nanda, 'India slips two spots to rank 131 in global Human Development Index', *Mint*, 16 December 2020, available at: www.livemint.com.

3   Prabhat Patnaik, 'Why Neoliberalism Needs Neofascists', *Boston Review*, 19 July 2021.

4   See Indranil Mukhopadhyay and Dipa Sinha, 'Painting a picture of ill-health', in Rohit Azad, Shouvik Chakravarty, Srinivas Ramani, and Dipa Sinha, eds, *A Quantum Leap Backwards: An Appraisal of the Modi government*, New Delhi: Orient Blackswan, 2019; Pritha Chandra and Pratyush Chandra, 'Healthcare, Technology, and Socialized Medicine', in Leo Panitch and Greg Albo, eds, *Socialist Register 2021: Beyond Digital Capitalism: New Ways of Living*, London: Merlin Press, 2020.

5   Santosh Mehrotra, *Informal Employment Trends in the Indian Economy: Persistent Informality, But Growing Positive Development*, International Labour Organization, Employment Working Paper #254, Geneva, 2019.

6   Jean Dreze and Amartya Sen, *An Uncertain Glory: India and its Contradictions*, Princeton: Princeton University Press, 2013.

7   Stranded Workers Action Network, *No Country for Workers*, 16 June 2021.

8   Lucas Chancel and Thomas Piketty, 'Indian Income Inequality, 1922-2015: From British Raj to Billionaire Raj?', World Inequality Lab, July 2017.

9   'India's Health Crisis', *Down to Earth*, available at: downtoearth.org.

10 Balarajan, Selvaraj, and Subramanian, 'Health care and equity in India', *The Lancet*, (377), 5 February 2011, pp. 505-15.

11   Dipa Sinha, 'There are many holes in the Ayushman Bharat health shield', *Money Control*, 17 August 2018.

12   'Daily new confirmed Covid-19 cases per million people: India, Asia, and World', *Our World in Data*.

13   Soumik Purkayastha, Ritoban Kundu, Ritwik Bhaduri, et al., 'Estimating the wave 1 and wave 2 infection fatality rates from SARS -CoV-2 in India', *BMC Research Notes*, (14), 2021.

14   Karan Thapar, 'Estimates Suggest 25 Lakh Indians Have Died of COVID, Not 4 Lakh', *The Wire*, 10 July 2021.

15   See the 'Co-Win Dashboard' at: dashboard.cowin.gov.in.

16   Mahesh Vyas, 'The jobs bloodbath of April 2020', *Centre For Monitoring Indian Economy Pvt. Ltd*, 5 May 2020.

17   '"India's success will help the entire world": PM Modi at WEF's Davos Dialogue', *Hindustan Times*, 28 January 2021.

18   There has been some speculation that even this could have been determined by political calculations, hoping for rewards from the religious faithful in the Uttar Pradesh Assembly elections due in 2022.

19   For example, states that were sourcing testing kits from within and outside the country were told to desist and wait for the centrally approved kits to be imported from China. When these eventually gave inaccurate results, the states were asked to stop using them and return the unused testing kits. See Teena Thacker, 'Centre decides to withdraw faulty Covid-19 antibody test kits, cancels import orders from China', *The Economic Times*, 27 April 2020.

20   *A Fair Shot*, International Monetary Fund Fiscal Monitor, April 2021.

21   Kalyani Raghunathan, Derek Headey, and Anna Herforth, 'Affordability of Nutritious Diets in Rural India', *IFPRI Discussion Paper 1912*, available at SSRN: papers.ssrn.com/sol3/papers.cfm?abstract_id=3552908.

22   Manika Sharma, Avinash Kishore, Devesh Roy, and Kuhu Joshi, 'A comparison of the Indian diet with the EAT-Lancet reference diet', *BMC Public Health*, (20), 2020.

23   See, for example, the Hunger Watch report described in Jagriti Chandra, 'Hunger continued even after lockdown, says report', *The Hindu*, 12 December 2020.

24   Manoj V. Murhekar, Tarun Bhatnagar, Jeromie Wesley, et al. 'SARS-CoV-2 seroprevalence among the general population and healthcare workers in India, December 2020–January 2021', *International Journal of Infectious Diseases*, (108), 1 July 2021, pp. 145-55.

25   Shaj Mohan and Divya Dwivedi, 'The Compassionate Revolution of Saint Stan Swamy (1937 – 2021)', *The Wire*, 11 July 2021.

26   Sudha Narayanan, 'The Three Farm Bills: Is This the Market Reform Indian Agriculture Needs?', *The India Forum*, 27 November 2020.

27   Atul Sood, 'The Silent Takeover of Labor Rights', *The India Forum*, 4 December 2020.

28   Adrija Roychowdhury, 'Vinayak Damodar Savarkar: He admired Hitler and other lesser-known facts about him', *The Indian Express*, 3 August 2021.

29   A description of these right-wing Hindu nationalist and often militant organizations can be found in Tapan Basu and Tanika Sarkar, *Khaki Shorts and Saffron Flags: A critique of the Hindu right*, New Delhi: Orient Longman, 1993; Christophe Jaffrelot, *The Hindu Nationalist Movement in India*, New York: Columbia University Press, 1996; and Aijaz

Ahmad, 'India: Liberal Democracy and the Extreme Right', in Leo Panitch and Greg Albo, eds, *Socialist Register 2016: The Politics of the Right*, London: Merlin Press, 2015.

30   See: www.makeinindia.com/sector/leather.

31   'Indian billionaires saw there [sic] wealth go up by Rs 12.7 trn during Covid-19', *Business Standard*, 25 January 2021.

32   Tenzin Zompa, 'Despite Covid, India adds 38 billionaires in 2021, Ambani & Adani retain top 2 spots', *The Print*, 8 April 2021.

33   Krishna Kant, 'Corporate profit to GDP ratio hits 10-year high of 2.63% in FY21', *Business Standard*, 31 May 2021.

34   I have discussed this in more detail with examples in: Jayati Ghosh, 'Hindutva, Economic Neoliberalism and the Abuse of Economic Statistics in India', *South Asia Multidisciplinary Academic Journal*, (24/25), 2021.

35   For example, the granting of bail to some student activists who had previously been denied bail, despite legal stipulation that bail should be the norm for all but exceptional cases. Shreya Agarwal, 'Delhi High Court Grants Bail To Devangana Kalita, Natasha Narwal And Asif Iqbal Tanha in Delhi Riots case', *Live Law*, 14 June 2021.

36   Amitabh Tiwari, 'In Charts: How Mamata Banerjee Scripted A Record Win In West Bengal', *Bloomberg Quint*, 6 May 2021.

EPIDEMIOLOGICAL NEOLIBERALISM IN SOUTH AFRICA

VISHWAS SATGAR

The Covid-19 pandemic inaugurated a new global conjuncture of the neoliberal class project. More than four decades of constant recalibration of financialized market rationality to deal with 'market failures' – market reform agendas, austerity, rising authoritarianism and exclusionary nationalism – have not ended the neoliberal project. The result is a set of contradictions ramifying through the entire capitalist system, its structures, its social relations and the ecological basis of its existence – a crisis of socio-ecological reproduction in its broadest sense. This crisis has become exemplified by the Covid-19 pandemic. As Mike Davis has pointed out, the current pandemic, as with previous ones, is 'directly the result of economic globalization',[1] which destroyed natural habitats and the natural commons; transmitted divisions between species; and deepened the divides of class, social inequalities, and nation states. More pandemics can be expected, thanks to factory farming, giant feedlots, fish farms and the ecocidal logic central to global accumulation. At the same time, the Covid-19 pandemic has demonstrated an incredible power to bring much of the world economy to a standstill. It has grounded airlines, tied up shipping, and disrupted global economic flows.

This is the pandemic's conjunctural significance. Within a short period of time the global power structure, national ruling classes, and capital had to find new modes of rule. A global public health emergency, foregrounding the need to ensure the well-being of societies and manage crisis-ridden globalized economies, brought a different set of imperatives to the fore. Decades of privatizing and underfunding public health care, sharp social inequalities, and externally dependent economies all fell short. It is in this context that Joe Biden's proclamation that 'trickle-down economics has never worked' has to be understood. While the Biden administration appears to be upending some of the key tenets of neoliberal ideology, the conjunctural shift propelled by the Covid-19 pandemic has been playing itself out differently in other parts of the world.

In South Africa the response to the pandemic took place in a context of more than two-and-a-half decades of neoliberal restructuring. Managing a crisis-ridden, globalized, and carbon-based capitalist economy, South Africa's deeply corrupt government continued to use a financialized market rationality as the basis for its response, including policies to mitigate the socio-economic impacts and challenges the pandemic presented. The ruling class is completely disconnected from the suffering in society, displaying a strong appetite for criminalized accumulation, while the crisis of legitimacy of the ruling African National Congress (ANC) and its allies intensifies. A failing class project has been rammed down the throat of a fear-ridden and vulnerable society.

THE ANC's CRISIS-RIDDEN CLASS PROJECT

In South Africa, neoliberalism took root in a conjuncture marked by the end of the Soviet Union, a triumphant US-led West, the crisis of the Bandung project, the second decade of defeat of radical pan-Africanism, and a national liberation movement – the African National Congress (ANC) – willing to demobilize mass politics and surrender the symbolic armed struggle for a negotiated compromize. In the resulting political trade-off, the embrace of neoliberalism and its financializing rationality was presented as a 'home-grown' attempt at structural adjustment – a political choice seen as far better than control by the World Bank and IMF. An indebted economy in a deep structural crisis was going to be stabilized through a policy regime that would be liberalized, globalized, and would limit risk to capital. The neoliberal moment was a means to an end – a temporary, contingent development.

However, neoliberalism persisted from the Mandela presidency (1994-1999) in a period of hegemonic rule, through the passive revolution of Thabo Mbeki's presidency (1999-2008), to a decade of criminalized accumulation and rule by the authoritarian populist Jacob Zuma (2009-2018). As a class project led by the ANC government, the neoliberal policy regime became increasingly shaped by primitive accumulation, financialization, the securitization of state-civil society relations, and the further weakening of an already 'thin' market democracy. In this time the hegemony constructed by the ANC-led Alliance (involving the Congress of South African Trade Unions and the South African Communist Party) underwent a further regressive transformation. The material base of this hegemony was a historic bloc linking the working class, elements of the middle class, aspirant black capital, and sections of white monopoly capital (the last actually increasing in the post-apartheid period) under the banner of a historical commitment to ending apartheid. At an institutional level these class relations were organized through trade unions, mass movements, and various social forces in the orbit of the ANC-led Alliance. All these institutions, including the organized formations of the Alliance, are in crisis.[2]

To maintain its grip on power, the ANC-led Alliance has utilized mythic historical representations, propaganda, co-option, division, rampant looting, and patronage networks. Corruption has criminalized politics to the point where 'transactional kick-backs' to the ruling party have become standard practice.[3] In communities, the practice of building voter banks, as part of criminalized accumulation linked to the local state, has fuelled widespread disaffection which is expressed through violent protest actions – the destruction of libraries, schools, and almost any public building – to draw attention to people's suffering and needs. In local government elections in 2016, this anger led to the ANC losing power in all major Metropolitan City governments in the country.[4] The rupturing of the national liberation bloc has also deepened institutionally, with the ANC-led Alliance experiencing three breakaways: the Congress of the People formed in 2008, a party of former ANC members linked to Thabo Mbeki; The Economic Freedom Fighters (EFF) made up of ANC Youth League members led by Julius Malema and formed in 2013; and the National Union of Metal Workers of South Africa (NUMSA), a break-away from the ANC-led Alliance after the Marikana Massacre of mineworkers, and the subsequent formation of its Socialist Revolutionary Workers Party in 2018. In class terms, these are elements of the aspirant black middle class and sections of the organized working class, realigning and organizing outside the ANC-led Alliance and historic bloc. None of these new forces, however, is necessarily emancipatory. For instance, Malema's EFF displays a black neo-fascist streak, and the NUMSA project is lost in unreconstructed Marxism-Leninism-Stalinism, with support even waning amongst NUMSA workers themselves. Ultimately the different periods of post-apartheid neoliberalization have been uncertain, politically fluid, and marked by the absence of a counter-hegemonic challenge to the ruling ANC-led Alliance.

The tactical embrace of neoliberalism became entrenched as a class project to ensure the de-racializing of capitalism. Its consequences have been, however, quite something else: various post-apartheid racisms; a failing capitalist state, with most parastatals inherited from the apartheid regime looted and bankrupt; an externalized accumulation model premised on high structural unemployment; income and wealth inequality (10 per cent of income earners have 65 per cent of household income, and 10 per cent own about 85 per cent of wealth, so that 14 million people were going to bed hungry even before Covid-19); increasing gender-based violence; and an incapacity to deal with climate shocks, such as the worst drought in South Africa's history (from 2014 till the present). These socio-ecological polarizations and contradictions are at the heart of the general crisis of South African capitalism. They interconnect, imbricate, and shape each other. The Covid-19 pandemic coincided with this general crisis.

THE SHIFT TO EPIDEMIOLOGICAL NEOLIBERALISM

By 23 January 2020, about 11 million people were put under strict quarantine in Wuhan, China. On 30 January, the World Health Organization (WHO) declared Covid-19 a Public Health Emergency of International Concern, and by 11 March the WHO declared the spread of Covid-19 a global pandemic. The world was now in the grip of an epidemiological emergency, affecting 7.6 billion people, all countries, and the world economy. On 6 March, South Africa confirmed its first Covid-19 case. The government did not have an effective protocol and strategy to deal with such a situation. Like many countries, its political leadership and ruling class invented a response based on its entrenched neoliberal imaginary, international experience and advice, its own capabilities (or lack of them), and the imperatives of the moment.

By 23 March, after infections had jumped to 51 cases, President Cyril Ramaphosa announced a 21-day lockdown effective from 27 March (on this day the Minister of Health also announced the first two Covid-19-related deaths, and infections were over 1000). This was a stay-home lockdown: only essential services could function, no alcohol and cigarette sales were allowed, and no large social gatherings were permitted.[5] Essentially, South Africa was brought to a halt and the normality of everyday life was suspended. Guided by the *Disaster Management Act*, a set of specific Covid-19 state structures were established (from the national to the local government level) to provide a focal point to coordinate the state's response. A more elaborate lockdown regime (with five alert levels – level 1 the least strict and 5 the strictest) was announced on 23 April, with each level having different regulatory standards for public behaviour (international travel, curfews, gatherings, mask wearing, social distancing, sanitization), and for the functioning of the economy. The WHO declared South Africa's initial level five lockdown a great success, commending the government for bringing the virus under control.[6] For the South African government, led by the presidency, an amplified narrative of care, public interest, and solidarity was constructed to legitimize the lockdown regime.[7] South Africa, it seemed, was now in the hands of a government that took human life seriously and was well positioned to protect society.

However, throughout the life of the top-down, cumbersome, and technocratic management of the lockdown regime, a sharp contradiction arose between managing the imperatives of accumulation and protecting public health.[8] After the level five lockdown, the South African state moved steadily towards easing the lockdown regime. By the middle of August 2020, South Africa was placed on level 2 and by September the country was moved to alert level 1, with minimal restrictions on public behaviour: the economy was open for business. In May 2021, the country was still at level 1 lockdown despite a looming third wave. The assumption at work was that a job-shedding and globalized private sector, even before Covid-19, was crucial for economic recovery. South Africa's tardy lockdown regime was the first policy element of the epidemiological neoliberal agenda.[9]

MITIGATING SOCIO-ECONOMIC HARDSHIP

Accompanying the lockdown regime was the second policy element of the agenda and an attempt to mitigate its economic and social impacts. Ostensibly, there was a sudden break with trickle-down economics: peoples' lives mattered. Various social relief policy tools, macroeconomic instruments, and philanthropic mechanisms were put to work: unemployment benefits, a temporary increase in social grants, additional funding for the healthcare response, a massive stimulus injection through re-prioritizing the budget of R130 billion, credit support for business, fiscal support to local municipalities to address water and hunger challenges, low interest rates (mainly benefiting South Africa's middle-class household bond-holders), mobilizing private sector solidarity funds, income support measures for workers, and a voucher system to support food provisioning. These measures were announced by President Ramaphosa in late April. The relief package, he said, 'with a total value of R500 billion or around 10 per cent of GDP, is the biggest on the African continent and compares favourably with other countries in the G20'.[10] For many political economists, this fiscal support still came up short as a proportional response to the economic fallout, and was much too small.[11] More critically, the sourcing of finance revealed a sleight of hand. Most of the so-called relief package was due to fiscal re-prioritizations of existing budgets. In addition, the Credit Guarantee scheme (R200 billion) made up the bulk of the promised relief, and was meant to be rolled out in partnership with banks, the Treasury, and the Reserve Bank. No consideration was given to a more progressive response, such as introducing greater income and wealth taxes on the top 10 per cent of South African incomes, for instance. At the same time, the most important symbolic gesture made to South African society was the establishment of the much-vaunted Solidarity Fund. This was the epitome of a public-private partnership, in which the government invited the private sector to donate to the fund. South Africa's plutocratic elites rose to the challenge to display their concern for the suffering of the people. The daughter of the late mining magnate Ernest Oppenheimer donated R1 billion to the fund, and substantial contributions were also made by several leading South African corporations.[12] This meant that capital had no other obligations to South African society and its suffering people; they had 'done their bit', so to speak.

RESPONDING TO THE ECONOMIC CHALLENGE

South Africa entered the Covid-19 pandemic with an economy already in recession. Its debt-to-GDP ratio was already forecast at 65.6 per cent, its unemployment rate (narrow definition) was at 29.1 per cent (6.7 million workers), and credit rating agencies had downgraded its investment status and thus pushed up borrowing costs. South Africa's neoliberal project was in crisis even on its own terms. The state understood that it needed to use the moment to address the structural challenges facing the economy. In this context, President Ramaphosa announced an Economic Recovery and Reconstruction Plan in mid-October 2020, at a joint sitting of the two houses of Parliament.[13] This plan explicitly declared its continuity with the neoliberal National Development Plan (adopted as a blueprint for the country's economy in 2012-13) with its emphasis on infrastructure-building for a carbon-based economy, accelerating economic reforms to unlock investment (mainly inward flows by transnational capital), promoting small-scale industrial manufacturing, intensifying the 'law and order approach' of the policing branches of the state, and building governmental technocratic capabilities. There was nothing new in this framework, only a re-affirmation of a commitment to deepen the financialized market rationality of an already deeply globalized economy. Moreover, the new plan was embedded in an austerity framework committed to 'fiscal consolidation,' and therefore to cutting public expenditure. The budget announced by the Minister of Finance in October 2020 reaffirmed this trajectory, with proposals to decrease expenditure by R300 billion over the next three years. The centrality of austerity in public finances was premised on managing the perceptions of credit rating agencies and potential sources of foreign direct investment, and their anxieties about a growing debt-to-GDP ratio (now forecast at over 80 per cent).

Institutional state failures were reflected in the fiscal crisis of the state:

notably in rampant criminalized accumulation in several major state-owned enterprises (SOEs), and similar activities in several ministries and sub-national tiers of government. Many SOEs are bankrupt, including the largest coal-fired power energy supplier Eskom, with debt at close to R500 billion. The extent of state corruption still has to be quantified, but this 'fiscal leakage' has unquestionably been staggering: the neoliberal state has consistently attempted to be taken seriously by global markets and finance, while rampant looting has continued at the nexus between the ruling party, the state, and capital – all at the expense of the working class and the poor. Moreover, over the past few years, the state's revenue-collecting capacity has been denuded and tax revenue shortfalls have become persistent. The criminalized Zuma period of rule actively weakened the institutional capacity of the South African Revenue Services by limiting its ability to identify and penalize corruption, organized crime, and tax evasion. In short, the third policy element of the epidemiological neoliberal agenda was an austerity-driven and globalized economic recovery strategy.

THE PANDEMIC, NEOLIBERALISM, AND RESISTANCE

Many movements, grassroots organizations, community networks, and campaigns existing before Covid-19, together with new Covid-19 civil society initiatives, have advanced grassroots resistance to epidemiological neoliberalism, and proposed what might be termed counter-hegemonic alternatives.

The healthcare system

Before Covid-19, South Africa's health inequalities and failing public healthcare system were already a matter of public concern. 50 million people depended on a corrupt, dysfunctional, and failing public healthcare system, while about 9 million had private medical insurance. A doctor in the public healthcare system handled about 2,457 patients a year, while a doctor in the private sector handled an estimated 429.[14] More generally, South Africa's dualistic healthcare system has not been able to address a host of challenges, ranging from 89,000 HIV/AIDS deaths per year, some 80,000 deaths from tuberculosis, a growing incidence of cancer, malnutrition (at least one in four children under the age of five is stunted), and obesity (with South Africa infamously sitting at the top of the charts for Africa). As Mark Heywood, co-founder of the Treatment Action Campaign, has pointed out,

> The crisis in our nation's health arises from an unconstitutional state of affairs; it is not preordained; it is not even a legacy of apartheid because there is much we could have done to improve it. It arose from bad

governance, corruption and planning that doesn't take account of human rights or equity.[15]

These arguments and calls for government to act on the healthcare crisis were made before Covid-19. Yet in 2019 major cuts to the public healthcare system were budgeted for. South Africa went into the pandemic with a public healthcare system that was already failing, and it faced the pandemic with only around 1,250 intensive care beds available for patients in the country's public hospitals.[16] Frontline healthcare workers had to remake their under-resourced and failing institutions into safe places of work.

As of 18 May 2021, according to an official government communication, South Africa had conducted 11,134,553 tests, with 1,615,485 positive cases identified, 55,260 deaths and 1,526,638 recoveries recorded, and 478,733 vaccines administered.[17] In comparative terms, by merely looking quantitatively at the US, Italy, Spain, Brazil or India where infection and death rates have been higher, it is easy to consider South Africa's Covid-19 response a success story. For the South African government, its hard, level 5, stay-home lockdown and its Covid-19 regulatory regime saved the country from the worst impacts, and also gave the country time to organize its healthcare response. This is the official narrative.

However, a closer look reveals that despite the initial level 5 stay-home lock-down in March and April 2020, South Africa has endured two waves of the pandemic, between May and September 2020 and November 2020 and February 2021, and was entering a third wave in May 2021. Many attribute the third wave to a failure of government to secure vaccines in a timely fashion. Even the first phase roll-out of vaccines, targeting over one million healthcare workers, floundered, with only about 478,733 reached in the first few months of 2021. This process was rolled out as a pilot study using Johnson and Johnson vaccines, but distributional bottlenecks, institutional failure, and even health concerns regarding the vaccine derailed this process. However, the two waves of the pandemic also showed the limits of a public healthcare system in crisis. While the government scrambled to set up emergency facilities in different parts of the country, after declaring the pandemic a National State of Disaster in March 2020, health inequalities, lockdown regulations and rampant corruption underpinned the state response.

To manage the crisis, the state banned or restricted alcohol sales at various moments. The government's argument was that such measures were necessary to limit the emergency pressures on hospitals, given that alcohol-related violence negatively impacted healthcare facilities, although it had itself done nothing to address the healthcare crisis and alcohol abuse challenges before the pandemic. At the same time, the lockdown regulatory regime was eased to keep the economy open, contributing to increasing infections and death rates. With the advent of a second wave from early November 2020 the government only moved the country back to level 3 lockdown regulations in late December, after the second wave had already taken a massive toll, and after the so-called Christmas shopping rush had happened. Even at that point it allowed businesses to self-manage customer and staff densities, and only after the realities of the second wave kicked in did the government make it a prosecutable offence not to wear a mask.

The ANC state also utilized the public health response as a looting opportunity. Procurement of Personal Protective Equipment (PPE), emergency 'pop-up' hospitals and 'sanitization' became opportunities for racketeering and the expansion of the parasitic middle class. Between April and November 2020 government institutions spent a total of R30.7 billion on PPE procurement contracts. According to the Special Investigating Unit, R13 billion worth of these PPE contracts were subject to investigations for corruption.[18]

The consequence of the state's haphazard, corrupt, and austerity-driven response to Covid-19 was one of the world's worst excess death rates, which hit the poor hardest of all.[19] According to the South African Medical Research Council, in the twelve-month period up to the 8 May 2020:

> The cumulative excess deaths from natural causes number more than 157,000 over the past 12 months. This is 3 times higher than the number of confirmed COVID-19 deaths (52,687) reported by the Department of Health ... The high temporal correlation between the excess deaths and the confirmed COVID-19 deaths nationally and in each province makes it clear that the excess deaths are mostly directly related to the pandemic. While some, particularly during the height of waves, may be collateral deaths associated with overwhelmed health services, it is considered that about 85% of the excess deaths are due to COVID-19.[20]

The same study also found that the age-standardized excess death rate in South Africa's Eastern Cape, the poorest province in the country, was 420 per 100,000 of the population, compared to the national excess death rate of 258 per 100,000.[21] As in other countries subject to neoliberal governance, the heaviest price was paid by the poorest.[22] In the midst of the pandemic waves, public hospitals collapsed, making people afraid to go to them. Covid patients in areas like the Eastern Cape would die at home and hence were often not recorded as deaths from Covid-19.

Nursing unions in both the public and the growing private healthcare sectors, facing casualization, inadequate wages, and difficult working conditions, have led resistance to the government's failing pandemic response, ranging from whistle-blowing against corruption and court challenges and protest actions outside hospitals to secure PPE and safer working conditions, to demands for proper health and safety requirements for community health workers.[23] However, the most intense struggle in the midst of the pandemic has been the response of public sector unions to the state's austerity budget, which envisaged three years of cuts in public sector wages directly affecting healthcare workers (as well as teachers and police officers). Wage negotiations deadlocked, with the government insisting that it did not have the resources for a wage increase. Despite healthcare workers rising to the challenges of the pandemic and placing their lives on the line, an extremely corrupt regime was unwilling to tax the wealthy, or cut the salaries of politicians and state managers, but was willing to squeeze the public sector working class.

Unemployment and hunger

Central to the crisis of South African capitalism is its unemployment crisis. South Africa's consistent structural unemployment rate is extremely high when compared to most middle-income economies. Its segmented labour market has not had an unemployment rate below 20 per cent since the 1970s. This was the situation before the pandemic struck. But by the end of 2020 South Africa's unemployment rate had jumped to 32.5 per cent (by the narrow definition), and the number of the jobless had risen to 7.2 million, mainly concentrated among the youth and the African working class.

In this context, the austerity-driven response to the pandemic was nothing short of barbaric, persisting on an economic trajectory and accumulation path that has not worked for over two-and-a-half decades, and which has certainly not addressed the ballooning unemployment and other socio-ecological contradictions. At the same time, the inadequate short-term public-private relief provision, and an uncaring approach to the lockdown, worsened already-precarious socio-ecological reproduction. The first lever that the government utilized was the Unemployment Insurance Fund. In October 2020, the government announced that the Covid-19 Temporary Employer-Employee Relief Scheme (Covid-19 TERS) had paid out more than R51 billion, covering over one million companies and about five million workers. But almost four million long-term unemployed and the four million in the informal sector (at least one million domestic workers and about three million informal traders) did not receive any relief. The level five hard lockdown (of March and April) also dramatically impacted working-class women engaged in informal trading and domestic work. Overnight the lockdown regulations meant that they could not feed their families.

At the same time, the public-private R200 billion Covid-19 Loan Guarantee Scheme (LGS) was not seriously taken up, since so many enterprises could not face carrying more debt. As of 27 March 2021, banks had approved 14,827 loans to the value of just R18.16 billion. This scheme was extended for another three months (till mid July 2021), but it has generally been perceived as a failure due to its onerous regulatory conditions and the uncertain and weak economic outlook. The government did maintain its social grant transfers to 18 million South Africans, mainly children (R440 per month per child, temporarily increased to R740), pensioners (R1780 per month), and people with disabilities (R1890 per month). But these transfers were far from adequate to deal with increasing food costs and the pressures of more unemployed family members.

For poorer working-class families, the impacts of high unemployment and austerity also registered in student politics. The National Student Financial Aid Scheme, providing finance to poor students, had its budget cut by about R6 billion due to austerity. Added to this was the increase in student debt of lower middle-class families, all contributing to an explosion of student protest across the country in early 2021. Financial exclusion has been a serious issue for over twenty years, and was sharply foregrounded in the #FeesMustFall protests between 2015-17. Yet the Minister of Higher Education (who was also the General Secretary of the South African Communist Party) failed to develop a serious and inclusive policy response. In reaction to the 2021 student protests, the same minister was forced to reprioritize his budget and find resources. This merely amounted to taking funds away from other urgent education needs and is a stop-gap measure reflecting a government incapable of adopting policy solutions to benefit the working class and the poor.

In this context, the campaign for a #UBIGNOW (universal basic income grant/guarantee), with its demand for a non-means tested basic income grant, backed by a coalition of the South African Food Sovereignty Campaign, Climate Justice Charter Movement, the #PAYTHEGRANTS campaign of the C19 Coalition, and the Black Sash, played a crucial role in forcing a government policy rethink on immediate social relief. The desperation in society also could not be ignored by the rulers. In response, the government announced a R350 special Covid-19 Social Relief of Distress Grant for the unemployed. This was a very small amount of money, and various administrative and capacity constraints hindered the roll-out. Nonetheless, it eventually reached about six million unemployed people. This grant commenced in May 2020 and ended on 30 April 2021, consistent with the Finance Minister's austerity budget requirements. However, campaigning for a #UBIGNOW continues, with the South African Food Sovereignty Campaign and Climate Justice Charter Movement launching a package of technical policy documents covering the case for the transition of the welfare system to a universal basic income grant/guarantee. The package makes the point that a fiscally neutral #UBIGNOW is possible and will not increase the public debt when funded by progressive taxation.[24] This is a direct challenge to the austerity budget of the finance minister, which actually lowered corporate tax rates.

Out of a total population of 59.6 million, 30.4 million people (of whom 29.9 million are Africans), live below the upper-bound poverty line (UBPL), which is R1,268 per person per month. About 13.8 million people live below the food poverty line (FPL), which is R585 per person per month. With casualization, fragmentation of the labour market, and limited enforcement, the reach of the minimum wage (R3264.93 per month) standards is limited. With poverty wages and high unemployment, most working-class families struggle to put food on the table. In the midst of Covid-19, at least 30 million families were in food distress. Child hunger was exacerbated when school closures meant that close to 9 million children stopped receiving hot meals in the government's school feeding schemes.

As noted, the government's social relief grants were extremely modest and temporary. In the course of 2020, news reports of communities in several parts of the country storming supermarkets and even hijacking food trucks circulated widely, reflecting the depth of the crisis. Grants also fell short in the context of increasing food costs. In the six months from September 2020 to March 2021, the average cost of the household food basket increased by R183.22 (4.8 per cent) from R3,856.34 in September 2020 to R4,039.56 in March 2021.[25] Working-class households relying on social grants, even social relief grants, with low wages and with unemployed members, have been squeezed by these increases.

At the same time, the much-vaunted public-private roll-out of food vouchers and parcels by the Solidarity Fund and the Department of Social Development was wholly inadequate, haphazard, and in some instances caught up in patronage politics. A food parcel valued at R700 was distributed by the Department of Social Development. The nutritional content, the period for which it was supposed to last, and the extent to which it was expected to have to feed an average household of four people were not clear. With the hunger challenge affecting close to 30 million people, by April 2020 only 250,000 households had been reached by the Solidarity Fund. The Social Development Department claimed that it had delivered food to 58,000 households, about 250,000 people, in April 2020.

In this context, resistance emerged across South African society. The South African Food Sovereignty Campaign (SAFSC) established a National Food Crisis Forum, which gained a great deal of media coverage when it messaged concerns about the worsening hunger crisis, challenged the government on high food prices, called for the building of community-level food sovereignty pathways, and pushed hard during the level five lockdown to open the food commons (informal markets, soup kitchens, community food distribution networks, and subsistence fishing in fresh water and the ocean, for instance).[26] The assumption of the government's lockdown regime was that everyone living in South Africa shopped at supermarkets. Yet local food systems depend on about 70,000 small-scale fishers and about three million informal traders. Thus, the demand for 'unlocking the commons' was crucial. The SAFSC backed the call of small-scale fisher organizations and informal traders for an amendment to the lockdown regulations. Media and public pressure eventually secured amendments that ensured that small scale fishers had access to the oceans (and fresh water sources), and that informal traders could trade in public spaces under public health guidelines, as the lockdown was eased after level five. A crucial legal challenge against the City of Cape Town to secure rights for informal traders, which opened the door to loosening up more generally, was also supported by these solidarity relationships.

Moreover, food relief efforts sprang up across society, and community solidarity kicked in. During and beyond level five lockdown of March and April 2020, soup kitchens, feeding schemes, gardening and food sovereignty pathway-building unfolded to plug the gap left by the failure of the state/ Solidarity Fund response. Community action networks, community NGOS, food sovereignty groups, C19 networks, and faith-based organizations all stepped up to meet household and community food needs. A strong tide of localizing and democratizing food systems, as well as advancing various kinds of commoning, was mainstreamed.

The pandemic and climate shocks

The Covid-19 pandemic coincided with the worst drought in the history of South Africa (2014 till the present). During the drought many big cities such as Cape Town and Nelson Mandela Bay, as well as smaller towns in different parts of the country, either experienced or came close to 'day zero events' (with taps running dry). Droughts in South Africa typically last three years, but this drought has lingered, mainly in the Eastern Cape province, for seven years. This is the country's first major climate shock since 2015, the year when the world overshot a 1°C increase in global temperature above the pre-industrial level. The Southern African region, including South Africa, is heating at twice the global average rate, and the current drought is directly attributable to this trend. As carbon emissions increase, and the world likely overshoots 1.5°C warming this decade, South Africa will be at 3°C, making some parts of the country unliveable and livestock and cash crop production difficult everywhere. Extreme weather events will be more frequent.

The drought has revealed how an unequal and polarized society, based on racialized accumulation during the era of apartheid and the post-apartheid period of neoliberalization, engenders climate injustice. Disproportionate impacts were felt in working-class households with increasing food prices, retrenchments mainly of farm workers, and increasing water costs. In rural working-class communities, the drought impact was life-threatening, with many forced to buy water from unscrupulous water traders, draw on distant springs and standpipes, and use rapidly depleting boreholes. The state only declared the drought a national disaster in early 2018, almost four years into the drought – simply too little and too late. The unjust impact of the drought was made worse by a corrupt and failing state, with local governments in South Africa being particularly vivid examples. According to a Ministry of Finance report to parliament in 2021, 63 municipalities were in financial distress, with 40 embroiled in financial and service delivery crises, while 102 more had adopted budgets they were unable to finance.[27] What the Minister failed to admit in parliament was that his party, the African National Congress, was largely responsible for this disastrous state of affairs. Many drought-affected communities could have mitigated the impact of the drought with more effective, responsive, and democratic local government.

In this context, the Minister of Human Settlements, Water and Sanitation opted to bypass local government when Covid-19 hit and rolled out a water tank programme to water-stressed communities. The government officially committed to targeting 2,000 communities. It was not clear how communities were prioritized, the roll-out was not communicated clearly, and there were numerous logistical problems over installation and maintenance. By 26 April 2020, it was announced that only 17,962 water tanks had been delivered to households and communities across the country, of which 11,978 had been installed, and 1,299 top-up tanker deliveries had been made.[28] This band-aid approach to meeting the water needs of communities served as a crucial symbolic gesture, and fitted in well with government's narrative that it cared for the people and was trying to prevent transmission of the pandemic. However, for the South African Food Sovereignty Campaign, which set up an online self-reporting tool for communities in water stress, the battles with the minister about water delivery showed consistently that there were gaps in the roll-out in terms of targeted communities. The need was far greater than the programme was capable of delivering, and more sustainable water infrastructure solutions were desperately needed.[29] The SAFSC worked in solidarity with close to 120 communities, provided four public reports to the minister and the Human Rights Commission on the dire water situation, and eventually threatened the minister with legal action before getting a written response explaining what the government had done and was willing to do. However, the terrible consequences of the state's historic failure to ensure investment in water infrastructure, functional local government, and democratic planning have again been exposed.

The climate crisis has to be 'mainstreamed' in state governance, and South Africa needs to be placed on a climate emergency footing. With its coal-dependent energy system, South Africa is the world's eleventh-highest emitter of carbon emissions, and this carries serious climate risks. The country should be leading the world in terms of decarbonization, systemic transformation, and democratic state capability-building. A deep just transition, creating socially-owned renewable energy, food and water systems, and climate jobs, and ensuring democratic planning should have been central to policy-making. Instead, the carbon-addicted ruling class, with its energy-intensive and extractive strategy of accumulation, is doing the opposite, notably in the President's Covid-19 Economic Recovery and Reconstruction Plan. This plan supports more carbon lock-ins through inflows of carbon-based investment, export-led mono-industrial agriculture, more extractivism, the building of carbon-based infrastructure, a coal-heavy integrated resource plan, and an extension of the minerals-energy-complex into the oceans. The president and his cabinet have declared offshore oil and gas extraction to be a 'game-changer'. An oil and gas bill is rapidly making its way through parliament together with policy support for a 20-year 'lock-in' for gas-based off-shore Karpowerships (the owner of floating energy plants) to deal with energy supply challenges. Yet there are cheaper renewable energy options for the country.[30]

Climate justice resistance, however, is intensifying on several fronts. Anti-extractivist struggles are coming to the fore. The NGO 350.org has a campaign for a Green Eskom, there is a climate jobs campaign, food sovereignty campaigning is widespread, legal actions are in the pipeline to tackle pollution being led by the NGO Groundwork, and there is the Climate Justice Charter process. This process began before the pandemic, and is grounded in six years of campaigning during the drought. In the midst of the pandemic, 238 organizations endorsed a Climate Justice Charter, which was presented to parliament in October 2020 together with a climate science document prepared by leading climate scientists and a memorandum of demands from communities to end hunger, water stress, pollution, and climate harm. But state violence is also being used in an attempt to silence such activists: on 22 October 2020, Fikile Ntshangase, who was central to a struggle in her community against the expansion of coal mining, was shot at her home.

THE LIMITS OF EPIDEMIOLOGICAL NEOLIBERALISM

The ruling-class response to the Covid-19 pandemic is reinforcing the crisis of socio-ecological reproduction. It does not provide solutions to the healthcare crisis, ballooning unemployment, hunger, or the intensifying climate shocks. As these systemic crisis tendencies interconnect, ramify, and amplify, South Africa is on a trajectory of socio-ecological systems collapse. The worsening climate crisis means more droughts, heat, and extreme weather shocks, thus more hungry and unemployed people, and more need for healthcare. The Covid-19 pandemic revealed the limits of more than two decades of neoliberalization. A corrupt and failing state was unable, or unwilling, to adequately cushion the shock to a deeply unequal society. Yet lessons were not learned. The ANC-led state and ruling class are continuing on a collision course with a fragile and desperate society.

At the same time, the general crisis of South African capitalism has weakened the ANC-led Alliance, fed into the rupturing of the national liberation bloc, and is giving rise to fluid re-alignments. Yet epidemiological neoliberalism creates the conditions for negative forces to thrive and grow in the midst of societal suffering and disaffection; the rising black neo-fascism of the Economic Freedom Fighters and the resurgent white neo-fascism of the Freedom Front Plus, both of which secured increased electoral support in the 2019 national elections, do not bode well. The current polarization within the ruling ANC, presented as a crude binary of the 'good Ramaphosa faction' versus the 'corrupt Zuma Radical Economic Transformation faction,' portends a further round of rupture in the national liberation bloc. If the Economic Freedom Fighters benefit from this, South Africa's second transition, beyond ANC dominance, is going to be fraught with racialized conflict, violence, and instability.

But the neoliberal response to the pandemic has also unleashed a new cycle of post-apartheid progressive resistance, advancing several counter-hegemonic responses to the systemic contradictions destroying the country. While the organized working class is weakened, many of the social forces that are emerging are expressing the racial, gender, and ecological relations of class struggle that could potentially converge around a new left class project. This project is threatened by NGO mentalities, business trade unionism, celebrity activism, competition for resources, and the usual personality conflicts. However, the realities of the general crisis of South African capitalism and its destructive trajectory are hard to ignore. The time for a left alternative has arrived. The coming period in South Africa will be defining for its future.

NOTES

I would like to thank the late Leo Panitch for his contribution to the *Socialist Register* and the global left. His connection to and solidarity with the South African left shall not be forgotten. I also want to thank Michelle Williams, Jane Cherry, Awande Buthelezi, Ferial Adam, and Charles Simane for comments on an earlier draft.

1   Mike Davis, *The Monster Enters: COVID-19, Avian Flu and the Plagues of Capitalism*, London: OR Books, 2020, pp. 47-8.

2   The ANC, for instance, has on numerous occasions been unable to pay its employees. This has made headline news.

3   This has been confirmed in the media but also by the recent Zondo Commission of Enquiry into corruption.

4   In the midst of Covid-19, the judicial capital of South Africa, Mangaung, was shut down in a three-day popular uprising as citizens took to the streets. They were frustrated by the collapsed city administration, corruption, and lack of service delivery.

5   The level five lockdown was extended for a further two weeks on 9 April, effectively keeping the country in a stay home lockdown for 35 days.

6   'WHO commends SA on COVID-19 response as death toll rises to 65,' *eNCA*, 23 April 2020, available at: www.enca.com.

7   South Africa's President, Cyril Ramaphosa, led the communication of the government's Covid-19 response with several televised addresses to the country.

8   South Africa could easily have had a three-level lockdown regime, with compulsory mask wearing for all levels of the lockdown and smaller numbers for gatherings at each level.

9   The term epidemiological neoliberalism was used initially to describe the problems with 'herd immunity' as a strategic basis to keep economies open. See: Isabel Frey, 'Herd Immunity is Epidemiological Neoliberalism', *The Quarantimes*, 19 March 2020, available at: https://thequarantimes.wordpress.com.

10   Cyril Ramaphosa, 'Address by President Cyril Ramaphosa to the joint sitting of Parliament on South Africa's Economic Reconstruction and Recovery Plan', *The Presidency*, 15 October 2020, available at: www.thepresidency.gov.za.

11   Duma Gqubule, 'The even greater depression', *Business Media Mags,* 2021, available at: businessmediamags.co.za.

12   Sibongile Khumalo, 'Mary Oppenheimer and daughters donate R1 billion to Covid-19 Solidarity Fund', *News24,* 1 April 2020, available at: www.news24.com.

13   Cyril Ramaphosa, 'Address by President Cyril Ramaphosa to the joint sitting of Parliament on South Africa's Economic Reconstruction and Recovery Plan', *The Presidency,* 15 October 2020, available at: www.thepresidency.gov.za.

14   Public Services International, '25 Years after apartheid: Health inequities persist in South Africa', 4 April 2021, available at: www.world-psi.org.

15   Mark Heywood, 'Ailing Nation – the things SONA won't say about the health crisis, *Spotlight,* 7 February 2019, available at: www.spotlightnsp.co.za.

16   Ryan Davids, N. Ahmed and D. Shead. 'Cry the beloved non-COVID country: A review of South African healthcare response to COVID pandemic', *Journal of Intensive and Critical Care* (6:4), 2020.

17   The official government website contains these figures and is available at: sacoronavirus. co.za.

18   Nicole McCain, 'Those guilty of PPE corruption will be found and prosecuted, Ramaphosa vows', *News24,* 8 February 2021, available at: www.news24.com.

19   This was headline news in one of South Africa's leading business newspapers: Tamar Kahn, 'SA's Covid death toll is one of the worst in the world', *Business Day,* 13 May 2021, available at: www.businesslive.co.za.

20   South African Medical Research Council, 'Report on Weekly Deaths in South Africa', 2-8 May 2021, p. 3.

21   South African Medical Research Council, 'Report on Weekly Deaths in South Africa', p. 3.

22   Nontsikelelo Mpulo, 'The Eastern Cape health Crisis', *Spotlight,* 23 July 2020, available at: www.spotlightnsp.co.za.

23   These struggles are documented in an essay by Christine Bischoff: 'Nursing and the Crisis of Social Reproduction: Before and During Covid-19,' *Democratic Marxism,* 7, 2022, forthcoming.

24   Climate Justice Charter Movement '#UBIGNOW policy approach and proposals', February 2021, available at: www.safsc.org.za; Asghar Adelzadeh, 'Fiscally Neutral Basic Income Grant Scenarios: Economic and Development Impacts', *The Bridge,* May 2021, available at: www.safsc.org.za.

25   Pietermaritzburg Economic Justice and Dignity Group (PMBEJD), 'Household Affordability Index', March 2021, available at: pmbejd.org.za.

26   See www.safsc.org.za for all its press releases during the Covid-19 pandemic. The SAFSC also crowd sourced a survey of food relief efforts in communities available at: www.safsc.org.za/food-relief-mapping/.

27   Thabo Mokone, 'Economic recovery a pipe dream until municipal ineptitude is tackled: Tito Mboweni', *TimesLive,* 21 May 2021, available at: www.timeslive.co.za.

28   An overview of the water tank roll-out and its challenges are provided in Nick Hamer, 'Communities and water: Covid19 changes everything, but will access stay the same?' available at: www.emg.org.za.

29   See: 'Water Stressed Communities Map', available at www.safsc.org.za.

30   A recent study by the University of Stellenbosch argues that South Africa can meet its energy needs eight times over through offshore wind power. See: Alec Basson 'Offshore

Wind energy could help solve SA's energy woes', 11 March 2021, available at: https://www.sun.ac.za. According to the International Renewable Energy Agency, the costs of renewable energy systems and unit costs of renewable energy generation have come down dramatically in comparison to fossil fuels such as coal. See: International Renewable Energy Agency, *Renewable Power Generation Costs in 2019*, Abu Dhabi: IRENA, June 2020, available at: https://www.irena.org/publications/2020/Jun/Renewable-Power-Costs-in-2019.

LOFT OFFICES AND FACTORY TOWNS: SOCIAL SOURCES OF POLITICAL POLARIZATION IN RUSSIA

ILYA MATVEEV AND OLEG ZHURAVLEV

From the United States to Great Britain to France, the capitalist societies of the West are increasingly politically polarized. The roots of the new divisive political climate are often traced to globalization.[1] Left of centre parties increasingly cater to the educated professionals in big cities – the 'winners' in the new, globalized economy – all but abandoning their traditional working-class base.[2] The 'losers' of globalization – lower-educated workers in deindustrializing small towns and rural areas – often turn to the radical right. The rise of right-wing populism is described as 'the revenge of places that don't matter';[3] scholars emphasize the political effects of the divide in levels of education.[4] While this new polarization is rooted in social and class dynamics, class conflict is displaced into endless culture wars that ultimately strengthen the position of the ruling class.[5] The revival of left social-democracy in various political forms partially counteracts this tendency, but its successes are limited and political breakthroughs have met with setbacks.

In relation to this new political conjuncture, Russia is both similar to and different from Western capitalisms. Economically, Russia has been shaped not just by globalization, but also by the transition from a command to a market economy. Just like globalization, this transition has created its own set of 'winners' and 'losers'. The 1990s witnessed unprecedented economic devastation and a dramatic rise in inequality (following a volatile pattern of growth within the so-called BRICS group of countries – see Figure 1). Economic recovery in the 2000s was highly uneven, creating new inequalities and divisions between regions, classes, and occupations. And the 2010s were a period of economic stagnation and renewed political contestation, when class and politics were complexly intertwined. As elsewhere, class conflict in post-Soviet Russia has never appeared in the political arena in its pure form;

Figure 1. Annual GDP growth, BRICS countries, 1991-2020.[6]

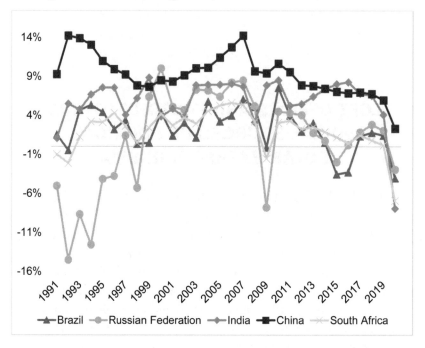

Figure 2. Russian Billionaires on the Forbes List, 1996-2015.[7]

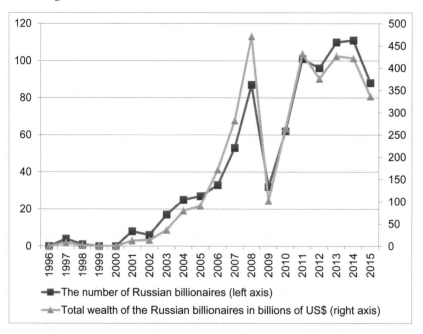

rather, it has been displaced into various ideologically and culturally driven mobilizations. Further, Russian politics has been transformed by growing authoritarian tendencies in the 1990s, and the emergence of a full-fledged autocracy since the early 2000s (with an astonishingly rapid growth of assets and concentration of wealth – see Figure 2). Conservative nationalism versus socially progressive cosmopolitanism; the regime versus the opposition; rich versus poor; all these divisions and polarizations overlap, intersect, and diverge in Russia's complex political reality.

Our goal here is to dissect this lived reality in Russia, relying on academic literature, social surveys, and economic statistics, as well as numerous interviews collected by the Public Sociology Laboratory (to which both authors belong). It is helpful to begin with a brief overview of Russia's economic geography and changing social dynamics, and then to explore political conflicts and polarizations in Russia from the early 1990s to the 2021 protests that unfolded across the country. In doing so, the focus is on the intersection of class and politics as well as the political articulation of social demands and, in this context, on the possible future of Russian politics and the potential salience of class conflict amidst changing social, political, and economic circumstances.

HOW MANY RUSSIAS?

Russia is the geographically largest country in the world, and one of the most regionally unequal in living standards. Per capita gross regional product (GRP) in the small oil-producing regions is comparable to that of Switzerland and Luxembourg; however, in the poor regions of the Caucasus, per capita GRP is closer to that of the Sub-Saharan African countries.[8] With 20 million inhabitants, the Moscow metropolitan area is one of the world's biggest urban agglomerations. In 2020, Moscow's budget was 44.2 billion dollars – almost thrice that of Tokyo. For the same year, the budget of the small Buddhist region of Kalmykia was only 367 million dollars. Moscow spent a comparable sum – 210 million dollars – on local state-run media alone. The capital spends more on urban improvement than all the other Russian regions combined.

According to economic geographer Natalia Zubarevich, regional contrasts in Russia are so dramatic that it is necessary to speak of 'four Russias' not one.[9] The 'first Russia' comprises the big post-industrial cities with relatively high living standards, advanced education systems, and significant white-collar employment. These urban centres concentrate social groups that have fared relatively well during the transition to the market economy since the early 1990s and continue to benefit from the country's integration into global markets. The population of this 'first Russia' grows with each year: Moscow and Saint Petersburg attract internal migrants from all over the country, while other big cities attract people from nearby areas. In fact, the metropolitan areas of Moscow and Saint Petersburg account for 60 per cent and 20 per cent of internal migration, respectively.[10] Regional inequality is supplemented by inequality within the big cities themselves. According to the official statistics, income inequality in Moscow in 2020 was second only to the small oil-producing regions, with the concentration of wealth that comes with resource rents and a clustering of highly skilled occupations. Unofficial figures are even higher: an estimation based on leaked tax documents (rather than population surveys) produced a Gini coefficient of 0.63 for Moscow – among the highest levels of inequality in the world.[11] Social polarization in Moscow increasingly resembles that of other global cities.[12]

The 'second Russia', according to Zubarevich, comprises industrial – or, rather, deindustrializing – cities with 50,000 to 250,000 inhabitants and a few larger urban centres built around manufacturing.[13] These cities are the product of the Soviet mode of urbanization, with the industrial production distributed among a large number of mid-sized factory towns. As opposed to the 'first Russia', the 'second Russia' concentrates the 'losers' of the transition – manual workers and skilled professionals whose jobs are connected to the local industry. Many such places were built around a single factory and, consequently, the fate of these 'mono-towns' *(monogoroda)* became one of the thorniest issues of the regional inequality in Russia over the last thirty years. The share of the population living in mid-sized industrial towns is declining, yet it is still very significant in Russia compared to the core capitalist states. According to Stephen Crowley: 'In the US, over 66 per cent of the urban population lives in metropolitan areas of one million or more; in Russia only 31 per cent do so.'[14] The population of such places is heavily dependent on the state: industrial jobs are subsidized and some factories were even re-nationalized in the 2000s, while the remaining jobs are concentrated in the public sector.[15]

The 'third Russia' is the vast rural periphery. Its population is rapidly shrinking, yet, as of 2020, Russia was still 25 per cent rural. Rural dwellers were among the hardest hit by the transition. What is more, they did not benefit as much as urban dwellers from the subsequent recovery: in the early 2000s, urban poverty declined at twice the rate of rural poverty, creating 'pockets of serious social and economic exclusion' in the rural areas. In 2000, poverty in Russia was 59 per cent urban and 41 per cent rural; by 2004, it was 40 per cent urban and 60 per cent rural.[16] Indeed, many, if not most, post-

Soviet rural dwellers depend on 'peasant-like farming, which is subsistence-oriented, based on family labour and traditional farming methods'.[17] The share of the rural population is particularly large in the Caucasian region as compared to the rest of the country.

Zubarevich argues that the North Caucasus and the South Siberian regions with large minority populations (Tyva and Altai) constitute the 'fourth Russia'. Even though some Caucasian regions have large metropolitan areas, as with Makhachkala, the capital of Dagestan, which has a population of over 600,000, they still have much smaller white-collar, professional employment than other big Russian cities.[18]

This brief overview of Russia's economic geography demonstrates that during the last thirty years of the post-Soviet transition it has acquired the key features of the socio-spatial development of the capitalism of the West, albeit often in a comically exaggerated form. Moscow and, to a lesser extent other big cities, especially Saint Petersburg, have developed vibrant post-industrial economies with significant employment in knowledge-intensive industries such as IT, finance, and consulting. Within these urban areas, entrepreneurs and educated private-sector professionals have generally benefited from the country's inclusion into global trade, financial, and intellectual flows, yet many others have been stuck with low-paying, dead-end service sector jobs. Beyond the encompassing ring roads of Moscow and Saint Petersburg lies the vast Russian 'rustbelt' – the 'second Russia' – with its uncompetitive, heavily subsidized industries, as well as the rural 'heartland' – the 'third Russia' – reduced to nineteenth century conditions. Inequalities abound, the social fabric torn apart. The conditions are ripe for the kind of right-wing populist backlash found in other countries, in the Russian case against Moscow-based elites. Yet the reality has proven to be more complex, not least due to the non-democratic nature of the Russian political system.

THE 1990s: CLASS AND POLITICS

For the purposes of this essay, political polarization is defined as a 'movement away from the centre toward the extremes' in political views and organization of the mass public.[19] In what follows, we will explore the dynamics of such movement – and its counter-movement – in Russia in the last 30 years.

In late 1991, on the brink of the collapse of the Soviet Union, the fault lines in Russian society were still only latent. A coup attempt by the military and the KGB leadership in August 1991 was singularly unpopular. Demonstrations against the coup were among the biggest in Russian history. Boris Yeltsin, just popularly elected as president, was widely seen as the person who prevented the coup. He enjoyed widespread legitimacy and the full support of the Supreme Soviet, the perestroika-era Russian parliament. Yet, with the start of the 'shock therapy' reforms in 1992, the situation quickly changed.

Amongst the devastation wreaked by the neoliberal reforms, the parliament, once Yeltsin's steadfast ally, became his mortal enemy.[20] The conflict between the two branches of government was reflected on the streets of Russian cities. The May First demonstration in Moscow in 1993 witnessed a seemingly impossible scene: red communist flags alongside the black, yellow, and white flags of the Russian Empire: the so-called 'red-brown' coalition of communist and nationalist forces was born. Within this loose alliance, social demands and opposition to market reforms were entangled with issues of identity, culture, and Soviet nostalgia. This contradictory fusion of left-wing and right-wing rhetoric was not just the product of a temporary alliance; it defined the political character of the Communist Party itself as well as most other opposition forces in the 1990s. Since its birth in early 1993, the Communist Party of the Russian Federation has combined social populism of a paternalistic kind with ethnic Russian nationalism.[21]

Political polarization reached new heights in September-October 1993, when Yeltsin, in an ironic twist of history, staged a coup of his own. His unconstitutional move to disband the parliament resulted in a small-scale civil war on the streets of Moscow. The parliamentary side included a motley crew of 'red-brown' forces, but also many ordinary people dismayed by Yeltsin's authoritarianism. At the same time, in the famous 'Letter of the 42', a few dozen writers and other cultural luminaries denounced the defenders of the parliament as 'fascists' and 'stupid scum who respond only to strength', and demanded a ban on the communist and nationalist parties.[22] This position was representative of a certain brand of pro-Yeltsin intelligentsia more generally. At the same time, the 'red-brown' camp had its own intellectuals and artists, such as the famous writer Eduard Limonov.

Yeltsin's victory in the conflict with the parliament, achieved by violent means, did not reduce the tensions in society or prevent their political articulation. Not a single party that could be meaningfully characterized as centrist cleared the 5 per cent voter threshold for representation in the Duma during the 1995 parliamentary elections, reflecting the polarization of the electorate between Yeltsin's pro-reform camp and the 'red-brown' opposition.[23] This polarization reached its peak during the subsequent presidential elections in 1996. For Michael McFaul, the divide in the Russian public did not have a social or class basis: '[T]he structure of societal interests alone cannot account for the prolonged polarization of Russian politics … When politics are polarized, all ideological differences, class divisions, and/or ethnic identities are subsumed by two broad categories: reform or anti-reform, *status quo* or *status quo ante*.'[24] However, subsequent research has refuted this claim. Using an original survey of the Russian population, Stephen Whitefield and Geoffrey Evans reported that an overwhelming 74.6 per cent of entrepreneurs supported Yeltsin during the 1996 elections, while only 7.5 per cent supported Gennady Zyuganov, the Communist candidate. At the same time, only 40.6 per cent of workers supported Yeltsin, while 34.2 per cent supported Zyuganov and 25.1 per cent supported the right-wing populist Vladimir Zhirinovsky. With peasants, the difference was even starker: 32.9 per cent supported Yeltsin, while 46.2 per cent supported Zyuganov.[25] In other words, despite Yeltsin's own populist cross-class appeal, the difference between his support, and support for Zyuganov, reflected class divisions in Russian society. According to Whitefield and Evans, different classes in Russia had vastly different experiences of the transition to the market: workers and peasants fared much worse than managers and entrepreneurs. This defined the collective attitude of different social groups towards the market economy which, in turn, dictated their political preferences. The varying experiences of 'shock therapy' mediated the political views of different social classes in Russia as well as the link between class and vote, which was undoubtedly present – and increasingly so – in the 1990s. Spatial voting patterns reflected class divisions: support for the pro-Yeltsin forces was strongest in the big cities, while the industrial 'rustbelt' and the rural areas supported the 'red-brown' opposition.[26]

To an extent, the Communist Party and other left-wing forces defended the interests of their class base in the legislative process: for example, they tried to increase the minimum wage and various social benefits. However, 'Yeltsin vetoed most of these measures, which government spokesmen condemned without exception as unaffordable, irresponsible, and populist'.[27] Due to the extraordinary weakness of the Russian parliament enshrined in the 1993 Constitution, the left-wing opposition's effective involvement in parliamentary politics consisted mostly of blocking Yeltsin's pro-market legislative agenda. (The Communist deputies also tried to impeach Yeltsin for the 'genocide of the Russian people' but could not muster the required majority.)

THE 2000s: DEPOLITICIZATION AND AUTHORITARIANISM

With Vladimir Putin's rise to power in 2000, Russian politics changed dramatically. In the 2000s, political polarization receded at the cost of widespread public apathy towards politics and the emergence of an authoritarian regime.

From the onset, Putin's political positioning was different from Yeltsin's. Gleb Pavlovsky, a long-time Kremlin spin doctor turned oppositionist, recalls: 'In the end, we stole the agenda from the left patriots. Putin came to power in a paradoxical way: as an establishment man with the opposition's program.'[28] Indeed, Putin was Yeltsin's designated successor. From a policy perspective, his first term in office (2000-04) was largely a continuation of Yeltsin's neoliberal reform agenda.[29] Discursively, however, he emphasized the key themes of the 'red-brown' camp, especially the need for a strong state and the return of Russia to 'great power' standing. In a highly symbolic – and illustrative – gesture, Putin changed the country's national anthem. In 1990, Russia replaced the Soviet anthem with a music piece by a nineteenth-century Russian composer Mikhail Glinka. However, in 2000 Putin brought back the music of the Soviet anthem with new lyrics (written by Sergei Mikhalkov, the author of the lyrics for the previous, Soviet anthem as well). Bringing back the Soviet anthem, albeit with new lyrics, was a conscious move on Putin's part with the aim of rising above the pro-reform, 'red-brown' divide on the level of culture and identity. This strategy was successful. Putin's own appeal transcended the political divisions inherited from the 1990s: he had a chameleon-like quality of appearing as a liberal reformer in one setting and a conservative statist in another.

Beyond the passive support for Putin and the government institutions generally, the aim of the Kremlin was to depoliticize Russian society. As Pavlovsky recalls, the strategy was to put a block on emotion in politics and on open conflicts of any kind, be they street protests or parliamentary disagreements.[30] Indeed, this was the time when the speaker of the Russian parliament, Boris Gryzlov, made the absurd claim that the 'State Duma is not the place for political battles, for the defense of political slogans and ideologies'.[31] Politics was replaced with the neutral language of technocracy and 'national interests'.[32] Again, this approach was successful: in the context of the sustained recovery, Russian civil society largely retreated into private life to heal its wounds from the traumatic decade of the 1990s. The Kremlin, meanwhile, was busy laying the groundwork for an authoritarian regime: bringing the media, parliament, and the electoral process under control. These efforts did not face any significant backlash from the public. Tightly controlled by the presidential administration, the Communist Party and Zhirinovsky's right-wing Liberal Democratic Party mostly catered to the narrow electoral bases that constituted the core of their support. Street protests in opposition to Putin's actions failed to gather more than a few hundred people. This led commentators on Russian politics to suggest the existence of an implicit 'non-intrusion pact' between the regime and the population.[33] In the next decade, however, this pact was broken by the emergence of a new protest movement.

WINTER OF DISCONTENT:
THE 'FOR FAIR ELECTIONS' MOVEMENT

In late 2011, the liberal opposition group *Solidarnost* (Solidarity) informed the authorities about a planned demonstration to protest the anticipated outcome of the parliamentary elections scheduled for 4 December. The group did not expect more than a few hundred people to show up. However, on 5 December, some 10,000 protestors turned to the streets, resulting in clashes with police and around 300 arrests. Five days later, more than 100,000 people showed up at Bolotnaya Square in Moscow to protest electoral fraud. This demonstration, the biggest since 1993, marked a new chapter in the history of post-Soviet Russia. Since December 2011, a mass movement of the opposition has always been present in one form or another on the streets of Russian cities. During its first phase from 2011-12, the movement was overwhelmingly focused on fair elections; and almost from the onset, it was strongly anti-Putinist in character.

The protestors were quickly labelled 'angry urbanites'.[34] At first glance, this was justified: the rallies were overwhelmingly held in big cities, especially Moscow and Saint Petersburg, where tens of thousands of people showed up. Rather uniquely, Levada Center, Russia's major polling agency, conducted surveys at the protests themselves, allowing researchers to compare the characteristics of an average protestor with those of the general population. The comparison revealed that one particular group was overrepresented at the protests: private sector professionals with a university degree.[35] On average, the protestors were also better-off than the rest of the country: around 30 per cent of the participants of the rallies were poor (struggling to afford anything beyond food and clothes), while in the total population of Moscow the share of the poor defined this way was around 50 per cent, and nationally it was 79 per cent.[36] Sociologically, then, these were protests of the 'winners' not the 'losers' of the transition to the market economy. The people who turned to the streets had generally benefited from the emergence of a booming post-industrial private sector in Moscow and other big cities during the economic recovery of the 2000s. Irina Busygina and Mikhail Filippov offered a plausible explanation as to why this particular group formed the core of the protestors:[37] the participation of public-sector workers and people without a university degree was low due to a fear of the economic turbulence that might accompany another attempt at democratization, with the government doing everything in its power to exacerbate these fears and anxieties. However, educated private-sector professionals participating in the demonstrations were much more competitive in the labour market, giving them more confidence that they could enjoy the benefits of democratization while adapting to and overcoming its possible downsides.[38] Our own interviews with the protesters revealed that this theory makes a certain sense, yet the reality is more complex.

The Public Sociology Laboratory has been conducting interviews and focus groups with the participants of the Russian opposition movement since 2011.[39] Our longitudinal study allows us to track the movement's evolution and identify the role it has played in the development of Russian society and politics over the last ten years. One of our basic conclusions is that the first phase of the movement against Putin's regime (2011-12) reflected the features of the society that developed under this regime: an apolitical mood, a lack of class identity and consciousness, and a significant discrepancy between actual social grievances and the slogans and demands articulated by the protestors. The participants of the movement either did not express individual grievances at all or considered them to be secondary to the movement's agenda of fair elections. Answering our question, 'Would you include any social demands or slogans in the movement's agenda?', they often said 'no', arguing that it could split the movement. In general, the protesters often seemed perplexed and unable to articulate what they wanted to achieve. The very association and solidarity between different people within the protest rallies turned out to be the value in and of itself for the protestors. Importantly, although the rallies took place in various Russian cities, it was a movement of the capitals. Moscow and Saint Petersburg were the cities where tens of thousands of people took to the streets, and where the leaders and organizers of the movement had been shaping the values and attitudes of different audiences through culture and journalism well before 2011.

What made a movement that lacked social and ideological consistency stable and reproducible? On the one hand, the displacement of social issues and ideological differences in favour of an abstract moral agenda, the concrete sociality of the movement, and the creative style of the protests, all played a role. On the other hand, our interviews revealed that two social groups were particularly influential in the movement: highly educated people (the intelligentsia) and the well-to-do (successful middle-class professionals and entrepreneurs). Furthermore, our interviews indicated that these two groups tended to identify with one another, even though the wealthier protestors did not necessarily work in intellectual professions, while the intelligentsia was often poorer than the successful middle class. In fact, many wealthier protestors claimed that it was the movement of 'smart', 'intelligent', and 'creative citizens and students'. At the same time, the intelligentsia pretended that they belonged to the middle class or strove to identify with the middle class. In many ways, this development was made possible by the sustained economic growth of the 2000s, which transformed the Russian social structure. On the one hand, the impoverished intelligentsia of the 1990s obtained at least a modicum of welfare in the 2000s, increasing their self-perceived social status as well. On the other hand, the professionals and entrepreneurs who prospered in the booming 2000s articulated a demand for their own cultural identity and political representation. In a sense, the rallies of 2011-12, although they were anti-regime, tended to confirm the tendency of the synchronization of cultural and economic capitals that characterized Putin's era.[40] *In other words, the protests themselves became the site of class formation.*

FROM PRO-PUTIN RALLIES TO THE 'CRIMEAN SPRING'

The Kremlin's response to the movement of 2011-12 was not only 'tightening-the-screws' through repression but also the counter-politicization of its loyalist electoral base. The regime organized mass rallies of its own, though largely through administrative mechanisms. Some participants were paid in cash for attending a rally; others were mobilized by their employers. People from the regions were offered a chance to see the capital; they were bussed to Moscow on condition that they participated in a Kremlin-organized demonstration.[41]

Our interviews with the participants in these rallies revealed their paradoxical character. Indeed, these demonstrations could be called 'mobilization without politicization'. The participants did not feel themselves part of a common political movement. While the protesters in the opposition camp downgraded their individual social grievances in favour of a common abstract liberal agenda of fair elections and civic freedoms, the participants in the pro-Putin gatherings were much more articulate about what they wanted ('to increase my salary', 'we lack social benefits', 'we need more measures to help small business'). However, these demands were clear precisely because they were individual. These people did not need to harmonize or integrate their grievances into the movement's common agenda because there was, in fact, no movement. The pro-Putin rallies were purely imitative, top-down performances with no grassroots component.

The next stage of the Kremlin's response to the protest movement turned out to be 'politicization without mobilization'. It consisted of a crude media campaign to delegitimize the protests in the eyes of the regime's supporters.

For example, during the 'direct line' with Putin on live TV, a foreman at the defence plant *Uralvagonzavod*, Igor Kholmanskih, offered to come to Moscow with his men and 'to defend our hard-earned stability' that the protestors presumably wanted to take away. Kholmanskih later received an important government position.[42] With such media spectacles, the regime sought to polarize the society by setting the population of industrial towns and rural areas against the 'big city liberals' who had joined the opposition movement – a familiar trope of right-wing populism across the world. However, the Kremlin-led populist campaign was partly successful because the cultural and symbolic elements of the opposition movement itself were, indeed, alien to many sections of the Russian population. As the cultural historian Ilya Kalinin has remarked:

> The stylistic and cultural element of the protest movement interpreted by the 'creative class' as its main achievement on the road to new forms of self-representation, possessed a completely idiosyncratic character … It was this artistic-stylistic specificity that in the main prevented the movement into development into a truly mass social protest. And it led to reinforcement of the logic of cultural distinctions … The turn of the regime, in response, to the language of culture … possessed a more inclusive character and was far more successful.[43]

Examples of such 'artistic-stylistic specificity' included playful costumes, banners, and slogans, as well as a general orientation towards a whimsical theatricality. The creative style of the protest rallies led by people with high levels of cultural capital was unfamiliar to the broader society. This fact was sophisticatedly exploited by the Kremlin, which turned the discrepancy between the protest movement's style and ordinary people's expectations into a kind of 'culture war', not dissimilar to the one that has raged for many years in the United States. The opposition itself supplied the Kremlin with more than a few weapons in this war. Many protest leaders, particularly cultural workers such as writers and journalists, espoused elitist views and presented themselves as an 'enlightened minority' within the broader population that was passive and backward.[44] It was easy for the Kremlin's media machine to seize on this elitism and to present the regime as the sole representative of the 'ordinary working people'. Overall, the new strategy of the authorities was to seek stronger, ideologically and culturally driven support from its core electorate instead of simply relying on mass apathy and depoliticization. As Pavlovsky remarked, the new populist rhetoric opposing the 'pathological minority' of protesters to the 'healthy majority' (the rest of the country) marked a return of conflict and strong emotions in the government-controlled media, particularly television.[45]

This counter-politicization of the regime's supporters reached its peak in 2014. The annexation of Crimea dramatically increased Putin's approval rating and transformed the relations between the regime and its supporters from a silent approval to a kind of genuine political representation through an unusual show of decisiveness that was met with enthusiasm by most groups in society. Nevertheless, even in the nationalist fervour of 2014, the regime stopped inches away from finally combining 'politicization with mobilization', that is, creating its own loyalist street movement. The most striking mobilization in support of the 'Crimean spring' happened in the territory of Ukraine, not Russia. Indeed, it was the war in Eastern Ukraine that attracted newly politicized conservatives – combatants, volunteers, and other civic supporters. Within Russia itself, the regime still preferred tight top-down control of any mobilization or street activity, even of a loyalist kind, organizing paradoxical 'demonstrations against demonstrations', that is, public rallies with a general message that the people should stay at home and not 'rock the boat' under any circumstances.[46] Deeply anti-populist at its core, Putin's regime is thus different not only from, say, Latin American 'left-populist' governments, but also from the European and North American right-wing populist forces that thrive on social polarization. The Kremlin reluctantly brought emotions and conflict back into politics, as Pavlovsky remarked, but strictly in a mediatized form, while doing everything in its power to isolate its own propaganda from grassroots activity of any kind; the authorities feared that any genuine, bottom-up loyalist movement could eventually escape control.

NAVALNY'S POPULISM

Since its emergence in 2011, the Russian protest movement has been changing and evolving. By 2017-18, it received a strong injection of populism.[47] The movement overcame its narrow liberal focus on fair elections and civic liberties, integrated some socio-economic demands, and attracted more people outside of the educated middle class. This evolution happened when Alexei Navalny became the main organizer of the protests after the state had persecuted several other leaders and activists. Navalny expanded the movement's agenda of protest against the usurpation of power by adding protest against the usurpation of wealth. He put forward a demand to double the minimum wage and began attacking the oligarchs in his anti-corruption investigations, promising to implement a tax on windfall profits from privatization. A slogan from his 2018 presidential campaign (he was eventually blocked from participating in the election) read: 'Prosperity for all, not wealth for the 0.1%'.

The 2017 rallies against corruption confirmed this evolution. Indeed, the 2011-12 demonstrations were a celebration of the self-expression of the educated and successful, the self-reliant and independent, the fair and courageous. In 2017 the self-perception and rhetoric of the protesters changed. They no longer articulated their moral and civic superiority in opposition to those in power. Instead, they stressed their subordinate position and deprivation. As shown above, in 2011-12 protesters avoided the articulation of social demands and their integration into the movement's agenda, arguing that such demands could threaten the unity of the movement. In 2017, on the contrary, social demands turned out to be an organic part of the movement's agenda, together with civic rights and liberties: '*Our salaries are so small … we can only have some food, poor clothes. If you have such a salary, you don't have any rights*'; and '*I started thinking not only about Putin, but also about our country in general. It is a wealthy country. It is a pity that our resources belong to the oligarchs. Navalny speaks about this.*'[48] Such statements are fairly common in our interviews with the 2017 protesters, many of whom belonged to lower-class stratums.

In 2018, the unpopular pension reform, of raising the retirement age from 55 to 60 for women and from 60 to 65 for men, led to a decline in Putin's approval rating, bringing it back to the pre-'Crimean Spring' levels. Despite the tightly controlled nature of the elections, United Russia, the Kremlin's party, lost the vote in several regions. Critical discourses delegitimizing those in power became widespread not only in civil society, but also among those who used to support the regime. Navalny created a network of branches of his organization, the Anti-Corruption Foundation, in tens of cities across Russia, widening the geographical scope of the opposition movement. These local structures often attracted poor and underprivileged young people. Thus, while Putin developed a populist media agenda while avoiding mobilizing the masses, Navalny adopted a quite different strategy: he transformed an elitist liberal protest movement into a populist one.

LATE PUTINISM:
STRUGGLE AND HOPE AMONGST VIOLENCE AND DECAY

This brings us to the current political conjuncture in Russia and three interrelated aspects that need to be explored – the state of the regime, the prospects and limits of the opposition, and whether a left that has been repressed by the regime (and has thus been absent or largely on the margins of the above events) can yet emerge.[49]

The Putin regime is undergoing a systemic crisis of legitimacy. Since the emergence of a mass protest movement in late 2011, it has become impossible for the Kremlin to rely on the apathetic indifference of the population and general appeals to social stability, as it did in the 2000s. In the presence of a critical counter-narrative and an alternative political force, such indifference can quickly turn into widespread dissatisfaction. However, the techniques of aggressive conservative and nationalist indoctrination, which the government has turned to in the last ten years, equally lose their effectiveness through time. The use of propaganda has diminishing returns: at some point, it only causes weariness, fatigue, and the desire to turn off the TV. Furthermore, the economic stagnation and turbulence of the last decade have slowly yet inexorably diminished support for the regime.[50] Importantly, the Kremlin stopped just one step away from creating its own loyalist street movement in response to the opposition rallies. The desire to mobilize the regime's passive supporters was overcome by the fear of the possible unintended consequences of such mobilization. This fear is not entirely unfounded: some of the people who are enthusiastic about the nationalist reawakening of the 'Crimean Spring' have become disillusioned and hold grudges against the authorities who betrayed their trust. Administrative actions, such as raising the retirement age without compensating increases in pension incomes, fracture the Kremlin's claims of being the provider of social stability, and dislodge political loyalties.[51]

The Kremlin's chief goal under Putin's rule has been to prevent independent political activity of any kind, even ones that might benefit the regime.[52] Russian society is not, in this sense, politically polarized as it had been in the 1990s: the opposition is mobilized, yet the pro-regime sections of the population remain largely passive. This leaves the government with one blunt instrument to deploy – repression. Indeed, in 2021 the repressive measures deployed by the state acquired an unprecedented scale. Tens of thousands of people were detained during the January protests. Prisons were overwhelmed and the police had to transfer the detainees to the migrant detention facilities. The authorities systematically closed down non-loyal media outlets. Independent candidates in elections of any kind are no longer simply blocked from participating, but rather sent to prison or into exile.[53] The general strategy is to completely rid the country of any organized opposition in advance of the parliamentary elections scheduled for September 2021.

The opposition movement itself has been transformed since the first mass rallies of 2011. Due to Alexei Navalny's influence, the movement has become thoroughly populist – a collective protest against the greed, lies and violence of the establishment. The January 2021 rallies, provoked by Navalny's imprisonment upon his return to Russia, as well as by the investigation of 'Putin's palace' on the shores of the Black Sea, had an unprecedented regional scope. Some 300,000 people took to the streets in 200 different locations across Russia. In some cities and towns, the January protests were the biggest in their entire history. While sociological data on the composition of the recent rallies is not available, anecdotal evidence suggests that the protest coalition is now far wider than its previous core of educated middle-class professionals. But Navalny's virtual monopoly over the organization of the protest movement made it vulnerable to the persecution of Navalny himself, and his organization. After Russian courts declared the network of Navalny's bases across the country to be 'extremist' (effectively giving it the same status as ISIS and other terrorist groups), the future of organized opposition is in doubt. What is more, the ideological vagueness and programmatic contradictions of the movement (a combination of social demands and occasional free market sloganeering) make it vulnerable to another threat. Even if Putin's regime is toppled, control could be seized by factions of the ruling class which advocate further neoliberal reforms, such as widespread privatizations. The movement could hardly resist such an agenda. Combined with the inevitable economic turbulence that would accompany democratization, such a scenario threatens the livelihoods of the working-class majority of the country. In many ways, this is what happened in Ukraine, where the anti-oligarchic Maidan uprising resulted in the local oligarchs maintaining or even expanding their power.[54] This makes the presence of an organized and militant left in Russia all the more vital.

Russia is one of the most unequal countries in the world, with 114 billionaires, some 250,000 millionaires, and 17.8 million people living below the official poverty line (150 USD per month). Due to widespread destitution, the traumatic experience of the transition to the market economy, and the residual Soviet ideological legacy, the population is generally very supportive of welfarist demands. The disillusioned youth who are now joining the opposition movement en masse are especially receptive to left-wing slogans. Yet the socialist camp is weak and disorganized. There are several reasons for this. One is state persecution. When left-wing groups such as Sergei Udaltsov's *Left Front* began making progress in 2011-12, they were broken up and decimated by the authorities. The regime understands full well the threat coming from the organized left. In fact, it can be argued that Navalny himself has been increasingly persecuted since 2017-18 precisely because he embraced certain social demands. However, beyond government pressure, the left suffers from ideological blind spots and makes strategic mistakes.

Many socialist groups are still tainted by 'red conservatism' of a nationalist and imperialist kind, with the Kremlin effectively coopting and assimilating their agenda. Numerous 'study circles' *(kruzhki)* limit their activities to reading the classics and waiting for the 'true Party' to come. Many left-wing media outlets, including popular YouTube channels, are stuck fruitlessly debating the Soviet Union with the liberals. When popular leaders and effective, militant organizations oriented towards real-world struggle do emerge in the socialist milieu, they are attacked with the full weight of the state.

But we have no choice but to carry on. Socialists work in trade unions and social movements, take part in elections, particularly on the local level (where a semblance of fair competition is still possible), engage in education and outreach, launch solidarity campaigns, and take to the streets, joining others in the opposition marches. The left has a consistent set of programmatic commitments that distinguishes it from Navalny's contradictory and eclectic populism. A programme based on workers' rights (especially the right to strike, currently denied by Russian law), social rights such as a stable minimum wage, progressive taxation, and massive public investment to restart economic growth and reverse the decay in public education and healthcare, has the potential to unite broad layers of the Russian society. It is this programme that we have to fight for in various opposition milieus to achieve a better future for our country and to make our contribution to the struggle for remaking a new left internationally.

NOTES

1   Hanspeter Kriesi, et al.,'Globalization and the Transformation of the National Political Space: Six European Countries Compared', *European Journal of Political Research,* 45:6, 2006; Dani Rodrik, 'Populism and the Economics of Globalization', *Journal of International Business Policy,* (1:1), 2018.

2   Thomas Piketty, 'Brahmin Left vs Merchant Right: Rising Inequality and the Changing Structure of Political Conflict', *WID World Working Paper,* 7, 2018.

3   Andrés Rodríguez-Pose, 'The Rise of Populism and the Revenge of the Places That Don't Matter', *LSE Public Policy Review,* 1:1, 2020.

4   Robert Ford and Will Jennings, 'The Changing Cleavage Politics of Western Europe', *Annual Review of Political Science,* 23, 2020.

5   Jacob S. Hacker and Paul Pierson, *Let Them Eat Tweets: How the Right Rules in an Age of Extreme Inequality,* New York: Liveright Publishing, 2020.

6   'GDP growth (annual %)', World Bank, available at https://data.worldbank.org/indicator/NY.GDP.MKTP.KD.ZG.

7   Daniel Treisman, 'Russia's Billionaires', *American Economic Review,* 106: 5, 2016.

8   'Valovoj Regional'nyj Produkt Na Dushu Naselenija', available at: fedstat.ru/indicator/42928.

9   Natalia Zubarevich, 'Four Russias: Human Potential and Social Differentiation of Russian Regions and Cities', *Russia 2025. Scenarios for the Russian Future*, Berlin: Springer, 2013.

10   Zubarevich, 'Four Russias', p. 74.

11   Sergei Guriev and Andrei Rachinsky, 'Neravenstvo: Rio-de-Moskva', *Vedomosti*, 15 May 2006.

12   Saskia Sassen, *The Global City*, Princeton: Princeton University Press, 2013.

13   Zubarevich, 'Four Russias', p. 75.

14   Stephen Crowley, 'Global Cities versus Rustbelt Realities: The Dilemmas of Urban Development in Russia', *Slavic Review,* 79:2, 2020, p. 369.

15   In the industry-heavy Kemerovo region, home to the largest number of 'mono-towns' in Russia, 22 per cent of the population work in manufacturing and resource extraction, while another 24 per cent work in state administration and public services. At the same time, the share of employment in small and medium enterprises (SMEs) is only nineteen per cent. These are aggregate numbers for the whole region – the concentration of jobs in the industry and the public sector is even higher in particular factory towns. In Moscow, on the contrary, only nine per cent of the population work in manufacturing and thirteen per cent work in state administration and public services, while the share of employment in SMEs is 34 per cent. See: 'Mosstat', available at: mosstat.gks.ru; 'KemerovoStat', available at: kemerovostat.gks.ru; 'Zanjatost' v MSP: daleko li do celej Strategii-2030?', *SberDannye,* July 2019, available at: nwab.ru/content/data/store/images/f_339_71958_1.pdf.

16   Christopher J. Gerry, Eugene Nivorozhkin, and John A. Rigg, 'The Great Divide: "Ruralisation" of Poverty in Russia', *Cambridge Journal of Economics,* 32:4, 2008, p. 606.

17   Natalia Mamonova, 'Understanding the Silent Majority in Authoritarian Populism: What Can We Learn from Popular Support for Putin in Rural Russia?', *The Journal of Peasant Studies,* 46:3, 2019, p. 11.

18   Zubarevich, 'Four Russias', p. 79.

19   Morris P. Fiorina, Samuel J. Abrams, 'Political Polarization in the American Public', *Annual Review of Political Science*, 11, 2008.

20   For a detailed account of the 1992-93 political crisis see David Kotz and Fred Weir, *Russia's Path from Gorbachev to Putin: The Demise of the Soviet System and the New Russia*, New York: Routledge, 2007.

21   Sirke Mäkinen, 'Political Parties and the Construction of Social Class in Russia', *Rethinking Class in Russia*, New York: Routledge, 2016.

22   'Pisateli Trebuyut Ot Pravitel'stva Reshitel'nyh Dejstvij', *Izvestia*, 5 October 1993, available at: vivovoco.ibmh.msk.su/VV/PAPERS/HONOUR/LETT42.HTM.

23   Michael McFaul, 'Russia between Elections: The Vanishing Center', *Journal of Democracy,* 7:2, 1996.

24   McFaul, 'Russia between Elections', pp. 321-2.

25   Stephen Whitefield, Geoffrey Evans, 'Class, Markets and Partisanship in Post-Soviet Russia: 1993-96', *Electoral Studies,* 18:2, 1999, p. 163.

26   Ralph S. Clem, 'Russia's Electoral Geography: A Review', *Eurasian Geography and Economics,* 47:4, 2006.

27   Linda J. Cook, *Postcommunist Welfare States: Reform Politics in Russia and Eastern Europe*, Ithaca: Cornell University Press, 2013, p. 123.

28   Andrei Goryanov, 'Pavlovskij: Real'nost' Otomstit Kremlyu i Bez Oppozicii', *BBC*, 31 December 2014.

29   Ilya Matveev, 'State, Capital, and the Transformation of the Neoliberal Policy Paradigm in Putin's Russia', *The Global Rise of Authoritarianism in the 21st Century: Crisis of Neoliberal Globalization and the Nationalist Response*, New York: Routledge, 2020.

30   Gleb Pavlovsky, 'Vlasti, Emocii i Protesty v Rossii', *Gefter.Ru*, 1 July 2014, available at: gefter.ru/archive/12661.

31   Boris Gryzlov, 'Remarks at the State Duma', 29 December 2003, available at: duma. gov.ru/media/files/Tph7rkFpnHaD1eSEvtAEop4zADR7pBl5.pdf.

32   Philipp Casula, 'Sovereign Democracy, Populism, and Depoliticization in Russia: Power and Discourse during Putin's First Presidency', *Problems of Post-Communism*, 60:3, 2013.

33   Nikolay Petrov, Maria Lipman, and Henry E. Hale, 'Three Dilemmas of Hybrid Regime Governance: Russia from Putin to Putin', *Post-Soviet Affairs*, 30:1, 2014.

34   Zubarevich, 'Four Russias', p. 72.

35   Bryn Rosenfeld, 'Reevaluating the Middle-Class Protest Paradigm: A Case-Control Study of Democratic Protest Coalitions in Russia', *The American Political Science Review*, 111:4, 2017, pp. 637-52.

36   Denis Volkov, 'Protestnoe Dvizhenie v Rossii v Konce 2011 - 2012 Gg.: Istoki, Dinamika, Rezul'taty', 2012, available at: www.hse.ru/data/2012/11/03/1249193438/ movementreport.pdf.

37   Irina Busygina, Mikhail Filippov, 'The Calculus of Non-Protest in Russia: Redistributive Expectations from Political Reforms', *Europe-Asia Studies*, 67:2, 2015.

38   Busygina and Filippov, 'The Calculus of Non-Protest in Russia'.

39   See the results of this research in: Oleg Zhuravlev, Natalia Savelyeva, and Svetlana Erpyleva, 'The Cultural Pragmatics of an Event: the Politicization of Local Activism in Russia', *International Journal of Politics, Culture, and Society*, 33, 2020; Svetlana Erpyleva, 'Freedom's children in protest movements: Private and public in the socialization of young Russian and Ukrainian activists', *Current Sociology*, 66:1, 2016.

40   This tendency towards bridging a gap between the intelligentsia and the well-to-do undoubtedly played a role in the neutralization of the polarization between the pro-reform liberals and the 'red-brown' camp that happened during the 2000s. In the 1990s, many members of the impoverished, frustrated intelligentsia joined the communist-nationalist opposition, while the economically successful people were staunchly pro-reform. In the 2000s, both groups moved closer to each other both economically and in terms of self-perceived social status thus helping to neutralize the ideological divide.

41   Maria Vasilieva, 'Massovka dlja mitingov v Moskve − po 1000 r za shtuku', *BBC*, 2 February 2012.

42   'I.Holmanskih Naznachen Polpredom Prezidenta Na Urale', *RBK*, 21 May 2012, available at: www.rbc.ru.

43   Ilya Kalinin, 'Why "Two Russias" Are Less than "United Russia"', in Birgit Beumers, Alexander Etkind, Olga Gurova, and Sanna Turoma, eds., *Cultural Forms of Protest in Russia*, New York: Routledge, 2017.

44   Ilya Matveev, 'The "Two Russias" Culture War: Constructions of the "People" During the 2011-2013 Protests', *South Atlantic Quarterly*, 113:1, 2014.

45   Pavlovsky, 'Vlasti, Emocii i Protesty v Rossii'.

46   Jardar Østbø, 'Demonstrations against demonstrations: the dispiriting emotions of the Kremlin's social media "mobilization"', *Social Movement Studies*, 16, 2017.

47   In this essay, we use the term 'populism' to denote a rhetorical strategy that opposes the people (as in 'ordinary people') to the corrupt and out-of-touch establishment. Following De Cleen and Stavrakakis, we differentiate between populism and nationalism. See Benjamin De Cleen and Yannis Stavrakakis, 'Distinctions and Articulations: A Discourse Theoretical Framework for the Study of Populism and Nationalism', *Javnost - The Public*, (24: 4), 2017. Unlike populism, nationalism emphasizes the in/out relationship between the people-as-nation and the individuals or groups that do not belong to it. At the same time, nationalist-populist hybrids are certainly possible, as with the ideological concepts of the 'globalist elites' and the 'Brussels establishment'. Within this analytical framework, Alexei Navalny's rhetoric has always been defined by the strong anti-establishment sentiment that is the essence of populism. In the beginning of his political career, he combined it with ethnic nationalist claims and even outright xenophobia. However, since 2011-12, he has almost completely eschewed nationalism. In recent years, his populism has acquired distinct left-wing undertones. See Ilya Budraitskis and Ilya Matveev, 'Putin's Majority?', *New Left Review*, 9 February 2021.

48   Interviews taken at the anti-corruption rally, 12 June 2017.

49   In the 1990s, the socialist left was overshadowed by the 'left-patriotic' camp. In the 2000s, it established a foothold in emerging independent trade unions and social movements. In the 2010s, the left was an important part of, but not the dominant force in, the opposition protests.

50   For a detailed analysis of the connection between the state of the economy and the support for the regime see: Ilya Matveev, 'Stability's end: The political economy of Russia's intersecting crises since 2009', in Felix Jaitner, Tina Olteanu, Tobias Spöri, eds., *Crises in the Post-Soviet Space. From the dissolution of the Soviet Union to the conflict in Ukraine*, London: Routledge, 2018.

51   These sentiments were increasingly voiced in the interviews taken by the Public Sociology Laboratory since 2018.

52   The aversion to any grassroots pro-regime activity is reflected in the way the Kremlin manages its political organizations. The United Russia Party is a strictly electoralist tool that is used to control the Duma and other legislatures as well as for distributing patronage to loyal elites. In 2011, Putin created another organization called the All-Russia People's Front, presumably to allow some genuine pro-regime activism. However, the Front became yet another government organized NGO-style bureaucracy with no grassroots component.

53   Fariza Dudarova, 'Letnie repressii', *Novaya Gazeta*, 18 July 2021, available at: novayagazeta.ru.

54   Oleg Zhuravlev and Volodymyr Ischenko, 'Exclusiveness of civic nationalism: Euromaidan eventful nationalism in Ukraine', *Post-Soviet Affairs*, 36, 2020.

FICTITIOUS POLARIZATIONS: THE FAR RIGHT, CORPORATE POWER AND SOCIAL STRUGGLES IN BRAZIL

ANA GARCIA, VIRGINIA FONTES AND REJANE HOEVELER

Studies of social polarization tend to refer to a set of political party forces and affirm an interpretation of politics that limits it to formal parliamentary electoral processes and institutions. While not ignoring social struggles, these analyses rarely account for the fact that a growing share of social and class struggles takes place outside the realm of electoral politics and government institutions, and that the actors involved maintain unequal relationships with the state. We call 'fictitious polarization' the false form of political contrast represented by electoral political parties portrayed as opposite poles, centred on disputes over cultural issues, which leave economic struggles to the side. Such a focus overshadows and mis-identifies the real polarization: that of social classes, whose struggles today encompass the economic and political spheres but also social and cultural realms.

The connection between the economic and the cultural was a crucial contribution of Antonio Gramsci in his emphasis on how civil society – conceived as a space of social and class struggles – expands the state and configures itself as 'a succession of sturdy fortresses and emplacements' in defence of class domination. In this essay, we will focus on political behaviour, represented not only by official parties but also by other organizations and 'parties' of the Brazilian ruling classes. Based on Gramsci's writings, we analyze polarizations that are promoted by private hegemonic apparatuses (PHAs). That is, the associative entities which really are a kind of 'party' and are sponsored by the corporate bourgeoisie, and whose day-to-day work has three particular emphases – internal bourgeois organization, policy formulation and dissemination, and capitalist-philanthropic aims. These associations are not limited to 'economic' decisions, but undertake organizational and political activities beyond the scope of the institutionalized, officially-registered parties.

WHICH POLARIZATION? THE BRAZILIAN CONTEXT

We start by looking at analyses of polarization in the United States. Without delving into the complex scenario in that country, we are interested in certain features of polarization which have had important consequences for the Brazilian and Latin American contexts. Firstly, the opposition between Democratic and Republican parties is directly associated with an opposition between a liberal camp and a conservative one, and has been characterized as fundamentally asymmetric.[1] They are not equally distant from a notional political 'centre' which is, in any case, strongly defended as a kind of social ideal in American politics. The growing radicalization of the right, inside and outside the Republican party, has led social liberals and social democrats alike, as represented in the Democratic party, to take up moderate and conciliatory political and policy positions, in an attempt to preserve institutional and constitutional stability. The GOP pole, in contrast, has hardly shown any willingness to compromise. Donald Trump's election consolidated the dominance of a reactionary political discourse amongst the core of the Republican base, openly aiming to restrict civil rights on racial, ethnic and gender grounds, as well as backing any number of authoritarian policy measures. In this sense, the far right has shifted the 'centre' of an already conservative political culture.[2] The GOP, and the far right in general, has taken to dismissing compromises and adopting 'clear, non-negotiable positions',[3] notably in policy positions set against black people, migrants, indigenous peoples, LGBTQ+, feminists, and others. The party leaderships that previously ran the establishment (the traditional right and liberal democrats) still attempt to move toward an ever more elusive moderate 'centre'. But the shifting of the political terrain has provided the grounds for the legitimization of far right and even proto-fascist ideas and positions.

The radicalization of political discourse by the far right did not, however, place liberals or social democrats and the traditional right in opposite positions with regard to economic policy and projects. Nancy Fraser demonstrates that progressive and conservative political forces have together 'shielded' the neoliberal economic project. This resulted in the incorporation of sectors of the left, present in socialist, labour, and social-democratic parties, into the economic and ideological agenda of neoliberalism in the 1990s and 2000s.[4] The consensus formed around the neoliberal policy regime meant that the main axis of political dispute abandoned the economic sphere and increasingly took the form of 'culture wars'.[5] Fraser contends that the rise to political prominence of far-right leaders expressed a crisis of the hegemonic neoliberal consensus.[6] Thus, the 're-politicization' of the political environment took place on the terms of the far right, that is, an asymmetric polarization in the field of ideas and values, leaving the economic sphere to the side. Ultra-conservative in social values and ultra-liberal in economics: this equation defined, at least initially, the governments of both Trump in the US and Jair Bolsonaro in Brazil.[7]

Other analyses see the rise of the far right as a consequence of four decades of the implementation of neoliberalism, and particularly of the transformations it has brought about in social relations, which have fuelled popular support for proto-fascist leaders.[8] Marco Boffo, Alfredo Saad-Filho and Ben Fine observe that the 2007-08 crisis resulted, paradoxically, in the strengthening of financial institutions and neoliberal economic policies. This contributed to a widespread mistrust of the political system, which saved banks but not people, houses, and jobs, and paved the way for an 'authoritarian turn'.[9] Politics was reduced to a competition 'between shades of orthodoxy in a circumscribed political market' —[10] a fictitious polarization. In this context, many pundits and leaders on the right – and even the far right – falsely appear as political 'outsiders' in opposition to traditional elites. A vast number of workers who were victims of neoliberal globalization suddenly became the objects of a systematic campaign by proto-fascist leaders who, as is customary with this brand of authoritarian politics, put forward popular demands blaming fictitious culprits. The institutions of liberal democracy, for example, were represented by the far right as the exclusive sphere of a corrupt elite (in the Brazilian case elites linked to the left then in power at the national level) and came to be seen as such by a large share of the working classes; and social rights won through popular political struggles for public policies that addressed inequalities (such as racial and gender quota systems or social inclusion programmes) came to be presented as conferring 'undue privilege' on the affected minorities.[11]

In Brazil, the financial crisis that began in 2008 was delayed, but eventually deeply affected the middle and working classes. Under Lula da Silva's Workers' Party (Partido dos Trabalhadores – PT) government these classes experienced citizenship through consumption, in the form of access to university, an increase in the minimum wage, and the alleviation of extreme poverty, but also increased indebtedness. Over the course of the crisis, these social strata lost these material gains in living standards and, for many, became part of a mass of workers without rights, notably in gig economy occupations like Uber drivers and delivery apps workers.[12] Faced with the absence or unreliability of public services, significant portions of the hard-hit middle and working classes channelled their anger and resentment towards the traditional political parties, and especially against the Workers' Party. Across a wide range of social sectors, conservative values emerged and gained strength, reinforced by the actions of organized groups of the far right,[13] often linked to the growing evangelical Pentecostal churches. In this cultural milieu the far right organizes systematically through the dissemination of 'fake news', and generates a politics of 'anti-communism without communists'.

Two other characteristics of the polarization process emerge here. The first is a change in the modes of information production and circulation. The 'classical' handling of information by traditional corporate media now has to compete with social media networks where there is little control over the dissemination of lies or the 'cyber-mobbing' of opponents.[14] The second is the growing cultural force of religion, as well as the intimate relations between political and religious leaders, with Christian fundamentalism in particular adopting an aggressive, ultra-conservative and, in many cases, science-denying position. In the context of the current pandemic, these two ideological terrains have had devastating effects on the lives of populations, in conjunction with the actions of presidents such as Bolsonaro and Trump. As of August 2021, Brazil and the US had achieved notoriety for the highest total number of deaths from Covid-19, not least thanks to the right-wing political leadership helping to spread distorted and false information about vaccines, alleging obscure origins for the new coronavirus, and peddling 'miraculous' and patently useless treatments and cures.[15]

The massive demonstrations that took over the streets of Brazil in June 2013 arose out of the contradictions and consequences of the 2008-10 economic crisis. It was in this context that the increasingly heated US debate on social polarization arrived in Brazil. On the one hand, the demonstrations marked the return to the streets of demands for effective social policies, as exemplified by calls for 'FIFA standard' public services (a reference to the plans in hand for the world soccer championship due to take place in Brazil the following year). On the other hand, they also revealed the emergence of a new right, more radical and organized.[16] As Paulo Arantes has remarked, the June 2013 outbreak was a surprise, as the protests erupted in a country that had been thought to be 'pacified' by the centrist 'social pact' arrived at by Lula. Discussions about polarization in Brazil until then focused on the divisions between parties of different shades of social democracy – the Workers' Party and the Brazilian Social Democratic Party (Partido da Social Democracia Brasileira – PSDB). This debate concealed fundamental historical and policy continuities between the two in their governance of Brazil in the 1990s and 2000s under the presidencies of Fernando Henrique Cardoso of the PDSB (1995-2003), Lula da Silva (2003-10), and then Dilma Rousseff of the PT (2011-16) .[17] Despite important differences, both parties upheld three pillars of Brazilian politics: liberal macroeconomic management, modest re-distributive policies, and a politics of recognition of cultural, racial and gender rights, each regime differing in the form and degree of these policies depending on the economic situation and their permeability by social pressure. In Nunes' words, it was 'a more progressive or more conservative neoliberalism according to the occasion'.[18]

The formation of a neoliberal consensus that included the parties of social democracy in Brazil is closely associated with the activities of private hegemonic apparatuses (PHAs): foundations and 'non-profit' associations linked to both national and international economic and financial groups. Located in civil society, they worked to 'depolarize' social life, attempting to carefully excise all organizational traces of the working classes from the formulation of policies, especially initiatives targeting the popular sectors. This strategy slowly eroded the centrality of official political parties as outlets for popular demands. The more PHAs evolved into 'quasi-parties' of the dominant elites in Brazil, the more party representation itself, in parliament and outside, lost status. Further, by directly influencing crucial policies, especially those aimed at the economy and the working youth, the PHAs eroded the principles these policies previously rested on: the notion of rights to services as part of citizenship was converted into 'access' by ability to pay, or to raise funds from somewhere or other; public management was converted into the private management of the public treasury; popular participation was reduced to subaltern incorporation – without rights – in social life and, perhaps, inclusionary representation in the hegemonic apparatuses themselves. In contrast, praise for 'entrepreneurship' by both the state and the PHAs was pervasive. The word became an incantation in the media, ranging from praise of the bourgeoisie for its entrepreneurial leadership, to the conception of education as human capital accumulation adapted to the needs of individual workers who must live their lives without any collective rights. In this ideological schema of the PHAs, the politics of parties and governments is replaced by direct capitalist management, either by the administrative norms adopted or by the privatization of state provisioning, further restricting political party representation to an electoral facade.

To a large extent, the 2013 protests were a rejection of the fictitious polarization that characterised a political process dominated in reality by the business classes, guided by the neoliberal policy consensus since the financial crisis, and administered by PT governments. As Nunes puts it, 'by transforming the private debts of banks into sovereign debt, passing on its cost to the population in the form of cuts in services and loss of rights, right and centre-left governments had shown they defended the interests of the market above all'.[19] The re-occupation of the streets did not, however, follow a leftist path. After initial police violence against protesters, and biased and manipulative media coverage, with the mass media being itself a frequent target of the protests, an 'anti-political' sentiment emerged – with chants of 'no party' and 'no flag' – which effectively re-polarized the streets towards the right. Following a year of a polarization falsely expressed in the electoral dispute between PT and PSDB in 2014, the streets were taken over in 2015 by massive protests against corruption and the PT, which continued through 2016 and the impeachment of Dilma Rousseff. If there are still debates about the nature and characteristics of the 'June Journeys' of 2013, there was no longer any doubt about the class character of the protests from 2015 onwards: they were led by the professional strata and the bourgeois classes, with support from corporations and private sources (and so did not encounter police repression), and often with funding from foreign organizations.[20]

As Nunes argues, the opposition to Rousseff was, in fact, not motivated by any 'radical measures' she took, much less because she moved in a socialist direction. For Nunes, the bourgeoisie saw the conjunction of the economic crisis with the demoralization of the PT as a 'historic opportunity' to unilaterally undo the 'social pact' which had underpinned the country's re-democratisation 'without having to negotiate with the left, the social movements or the working class'. The parliamentary coup through the successful impeachment of Dilma in August 2016 was thus another expression of the 'asymmetric polarization between an opposition moving towards the right and a PT increasingly at the centre', obscuring and misdirecting the real class antagonism.[21]

What Brazil experienced was a phenomenon described by British Marxist David Renton as a 'convergence': an alliance between traditional strands of the right and an emerging extreme right.[22] The political process adopted to remove Rousseff and the PT from government without going through an election expressed a willingness on the part of the bourgeoisie (facilitated by their private apparatuses of hegemony), and the traditional conservative and neoliberal parties, to accept far-right ideas, programmes, and leaders. As Paulo Arantes put it, the 'pacification pact' sustained across the Lula era was breaking down on the right-wing side of the tacit agreement, to the point where a moderate wing of the PSDB 'declared that the doors of the party were open to the people who demonstrated, with guns in their waistbands, their horror of the colour red'.[23] Historical examples of such 'convergence', analyzed by Renton, can be found in crucial moments since the 1950s in the United States and Britain, when traditional parties served as 'umbrellas' for far-right groups aiming to subvert the liberal democratic institutional order, rather than function as 'dikes' protecting that order by refusing to grant political credibility to such forces of instability. A similar process can be observed in Brazil in the activities of the traditional parties of the right and corporate organizations that promoted the impeachment of Rousseff and backed the subsequent election of Bolsonaro.

GRAMSCI AND BOURGEOIS PARTIES

To understand how such 'truncated polarizations' have been achieved, it is helpful to look beyond the formal political system and electoral disputes. Gramsci referred to private apparatuses of hegemony, the varied individual and groupings of civil society associative entities, as 'parties', since they had as one of their functions organizing and directing the political struggle. The term could refer both to the entities organized by the ruling classes and to those of the subaltern classes.

Analyzing post-1870 French politics, Gramsci noted that the most important initiatives did not emerge from vote-based political organizations, but from private bodies or relatively unknown offices deep inside the bureaucracy. From this he concluded that 'there was a proper relation between state and civil society, and when the state tottered, a sturdy structure of civil society was immediately revealed'. The state served as 'just a forward trench, behind it stood a succession of sturdy fortresses and emplacements'.[24] Awareness of the historical class struggle – a 'spirit of cleavage' – would be the necessary foundation of an effective polarization by the working class. Gramsci adds,

What can an innovative class set against the formidable complex of trenches and fortifications of the ruling class? The spirit of cleavage – that is, the progressive acquisition of the consciousness of one's historical identity – a spirit of cleavage that must aim to extend itself from the protagonist class to the classes that are its potential allies: all of this requires complex ideological work …[25]

In *Americanism and Fordism*, Gramsci analyzed the role of the Rotary Club as an example of the particular combination of coercion and persuasion that provides the historical conditions for the emergence of a completely 'rationalized' production, which required a way of life and a social type that was adequate for it. Having analyzed various press sources about the Rotary, Gramsci wrote: 'Its basic problem seems to be the dissemination of a new capitalist spirit: in other words, the idea that industry and trade are a social *service* even prior to being a business and that, indeed, they are or could be a business insofar as they are a "service".'[26]

There is today a proliferation of foundations, institutes, and associations – all formally non-profit – which are funded and maintained by the corporate sector. Following Gramsci, these private apparatuses of hegemony express positions that go beyond immediate economic-corporate interests, and seek to build consensus, educate their own class, and act politically. Despite representing specific economic sectors, they are the setting for making compromises out of conflicts of interest within a sector or between sectors. These private apparatuses of hegemony can be found at all scales, from the local to the international, and Gramsci notably includes religious entities amongst them.

The corporate associative networks remain outside the scrutiny of the mainstream media, even while often integrated into them. This permits the participation of these PHAs in policymaking in states, often with special access to the executive but also to key offices in departments, as well as aiding the development of a ubiquitous pedagogy of capitalist domination in the media and cultural sectors that has helped to make neoliberal thought 'common sense'.

Even if formally outside the state, association members recognize their actions as political, although not partisan. They organize national interest groups and link to similar international entities, from the corporate level to broader interest groups, bringing together sectors such as manufacturing, agri-business, and development. In the case of the Trilateral Commission, created in 1973, an attempt was made to organize the international socio-economic order itself, and to rid 'overloaded' democracies of their substance (the annual Davos World Economic Forum continues in this vein).[27]

PHAs intersect and act as networks, co-participating in other associations. They prepare intellectual cadres, select and train managers and leaders to work in the state, and have an intense media presence with an intellectual profile, as seen in the activities of corporate think tanks. They often approach conservative religious groups, incorporating or funding their leadership (an important organizational role in Brazil). Some act with an international and 'philanthropic' content, such as the American-based Ford, Rockefeller, Carnegie, and Kellogg Foundations.

Some PHAs even take on a capitalist-philanthropic profile, as they claim to assist in the mitigation of impoverishment resulting from privatization and the withdrawal of social rights. This pattern was strengthened after 1968, with the intensification of social struggles, as countless associative forms were established. While business-sector PHAs institute practices to disqualify, contain and block trade union organizations, capitalist-philanthropic PHAs develop a rhetoric about alleviating social problems, while deepening inequalities, oppression, and environmental destruction through their associated companies. In other words, while supporting certain social organizations and their 'demands' (as long as they stay clear of attacks on private property), these apparatuses seek to contain the 'spirit of cleavage', or class consciousness, and reduce the capacity for class organization.

POLARIZATION AND BOURGEOIS PARTIES IN BRAZIL

The origins of PHAs in Brazil date back to the late 19th century.[28] Until the 1960s they were mainly directed towards the defence of sectoral economic interests, organizing different bourgeois fractions and maintaining a strong presence in the state structure. The intensification of social struggles has favoured a new organizational level, through an association between the Brazilian Institute of Democratic Action (IBAD), directly financed by the US, and the Institute for Research and Social Studies (IPES), which organized a large portion of the Brazilian bourgeoisie and military personnel for the 1964 coup d'état and functioned as a headquarters.[29] Throughout the dictatorship (1964-88) strategic PHAs continued to prosper and multiply, with a strong sectoral character and easy access to the formulation of economic policies inside the state.[30]

After 1989, alongside the permanence and growth of PHAs that served the internal organization of the bourgeoisie, new entities were created in various social sectors, some with a capitalist-philanthropic character targeted at 'harm reduction' in the face of liberal policies. They were largely focused on the production of social consensus through 'concerted action' between business associations and unions or other popular sectors.[31] Their main policy target was education: by influencing public schools, public procurement, management systems, and weakening labour ties; through the training of workers without rights; and through the inclusion of 'entrepreneurship' in public school curricula, and the dissemination of a corporate pedagogy.[32] More recently, PHAs have also educated their own cadres for parliamentary roles and lobbying.[33] Like other capitalist-philanthropic PHAs, they promote a peculiar form of 'meritocracy' – the active recruitment and training of young people from disenfranchised sectors so as to convert them into 'popular' leaders.

The number of PHAs has grown significantly in the last two decades.[34] In 2003, the accession to the presidency of Lula da Silva and the PT spurred the creation of larger and more powerful PHAs, which began to make detailed proposals in many policy fields, and to monitor policy implementation.[35] PHAs also began to play an important role in the evaluation of public policies, including engaging in widespread media propaganda for a reduction in the size of the state sector, and lobbying for the adoption of the 'New Public Management' favouring privatization of the most diverse public resources and functions.[36] The PT, in this context, often behaved as a 'pro-capital left' by taking up the proposals of the corporate sector.[37] New administrative practices evolved in response to the PHAs' main demands. On the one hand, the PHAs demanded discipline from legislators, in the form of measures of fiscal austerity, limitations on universal policies of social security, and, above all, an increase in the ruling class's share of public resources. On the other hand, the capitalist-philanthropic PHAs proposed turning the social catastrophe these policies produced into an opportunity to transform workers stripped of social rights into 'entrepreneurs'.

Following the dismantling of party politics by the judicial-parliamentary coup of 2016, which ushered Michel Temer into the presidency, the Brazilian bourgeoisie ceded political control to far-right groups, increasingly aligned with conservative religious sectors. The PT, including Lula himself, were raised to the status of public enemies, a status magnified by the so-called 'car wash' money-laundering scandal, involving the state-owned oil company Petrobras and the leading political parties, and enflamed by the media as an indictment of the entire political system. This led to the peculiar 'polarization around a single pole' in Brazilian politics.[38] Business-sector PHAs devoted to the defence of sectoral or general capitalist interests joined in 'anti-communist' activism, while those with a 'capitalist-philanthropic' profile retained a deferential silence with respect to the state. The anti-PT discourse mutated into a visceral anti-communism completely at odds with the many pro-business and pro-capital policies that the PT had pursued, even if it had also made some concessions to the popular sectors.

In the 2018 presidential elections, Jair Bolsonaro's openly fascist, xenophobic, racist, anti-democratic behaviour led to an intense popular mobilization against his candidacy. But many PHAs supported Bolsonaro, while the corporate media portrayed the conciliatory candidacy of Fernando Haddad of the PT and former mayor of São Paulo as if they were equivalent poles of political extremism. Threats by the armed forces, militias linked to the Bolsonaro family, and the Pentecostal churches allied with Bolsonaro's social conservatism, intensified this new polarization. Indeed, the anti-communism that had animated a resurgent hard right in Brazil became co-joined with a concerted attack by historical far-right forces against bourgeois institutions – including representative institutions – with the complicity and support of the business sector.[39]

Once in government, Bolsonaro fulfilled his promise to dismantle many of the popular and cultural achievements that were the progressive legacy of the PT, and he has remained dogged in pursuing this destructive agenda. His ultra-neoliberal economic policy regime, including direct assaults on the working classes through minimum wage cuts and labour legislation rollbacks, has secured support from the business sector, although they have limited options in any case.

There are, however, contradictions in Bolsonaro's political agenda. His attacks – including economic attacks – against the country's largest corporate media have helped him maintain the loyalty of his most radical right-wing bases. But the constant anti-media barrage has also opened fissures within the business sector, especially as the Covid-19 pandemic demonstrated his profound inability to provide any of the necessary verbal guidance needed to manage an emergency situation.[40] The inept handling of the pandemic response has meant that opposition to Bolsonaro has been growing even within right-wing parties, as illustrated by the recent 'impeachment super request' which unified parties from different camps.[41] In addition, a parliamentary commission of inquiry is currently underway in the Brazilian Senate with the aim of investigating the health policies of Bolsonaro's government in relation to the COVID-19 pandemic. These developments have been undercutting, to some degree, Bolsonaro's framework of parliamentary alliances and support.

However, there remains no major disagreement amongst the social forces on the right with respect to the economic policies of the government. The corporate media groups at odds with Bolsonaro criticize his health policy and pandemic management but not his economic programme.[42] A few capitalist-philanthropic PHAs keep some distance from the most belligerent 'Bolsonarist' practices. But there has been no substantive break with Bolsonaro in the political positioning of the most important PHAs devoted to internal bourgeois organization, including the most important one, the Federation of Industries of the State of São Paulo (FIESP).

Could there be a new polarization, of a quite different kind, initiated by the left in Brazil? The fascist discourse and practices of the Bolsonaro government have led the small left-wing parties, and the more combative sections of the PT, as well as many social movements, to include self-defence as part of their organizational arsenal, since they have been subject to direct attacks. So far, all mobilizations against Bolsonaro have come from anti-fascist groups and various social movements, many of them gathered in two large fronts – *Frente Brasil Popular* and *Frente Povo Sem Medo* (People Without Fear) – each including combative leftist groups and a small portion of the cadres of the institutionalized left-wing parties. Their organizational expression on a national scale is small but growing, despite the restraints imposed by the pandemic. The central issue for these fronts is the fight against the government's genocidal policies, and 'Fora Bolsonaro' (Out with Bolsonaro).[43] Although they are united in anti-fascist struggle, there remains a strategic bifurcation in the fronts. Some defend a broad front that would include all social and bourgeois sectors that oppose Bolsonaro, given the urgency of the pandemic and the ongoing socio-environmental devastation (not least of the Amazon) – a perspective that tends to minimize the character of the class polarization cutting across Brazilian society. Others support a united front with an explicit class profile, aggregating anti-capitalist forces and popular parties and movements, with a more organizational emphasis – the focus being on forcing Bolsonaro out of office, or even overthrowing him.

The legal turnaround by the Brazilian Supreme Court in April 2021 that allowed Lula to be the PT candidate in the next presidential election has led to the re-emergence of the term 'polarization', particularly invoked again by the large corporate media. This reactivates the old notion of an electoral polarization between Lula and Bolsonaro which had previously been pushed to the side by the 'car-wash' scandal. But the retrieval now carries a dramatic significance, since defeating Bolsonaro – and his fascistic politics – is a fundamental condition for the survival of Brazilian democracy.

The 'spirit of cleavage', as Gramsci would say, or an effective class polarization, still seems far off in Brazil. The anti-fascist struggle opens up the possibility for a reconstitution of class politics, especially since anti-fascist demonstrations for Bolsonaro's impeachment, and for 'vaccines in the arm and food on the plate', may become the source of an effective left-wing front that aggregates multiple struggles, and is able to confront the power wielded by the capitalist classes through their varied apparatuses of hegemony.

POLARIZATION AND THE FAR RIGHT IN LATIN AMERICA

What are some of the expressions of polarization found in other Latin American scenarios? The region is currently the scene of intense social struggles and the emergence of new political actors. A suggestive expression formulated by Maristela Svampa, which is not unlike the use here of the concept of fictitious polarization, is 'toxic polarization'.[44] She refers to the polarization between, on the one hand, the 'old progressivism', personified by former Ecuadorian President Rafael Correa, and consisting of self-proclaimed socialist sectors, businessmen, and even social conservative groups, giving rise to a contradictory 'conservative progressivism'; and, on the other hand, the more reactionary and 'ultra-liberal right'. The struggle between them concerns the rhythm and intensity of capitalist exploitation, present in both programmes, and the admission of a larger or smaller range of subaltern and indigenous partners into the progressive pole, most of whom are ideologically excluded by the reactionary right.

At the outset of Latin America's so-called 'pink tide' challenge to neoliberalism in the early 2000s, Ecuador and Bolivia drew up innovative political constitutions whose corollary was the expansion of rights, with great popular participation. Amidst the commodities boom, these governments consolidated popular leadership and an electoral base responding to economic growth and poverty reduction, through strategies adapted to each local context. In each case, the growth and redistribution strategy pivoted on the expansion of extractive activities in the mining and oil industries, benefiting from high prices in the international market driven by Chinese demand.

According to Svampa, this led to contradictions and clashes with indigenous and environmental movements which promoted a plurinational state, defended the rights of nature, and sought alternatives to extractivism. Correa's government reacted to these socio-environmental conflicts with the criminalization and judicialization of social movements, as well as the removal of the legal status of foreign NGOs, and their expulsion. For Svampa, Ecuador became not only an 'extractivist state', but also an anti-indigenous and authoritarian government 'with unmistakable patriarchal traits and practices'.[45] This fuelled growing opposition forces ideologically oriented to Correa's left, especially among indigenous movements, which promoted Yaku Perez's losing presidential candidacy for the eco-socialist Pachakutik party in 2021.[46]

Thus, the 2021 electoral context in Ecuador revealed a struggle between three main social forces. The first two were a more statist 'progressive' force, and the 'ultra-liberal' right against which it was polarized, although both were socially conservative (against abortion, for instance) and supported various forms of 'developmentalism' and promoted the expansion of capitalism, at different intensities and in different ways. The third force is popular, autonomously organized, anti-development, and anti-capitalist (if in quite distinct forms), and it struggles against the other two forces. This framing design could be extended to other countries, with some adjustments, assuming that the countless disputes loosely-designated as 'identity struggles' configure as part of a third force alongside revolutionary left-wing parties which have importance but limited social and political expression. For Svampa, the previous election in Ecuador in 2017 had already led to 'extreme and indefensible' positions, leaving such deep political wounds that, for an important sections of the indigenous movement, Correa was no longer considered a progressive, or leftist, much less a socialist politician.[47] The result of this difficult Ecuadorian context was the victory in May 2021 of the neoliberal right pole, led by Guillermo Lasso and his revealingly-named 'Creating Opportunities' party (Creando Oportunidades).

The Latin American scenario adds complexity to the asymmetric polarization process discussed earlier, and to the division between a more progressive neoliberalism and a more conservative one. Some of the 'progressive' Latin American leaders hold more conservative positions in relation to social values, especially when it comes to gender issues and abortion rights.[48] Svampa notes that Correa's government dismantled a family planning and teenage pregnancy prevention programme guided by public health criteria, even going so far as to place it under the control of people associated with the ultra-conservative Catholic organization Opus Dei.

The proto-fascist far right that emerged in Brazil has found peers in the rest of Latin America. The crucial year is 2015, when a populist hard right returned to the streets in protests and began taking power in a series of elections across Latin America in a 'conservative wave', in direct reaction to the 'pink tide'. Argentina saw the arrival at the presidency in November 2015 of the right-wing coalition led by Mauricio Macri, now called *Juntos por el Cambio* (Together for Change), after twelve years of governments headed by Néstor Kirchner and then Cristina Fernández de Kirchner. Macri was not elected, however, on a platform of polarizing the electorate; on the contrary, in the middle of the electoral race Macri declared himself a Peronist. Even though the right-wing opposition to the Kirchner governments was far from weak, and was able to launch a (failed) corruption investigation against Cristina Kirchner, until recently there were no political forces that clearly identified as far-right movements. Amid the rise of the so-called 'new right' on the continent, Cristina Kirchner's return as vice-president, in the 2019 election that brought the left-leaning Alberto Fernández to the presidency, was the political fact that awakened an actual far right in Argentina.[49]

In Chile, there was no fundamental rupture with the far right in state institutions after the Pinochet dictatorship (with Pinochet becoming a senator for life), or the neoliberal policies the far right had mandated. For instance, the cadres of UDI (*Unión Demócrata Independiente*, the party founded in 1983 by Jaime Guzmán and the architect of the 1980 Constitution that is now being overturned) remained in powerful positions even during the *Concertación* (coalition of parties for democracy) governments of the centre-left in power from 1990-2010. The Chilean far right, through the candidacy of José Antonio Kast, obtained a significant number of votes in the elections that returned businessman and former president Sebastián Piñera to power in 2018. The social mobilizations (*estallido*) that took to the streets of Santiago in October 2019 were directed against both the legacy of Pinochet's dictatorship and the enduring neoliberal policy regime. The defenders of the former dictator, however, did not watch in silence. In addition to the brutal state violence that led to the death of over thirty young people, and blinded hundreds of others, there was also 'private violence' by the far right through attacks, death threats, and so on. For instance, during campaigns for the Plebiscite on the Constitution, held in October 2020, weapons were found in bunkers linked to the 'no' campaign opposed to the formation of a new constituent assembly. The discourse of the 'no' campaign was representative of a broad sector of the Chilean ruling classes, pressuring President Piñera, who had always politically condemned the past dictatorship, to offer a series of nods and concessions – what Renton refers to as 'convergence' – to the far right in the rest of his term. In a deeply symbolic gesture, Piñera appointed to the Ministry of Education a great-niece of Pinochet, who would soon defend a ban on 'gender ideology teaching'.[50]

In contrast to Brazil, in neither Argentina nor Chile has the cult of the dictatorial past become as widespread or as much part of the common sense. It has been much more difficult for the far right in these countries to maintain a symbolic and even intimate connection to the violent dictatorial regimes of their past as explicitly as Bolsonaro does in Brazil. Still, the hard right in Latin America is increasingly open about their anti-democratic instincts. For example, the former Argentine president Eduardo Duhalde spoke in August 2020 (just eight months after Alberto Fernández's inauguration as president) of the supposed 'need' for a coup d'état.[51]

If we can see a political renewal of the radical right in Latin America from 2015 onwards, the big corporate media in Latin American countries also started to give more space around that time to an 'intellectual renewal' of the far right through such figures as Agustín Laje (Fundación Libre) and Javier Milei in Argentina; Axel Kaiser in Chile; and Gloria Alvarez (Atlas Foundation) in Guatemala. The 1996 bestseller, *Manual del perfecto idiota latinoamericano* (*Guide to the Perfect Latin American Idiot*) by Álvaro Vargas Llosa, Carlos Alberto Montaner and Plinio Apuleyo Mendoza, had already begun to lay a foundation for a cultural resurgence of a radical right. And the more recent 2016 missive, *El libro negro de la nueva izquierda: Ideología de género o subversión cultural* (*The Black Book of the New Left: Gender Ideology or Cultural Subversion*') by Agustín Laje and Nicolás Márquez, was equally fundamental in spreading this new right agenda across the region, as was the pervasive presence of all these authors in social media. In this way, a leader like Macri could take office in Argentina as a 'pragmatic' neoliberal, but be pushed further to the right by other social forces that were building a base for the radical right – and themselves – on the terrain of so-called 'culture wars' against anything that might refer to liberal and leftist agendas.

In this respect, the influence exerted in Latin America by the far-right Spanish party Vox is also noteworthy in setting up the broad left as the target for the radical right. By founding the 'Anti-Foro de São Paulo' (the conference of leftist political parties across South America initiated by the PT in 1990) in Madrid the party, led by Francoist and neo-fascist deputy Santiago Abascal, has managed to bring together different expressions of the Latin American radical right.[52]

IN THE FACE OF THE PANDEMIC

The legacy of asymmetric polarization in the Brazilian party system, and the fictious polarizations successfully pursued by the far right, have been brought into sharp relief by the arrival of the pandemic. Faced with a devastating loss of more than 500,000 lives in Brazil from Covid-19, the result of the genocidal policy promoted by Jair Bolsonaro's government, the social problems and grotesque inequalities of Brazil have become even more dire. By the end of 2020 the most elementary degree of poverty – hunger – was experienced by fifty-eight million people (27.7 per cent of the population) in Brazil.[53] In addition, while unemployment reached 15 per cent of the population, the pandemic has raised the proportion of the adult population that work via digital platforms (such as Uber drivers, food delivery workers, and personal caregivers) in Brazil to 20 per cent.[54]

The situation is even more serious for women: thirteen million women lost their jobs in Latin America during the pandemic, today amounting to twenty-five million unemployed women in the region.[55] At the same time, the number of Latin American billionaires has increased by 40 per cent during the pandemic.[56] Sixty-five Brazilian billionaires are on Forbes Magazine's list – twenty of whom have been bumped on to it during the pandemic.[57] This is the *true polarization* that is at the centre of Brazilian, and indeed Latin American, capitalism. It is the setting in which social struggles will need to be rebuilt to face the economic and social wreckage aggravated by the pandemic.

To confront the emergence of a far right with its proto-fascist elements, it is essential to recompose the organizational forms of anti-capitalist struggle. These forms are being renewed by anti-racist, feminist, indigenous, LGBTQ+ struggles, as well as by anti-fascist and anti-imperialist struggles. But they need to maintain, above all, their working-class 'spirit of cleavage', that is, their anti-capitalist character.

NOTES

1   Rodrigo Nunes, 'Todo lado tem dois lados', *Revista Serrote*, 16 June 2020, available at: www.revistaserrote.com.br.

2   Nunes, 'Todo lado tem dois lados'.

3   Paulo Arantes, 'Entre destroços do presente' (entrevista), *Blog da Boitempo*, 10 April 2015, available at: blogdaboitempo.com.br.

4   Nancy Fraser, 'From progressive neoliberalism to Trump and beyond', *American Affairs*, 1(4), 2017.

5   Nunes, 'Todo lado tem dois lados'.

6   Nancy Fraser, 'From progressive neoliberalism to Trump and beyond'.

7   According to Paulo Arantes, 'the new right ended up leading a wave of re-politicization, on its own terms, of course, but no less real, by reintroducing the enemy into the crony game of current political affairs'. And for Rodrigo Nunes, with the economy 'shielded' by the neoliberal consensus, the polarized dispute of politics – and therefore, its 're-politicization' – took place in the field of culture, in what came to be called 'cultural wars'. See Paulo Arantes, 'Entre destroços do presente'; and Rodrigo Nunes, 'Todo lado tem dois lados'.

8   See Pierre Dardot and Christian Laval, *The New Way of the World: on Neoliberal Society*, London: Verso, 2017; Wendy Brown. *In the Ruins of Neoliberalism: The Rise of Antidemocratic Politics in the West*, New York: Columbia University Press, 2019; Marco Boffo, Alfred Saad-Filho, and Ben Fine, 'Neoliberal Capitalism: The Authoritarian Turn', in Leo Panitch and Greg Albo eds, *Socialist Register 2019: A World Turned Upside Down?* London: Merlin Press, 2018.

9   Boffo, et al, 'Neoliberal capitalism: the authoritarian turn'.

10   'Neoliberal capitalism: the authoritarian turn', p. 257.

11   'Neoliberal capitalism: the authoritarian turn', p. 259.

12   The informality rate in Brazil rose from 32.5 per cent in 2012 (when the crisis effectively took hold in the country) to 41.6 per cent in 2019. Brazilian sociologists Ruy Braga and Ricardo Antunes have produced extensive research on struggles of 'uberized' workers in Brazil and elsewhere, discussing both contemporary labor relations and the new struggle of precarized workers, or 'Infoproletarians'. See 'IBGE: informalidade atinge 41,6% dos trabalhadores no país em 201', *Agência Brasil,* 20 November 2020; Ricardo Antunes and Vitor Filgueiras, 'Plataformas digitais, uberização do trabalho e regulação no capitalismo contemporâneo', *Contracampo*, 39(1), 2020; and Ruy Braga and Ricardo Antunes, *Infoproletários: degradação real do trabalho virtual*, São Paulo: Boitempo, 2009.

13   The growth of these groups was, to a large extent, encouraged by organizations of the Brazilian bourgeoisie. The Federation of Industries of the State of São Paulo (FIESP),

for instance, carried out a campaign for the impeachment of Dilma Rousseff using a yellow duck as a symbol, which became a reference for right-wing protests. See:. 'Empresários redobram pressão contra Governo Dilma e cobram apoio do Congresso', *El País*, 16 March 2016.

14   According to Nunes, 'the journalistic reflex of "telling both sides of the story", even when the statements of one side have no basis in reality, helps manipulators in the creation of a false appearance of symmetry, which is instrumental for those who feed on polarization. Thus, the debunking and apologies of controversial characters will never receive as many shares as the impact headlines in their speeches.' Nunes, 'Todo lado tem dois lados'.

15   A study published by researchers from several areas, including a renowned group from the Paulista School of Medicine at USP, has demonstrated how Jair Bolsonaro's actions have resulted in the spread the new coronavirus. These included: vetoes of state laws on the mandatory use of masks; authorization for churches and temples to operate unrestricted; the inclusion of sectors such as gyms and beauty salons as 'essential' activities; and the distribution, especially among indigenous peoples, of hydroxychloroquine, ivermectin, and other drugs proven ineffective in combating Covid-19. This study supports the work of the Parliamentary Inquiry Commission currently underway in the Brazilian Senate. Together with other research, has served as the basis for four petitions to investigate Bolsonaro filed at the International Criminal Court in the Hague. See: Deisy de Freitas Lima Ventura and Rosana Reis, 'A linha do tempo da estratégia federal de disseminação da covid-19', *Direitos na pandemia: mapeamento e análise das normas jurídicas de resposta à Covid-19 no Brasil*, 10, São Paulo, 2021, pp. 6-31.

16   Nunes, 'Todo lado tem dois lados'.

17   Arantes, 'Entre destroços do presente'.

18   Nunes, 'Todo lado tem dois lados'.

19   Nunes, 'Todo lado tem dois lados'.

20   There were allegations of obscure funding coming from the Koch family in the US to far-right groups in Brazil and Latin America. See: Carolina Schiavon and Katya Braghini, 'Os irmãos Koch miram a América Latina', *Outras Palavras*, 24 Agosto 2020; and 'Irmãos Koch, os donos do mundo, *El País*, 23 September 2019.

21   Nunes, 'Todo lado tem dois lados'.

22   David Renton. *The New Authoritarians: Convergence on the Right*, Chicago: Haymarket Books, 2019.

23   Arantes, 'Entre destroços do presente'.

24   Antonio Gramsci, *Prison Notebooks*, Vol. 3, translated by Joseph A. Buttigieg, New York: Columbia University Press, 1992, Q7 § 16, p. 169.

25   Antonio Gramsci, *Prison Notebooks*, Vol. 2, translated by Joseph A. Buttigieg, New York: Columbia University Press, 1992, Q3 § 49, p. 53.

26   *Prison Notebooks*, Vol. 2, Q 5 §2, p. 269. The Rotary Club is a US-based decentralized association of business and professional leaders undertaking charitable services.

27   Rejane Carolina Hoeveler, *As elites orgânicas transnacionais diante da crise: os primórdios da Comissão Trilateral (1973-1979)*, Niterói: UFF, Masters' Thesis, 2015, pp. 92-173.

28   Sonia Regina de Mendonça, *O ruralismo brasileiro*, São Paulo: Hucitec, 1997.

29   René Armand Dreifuss, *1964: a conquista do Estado. Ação política, poder e golpe de classe*, 5. ed., Petrópolis: Vozes, 1987; and Elaine de Almeida Bortone, *O Instituto de Pesquisas e Estudos Sociais (IPES) e a ditadura empresarial-militar: os casos das empresas estatais federais e*

da indústria farmacêutica (1964-1967), Rio de Janeiro: UFRJ, Doctoral Thesis in History, 2018.

30 It was particularly the case with associative entities linked to engineering and construction companies. See: Pedro Henrique Pedreira Campos, *Estranhas Catedrais*, Niteroi: EDUFF, 2017.

31 Flavio Henrique Calheiros Casimiro, *A nova direita – aparelhos de ação política e ideológica no Brasil contemporâneo*, São Paulo: Expressão Popular, 2018.

32 André Silva Martins, *A direita para o social: a educação da sociabilidade no Brasil contemporâneo*, Juiz de Fora: Editora UFJF, 2009.

33 For example, the *Líderes do Amanhã* program, offered by the *Instituto de Estudos Empresariais-Forum da Liberda*de in association with US-based organizations such as the Atlas Institute, is focused on the training of heirs. More recent initiatives include: *Politize!* (led by 'young entrepreneurs'); *RenovaBR* (founded by a financial sector entrepreneur who works in education); the *RAPS-Rede de Ação Política Pela Sustentabilidade* (created by one of the owners of the Brazilian multinational corporation Natura); and several programs carried out by the Lemann Foundation (co-owner of several companies, including AB InBEV). All have aimed to form 'leaders that promote social impact'. See: Lísia Nicoliello Cariello, *Construindo redes de intelectuais orgânicos: o Programa de Bolsas de Estudos Lemann Fellowship da Fundação Lemann (2007-2018)*, Niterói: UFF, Masters Thesis in History, 2021.

34 From 105,000 in 1996 to 276,000 in 2002, and in 2018 reaching 820,000 entities. See: Instituto Brasileiro de Geografia e Estatística (IBGE), *As Fundações Privadas e Associações sem Fins Lucrativos no Brasil 2005*, Estudos e Pesquisas de Informação Econômica 8, Rio de Janeiro: IBGE, 2008; IBGE, *As Fundações Privadas e Associações sem Fins Lucrativos no Brasil 2010*, Rio de Janeiro: IBGE, 2012; and Felix Garcia Lopez, Org., *Perfil das organizações da sociedade civil no Brasil*, Brasília: IPEA, 2018.

35 André Pereira Guiot. *Dominação burguesa no Brasil: estado e sociedade civil no Conselho de Desenvolvimento Econômico e Social (CDES) entre 2003 e 2010*, Niterói: UFF, Doctoral Thesis in History, 2015.

36 For examples: *Todos pela Educação* (formulation, control, evaluation and implementation of basic educational policies shaped by the business sector); *Movimento pela Base* (formulation and implementation of new curriculum for public schools with a capital-led pedagogical structure); *COMUNITAS* (contracts with municipalities and state governments to monitor the integral management process of public entities); *Movimento Brasil Competitivo* (partnership with the federal government to 'modernize' public management centered on managerial models). See: Nivea Silva Vieira and Rodrigo Lamosa, *Todos pela Educação? Uma Década De Ofensiva Do Capital Sobre As Escolas Públicas*, Appris: Curitiba, 2020; and Anderson Tavares, *Transformações no aparelho de Estado e dominação burguesa no Brasil (1990-2010)*, Niterói: UFF, Doctoral Thesis in History, 2020.

37 Eurelino Teixeira Coelho Neto, *Uma esquerda para o capital – o transformismo dos grupos dirigentes do PT (1979-1998)*, São Paulo: Xamã, 2012.

38 Anticommunism in Brazil is constitutive of, and in practice constitutes, a deep rejection of any popular democratic participation and to forms of popular nationalism. The only pole – anti-communism – did not confront revolutionary organizations.

39 A masterful study that analyzes the network of intersections between the Brazilian and international far rights, the American CIA, and various Brazilian state agencies between

1936 and 1964 is: Vicente Gil da Silva, *Planejamento e organização da contrarrevolução preventiva no Brasil: atores e articulações transnacionais (1936-1964)*, Rio de Janeiro: UFRJ, Doctoral Thesis in History, 2020.

40   Recently, an editorial in one of the largest corporate media newspapers in Brazil wrote: 'No more blackmail. The Nation can no longer stand blackmail. Enough with the threats to Republican institutions and to the democratic regime that Brazilians have recovered through great sacrifice. It is time for courage and determination in defence of freedom. President Jair Bolsonaro no longer meets the conditions to remain in office.' Antonio Carlos Pereira, 'Chega de chantagem', *O Estado de São Paulo*, 7 November 2021.

41   'Super pedido de impeachment de Bolsonaro: quais os 23 crimes de responsabilidade listados no documento', *BBC Brasil*, 1 July 2021.

42   The Globo TV network and corporate national newspapers have come to oppose Jair Bolsonaro's government for the criminal neglect of the pandemic. Yet, the same media support the government's liberal economic policy, including fiscal austerity, pension reform, and ongoing privatizations. Such media also integrate and promote PHAs in various fields, such as education, agri-business, and social sectors.

43   Bolsonaro is being accused of crimes against humanity at the International Criminal Court in the Hague for the criminal mismanagement of the pandemic. There was already an accusation, presented at the Hague court in 2019, for human rights violations committed against indigenous peoples during his first year in government. See: 'Ação contra Bolsonaro avança em Haia, e indígenas vão denuncia-lo por genocídio e por ecocídio', *El País*, 30 June 2021.

44   Maristela Svampa. 'Yaku Perez y otra izquierda posible', *El DiarioAR*, 8 February 2021, available at: www.eldiarioar.com

45   Svampa 'Yaku Perez y otra izquierda posible'.

46   'Yaku Perez y otra izquierda posible'.

47   'Yaku Perez y otra izquierda posible'.

48   Paul Angelo and Will Freedman, 'A socially conservative left is gaining traction in Latin America', *Americas Quarterly*, 23 June 2021. The article expresses a US liberal vision that we do not share, but it synthesizes conservative positions in terms of gender and LGBTQ+ rights among progressive leaders on the continent and praises, in turn, those leaders that were closest to the US, in countries such as Chile, Costa Rica, Colombia, or Lula's Brazil, for liberal positions in this regard.

49   Pablo Stefanoni, *¿La rebeldía se volvió de derecha? Cómo el antiprogresismo y la anticorrección política están construyendo um nuevo sentido común (y por qué la izquierda debería tomarlos en serio)*, Buenos Aires: Siglo Veinteuno, 2021.

50   'Piñera nombra a sobrina nieta de Pinochet a cargo del Ministerio de la Mujer', *El Mostrador*, 5 May 2020.

51   'Eduardo Duhalde: La Argentina puede tener um golpe de Estado', *La Nación*, 25 August 2020.

52   'O VOX aterrissa na América Latina', *Revista Ópera*, 7 June 2021.

53   'Fome no Brasil cresce e supera taxa de quando Bolsa Família foi criado', *Deutsche Welle Brasil*, 13 April 2021.

54   'Do WhatsApp ao Uber: 1 em cada 5 trabalhadores usa apps para ter renda', *UOL Economia*, 12 May 2021.

55 'OIT: Covid deixou 13 milhões de mulheres da América Latina sem emprego', *UOL Economia*, 3 March 2021.

56 A mere 107 people have accumulated US$ 408 billion in assets in Latin America and the Caribbean. See: 'Número de bilionários latino-americanos aumenta 40% durante a pandemia de coronavírus', *El País*, 28 May 2021.

57 'Lista de bilionários da Forbes ganha 20 brasileiros e tem crescimento recorde na pandemia', *BBC Brasil*, 7 April 2021.

IDENTITY CRISIS:
THE POLITICS OF FALSE CONCRETENESS

SAMIR GANDESHA

The global emergence of authoritarianism has, unsurprisingly, provoked analogies with the Weimar period.[1] Yet caution must be exercised when reasoning by historical analogy.[2] Capitalism has always embodied a sacrificial logic, and the deepening of such logic lies at the heart of its redoubled authoritarian potential today. But how are we to understand the logic of new forms of polarization based on the contradictions produced by neoliberal globalization? While we ought not so easily be swayed by analogical reasoning, the European interwar period might yet hold some unexpected lessons for us today.

Accordingly, it is worthwhile to turn to Max Weber's account of rationalization and the responses to this phenomenon by thinkers of the German 'conservative revolution'. Weber and his critical interlocutors can help us to grasp some of the key dimensions of the contemporary contradictions of globalizing neoliberalism, and the political polarization generated in its wake with the waning of a politics grounded in critical analysis of capital, class, and social totality. As Ray Kiely observed in the *2019 Socialist Register*: 'There are some parallels here with the radical conservatives of 1930s Germany, as Trump can be seen as an attempt to re-enchant a world of bureaucratic rationalization (albeit this time where the rationalization has occurred through the market).'[3]

Neoliberalism exacerbates the rationalization tendencies of capitalist modernization through heightened processes of institutional and ideological abstraction. This means the unceasing subordination of qualitative human needs and aspirations to the quantitative monetary values of the market and the dynamics of capital accumulation. Such processes come under pressure in moments of crisis, giving rise to a fragmentation of the universalism that had historically underwritten the struggle for socialism, leading to aspirations to what could be called a false concreteness centred on a particularistic form of identity on both the contemporary right as well as the left. Each of these forms of 'false concreteness' eschews universalism, and has thus contributed to the crippling polarizations of our times. On the right, this has taken the form of authoritarian ethno-nationalism. On the left, identity politics, far from challenging the neoliberal consensus, only reinforces its iron grip.[4] In these ways, neoliberalism's deepening of the increasingly abstract nature of social life under capitalism redoubles tendencies towards re-enchantment as a way of providing *false* solutions to *real* problems.[5]

After looking at the radical conservative response to Weber's diagnosis of modernity, I turn to neoliberalism's heightening of abstraction, before showing the way in which identity politics represents an ostensible response to this logic by seeking to grasp the concrete or the particular in its immediacy. In conclusion, I suggest a way in which class analysis can provide a genuine alternative to such a politics, one that articulates what Ato Sekyi-Otu calls 'left universalism'.

RATIONALIZATION AND ITS DISCONTENTS

In his famous lectures 'Politics as a Vocation' and 'Science as a Vocation', delivered at the University of Munich in the midst of the ill-fated German Revolution in 1918, Max Weber sums up certain key themes of his research agenda:

> ... the growing process of intellectualization and rationalization does *not* imply a growing understanding of the conditions under which we live. It means something quite different. It is the knowledge or the conviction that if *only we wished* to understand them we *could* do so at any time. It means that in principle, then, we are not ruled by mysterious, unpredictable forces, but that, on the contrary, we can in principle *control everything by means of calculation.* That in turn means the disenchantment of the world. Unlike the savage for whom such forces existed, we need no longer have recourse to magic in order to control the spirits or pray to them. Instead, technology and calculation achieve our ends. This is the primary meaning of the process of intellectualization.[6]

What Weber suggests is that the very emergence of science as a form of intellectualization means that the totality of the world is subject to rational calculation. Rationalization, in Weber's view, entails a further assumption: disenchantment, or the idea that the world is no longer to be understood as governed by inscrutable forces. It is through rationalization that the world becomes subjected to ever greater control which, in an important sense, furthers human freedom, understood as the increasing subjection of the natural world to human aims and intentions. This form of freedom, however, is purchased at a tremendous cost, and this cost, paradoxically, extends to, and puts into question, the very meaningfulness of the practice of scientific activity itself. If scientific research, itself premised upon a logic of ever-increasing specialization, is chained to a notion of progress in calculability and mastery of an increasingly disenchanted nature (this includes human 'nature'), then this activity becomes subject to a deep crisis of meaning, insofar as the results of scientific activity are rendered obsolete at an ever-quickening pace.[7]

Consequently, the relationship between the different spheres of value that were once closely integrated – namely, science, morality, and art – are now separate from each other and occasionally conflicting. It is precisely such a differentiation of value spheres, in Weber's view, that produces the modern crisis of meaning.[8] Thus intellectualization generates the following question: Why ought scientists engage in research that is certain to be superseded by the heady rush of historical progress? The formal nature of the scientific method employed by myriad disciplines beyond the natural sciences deeply affects aesthetics, jurisprudence, the historical and cultural sciences, as well as the social sciences. The formal and specialized nature of the sciences that are increasingly obsessed with questions of method generate a need for answers to the fundamental questions of life: 'What shall we do? How shall we live?'[9]

It was within the context of the Weimar Republic that we see a very different attempt to address the empty procedural form of liberalism, now not from the left but from the right. In the very year that Weber's lectures were published, Carl Schmitt came out with a book in which he takes direct aim at what he calls 'political romanticism'. In The Concept of the Political, Schmitt responds to Weber's articulation of the crisis of political meaning. Such a crisis results, not just from the domination of science and technology, but more generally from the process of formalization of reason within that novel structure of power that, according to Weber's typology, displaces both charismatic and traditional forms: namely, legal-rational authority.[10] The authority of government is simply an outcome of correct procedures and rules.

In this text, Schmitt attacks the bourgeois, liberal-parliamentary conception of politics as based on empty and inconsequential discussion and compromise, and defends a form of political existentialism, which responds directly to the crisis of authority – itself rooted in the crisis of meaning. With such a conception, Schmitt infamously defines what he calls 'the political', by which he means the essence of politics, as the moment at which the enemy comes into view as such; the latter threatens our entire way of life.[11] The contemporary period of polarization based on an ethno-nationalist opposition of friend and foe owes much to the spirit of Carl Schmitt.[12]

In the interwar years, a period of massive geopolitical, social and economic dislocation, Martin Heidegger, another thinker who would, like Schmitt, infamously join the ranks of the Nazis, registered the crisis of meaning most directly in his early opus *Being and Time*.[13] Eschewing historical explanations of such a crisis in a manner that would profoundly influence contemporary post-structuralism and, by extension, post-colonial theory, Heidegger argues that one ought to look at the tradition of Western metaphysics for its 'forgetting of being'. In other words, meaning was in crisis because of a conflation of the human being – the being for whom meaning is constitutive – with other mere beings or mere things. Heidegger's account of the situated, meaning-oriented nature of the human being (what he calls *Dasein*) implicitly answers Weber's analysis of the crisis of meaning stemming from the logic of specialization in the sciences, insofar as it states that prior to any objective, or what he dismissively calls an 'ontic' account of the nature of reality, comes the question of the 'meaning of being'. Keeping in mind Heidegger's invocation of the German 'volk' in *Being and Time* as, at least, a partial answer to the crisis of the meaning of Being, it is not difficult to see how contemporary identity politics, in its own emphasis on collective cultural identities, represents a modern version of false concreteness.[14]

While the historical analogy of the Weimar period clearly has its limits, one can say that, each in their own way, these thinkers of the German far right, among others, were responding to the failure of the German Revolution. Each could be said to represent an attempt to address or confront the increasingly abstract nature of modern society as Weber had defined it, in terms of rationalization, disenchantment, the domination of a procedural form of rationality indexed to a legal-rational form of authority. Such abstraction, for these far-right intellectuals, led to a deep crisis of political, aesthetic, and ontological meaning. Each appealed to concrete experience in providing alternatives to the growing power of abstraction in the early twentieth century. Yet, all these thinkers provide a false or a pseudo-response to the crisis because they failed, like their interlocutor Max Weber, to get to the root of the matter. This was the increasing domination of capital, and what Alfred Sohn-Rethel called the logic of 'real abstraction', which is to say, *the domination of the commodity form*.

In a chapter entitled 'The Commodity Abstraction' in his book *Intellectual and Manual Labour*, Sohn-Rethel argues that abstractness governs the commodity in three ways: (1) it is abstract insofar as it is the bearer of exchange value; (2) the concrete appearance of commodity-value is money, which is to say an 'abstract *thing*', and therefore a contradiction in terms; and the key point, (3) 'Lastly a society in which commodity exchange forms the *nexus rerum* (social bond) is a purely abstract set of relations where everything concrete is in private hands'.[15]

Sohn-Rethel's argument about the division of intellectual and manual labour, a division that is inextricable from the deepening of commodity exchange, is taken up in Adorno's *Dialectic of Enlightenment* and expanded in the genealogy of the logic of the self-subverting drive towards self-preservation: Idealism as 'belly turned mind'.[16] For Adorno, in contrast to the philosophies of 'bourgeois interiority', a genuine grasp of materiality or the concrete entailed an understanding of the 'preponderance of the object'.[17] This means that the concrete was not accessible directly through *immediate experience* but, rather, was revealed in the form of a constellation comprised of three dimensions: the relation (what Marx calls 'metabolism') between forms of human society and nature; relations between subjects within society (i.e. class relations); and the relation of subjects to themselves, which entails not just the internalization of ideological formations, but also the dimension of psychodynamics: libidinal and aggressive drives, eros and thanatos.

The implication was that, in his very attempt to move beyond idealism, Heidegger re-inscribes it insofar as he places the question of the subjective category of historicity above a materialist understanding of the entwinement of nature and history, object and subject, understood as the progressive mastery of external and internal nature. As a result, what we see in Heidegger is an elision of the question of *the socio-historical sources of the problem of abstraction*. Heidegger's inability to grasp the situated human being as a form of what Adorno calls 'society unaware of itself', which is grounded in the division between intellectual and manual labour, merely repeats such abstraction, so that the attempt to grasp the concrete falls short. The ontological critique of reification becomes, as a result, reified.

Each of the dimensions of existentialism has returned in forms of identity that attempt to re-territorialize what had, through a constellation of crises amidst the contradictions of a global neoliberal order, become de-territorialized.[18] At the heart of this development is a claim to 'authenticity' that answers the problem of a nihilistic crisis of meaning in a period ever more subject to violent, yet ever-more inscrutable, permutations of logic of abstraction. What we see, with the global spread of neoliberal forms of abstraction is an increasing drive to gain access to the 'concrete'. Such a drive takes the form of the rise of new or atavistic forms of collective identity, precisely in such a drive to grasp the concrete, including in left 'identity politics'.[19] Before analyzing contemporary identity politics, it is important to look somewhat more closely at neoliberalism.

NEOLIBERALISM AND THE DEEPENING OF ABSTRACTION

Neoliberalism, it has often been remarked, is notoriously difficult to grasp, and a common pitfall is to overstate its novelty. It has often been defined as a set of four overlapping and mutually reinforcing policies and practices: deregulation, privatization, polarized redistribution of wealth and income, and accumulation by dispossession.[20] To this, a fifth could be added: financialization, burgeoning household and sovereign debt linked to a reduction of all human action to decisions about an abstract portfolio of assets.[21] Neoliberalism has, therefore, also been characterized as a new form of construing the 'conduct of conduct' or 'governmentality'.[22] It has been conceived, moreover, as the displacement *of homo politicus* by *homo economicus,* amounting to a pervasive and total marketization of politics.[23] None of which, as Leo Panitch and Sam Gindin have suggested, should prompt us to think of these processes as somehow rolling back the capitalist state. Rather, they are tied to distinct class forces operating both within and through states themselves.[24]

In fact, ordo-liberalism (the immediate post-war German forerunner to modern neoliberalism) was identified in the post-war writings of Carl Schmitt as consisting of a 'strong state and free market'. Ordo-liberalism, in other words, required strong state intervention to maintain market freedom. It was, in this sense, the opposite of laissez-faire. It was through these means that ordo-liberalism was geared to transforming potentially rebellious workers, acting in solidarity according to a logic of class conflict, into atomized subjects competing with one another as individuals.[25] As we shall see, this logic of difference and division crystallizes in identity politics as the ideology of neoliberal capitalism in which an increasingly precarious working class turns against itself.[26]

While discussions of neoliberalism are quick to indicate the way in which it represents a dramatic break with the Keynesian welfare state it supplants, its novelty must not be overstated. Rather than a qualitatively new form of society, neoliberalism represents a social order in which existing tendencies within capitalism are deepened and sharpened. The most important such tendency of which is the acceleration of the logic of abstraction.

A cursory examination of the genealogy of the concept of abstraction in the previous century bears this out, from Marx's account of commodity fetishism, through Lukács' theory of reification, to Debord's concept of the society of the spectacle.[27] It also, of course, underlies Sohn-Rethel's argument about 'real abstraction'. Each one shows the increasing pervasiveness of *abstract labour* as the principle means of social mediation.[28] Such pervasiveness has generated a tendency to understand the key political fault-line as that between abstract and concrete labour, which has led all too often to the personification of the former in opposition to the latter. Such an understanding negates the possibility of conceiving of the unity of both.[29]

The original version of this argument can be found in Horkheimer and Adorno's *Dialectic of Enlightenment,* which could be said to uncannily anticipate key dimensions of neoliberalism, not least the damage it does to subjectivity and the way in which such damage leads to a tendency to embrace destructive identitarian and collectivist fantasies.[30] Faced with a social world marked by a Hobbesian war of all against all, an apparent state of nature that is, in fact, the natural–historical reality of capitalism,[31] individuals must divest themselves of empathy and become cold and hard to be able to compete against others in the interest of self-preservation. They must subordinate themselves to, and therefore identify with, the external imperatives of the prevailing performance principle. At the same time, to do this successfully, such an adaptation to the outside must be introjected or internalized. This takes the form of an internalization of sacrifice or self-renunciation.

The neoliberal subject is, therefore, at its core self-sacrificial, and fundamentally constituted by guilt. The psychic cost of this dialectic of identification with, and introjection of, external forces in the interest of self-preservation is a diminution of the capacity of the self to fully experience the world, and to think and act within it. The self is reduced to a bundle of unreflective, quasi-automatic reactions to external stimuli. And this entails dissociation. The life that is to be preserved at all costs turns, paradoxically, into mere existence; it becomes a kind of living death. The accumulation of aggression that results from deepening repression and sublimation is unleashed on 'out-groups', or what Schmitt calls political 'enemies', a term which has returned with particular valency and force in the contemporary period.[32]

In intensifying the process of disenchantment and rationalization Weber identifies, neoliberalism thus generates a retreat to ethno–national identities to re-enchant a world increasingly governed by what is perceived to be a cold, empty, and oppressive rationality. This contradiction, which was always at the heart of capitalism, is produced out of, on the one hand, the ideal of individual freedom and autonomy, whereby individuals are held increasingly responsible for their lives. Yet, on the other hand, there is a drastic diminution of the resources necessary for that responsibility to be properly assumed, as public goods and social services are re-commodified.[33] As a result of the widening gap between subjective imperatives and objective conditions, as Michael Kidron put it, neoliberal capitalism produces 'injured selves'. Such injured selves are increasingly susceptible, psychologically, to an 'identification with the aggressor'.[34]

THE POLITICS OF FALSE CONCRETENESS

Along with a raft of articles and books on the subject in the aftermath of the 2016 election, one of the best accounts to date of identity politics is Asad Haider's book, *Mistaken Identity: Race and Class in the Age of Trump*.[35] Haider offers a genealogy of an identity politics as being initially central to a revolutionary transformation of a racist, patriarchal-capitalist order, to its recent cynical appropriation by the Democratic Party.[36] Absent a structural critique of capitalism, Haider argues, identity politics ends up taking bourgeois, heterosexual, white, masculinist subjectivity as normative. He poignantly shows how identity politics has not only become the ideology of the prevailing neoliberal order, as critics such as Walter Benn Michaels and Adolph Reed Jr. have also cogently argued,[37] but also short-circuits genuine movements on the left seeking to transform it.[38] This is a key point to which I shall return in my conclusion.

Haider addresses the deep paradox of the tenacious attachment among young activists to the idea of race, although it has been thoroughly demystified as possessing little or no substance in biological terms. Haider seeks to understand the rise of Trump through Stuart Hall's pioneering work on authoritarian populism as well as Wendy Brown's development of Walter Benjamin's notion of 'left-wing melancholy' – the full-scale embrace by the left of its own marginality and failure, and its stubborn refusal to innovate a new form of 'cultural politics' to meet the challenges of the present.[39] Haider develops an alternative that returns to the original spirit of the earliest statement of identity politics by articulating a case for an 'insurgent universality', based not on an abstract concept of rights-bearers but, rather, on 'particular and concrete individuals – women, the poor, and slaves – and their political and social agency' in making history as in, for example, the Haitian Revolution. Haider locates the origins of identity politics in the black radical tradition, in the earlier, pioneering work of the black lesbian feminist Combahee River Collective.[40] At the same time, however, Haider articulates a concern about the capacity of identity politics today to serve as the basis for a radical political agenda. In contrast to dismissals based on a reconstructed liberalism, Haider engages in a genuinely immanent critique of identity politics; that is, he criticizes its contemporary *practice* based on its own best and strongest *theoretical* self-understanding.

In attempting to understand identity politics, Haider makes the correct claim that it is of vital importance to get the relation between the abstract and the concrete right. He argues that 'A materialist mode of investigation has to go from the abstract to the concrete – it has to bring this abstraction back to earth by moving through the historical specificities and material relations that have put it in our heads'.[41] In my view, it is vital to situate identity politics, however, in a somewhat different understanding of the relation between the abstract and the concrete. In contemporary identity politics, race, gender, ethnicity, sexual orientation, and other identities demand recognition and affirmation, and in societies constituted, in part, by the misrecognition or non-recognition of these identities. This is not unreasonable.[42] Indeed, the desire for such recognition and affirmation is a desire for immediate access to the concrete and the meaningful in a world dominated by inscrutable abstractions. Yet 'class identity' cannot be understood in quite the same way. Thought in radical terms, class identity is not simply an empirical sociological category, but manifests a form of structural negativity that, as such, demands its own *negation*. Just as people who are homeless, far from wanting their homeless condition to be recognised and affirmed, want it to be eliminated through, amongst other things, the provision of adequate employment, housing, and other public goods. Capital cannot properly 'include' the proletariat on whose un-remunerated surplus labour its own expanded reproduction is premised.

In other words, while other identity markers may have a legitimate interest in recognition and affirmation that can be met within the existing order, the 'identity' of the working class simply cannot be so affirmed. *It is a structural impossibility*. The identity of the working class, Adorno would argue, is precisely non-identical. The realization of proletarian identity is therefore, in the final instance, negative rather than affirmative. Such 'identity', unlike most other identities, has an interest in its own self-dissolution, along with that of class society as such. I would suggest that rather than an individualistic, rights-based model, as Haider argues in invoking Butler, identity politics is based on the false appearance of a viable, *concrete* alternative to the rule of abstraction. Insofar as identity politics rejects the critique of political economy, it cannot but repeat and reinforce the very form of abstraction it ostensibly opposes and contests.

This can be seen in the way in which identity politics entails a *proprietary* relation to a reified form of experience – unchanging, fixed, substantive – understood as the possession or property of a given group that is, paradoxically, constituted by that very form of experience. In German, the word for authenticity, or *Eigentlichkeit,* is closely associated with the word for property, or *Eigentum*. Identity politics often makes an exclusionary claim to authenticity and therefore concreteness, and such claims are closely linked to questions of ownership rights.[43] Such an exclusionary claim lies at the heart of the contemporary politics of polarization.

BACK TO THE FUTURE: FROM IDENTITY TO CLASS POLITICS

While in the guise of 'intersectionality' identity politics appears to be cognizant of class difference, if one looks more closely this is not necessarily the case. Indeed, attempts to centre structural analysis are met with the charge of 'class reductionism'.[44] And the elision of class undermines a universalistic and solidaristic counter-hegemonic politics based on, for example, the kind of cross-racial alliances envisioned by the Black Panther Party as articulated by one of its most inspiring young leaders, Fred Hampton, who was brutally murdered in his prime by the FBI. It negates the very possibility of what philosopher Ato Sekyi-Otu, writing from a post-colonial African context, calls 'left universalism' or the idea that universalism is 'an inescapable presupposition of moral judgment in general and critique in particular'.[45] In the absence of such a possibility, we can only expect the logic of polarization to drive an already accelerating authoritarianism, as right-wing demagogues mobilize support based on racialized grievances. Nonetheless, there are important countervailing tendencies that can be built upon.

For example, the African-American author and activist Kimberley Jones recently provided incisive and urgent class analysis of the insurrections that coursed through the US in the wake of the murder of George Floyd in a short, widely-viewed YouTube clip entitled 'How Can We Win?'.[46] It is clear that, while race is a central concern, Jones doesn't make it into a fetish. In a manner that resonates with the crucial work of Keeanga-Yamahtta Taylor, Jones seems to suggest that if we see what has been going on in the wake of the murder of George Floyd in exclusively racial terms, we miss something very important analytically and this, in turn, can lead not only to tactical and strategic missteps, but it can also contribute to fanning the flames of white identity politics. *Indeed, far from confronting the structure of white supremacy, the failure to break with a fetishized idea of race can lead to strengthening, rather than weakening, its iron grip on society, not least because it undermines the possibility of the cross-racial solidarity that has come to be so imperilled by the language of 'allyship'.*[47]

Four aspects of Jones's analysis are especially noteworthy. First, she begins with a withering attack on the condemnatory response of wealthy blacks to the uprising which is, to cite Langston Hughes, 'Go Slow'. Jones is clear that she is viewing things not from the perspective of black people as such, but from the perspective of *poor* blacks. So, her focus isn't simply on the difference between identities, that is, black and white, but also the differences with them, i.e., the differences within the black community, which includes substantive class differences and conflicts. Middle-class blacks who condemn the protestors, rioters, and looters, and, in the process, offer an apology for an unjust and structurally violent social order, like colonial and post-colonial elites, *identify with the aggressor* as a response to the traumatic material of history.

Second, Jones's discussion of the boardgame Monopoly as an analogy for the failure of the social contract in the United States is powerful, and her invocation of Tulsa and Rosewood show the extent to which black socio-economic and political gains have resulted in a white backlash, or 'Whitelash' for short.[48] Donald J. Trump may be regarded as the personification of this, in his rancorous attempt to systematically undo the legacy of the Obama White House, including and especially the Affordable Care Act, even if, at the end of the day, under Obama the socio-economic conditions of black Americans actually worsened to a greater extent than their white counterparts.[49]

Third, Jones claims that the social contract is broken. Here, it is possible to argue the opposite, with reference to Jamaican political theorist Charles Mills's concept of the *racial contract*.[50] This is the idea that the contractarian tradition from Hobbes through Rawls is premised upon the unacknowledged exclusion of black and brown people, and therefore a hidden yet no less consequential white supremacy. One could say that this is the repressed content of political theory. For example, the Lockean idea that North America was *terra nullius* – that the land was 'nobody's' – lent legitimacy to the settler colonial project which, by the way, was a project that consisted of little other than *looting* on a grand scale. So perhaps it's not a matter of the contract being broken at all, but rather its functioning as intended. The point is not that the liberal-democratic social contract ought to be adhered to by way of equal treatment under the law, but fundamentally reconstructed to move beyond the premises of liberal-democracy towards a genuine, which is to say, *socialist* democracy. Liberal-democracy's dreams appear to be deferred infinitely for Black and Indigenous peoples. As Langston Hughes so appositely put it: 'The prize is unattainable.'

The last and most important claim worthy of note is that Jones' rejoinder to wealthy blacks takes the form of a defence of the figure of the 'looter', which she de-fetishizes by refusing a fixation on *what* it is they're doing, i.e., egregiously smashing and grabbing consumer goods, but rather focusing on *why* they are doing it. And this leads to an indictment of capitalism as such. As Marx indicates with his concept of primitive accumulation in Part 8 of

Capital, this is a system that is made possible by looting on a truly spectacular scale, embodying the very real primitivism that is subsequently projected onto its victims:

> The discovery of gold and silver in America, the extirpation, enslavement and entombment in mines of the aboriginal population, the beginning of the conquest and looting of the East Indies, the turning of Africa into a warren for the commercial hunting of black-skins, signalled the rosy dawn of the era of capitalist production.[51]

Jones' argument echoes Guy Debord's essay, 'The Decline and Fall of the Spectacle-Commodity Economy'.[52] Debord draws attention to the almost universal condemnation of the riot – in this case the Watts Uprising of 1965. He singles out remarks by the head of the NAACP at the time, Roy Wilkins, who argued that the riot 'ought to be put down with all necessary force'. Like Jones, Debord understands the uprising not in racial but in class terms, referring to MLK Jr's statement in a recent Paris lecture that Watts wasn't a 'race' but a 'class' riot. What drove the blacks of Watts, according to Debord, is *proletarian* consciousness, which means consciousness that they neither are masters of their own activities nor of their own lives.

The crux of Debord's analysis aims at an inversion of the characterization of looters as the embodiment of animalistic drives. He does so by deploying a concept that he would elaborate in his most famous book one year later, which, in fact, gave direction to the events of May '68 – the concept of the *spectacle*. According to Debord, 'the spectacle is *capital* accumulated to the point where it becomes images'.[53] The spectacular society is the society that creates, amidst real misery and deprivation, the appearance or fantasy of affluence and abundance. Neoliberalism, to reiterate, has only intensified and amplified the spectacular nature of capitalist society.

The spectacle represents a new level of the fetishism of the commodity form, which is an object with a certain use value that satisfies determinate human needs but that is, nonetheless, produced in order to realize its exchange value or profit. For Debord, the looters, far from being animals, represented a human response to dehumanizing conditions, namely, the fact that capitalist society, characterized by generalized commodity production, is a society in which relations between things appear as relations between people and relations between people seem like relations between things.

By challenging the almost theological sanctity of the commodity, the looters re-establish human relationships grounded in gift and potlatch economies. For Debord the racist and colonial 'hierarchy' of the society of the spectacle, people of colour, but particularly black people, are reduced to the status of things. The looters directly circumvent the logic of exchange with the demand for use, which is to say, the satisfaction of needs, however false such needs may be. As he argues, 'The flames of Watts *consummated* the system of consumption … Once it is no longer bought, the commodity lies open to criticism and alteration, whatever particular form it may take.' Yet, such flames immediately call into action the police. The policeman is,

> … the active servant of the commodity, the man in complete submission to the commodity, whose job it is to ensure that a given product of human labor remains a commodity, with the magical property of having to be paid for, instead of becoming a mere refrigerator or rifle – a passive, inanimate object, subject to anyone who comes along to make use of it. In rejecting the humiliation of being subject to police, the blacks are at the same time rejecting the humiliation of being subject to commodities.[54]

Far from being broken, the social contract, as a 'racial contract', to reiterate, functions all-too well: for it is a contract geared to the maintenance of private property, with all the necessary violence and force necessary.[55] An identity politics of authenticity that takes private property as its model, it should go without saying, not only cannot challenge such a contract, but represents a false concreteness that only reinforces its dubious validity.

It is of vital importance to grasp the particular and universal significance of the uprisings, and in the process to make of it more than a 'racial' event, for this is exactly what the far right wants. Rather, we must situate the uprisings that we're seeing within the larger context of a society in which inequalities are deepening. It is also important to place recent developments in the context of a history of social struggles, from Watts in 1965 to Paris in 1968 to Minneapolis in 2020. Police violence is not an effect of a mystical, transhistorical white supremacy, but rather is a manifestation of a racism that flows from the vicissitudes of a social order mediated by the commodity-spectacle, grounded in the sanctification of private property under deepening forms of a socio-economic inequality that, nonetheless, hits black and indigenous communities especially hard. This social order is a historical one – an order that came into being and one from which it is still possible for us to emancipate ourselves.

NOTES

I would like to thank Charles Reeve for his valuable comments on a previous version of this essay. This essay is dedicated to the memory of a chance encounter with L.P. and G. A. in London in November 2018.

1   For an overview of this tendency, see Daniel Bessner and Udi Greenberg, 'The Weimar Analogy', *Jacobin*, 17 December 2016.

2   Alberto Toscano cautions against such analogical reasoning and suggests that, if we look at the temporality of fascism, what he usefully differentiates into an objective 'time for fascism', 'time of fascism', and 'time in fascism', one notices a key difference between our time and the 1930s. This has to do with the fact that in the latter it is possible to argue that fascism was comprised of what Ernst Bloch calls distinct 'non-synchronous' temporalities wherein its 'utopic' content resided, whereas today fascism seeks a completely synchronous temporality. While Toscano's incisive analysis is perhaps applicable to the global north, it is not clear that it can illuminate tendencies in global south, for example in Turkey with Erdogan's dream of the rise of a much vaunted 'Second Caliphate', or in India with Modi's vision of a Hindu Rastra (polity). In other words, the putatively forward-oriented logic of neoliberal capitalist rationalization is combined with a backward-looking attempt to rehabilitate the 'good old days'.

3   Ray Kiely, 'Locating Trump: Paleoconservatism, Neoliberalism, and Anti-Globalization', in Leo Panitch and Greg Albo, eds, *Socialist Register 2019: A World Turned Upside Down?*, London: Merlin Press, 2018, p. 135.

4   See, for example, Adolph Reed Jr., 'Antiracism: A Neoliberal Alternative to the Left', *Dialectical Anthropology*, 42, 2018, pp. 105-15.

5   See Ralph Miliband and Leo Panitch, eds, *Socialist Register 1993: Real Problems, False Solutions*, London: Merlin Press, 1992.

6   Max Weber, *The Vocation Lectures*, translated by Rodney Livingstone, Indianapolis, Indiana: Hackett, 2004, pp. 12-13.

7   Weber, *The Vocation Lectures*, pp. 11-12.

8   Weber, *The Vocation Lectures*, p. 23.

9   Weber, *The Vocation Lectures*, p. 17.

10   Carl Schmitt, *The Concept of the Political*, translated by George Schwab, Chicago: University of Chicago Press, 2007.

11   Schmitt, *The Concept of the Political*.

12   See, for example, Trump's speech on foreign policy from April 2016, in which he claims that Obama treated the US's enemies like friends and its friends like enemies, available at: www.youtube.com/watch?v=ePlopVAV6Hc.

13   Martin Heidegger, *Being and Time*, translated by Joan Stambaugh, Albany, NY: SUNY, 1996.

14   Heidegger states in *Being and Time*: 'But if fateful Dasein, as Being-in-the-world, exists essentially in Being-with Others, its historizing is a co-historizing and is determinative for it as destiny [Geschick]. This is how we designate the historizing of the community, of a people. Destiny is not something that puts itself together out of individual fates, any more than Being-with-one-another can be conceived as the occurring together of several Subjects. Our fates have already been guided in advance, in our Being with one another in the same world and in our resoluteness for definite possibilities. Only

in communicating and in struggling does the power of destiny become free. Dasein's fateful destiny in and with its "generation" goes to make up the full authentic historizing of Dasein' (p. 436). See also the brilliant Simon Fraser University M.A. thesis, written by Stephanie Yu, entitled, 'A Materialist Approach to Heideggerian Anxiety' (2020).

15   Alfred Sohn-Rethel, *Intellectual and Manual Labour*, translated by Martin Sohn-Rethel, London: Macmillan, 1978, p. 19.

16   Theodor W. Adorno, *Negative Dialectics*, translated by E.B. Ashton, New York: Continuum, 2008, p. 23.

17   *Negative Dialectics*, p. 183.

18   This is the meaning of the word revanchism, from the French word for revenge (*revanche*). For an account of the logic of deterritorialization and reterritorialization, see Gilles Deleuze and Félix Guattari, *Anti-Oedipus: Capitalism and Schizophrenia*, translated by Mark Seem and Robert Hurley, London: Penguin, 2009.

19   Yet, there is good reason to suspect that these figures of the German far right haunt our present insofar as they have been brought into the discussion, not least in the pages of a journal that was once devoted to introducing Critical Theory to a North American audience, namely *Telos*. Indeed, one of their regular contributors, who is also an expert on the political theory of Carl Schmitt, is a mentor to Richard Spencer and coined the term 'alt-right'. Moreover, two of the journal's editors, David Pan and Russell Berman, served on the Trump Administration's Committee on Inalienable Rights. The influence of Schmitt on his administration was unmistakable. See note 12.

20   David Harvey, *A Brief History of Neoliberalism*, Oxford: Oxford University Press, 2007.

21   See Costas Lapavitsas, *Financialization in Crisis*, Leiden: Brill, 2011; and Maurizio Lazzarato, *The Making of Indebted Man: An Essay on the Neoliberal Condition*, Cambridge, MA: Semiotext(e), 2012.

22   Michel Foucault, *The Birth of Biopolitics: Lectures at the College de France, 1978-79*, London: Palgrave Macmillan, 2008.

23   Wendy Brown, *Undoing the Demos: Neoliberalism's Stealth Revolution*, Cambridge, MA: Zone Books, 2015.

24   Leo Panitch and Sam Gindin, *The Making of Global Capitalism: The Political Economy of the American Empire*, London: Verso, 2012; and 'Trumping the Empire', in Leo Panitch and Greg Albo, eds, *Socialist Register 2019: A World Turned Upside Down?*, London: Merlin Press, 2018.

25   Werner Bonefeld, *The Strong State and The Free Economy*, Lanham, MD: Roman and Littlefield, 2017, p. 25.

26   See 'Misery and Debt: On the Logic and History of Surplus Populations and Surplus Capital', *Endnotes 2*, April 2010, available at: https://endnotes.org.uk/issues/2/en/endnotes-misery-and-debt.

27   Samir Gandesha and Johan Hartle, eds, *Spell of Capital: Reification and Spectacle*, Amsterdam: University of Amsterdam Press, 2017.

28   See Anselm Jappe's reading of the work of Debord through the concept of value-form in *Guy Debord*, Berkeley: University of California Press, 1999.

29   Moishe Postone, 'Anti-Semitism and National Socialism: Notes on the German Reaction to "Holocaust"', *New German Critique*, 19, 1980, pp. 97–115.

30   Max Horkheimer and Theodor W. Adorno, *Dialectic of Enlightenment*, Palo Alto, CA: Stanford University Press, 2010.

31   See C. B. Macpherson, *The Political Theory of Possessive Individualism from Hobbes to Locke*, Oxford: Oxford University Press, 1962.

32   Horkheimer and Adorno provide a historical genealogy of Schmitt's normative friend-foe opposition.

33   This is incisively documented in the films of Ken Loach, in particular his *I, Daniel Blake* (2016) and *Sorry We Missed You* (2019).

34   Samir Gandesha, 'Identifying with the Aggressor: From the "Authoritarian" to the "Neo-Liberal" Personality', *Constellations*, 25, 2018, pp. 147–64.

35   Asad Haider, *Mistaken Identity: Race and Class in the Age of Trump*, London: Verso, 2018. See also: Mark Lilla, 'The End of Identity Liberalism', *New York Times*, 18 November 2016; Mark Lilla, *The Once and Future Liberal: After Identity Politics*, New York: Harper, 2017; Francis Fukuyama, *Identity: The Demand for Dignity and the Politics of Resentment*, New York: Farrar, Straus and Giroux, 2018; and Kwame Anthony Appiah, *The Lies That Bind: Rethinking Identity*, New York: Liveright, 2018.

36   Haider, *Mistaken Identity*, p. 9. See also: Keeanga-Yamahtta Taylor, *From #Black Lives Matter to Black Liberation*, Chicago: Haymarket Books, 2016; and *How We Get Free: Black Feminism and the Combahee River Collective*, Chicago: Haymarket, 2017.

37   See for example the Special issue of the *The Nation: What Is the Left Without Identity Politics*, 16 December 2016.

38   Haider provides the example of the counter-productive and occasionally comical debates amongst people of colour on the campus of UC Santa Cruz, where Haider was a graduate student, over the use of the word 'occupy' in reference to protests against the administration which had recently raised tuition fees. He also considers the much more serious political conundrum of the 'Afro-Pessimism' of Frank Wilderson that was to exercise growing influence on #BlackLivesMatter insofar as it refused to reciprocate the solidarity offered to the movement by Palestinian activists. This, I think, is the most important aspect of Haider's argument but one that he fails to develop fully enough.

39   Wendy Brown, 'Resisting Left Melancholy', *boundary 2*, 26 (3), 1999, pp. 19-27.

40   See Taylor, *How We Get Free*.

41   Haider, *Mistaken Identity*, p. 11.

42   This is especially the case with black, 'trans', and indigenous identities that have asserted and reasserted themselves, respectively, in recent years with particular force.

43   Such a proprietary relation to experience is especially well exemplified by Hannah Black's infamous open letter attacking White painter Dana Schutz's painting of Emmett Till, the African-American boy beaten to death by white supremacists for allegedly looking at a white woman in 1955, and entitled *Open Casket* (2016), during the Whitney Biennale in 2016. 'The painting,' the letter reiterates several times, 'must go'. Co-signed by some 47 artists, curators, and critics, it demands not only that the painting be removed from the exhibition, but also that it actually be *destroyed*. The key reason for this, according to Black, is that Schutz has *no right* to the experience of black suffering. This demand for the work's destruction, informed by Afro-pessimism, is the logical conclusion of the radical particularism of identity politics, or the idea that identity-based groups are unified by certain experiences that other groups simply have no *right* to. The relationship is one suggestive of property ownership, yet a relationship also overdetermined by a sense that the loss of such property entails not just a monetary loss but an ontological one – a loss of being itself. From this perspective, claims or representations made by members of one group about another are not simply

to be addressed by judgments, and, therefore, criticisms, because such claims and/or representations constitute hateful and harmful attacks on these very groups.

44   As was made clear in the bizarre 'de-platforming' of Adolph Reed, Jr., by the Philadelphia and New York City chapters of the DSA, on the basis of his ostensible 'class reductionism'.

45   Ato Sekyi-Otu, *Left Universalism: Africacentric Essays*, London: Routledge, 2018, p. viii.

46   Available at www.youtube.com/watch?v=llci8MVh8J4. The foregoing analysis draws upon my 'The Consummation of Consumption 1', *openDemocracy*, 2 October 2020; and 'The Consummation of Consumption 2', *openDemocracy*, 3 November 2020.

47   This is the argument of Jodi Dean's *Comrade: An Essay on Political Belonging*, London: Verso, 2019.

48   See Terry Smith, *Whitelash: Unmasking White Grievance at the Ballot Box*, Cambridge: Cambridge University Press, 2020.

49   Taylor, *From #BlackLivesMatter to Black Liberation*. Referring back to the Obama Administration, as sociologist and long-time anti-fascist organizer Helmut-Harry Loewen recently suggested in a private communication, perhaps we could rephrase Michelle Obama's famous bon mot from the 2016 Democratic Convention: 'When they go low, we go slow.'

50   Charles Mills, *The Racial Contract*, Ithaca, NY: Cornell University Press, 1997.

51   Karl Marx, *Capital Volume I: A Critique of Political Economy*, translated by Ben Fowkes, London: Penguin, 1992, p. 915.

52   Guy Debord, 'The Decline and Fall of the Spectacle Economy', translated by Ken Knabb, *Internationale Situationniste*, 10, 1966.

53   Guy Debord, *Society of the Spectacle*, Canberra: Hobgoblin Press, 2002, p. 34.

54   Debord, 'The Decline and Fall'.

55   This recently became amply clear in the actions of the seventeen-year-old, white shooter in Kenosha on 25 August who was there, according to his own account, to help the police defend private property. See Paige Williams, 'Kyle Rittenhouse, American Vigilante', *The New Yorker*, 28 June 2021.

THE DOUBLE CONSCIOUSNESS OF CAPITAL

DAVID HARVEY

In the *Grundrisse,* Marx provides two seemingly antagonistic visions of the role and significance of capital in the history of humanity. In the first, he builds a laudatory account and up-beat assessment of how, through its penchant for creative destruction and technological revolutions, capital can bring us to the cusp of a new form of society, a civilization in which the human species can flourish as never before. I cite the passage at length.

> Capital creates the bourgeois society and the universal appropriation of nature, as well as of the social bond itself by the members of society. Hence, the great civilizing influence of capital; its production of a stage of society in comparison to which all earlier ones appear as mere local developments of humanity and as nature idolatry. For the first time, nature becomes purely an object for humankind, purely a matter of utility; ceases to be recognized as a power for itself; and the theoretical discovery of its autonomous laws appears merely as a ruse, so as to subjugate it under human needs, whether as an object of consumption or as a means of production. In accord with this tendency, capital drives beyond national barriers and prejudices as much as beyond nature worship, as well as all traditional confined, complacent encrusted satisfactions of present needs, and reproductions of old ways of life. It is destructive towards all of this, and constantly revolutionizes it, tearing down all the barriers, which hem in the development of the forces of production, the expansion of needs, the all-sided development of production and the exploitation and exchange of natural and mental forces.[1]

To be sure, this does not mean there is no serious work to be done in engineering the transition to socialism. Marx immediately focuses on the struggle to dissolve the contradiction between productive forces and social relations, but there seems to be nothing seriously problematic about the legacy of capital in pursuing the transformation to socialism. I will refer to this mode of thinking about capital and the path to socialism it presages, as Model 1. But later on, in the midst of his attempt to reconstruct the various pre-capitalist modes of production, Marx offers some very different reflections on how the history of humanity has unfolded with the rise of capital. Here that legacy is seen as deeply problematic, to the point where it constitutes a primary and perhaps insuperable barrier to founding a rosy socialist future.

> The old view, in which the human being appears as the aim of production, regardless of his limited national, religious, political character, seems to be very lofty when contrasted to the modern world, where production appears as the aim of mankind and wealth as the aim of production. In fact, however, when the limited bourgeois form is stripped away, what is wealth other than the universality of individual needs, capacities, pleasures, productive forces, etc., created through universal exchange? The full development of human mastery over the forces of nature, those of so-called nature, as well as of humanity's own nature? The absolute working out of his creative potentialities, with no presupposition other than the previous historic development, which makes this totality of development, i.e. the development of all human powers as such the end in itself, not as measured on a predetermined yardstick? Where he does not reproduce himself in one specificity, but produces his totality? Strives not to remain something he has become, but is in the absolute movement of becoming? In bourgeois economics – and in the epoch of production to which it corresponds – this complete working out of the human content appears as a complete emptying out, this universal objectification as total alienation, and the tearing-down of all limited one-sided aims as sacrifice of the human end in-itself to an entirely external end. This is why the childish world of antiquity appears on one side as loftier. On the other side, it really is loftier in all matters where closed shapes, forms and given limits are sought for. It is satisfaction from a limited standpoint; while the modern gives no satisfaction; or, where it appears satisfied with itself, it is vulgar.[2]

Note the centrality of alienation, of hollowing out, of loss of meaning, of the sacrifice of all human potentiality to Molloch, the god of money power, and the descent into vulgarity of capitalist developmentalism. In this account the raw materials out of which socialism must be built are toxic and tainted to their very core. I will refer to this theorization of capital and the tasks it sets for any socialist transition as Model 2.

DOUBLE CONSCIOUSNESS

The easiest way to interpret and in a sense 'reconcile' these two statements is to suggest that the first is Marx's representation of the bourgeois utopian vision as to what they were achieving and what they were destined to achieve, while the second is a dramatic rendition of Marx's dystopian vision of what the bourgeoisie was actually accomplishing. There is nothing in the context of either statement, however, to support this interpretation. There are, in addition, plenty of other passages in his works where Marx does express open admiration for the very real historical achievements of capital and the bourgeoisie even as he excoriates them for their material practices.

Marx seems to have internalized both visions as parallel tracks within his own mode of thought. In a way, this should not be surprising. He was, after all, deeply sensitive and attuned to the external and the internal contradictions of capital as these played out in the world around him. He was almost certainly powerfully and permanently marked by the contradiction between his bourgeois (albeit Jewish) origins and his revolutionary desires. The *Grundrisse* documents in part his struggle to free himself from the dominant bourgeois interpretations (particularly from Hegel and Ricardo) that he had earlier absorbed. A radicalized bourgeoisie (which was Marx's burden) has, it is worth remarking, played a major role in both shaping and leading revolutionary movements, and in the process it has frequently been dogged by what I choose to call a 'double consciousness' derived from these divergent accounts of capital's nature. By exploring this double consciousness, we stand to learn something important about the ambivalences that characterize thinking about the socialist project today. It may also help us understand why so many past socialist projects have had so much difficulty in living up to their promise and either turned authoritarian or succumbed to bourgeois revisionism within a short space of time. The choice, it sometimes seems, is not between socialism or barbarism, as Luxemburg and Kautsky thought,[3] but between barbaric and humanistic forms of socialism. In this the question of how the double consciousness is negotiated politically plays a central role.

There is a lot going on in the two statements quoted above. The second is full of question marks while the first is not. The second lists unfulfilled potentialities while the first sees no insuperable barriers to fulfillment. It is interesting to sit back and think about which of these two worlds we currently inhabit. In practice we find ourselves perpetually negotiating between creative and emancipatory possibilities, cut across by demonic and self-destructive threats. Social media has become exhibit one in which this sort of conflict is playing out before our very eyes.

This is what Du Bois famously dubbed 'double consciousness'.[4] For Du Bois this arose as he defended the United States against its bourgeois European critics while excoriating the racism he experienced at home. His dual identity was that of American and African American, and the two could not be reconciled. In the recent political turmoil in the United States some of the most articulate defenders of US constitutionality have, interestingly, been African Americans, like the late John Lewis and the late Elijah Cummings, both of whom had a history of having to fight tooth and nail for the rights of African Americans in a lifelong struggle against the white racism which is elided in the very constitution they defend. In an interesting entry in the *Stanford Encyclopedia of Philosophy*, Du Bois' embrace of the theory is traced back to 'the European romantic opposition', to be found in both Goethe and Hegel, 'between an innate human affinity for the transcendent' on the one hand, 'and a pragmatic "materialism" grounded in a utilitarian attitude to life, to mundane needs and commercial enterprise' on the other. It was 'this anti-bourgeois romanticism', the *Stanford Encyclopedia* entry suggests, that formed the 'figurative background' for Du Bois' embrace of the term 'double consciousness'.[5] Marx was deeply familiar with and affected by both Hegel's and Goethe's positions and in his youth, as evidenced from his notebooks, and was attracted to rather gothic forms of 'anti-bourgeois romanticism'. Much later in his life he reputedly identified with the central protagonist in Balzac's darkly romanticist story *The Unfinished Masterpiece*, as he recognized that the multiple plans he had for *Capital* were unfinishable.[6] Marx also took from Hegel the insight that tragedy is not the outcome of struggle between right and wrong, but the inevitable outcome of a conflict between two equal rights between which, as he puts it in *Capital*, only force can decide.[7] It will therefore be helpful to confront and elucidate the double consciousness (or what Marx more coyly refers to as 'double positing'[8]), within his theorization of capital and the political consequences of embracing this disjunction.

ALIENATIONS

In *The Economic and Philosophical Manuscripts of 1844*, Marx had advanced the concept of humanity as a 'species being' struggling to emancipate itself from the alienations largely imposed by capital.[9] Many hold that Marx subsequently abandoned these postulates as too tainted by humanist idealism and transcendental romanticism. Althusser, for one, vigorously condemned both 'species being' and 'alienation' as unscientific concepts that should be expelled from the Marxist lexicon.[10] But in the second passage in the *Grundrisse*, it seems that the concepts of both species being and alienation are being revived, in order to acknowledge capitalist blockages to true emancipation and to underline the way in which capital 'moves in contradictions which are constantly overcome ... but just as constantly posited'.[11]

Most subsequent critical attempts to resurrect the concept of alienation have focused on Marx's early works. Little attention is paid to the radical reformulation of the concept in the *Grundrisse*. The 'scientific' presentation of the concept in the *Grundrisse,* writes the Chinese scholar Zhang in his monumental work *Back to Marx*, was

> fundamentally different from his past use of the humanist alienation conception ... In fact, these were two completely different conceptions of alienation; the labor alienation in the *1844 Manuscript* was a humanist value postulate; the idealized essence that it formed was at odds with reality. This was a contradiction between imaginary and the real ... The self-alienation of labor was a logical reflection, established in ideas ... The labor alienation in *Grundrisse*, on the other hand, was fundamentally Marx's reflection on real history. The objectified results of workers' past labor actually became the rulers and exploiters of today's workers. The 'past' created by workers becomes the ruler of the 'present' ... Hired labor necessarily created a ruling power transformed out of itself: capital. This is the actual alienation of capital and labor relations that Marx describes.[12]

This is the concept of alienation that we perforce must work with. Yet its relation to the earlier initial conception cannot be totally ignored.

In the early Marx the universality is rooted in the supposed inherent qualities of our species being. The potentiality for realizing those qualities (which, by default, are tacitly presumed to be noble and good) is frustrated by capital. The labourers who produce capital are denied the fruits of their labour (they stand in a relation of alienation to their product, to the value they produce, and to the labour process in which they engage). The individual potential to achieve self-perfection (in social relations, in the relation to nature, and in the experience of the labour process) is denied. The advantage of such a formulation is that it is forward looking and aspirational. It is expressive emotionally of the frustration of human possibility. In politics, exhortations based upon such thinking often play an important role. A contemporary example of this idealist and moralizing response is to react to the bigotry and violence of white supremacy in the United States with the exhortation that this is 'not who we Americans truly are'. All we need do is to re-gain our moral compass and practice what it means to assume the identity of a 'true American' (predicated upon the exceptionalism of American species being), then all will be well. This is rank idealism at work at its blatant worst. It is also politically ineffective.

THE RULE OF ABSTRACTIONS

In the *Grundrisse*, alienation arises out of the historical tendency within capital to create the world market, to establish its social (class) and metabolic relations everywhere, and to inscribe certain identifiable laws of motion into human history under the rule of the coercive laws of competition. The problem from the *Grundrisse* onwards is to identify the laws of motion of capital and to understand how these laws govern the conditions of daily life and labour for the mass of the working population. The question of goodness and morality does not come into it.[13] The keystone of the theory of alienation in the *Grundrisse* is the statement that: 'individuals are now ruled by abstractions, whereas earlier they depended on one another. The abstraction, or idea, however, is nothing more than the theoretical expression of those material relations which are their lord and master.'

Marx then follows this observation with an interesting coda:

Relations can be expressed, of course, only in ideas, and thus philosophers have determined the reign of ideas to be the peculiarity of the new age and have identified the creation of free individuality with the ideological overthrow of this reign. This error was all the more easily committed from the ideological standpoint, as this reign ... appears within the consciousness of individuals as the reign of ideas, and because the belief in the permanence of these ideas, i.e. of these objective relations of dependency, is of course consolidated, nourished and inculcated by the ruling classes by all means available.[14]

While we may all passionately believe ourselves to be free individuals, we are in practice ruled in our daily lives by the abstractions of capital. Was Thatcherism or Reaganism anything more than 'the theoretical expression of those material relations which are their lord and master'? And when Thatcher confidently asserted that 'there is no alternative' in the name of individual liberty and freedom (she meant in the marketplace), was she not simply articulating the ruling ideas of the ruling classes of her time?

The two models with which we began jointly point to how the 'universality towards which (capital) irresistibly strives encounters barriers in its own nature'.[15] Marx strives to come to terms with what the human species has achieved and what it might have lost. The fact that 'something's lost and something's gained' in capitalist modernity's relation, for example, to the world of antiquity or, in our times, to indigenous or religious thought, beliefs and cultural practices is a very real issue. There are social and political movements all over the world these days desperately seeking to regain that which they feel they have lost. For them, the Model 2 interpretation makes overwhelming sense.

SOCIALISM

Taken together, the two statements also say something about the future: there is no idealist or romanticist resolution (such as a perfected utopian communism) that can be distilled from them. Marx almost certainly gave up on that idea. There is no stable harmonious endpoint for human evolution, only the prospect of a continuous unfolding of contradictions between our collective capacities and our desires, on the one hand, and the desecrated nature of the world we actually produce and reproduce (including its class relations), on the other. 'The working class', Marx tells us,

> did not expect miracles from the (Paris) Commune. They have no ready-made utopias to introduce '*par dècret du people*'. They know that in order to work out their own emancipation, and along with it that higher form to which present society is irresistibly trending by its own economical agencies, they will have to pass through long struggles, through a series of historical processes, transforming circumstances and men. They have no ideals to realise, but to set free the elements of the new society with which old collapsing bourgeois society itself is pregnant.[16]

Marx could proffer this startling opinion in the midst of a barrage of bourgeois protestations across the whole European space, railing against working-class international conspiracies and the sheer futility and impossibility of any attempted transition to communism. In our own times, a cacophony of similar objections to even the mild-mannered social democracy of a Bernie Sanders or a Jeremy Corbyn is accompanied by repeated assertions that, to the degree that socialist, let alone communist, alternatives to capitalism have been tried they have proven to be a miserable, incompetent, often murderous utter failures. So exercised has the European political establishment become about such matters that the European Parliament recently voted overwhelmingly to declare Communism equivalent to Nazism, and to ban both forms of discourse from the political arena. Leaving aside the patent absurdity of such an equivalence, this historical judgment flies in the face of the astonishing rise of China to be the largest and increasingly most technologically sophisticated capitalist economy in the world, in the name of a political tradition anchored in the revolutionary theories of Marx, Lenin, and Mao, as interpreted through the thought of Deng and now Xi Jinping. That, surely, is double consciousness in action. Chinese developmentalism in broadly hewing to the Model 1 line is running afoul of Model 2 problems that are only now beginning to emerge. Behind the scurrilous right-wing attacks against communism in general, and Chinese communism in particular, there lurks a crucial question: what do we do when the pregnant elements of the old society are so toxic as to give birth to socialist monsters like Stalin and Pol Pot? The first model begs that question while the second provokes it.

THE CONTRADICTIONS AT THE HEART OF SOCIALIST PROJECTS

It would be wrong to see the two models as mutually exclusive. They are at some level two sides of the profoundly contradictory nature of the project of humanity, in our time largely held captive by capital, as it seeks material well-being, an impossible unalienated existence, deep socio-cultural satisfactions, and profound meanings in the face of its own banal materialist laws of motion which point in an entirely different and 'vulgar' direction.

This tension is internalized in the aesthetic traditions of bourgeois culture that perpetually seek some reconciliation between capital's vulgar despoliation of the world and the desire for re-enchantment in the relation to nature, along with attempts to appropriate for current monetized consumption the loftier products of humanity's history.[17] The great bourgeois philanthropist builds a sumptuous art museum to exhibit classical treasures. The owner of the dark satanic mill retires to a country estate that is so immaculately landscaped as to become an icon in national culture, access to which on weekends is now duly monetized. The working-class version of such sentiments in Britain used to be the rose garden in the tiny front yard or the breeding of homing pigeons, all in the midst of the industrial city. The current fascination with indigenous rights and philosophies of being and nature is further testament to the search and longing for alternative meanings in an alienated world. Both bourgeois and worker alike seek an unalienated and more enchanted relation to the nature they both pollute and desecrate on a daily basis. In this and other regards both capital and labour are equally alienated in their relation to each other as well as in relation to their natural and cultural-historical foundations.

The 'loftier', if 'childish' sensibilities and satisfactions achievable in the ancient world or in traditional ways of life contrast with the 'emptying out' of all meaning as the singular achievement of capitalist modernity, accompanied by the narcissism of a contemporary philosophy rooted in the reductionist individualism implied in the Cartesian dictum that 'I think therefore I am' (an invitation to mental bedlam if ever there was one, and to which Marx sensibly replies that you had better eat dinner first). The contemporary choice, therefore, is not, as some have occasionally argued within the confines of a long Marxist tradition stretching back to Kautsky and Rosa Luxemburg, between socialism and barbarism (Socialisme où Barbarie was a French political movement for a while).[18] The real future choice is between a humanistic or authoritarian socialism.

What is meant by this? Humanity has arrived at a point where it has no option except to find a collective social way to manage its metabolic relation to nature, its production of material goods, its shaping of adequate mental conceptions of the world and, above all, the production and reproduction of its own human nature through material practices. This collectivity has to give expression to a communist politics whether it likes it or not, and to accept the ruthless imposition of its policies if we are to address, for example, the proper management of the global commons to provide a decent life in a decent living environment for ten billion people on planet earth. In other words, Lenin, who certainly understood his Hegel very well, was and is right. 'Trust is good, control is much better.'[19]

TRUST VERSUS CONTROL

Many years ago, Garrett Hardin wrote a highly influential article on 'the tragedy of the commons' in which he pointed out that the common use of a pasture by individual stock breeders would ultimately lead to the degradation and impoverishment of the commons since each herder would gain all the benefits and bear only a small fraction of the costs attached to adding another head of cattle to their herd. The rational economic choice for the individual was irrational for the collective good.[20] This problem was immediately seized upon by bourgeois economists to favour and justify privatization of the commons. The herder would then have to internalize the costs of adding another head of cattle to the herd. This was not, however, Hardin's political point. He was primarily concerned with population growth. The only solution to the fact that millions of families would gain from an extra child but not have to bear all the environmental and other costs was the draconian use of absolute power.

This was what the Chinese did through their largely successful one child policy. Privatization and marketization cannot solve problems of excessive population growth, greenhouse gas emissions, habitat destructions and the like. It will require an exercise of global repressions and authority of an analogous sort to that which the Chinese government successfully imposed in its one-child policy. Trust will not work but control does. Only repressive humanism will work. This happened in China. In the West such an option is unthinkable because it is there axiomatic that any solution has to be market and private property based. It cannot go against the supposed sacrosanct rights for individuals to do exactly as they please, believe in anything they like, and perform any acts dictated by their feelings (however ill-considered and of the moment). This guarantees that any collective solution will fail, except, of course, one which favours the top one percent. We are left with the overwhelming but empty and alienated privileges of an immensely wealthy oligarchy wallowing in a consumerist's cornucopia of often useless commodities in a rapidly disintegrating ecological and social world of universal alienation.

While the ruling oligarchy and its ideological apologists and analysts are dangerously close to power in China, they have yet to wield enough power to dominate the cadres of a ninety-million-strong Communist Party that has not yet abandoned Maoist and Leninist principles. But China now has to confront Marx's law of capital accumulation, which requires population growth as its basis; and as the more than fifty countries (such as Japan and Italy, which have low if not negative population growth rates) experience chronic economic difficulties, the demand arises to increase population to match the needs of capital for both labour supply and an ever-expanding market.[21] China now permits and even exhorts couples to have three children! But the demographic response has been minimal. The double consciousness which Marx articulates is plainly in view. But do people, policy makers, and political movements see it and acknowledge it?

THE ROLE OF REPRESSSIVE TOLERANCE

For this issue to become both visible and actionable requires the active embrace of what Herbert Marcuse and Barrington Moore negatively critiqued as 'repressive tolerance'.[22] In the 1960s it was impossible in the 'tolerant' United States to have access to the mainstream media if you were a socialist or a communist. The 'faux' tolerance of the US regime at the time was repressive towards the left. But some form of repressive tolerance is essential to any social order. The big question is who sets the boundaries and how they are enforced. Repressive tolerance that excludes leftist and particularly Marxist thinking has long prevailed in bourgeois society. On the other hand, the world's central banks and Treasury departments manage the global monetary system in an authoritarian and exclusionary way, albeit in the class interest of capital and under the convenient cloak of neutrality, as they try to make sure the market works smoothly. This, they claim, is supposedly to everyone's material benefit, even though it clearly is not.

The central banks do not have to rely on military power to do their invidious task (though military back-up is always available if any group or faction protests too much). But regulation is tightly orchestrated to support a class interest. The contemporary organization of repressive tolerance in the United States mandates that anyone designated 'Marxist' is excluded from the mainstream and relegated to social media. Boundaries can shift, however, as illustrated by recent shifts in norms in the United States regarding sexual harassment, sexual identities and racial disparities.

These boundaries can be strictly patrolled and tightly defined. In a newsletter that accompanies his regular opinion pieces in the *New York Times*, Paul Krugman complained that 'powerful interests try to block the dissemination of ideas they find threatening'. Twice in recent history, he tells us, there have been serious political attempts 'to block the teaching of Keynesian economics'. The first was 'an organized smear campaign' in the late 1940s, 'with many university trustees and donors' demanding that 'the Keynesian textbook be cancelled'. But the publication of Paul Samuelson's authoritative and popular text made this almost impossible. The second attempt began in the 1970s, 'when some economists began arguing that Keynesianism must be wrong, because the phenomena that Keynes described could not happen in an economy of perfectly rational individuals and perfectly functioning markets'. Within a few years, anyone who talked Keynesianism was being ridiculed and 'major journals would not publish anything overtly Keynesian'. Budding economists understood that

> if you wanted to get tenure, you would have to build your publication record in subfields that steered clear of the core field of depressions and how they happen. Then came the 2008 crisis and its aftermath which demonstrated that Keynes had been right all along [and that] the anti-Keynesian theories that had dominated the journals for several decades proved perfectly useless ... Many economists entered the crisis ignorant of basic concepts that had been worked out many decades earlier, because you couldn't publish those concepts in the journals or teach them in many (not all) graduate programs.[23]

If this was true for Keynes, imagine how it was for Marx, who all along noted that economists had a habit of proclaiming, when faced with a crisis, that such things could not happen if only the economy performed according to their textbooks.[24] To this day, economists remain ignorant of basic concepts that Marx worked out a century and a half ago, that illuminate how the capitalist world works.

POLICING REVOLUTION

The left, if it comes to power, has to define its own forms of repressive tolerance. Inevitably the left has to face the power of reaction, and to the degree that it often comes to power with a promise to deepen democratic freedoms, it finds itself hamstrung in dealing with the proliferation of oppositional doctrines and discourses which will use democratic openness (along with its often concentrated power in the media) to plot and plan counter-revolution in the name of bourgeois freedoms and interests. The left cannot afford to be squeamish in principle about suppressing the founts of counter-revolution and neo-fascism. But it must be sure to do so in ways that at least touch upon the issues raised in the Model 2 account if it is to consolidate and sustain popular support.

This issue of necessary repressive tolerance lies at the centre of the ongoing struggle and argument over China's developmental path. The orchestration of centralization and decentralization within the Chinese political system is one of the more remarkable features of its political economy. The clash between the drive for an emancipatory economics (which seeks to eradicate poverty and enhance social provision while growing the wealth and power of the state on the world stage) and repressive surveillance politics underlies the perpetual merging and sometimes fusion of authoritarianism and humanistic freedom. The response to and management of the global pandemic in China relative to elsewhere signals something important about the potential future for humanity. It was, after all, China that saved global capitalism from collapse in the crisis of 2008 through its collective action, and that astonishing accomplishment is now being followed by an equally astonishing absorption of both the viral spread that originated in China and its economic effects (both national and global). We may well be witnessing (though nobody in the West wants to mention it) China again rescuing global capitalism from collapse. In the Chinese case, the political tension/fusion between humanism and barbarism within the framework of communism seems stark and obvious. It is a product of the conflict between China's longstanding political and social ambitions and the need to understand and neutralize, if possible, the power of the abstractions, the laws of motion of capital. When China acceded to the rules of the World Trade Organization in 2001, it agreed in effect to obey the rules of capital's game, thereby conceding some (but by no means all) of its sovereignty to international capital. Fortunately for China, Donald Trump did not abide by the rules of the WTO, and in flouting them at will gave license to others to do the same.

THE MALFEASANCE OF CAPITAL

The ideological classes of the so-called capitalist democracies of the world, on the other hand, cannot locate any such internal tension, thanks to the ever-increasing ideological fog of alienations and conspiracy theories deliberately fostered, not only by the radical right, but even more perniciously by the liberal left, to protect the privileges of private property and, more covertly, absolute class power often at the expense of collective interests and needs. A simple example of this systematic misrepresentation and misreading of the situation and its possibilities lies in the obvious need to confront and manage climate change on a global basis. Hardin's conclusions apply with force in this case. Free markets and private property plainly cannot do it.

Meanwhile, the 'universal objectification as total alienation, and the tearing down of all limited one-sided aims' sacrifices the human end in itself to 'an entirely external end', that of the accumulation of money power. Small wonder that suicide rates around the supposedly 'free' world, most disturbingly among the young as well as among farmers and peasants (from India to South Korea and even among British hill farmers), are an indicator of the spreading meaninglessness that contemporary capital increasingly signifies. Small wonder either that 'the childish world of antiquity appears on one side as loftier' while 'the modern gives no satisfaction'. Small wonder either that in the midst of the most astonishing technological possibilities, we are witnessing the birth of incoherent movements expressive of mass discontents.

In the ancient world, Marx postulates, the supreme question for elites was: what makes for good citizens? Not: how much monetary wealth can I accumulate? To be sure, there are many individuals and even whole social movements devoted to recovering the moral compass of antiquity and a sense of bourgeois virtue, who pursue the holy grail of a political economy concordant with the requirements of 'good citizenship'.

The double consciousness that Marx was confronting defines and confines his radicalism. Are we more interested in being viewed and judged as good citizens than as rich and all-powerful in money terms? So what, then, is wealth? And what should we do with it when we have it? Under modernity, we have an account of wealth that reduces it to the universality of money power. Marx proposes free time as its proper measure.[25] Capital produces the potentiality for free time but converts it into surplus value in order to expand and reinvigorate itself. Thus we get not a 'complete working out of the human content', but a complete emptying out. This is the emptiness and the anxiety felt in the midst of technological wizardry and a cornucopia of commodity choices. We have never been so blessed as now with technological prowess, but the pursuit of wealth under capitalism is the pursuit of emptiness. The nothingness at the heart of capitalist enterprise is overwhelming. When we compare the current pursuit of wealth with what happened in the 'childish world' of antiquity, we start to understand how the latter appears so much loftier even though restricted and confined. But even here there is a warning sign. The ideology of contemporary fascism roots itself (whether legitimately or not does not matter) in the imaginaries of classical antiquity. That is part of its emotive appeal.

Capitalist society, supposedly based on freedom to choose, currently has no real or meaningful choices. Minor things can shift. Technological options and compensatory consumer choices abound. But the option not to embrace the pursuit of surplus value, not to obey the laws of motion of capital, and to flout the abstract ruling law of value (already technically obsolete) is by definition not available in a bourgeois world. The essence of capital is the pursuit, both individual and collective, of material and monetary wealth. It is about endless alienation through growth, growth, and more growth; accumulation, accumulation, and more accumulation. The abstract spiral of perpetual accumulation rules requiring, as the Communist Chinese have now discovered, population growth and further consequent environmental degradation. Far from being 'a complete working out of the human content', a complete exploration of all that we're capable of doing as a species, capital has deepened its pursuit of universal objectification and commodification of the world, it is about total monetization and total alienation and the tearing down of all limited one-sided aims, the sacrifice of the human end in-itself to an entirely external end. This is why it is an emptying and hollowing out. This 'emptying and hollowing out' along with 'universal alienation' every day becomes more and more evident and politically salient. The recovery of meaning becomes the holy grail. The only meaning that makes sense is the hunt for the narrow passage that takes us from the totalizing world of capital through to an anti-capitalist world so as to organize the economy to take adequate care of material wants, needs, and desires, and to release the free time to pursue what 'a complete unalienated working out of the human content' might mean for every individual on planet earth.

POLITICAL IMPLICATIONS

The political significance of this double consciousness is everywhere apparent. Consider the example of Andean socialism in general, and Ecuador in particular.[26] The first round of the 2021 election for President in Ecuador produced three viable candidates. Andres Arauz emanated from the progressive left tradition established by Rafael Correa, who was President from 2007 to 2017. The neoliberal Opus Dei business candidate Guillermo Lasso, came a far-away second. A close third behind him was Yaku Perez, who had indigenous backing through the Pachakutik (plurinational) movement. In the run-off many leftist outsiders presumed that the indigenous candidate would endorse and support Arauz, much as the indigenous organizations had initially supported Correa and the rewriting of the Ecuadorian constitution in 2008. That new constitution declared Ecuador to be a plurinational state that acknowledged both the rights of nature and the rights of indigenous populations. Bolivia adopted a similar constitution a year later. These were landmark, even revolutionary transformations in bourgeois constitutionality that went beyond the constitutions that rested on the foundational but empty market logic of equality, freedom, and reciprocity. But once securely in power, Correa pursued a left developmentalism (Model 1) that sought to take all that was positive from the bourgeois tradition and reshape Ecuador's nature and people to facilitate the move towards socialism. This resulted in some economic redistribution, while breaking from incorporation in the global system of US hegemony (at the expense, however, of relying upon China). But in so doing Correa went against his indigenous base. He marginalized CONNAI (the Confederation of Indigenous Nationalities of Ecuador), abandoned all modes of indigenous thinking (Pachamama, *sumac kawsay*, and even *buen vivir*), repressed and jailed the leaders of the more militant environmental organizations, such as Accion Ecologica, attacked the ecofeminists, abandoned the Yasuni initiative that sought to protect one of the most diverse ecologies on planet earth in Amazonia, and opened up Ecuador to oil and mineral extractivism (using the army to ride roughshod over indigenous protests in southern Ecuador). This 'complete working out of the human content' increasingly appeared (Model 2) as 'a complete emptying out', and 'this universal objectification' of nature and culture 'as total alienation', which explains why the indigenous view increasingly appeared to many (beyond the indigenous) as far 'loftier in all matters', though limited and circumscribed in scale, than the results of the Correa programme which 'gives no satisfaction; or, where it appears satisfied with itself, it is vulgar'. This helps to explain why major thinkers in the indigenous tradition balked at supporting Arauz, making the not unsupported claim that they have suffered more at the hands of left developmentalism than at the hands of the neoliberal oligarchy.[27]

The same tensions between Model 1 and 2 thinking are observable in Bolivia, where Evo Morales adopted a left developmentalism and extractivism at the cost of support from some of his indigenous base. This contributed to the right-wing coup against him. But Luis Arce, the current president of Bolivia who came to power through support from Morales' socialist party, was a successful Finance Minister much praised by the IMF during the Morales years.

For both Arauz and Arce, the tension within the double consciousness that Marx depicts houses a critical contradiction that they will have to address. Arauz lost the election by a significant margin. While there are doubtless many reasons for this (including all kinds of dirty tricks by his opponent), the lack of enthusiasm in the indigenous base was surely prominent among them. The 16 per cent of the voters who cast null votes far exceeded the five-point margin that the right wing achieved. The result has been disastrous for the left, as the right wing in true Opus Dei fashion has pursued a vindictive vendetta against anyone who supported Arauz. In this regard it is important also to remember that it was Sandinista left developmentalism applied to the indigenous Mesquite populations of the Pacific coast in Nicaragua that opened a path for the CIA-supported 'Contra' movement that proved so troublesome – both to the course of the now failed and increasingly authoritarian Sandinista Revolution in Nicaragua, as well as to the Reagan administration in the USA (i.e. the Iran-Contra scandal).

Problems can be solved but contradictions, particularly those of the double consciousness sort, never go away. The answer is not to abandon left developmentalism as a stepping stone to socialism, but to assure that it is less vulgar, and to create spaces and opportunities within that re-jigged developmentalism to permit the search for meaning, for unalienated sociality and physicality, for opening up to the 'complete working out of the human content'. Revolution, like almost everything else that we do, requires some mix of inspiration, perspiration, and long-term patience with the dialectics of the primary contradictions. Getting the balance right, both in thought and in practice, even if only for a time, is critical for socialism to have some future. The radical right justifies and legitimates its turn to fascism as the only possible antidote to a socialism that is for them by definition authoritarian, barbaric and suppressive of individual rights. The socialist left cannot respond simply by denial. It needs to reaffirm its objective of securing the free development of individual capacities and powers through collective action. The first step of the radical right, with its roots in ruling-class culture, is to unleash forces of counter-revolution in the name of bourgeois liberties and freedom (including of course the freedom to exploit labour without restraint), forcing the socialist left to exercise a collective discipline and respect for authority which internalizes the seeds of authoritarianism and barbarism within its body politic. It is exactly at this conjuncture that the consciousness of double consciousness within the left needs to be invoked, not as a vapid moral stance but as a comprehensive long-term best political praxis, drawn from the whole history of emancipatory movements. The long two hundred or more years of African-American struggle for emancipation from racism in the United States, and the double consciousness it has all along entailed and embraced within that troubled history has, as Du Bois, John Lewis and Elijah Cummings well understood, much to teach us in this regard.

NOTES

Acknowledgement: I thank Leo Panitch who over the years generously opened the pages of *Socialist Register* to me, while personally offering much helpful advice and endless encouragement.

1   K. Marx, *Grundrisse*, translated by Martin Nicolaus, London: Penguin Books, 1973, pp. 409-10. The context to these and subsequent remarks is detailed in David Harvey, *A Companion to Marx's Grundrisse*, London: Verso, forthcoming.

2   *Grundrisse*, p. 488.

3   The origins of the slogan 'socialism or barbarism' in the works of Kautsky and Luxemburg are identified in Ian Angus, 'Socialism or Barbarism: An Important Socialist Slogan Traced to an Unexpected Source', *Links: An International Journal of Socialist Renewal,* 21 October 2014.

4   Du Bois makes free use of this concept in W.E.B. Du Bois, *The Souls of Black Folk*, 1903.

5   'Double Consciousness' entry in *Stanford Encyclopedia of Philosophy*, 21 March 2016, available at https://plato.stanford.edu/entries/double-consciousness. There is a loose connection here with Karl Polanyi's subsequent formulation of a 'double movement' in the dialectical relation/tension between *laissez-faire* and state management in the history of capital. See: Beverley Silver and Giovanni Arrighi, 'Polanyi's "Double Movement": The Belles Epoques of British and U.S. Hegemony Compared,' *Politics & Society,* 31 (2), 2003, pp. 325-55.

6   Honoré de Balzac, *The Unfinished Masterpiece*, New York: New York Review of Books, 2001. Also see: Marcel Van der Linden and Gerald Hubmann, *Marx's Capital: An Unfinishable Project*, Chicago: Haymarket Books, 2018.

7   Karl Marx, *Capital,* Volume 1, London: Pelican Books, 1976, p. 344.

8   *Grundrisse*, pp. 94-5.

9   Karl Marx, *The Economic and Philosophic Manuscripts of 1844*, New York: International Publishers, 1964.

10   Louis Althusser, *On the Reproduction of Capitalism: Ideology and Ideological State Apparatuses*, London: Verso, 2014.

11   *Grundrisse*, p. 410.

12   Yibing Zhang, *Back to Marx: Changes in Philosophical Discourse in the Context of Economics*, Gottingen; Universitatsverlag, 2014.

13   David Harvey, 'Universal Alienation,' *Journal for Cultural Research*, 22: 2, 2018, pp. 137-50.

14   *Grundrisse*, p. 165.

15   *Grundrisse*, p. 150.

16   Karl Marx, and Vladimir I. Lenin, *Civil War in France: The Paris Commune*, Moscow: International Publishers, 1940, pp. 61-2.

17   Terry Eagleton, *The Ideology of the Aesthetic*, Oxford: Basil Blackwell, 1991.

18   Jean Amair, Hugo Bell, Cornelius Castoriadis, et al., *A Socialisme ou Barbarie Anthology: Autonomy, Critique and Revolution in the Age of Bureaucratic Capitalism,* London: Eris Publications, 2018.

19   This saying is widely attributed to Lenin but may be apocryphal since no one can locate it in any of his works.

20   Garrett Hardin, 'The Tragedy of the Commons,' *Science*, 162, 1968, pp. 1243-8.

21   Marx's presumption (particularly throughout the *Grundrisse*, e.g., p. 610) that continuous capital accumulation has to rest upon a perpetually increasing population (as both a source of labour and as a market for commodities) is rarely mentioned let alone taken seriously.

22   Herbert Marcuse in Robert Paul Wolff, Barrington Moore, Jr., and Herbert Marcuse, *A Critique of Pure Tolerance*, Boston: Beacon Press, 1969, pp. 95-137

23   Paul Krugman, '*Newsletter* on "Cancel Culture",' *New York Times*, 1 June 2021.

24   Karl Marx, *Theories of Surplus Value,* Part 2, London: Lawrence and Wishart, 1969, p. 468.

25   Harvey, *A Companion to Marx's Grundrisse*.

26   The travails of Andean socialism have been well represented in: Jeffrey Weber, 'Struggle, Continuity and Contradiction in Bolivia,' *International Socialism*, Winter 2010; and T. Wood, 'Retrocession in Ecuador,' *New Left Review,* 129 (May/June), 2021.

27   The no-holds-barred intellectual attack against left developmentalism has long been led by Arturo Escobar, *Encountering Development: The Making and Unmaking of the Third World,* New Jersey: Princeton University Press, 2011.

FINDING A WAY FORWARD: LESSONS FROM THE CORBYN PROJECT IN THE UK

JAMES SCHNEIDER
INTERVIEWED BY HILARY WAINWRIGHT

In 2015, the year of Jeremy Corbyn's election to the leadership of the British Labour Party, James Schneider was 28, working as a journalist specialising on Africa. Later that year, after he and others had spontaneously mobilized to help organize the campaign that powered Corbyn to the leadership, he co-founded a new left-wing organization, Momentum, to give backbone and direction to the diffuse initiatives and energies released by the campaign. A year later he started work in the Labour Party Leader's office as Corbyn's spokesperson and Head of Strategic Communications.

Working closely with the new leadership team he daily faced the forces in the Parliamentary Labour Party (PLP) and their close allies in the mainstream political media that were bent on seeing Corbyn replaced as leader. The Labour Party's domination by the PLP has plagued the left in Britain for a century. The party's monopoly of political representation in Britain's 'first-past-the-post' electoral system means that there is no other route to credible political representation. Labour's 'parliamentarism', pervading every level of the party, has effectively blocked or smothered the moments of insurgent working-class militancy that periodically threaten the interests of the British ruling class. Corbyn's leadership victory seemed to break that pattern, and constituted a major threat to the interests for which the Labour Party has always provided a protective barrier.

Within hours of Corbyn becoming leader, the gloves were off. The PLP, the mainstream media (assisted by much of the Labour Party's administrative apparatus) and the British capitalist class were all intensely hostile and launched a relentless attack that constantly stymied Corbyn's project of a transformative socialist government, culminating in the party's heavy defeat in the general election of December in 2019, in which the right-wing populist project of

'Brexit' (leaving the European Union) split Labour's members and its electoral base. Corbyn and his supporters were quickly marginalized, as the right wing reasserted its grip under the new leader, Keir Starmer.

Schneider not only had a ringside seat at all these events, but was sufficiently part of the team to feel keenly the moments of exhilaration, sweat and pain of the five-year struggle, while all the time knowing, from his year as Momentum's National Organizer, the vast untapped potential for movement initiative and mobilizations that lay beyond the 'tyranny of the immediate' which dominated life in the Leader's office in Westminster.

In this interview he assesses the strengths and weaknesses of the extra-parliamentary forces that backed Corbyn, from the low ebb of trade union organization when Corbyn first became leader to the limited but important ways in which the new leadership of the Labour Party revalidated trade unions, and the positive legacy of the Corbyn leadership in encouraging popular self-confidence and politicization.

At a time when many on the left are leaving or considering leaving the Labour Party, Schneider urges a strategy which transcends the 'inside the party or out of it' dichotomy which has constantly exhausted left thinking in the UK. Instead, he outlines the idea of a hybrid movement rooted primarily in communities and workplaces while at the same time, without compromising its mobilizing and campaigning energies, continuing the struggle for democratic control of the Labour Party. This response to the problem facing the left at a time of acute political polarization, while the 'centrists' offer no alternatives, has relevance to the left throughout Europe.

James Schneider was interviewed in May by Hilary Wainwright, editor of Red Pepper and contributing editor to the Socialist Register, and author of numerous books on the politics of the left.[1] Hilary has long been an advocate of the need for the left across Europe to experiment in 'parties of a new kind' that would break from both traditional social democracy and the vanguard party models of the far left.

Hilary Wainwright (HW): Let's start with the strategic vision for socialists that you first set out in 2017. You said:

> The long run aim is to achieve a radical shift in the balance of power, income and wealth, transforming the political, economic, and social levels. You then work backwards on how to get there. A necessary step is winning elections within the current system and balance of forces, to make major changes that noticeably improve the lives of the overwhelming majority. With power, you have to make more fundamental structural

and institutional changes: politically, by democratizing the state; economically, by expanding the commons, shifting the distribution of ownership towards the majority, and giving workers and communities control over work and economic life; and socially, through a concerted shift in the balance of social forces, with race and gender justice playing a vital role.

From this analysis, it follows that you must pass three categories of measures in the first term of office – and get the balance right. The first is a broad swathe of immediate, ameliorative measures, mainly using the state's existing policy levers, such as tax and spend, to noticeably and swiftly improve lives. There must be several major measures that fall into the second category of contributing to shifting hegemony – they must be radical, explicit, and difficult to reverse. They attract opposition – not reforms by stealth like Brown's tax credits, which are now being undone. The third category is non-reformist reforms, those which push at the boundaries of the possible and therefore open up new horizons, such as the National Health Service in the 1940s or expanding workers' ownership and control. The number of reforms of the third kind that can be achieved will depend more on the balance of forces in society and within the movement itself than on capacity within the state administration.

If implemented effectively to overcome elite opposition, this package could have a ratchet effect, creating a dynamic momentum in a progressive direction. Every action must be situated in an understanding of where we are now and where we want to be. The essence for all reforms is to be radical and reflect common sense, while at the same time pushing it in a socialist direction.[2]

HW: Were you describing the thinking of the Corbyn team, or what you thought the thinking should have been?

James Schneider (JS): I was describing an ideal, rather than what we actually had.

HW: How would you describe the reality?

JS: Well, we never made it into government, so it's hard to say exactly what the reality would have been. But this type of strategic thinking was not shared across the Corbyn team. Our approach was usually more ad hoc, more short- to medium-term because of the sheer weight of things to deal with every day, and we were hemmed in by lack of capacity. Not many people on the left had significant experience of strategic thinking or the hand-to-hand combat we had to engage in. We learned on the job.

HW: You're clear about what's to be done once the left is in government – but does it have any implications for how to get there?

JS: It very much does. Take the first level, immediate ameliorative measures: you have to foreground policies like raising the minimum wage, ending the public sector pay cap, immediate funding for schools, hospitals, social care, childcare, ending tuition fees and so on – the reforms from which big groups of the electorate will immediately benefit. That first element can be relatively top-down and 'mediatized', and can be conducted, more or less, within the parameters of Westminster politics – but tilting it substantially to the left.

Then there is the second category, which I'd call strong reforms – things that will face intense opposition and, for that reason, once in place are not easily undone. Compare two New Labour policies: the introduction of the minimum wage in 1998, and tax credits. The latter policy was more redistributory than the former, which was fiercely resisted by capital. The successor Conservative government could dramatically reduce tax credits within a year of coming to power, while the minimum wage has been extended. The minimum wage was a strong reform, the purpose of strong reforms is to shift the country's social settlement lastingly in a progressive direction.

They are going to face serious conflict, so they need to be something that an organized section of society is pushing for as its key demand, so that they can be forced through. These reforms bring social conflict to the fore prior to being in government. A politician can't just simply announce this sort of policy as a great idea.

Consider the experience of the universal free broadband policy in the 2019 Labour election platform. It's a strong reform that would expand the social settlement in a progressive direction. It would provide a service that would then be held onto and fought for. But in 2019, that policy was not a popular demand. It hadn't come up from any organized force in society.

Ahead of being in government the party needs to work out what areas it wants strong reforms in because they will advance the socialist project, and how demands for them could be stimulated. And then you set about trying to stimulate them. To do that now with broadband, for example, you would create an organization that was putting forward that demand, pressuring for that – an alliance of the interests that would benefit. If that got sufficient salience in the country, you could make that one of your strong reforms.

The third category, non-reformist reforms of the kind called for by André Gorz fifty years ago, has the potential for maximum social conflict and therefore requires the largest stimulation of social forces in support of them beforehand.[3] Rather than just shifting the social settlement, such reforms contain a dynamic within them to carry on shifting the balance of forces in the progressive direction. Imagine, for example, a policy of a People's Investment Fund that brought strategic companies and sectors into public ownership and took significant stakes in infrastructure and investment projects. If that fund paid out a Universal Basic Dividend to everyone in the country, you would create a constituency with a short-term material interest in expanding public ownership. But for that to be delivered, it would have to overcome heavy resistance from capital and its allies. So non-reformist reforms require high levels of understanding and organization.

HW: This relationship between a radical programme for government and the strategy of extra-parliamentary mobilization necessary to implement it is common to the European left, even though the left in the UK face a special problem of the Labour Party's monopoly of working-class political representation, and its parliamentarism. In response to the left's entrapment in this, John McDonnell (the Labour Shadow Treasury critic under Corbyn) used to say: 'We need mobilization.' How far was there a strategy to develop that and, if so, what did it come up against?

JS: Not particularly, or not particularly coherently. This partly comes down to questions of capacity and what is in front of you every day. That's a significant factor. A mobilization strategy would have to assess the organized blocs we're trying to knit together – the environmental movement, the labour movement, the feminist movement, the anti-racist movement, and so on – the unorganized groupings of people that those movements can reach and pull into the bloc, and the currently unorganised groups that could become organized, like tenants: what key demands will arise from these groups and how can the party tell a story that brings them all together under one banner? You might have three or four themes within it but there's one overarching story so that these demands all come under the banner, and the role of the party is to stimulate those forces, and to drive politics in that direction. The overarching story might be a simple slogan, such as 'Peace, Land, Bread' that brought together workers, peasants, and soldiers in Russia in 1917.

Writing about Tony Benn in the early 1980's Tariq Ali said: '[Benn] has understood that Labour's only serious electoral chance lies in turning the entire organization into a giant lever of popular political mobilizations, championing the causes of all sectors of the oppressed, and offering a governmental perspective of real change.'[4] It's all there, really.

A POLITICAL TRADE UNIONISM

HW: I want to come onto some of the structural constraints that are deeper than the day-to-day 'tyranny of the immediate'. For unions to organize around Labour's 2019 proposal to create Inclusive Ownership Funds, for example, would require a trade unionism that was itself political. How could that have been stimulated?

JS: By 2015, you've had 35 years of year-on-year reduction in trade union membership – every year – and very few strike days. Withering is not the right word, because it makes it sound passive. It's a destruction and a squeezing – hacking off bits of the movement and then squeezing it down.

After decline, loss, shrinking, being under attack, and so on, your horizons adapt. If your expectations are, 'Hold the fort, box clever, hold onto position as much as we can', then you get shrunk down to that. There's the great quote attributed to Rosa Luxemburg: 'Those who do not move, do not notice their chains.'

HW: But wasn't the vote for Jeremy amongst individual union members a sign of some increased confidence, or at least a level of discontent that produced confidence or determination? After all, the Blairites expected that opening up of the union block vote to individual members in leadership elections would mean the voice of the normally silenced moderate majority would be heard, whereas in fact this opening up actually unleashed a hidden desire for radical change. Wouldn't this have been a stimulus to confidence building?

JS: It was just from an extremely low base. I also think we must be realistic about what most of the trade unions probably thought they were doing when they backed Jeremy. The trade union nominations for Jeremy as Labour leader in 2015 for the most part did not indicate support for a thorough-going socialist strategy, transforming Labour into a movement–party. I think it was: 'We need to shift the party back towards at least some form of actual labourism and the needs of working-class people.'

HW: Was there any thinking about how far Jeremy and John McDonnell – and I suppose also Momentum – could play a role in building up confidence and capacity in the unions?

JS: Yes, with regards to confidence. I think the way Jeremy and John did that was by having lots of meetings with the trade unions; making sure that on most visits around the country they went to a workplace and met trade union reps; speaking at all the trade union conferences; praising trade unions in public; having policies that support trade unions; bringing on their demands, and so on. Basically, through communication rather than through organizing. I think that was the necessary first step.

Momentum shied away from organizing socialists within trade unions. It was not in a position to engage in what does have to happen at some stage: that is, increasing the political engagement of trade union members, or the engagement of trade union members with political activity, broadly defined – not just focused on cheerleading the red tie at Westminster or campaigning for the red rosette at elections.

HW: Sam Gindin and Leo Panitch often stressed the need within the unions for a layer of socialists who are not primarily focused on winning positions in union elections, but on the politicization of union activity. For example, from what you're saying, it's almost like there needed to be an organic bridge to people working on policies like inclusive ownership, and workers' control in public industries and union workplace organizations. Surely unions in sectors like the railways, energy, and water could have been more engaged in preparing and campaigning for plans and proposals for how they would run the industry?

JS: You make a good point and rail is a good example. We had an incredibly popular policy – public ownership – and there were several industrial disputes with privatized rail. We could have taken more advantage of this situation with more thinking-through of how workers – and users – could play an active role in running the industry. Stimulating this from a low base, however, isn't easy. You've got to see and grasp the openings. We did not have enough of that approach. But, again, I think that generally comes down to internal capacity. I think if we had had more people who had been able to do that, maybe we would have been able to take those things on.

HW: Now privatization of the National Health Service is a central issue, with everything we're learning about what has gone wrong during the pandemic. You could imagine the impact if we focused on control and participation, and had a massive campaign for a democratic NHS – a transformative polarization, in place of the diversionary polarizations of the populist right.

JS: The tip of that spear – and this is the easy bit, where you don't need masses of people – is that we should be occupying the offices of all the companies that are involved in the outsourcing and privatization of the NHS. Not their health facilities, obviously, because people need those, but their finance offices, their lobbyists. They should all be occupied.

HW: You're beginning to inspire me, not that you weren't before! There is a power in our physical presence, our bodies on the line as it were. You could occupy until there is an agreement that a contract be brought back into public control. You could use the anger that is more than the sum of the trade unions.

JS: One of the outcomes of Corbyn's leadership is that trade unions have a more normalized role in society than at any time since around 2000. Public understanding of trade unions is more normalized, just because in the last five years people have heard some good things about trade unions.

And there have been recent important victories: take GMB (a general union) against fire-and-rehire by British Gas, and Unite have a national campaign on that too, and there's going to be way more of that, with big pressure to outlaw fire and rehire. And there's the Deliveroo workers' victory recently in the Supreme Court; there are newer organizing efforts in the Amazon warehouse and with delivery drivers with GMB, IWGB (Independent Workers Union), and Unite; and the CWU (Communications Workers) just keep on winning ballot after ballot for industrial action on extremely high turnouts.

Moreover, we've now had four years in a row – for the first time in over 40 years – in which trade union membership has increased. Not by massive amounts, but nevertheless it's significant that it's no longer in decline. There is also an influx of a greater number of politicized socialist activists within the labour movement, orientated to re-politicizing trade unions at the base and, amongst some of the leadership there is a greater sense of being important political actors in their own right.

There are all these green shoots. Militancy levels are still low and membership engagement is low, but for the first time for a while, it seems, the trajectory is pointing up a bit.

BEYOND PARLIAMENTARISM

HW: Turning to the British Labour Party, what structural constraints would you point to as being particularly important? How far did constraints in people's mentality, the pervasiveness of parliamentarism at every level of the party, and the separation of the unions from political engagement, make it difficult or perhaps impossible to make advances in the strategic direction that you've outlined?

JS. Within the Labour Party, a mixture of two things took over from 2017 onwards, first, within the party's machinery, and then within the movement around the party, including the think tanks and campaign groups and so on. First, in the party machinery: members of the shadow cabinet, their staff, people in Jeremy and John's office, the staff in Southside [the unofficial name for the party's headquarters], and so on had an overly left-technocratic approach. We treated the policies we were developing in a slightly utopian way. The thinking behind the 2019 manifesto is genuinely very impressive, including the big documents that stand behind them. Take the policy on pharmaceuticals: it's two sentences in the manifesto, but there's a detailed 50-page report that sits behind it. Now that my work with Progressive International leads me to talk to movements, parties, activists, and unions all over the world, I can see that our policy documents really stand up for their rigour and quality. But that work needs to be combined with an idea of how these policies are going to become reality, that isn't just: 'This bill has to be written in this way, and we might have to create a new agency within the department to deliver this policy, and we'll need this new reporting standard so that there is feedback in this way, and we'll judge these things by these metrics rather than those metrics.' All of those things are very, very important but they don't take into account how change actually happens.

The state is an enormous site of struggle, and we aren't just going to be able to do what we want. Once we are in government, the main forces acting on us, every single day, are from the establishment and the ruling class, not from the people – who have less access to the state. One of the areas on which our strategy was, to be honest, poorly developed was the opening up of the state. Democratization, and opening up the state, was a lacuna in our programme – in contrast to, for example, the Greater London Council (GLC) or the ideas of the previous left in the 1970s and '80s which placed premium on those things.[5]

Then the second development was one that you could see within the wider movement – and this is a double-edged sword, both a very good thing, but it also shows how the party wasn't really set up to be a democratic movement party by that time again – another type of utopianism. You could see it at the 2019 Labour Party Conference in Brighton. It was unbelievably exciting because, for the first time, the base of the party was more advanced than the leadership. The conference floor pushed beyond the leadership and voted for a Green New Deal 2030, for abolishing private schools, for a national care service, and so on.

That was incredibly exciting but I have to say that most people within the leadership team were not so delighted about it.

HW: Because it had a momentum of its own?

JS: Yes, and that causes headaches. The members' motions might not be written that coherently. Let's take the motion to abolish private schools – a brilliant campaign, but a very poorly written motion: the three policy points were mutually contradictory. It comes back to this: if you're going to have a democratic movement party, what mechanisms are you going to have to channel the democratic movement? So, it was very exciting, and it was one of the effects of having opened up the priorities ballot – it went from a maximum of eight subjects to be debated to twenty-four. The idea that a conference can take that many major strategic decisions is implausible. The idea that a government, a party, can have twenty-four major policies that get brought forward each year, is also, I think, implausible. It was fizzing with ideas that were also not necessarily connected to either popular demands or organizing.

We simply didn't have a structure for democratic policymaking and, other than expanding the number of issues debated at conference, little changed under Corbyn's leadership.

HW: Why couldn't that be changed? Did you have a vision of a different policy process?

JS: It wasn't changed because it was never made a priority and no one could agree on what the replacement would be. In my view, the role of conference should be setting the big strategic direction. It shouldn't be the detailed specification of policy. Strategic questions need to be ones that are really debated by the movement through conference; you then get a resolution and a direction. Take, for example, the national care service. I don't think it's the role of conference to work out precisely which taxes would have to be raised, how different types of private care homes would be brought into a public system, the oversight models, the forms of worker-management, and so on. The role of conference is to decide: do we want a strategic priority to be having a national care service, which must be universal and free at the point of need like the NHS? Then I think it would be incumbent on the leadership of the party to have some kind of committee to develop a detailed policy which includes the relevant trade unions, social movements, and members with knowledge about the sector, alongside staff and technical advisors and think tanks and so on. The relevant politician should then have to report back to conference the following year about how far they've developed the policy in all ways: popular support for it, a movement behind it, the technical implementation, the outline of how it will work with government machinery, the funding for it, and so on. That is presented to conference which either says, 'Yes, you're on the right track, carry on,' or no.

Conference would be taking the big decisions on the top line policies and then providing scrutiny over whether it is on track. Because, really, how do you move a party away from being a Westminster politics-as-game vehicle towards being the tip of a movement that is trying to bring forward a set of radical reforms? That requires an active, self-advancing, self-educating movement-party that is trying to push these radical reforms up the political agenda – that is trying to make them common sense, trying to win people over in workplaces and communities for these policies, and to develop the organized strength of the social forces behind them.

My thinking here comes after the fact. No one had been seriously thinking what a democratic socialist movement-party would look like in the twenty-first century, because it seemed there was zero chance of there being one. The knowledge that people had – people who know a lot about party processes, the Campaign for Labour Party Democracy (CLPD) and so on – was generally: 'How can you operate within the existing rules and the existing structure to defend as much as you can and occasionally advance here and there?' That's a very different type of thing to: 'What would we do if we were starting from scratch?

HW: Could more have been done about how a party leadership committed to socialist politics encourages direct action? If there is a left leader in the future – or even now in local councils – how can they be more encouraging and collaborating in spreading direct action?

JS: The Labour Party had 400 employees and 600,000 members but was not designed to do that kind of militant campaigning. I'll give one example. In December 2017, John McDonnell wanted to develop a campaign on public ownership of water, which was our policy. I remember being called into a campaign planning meeting and everyone's saying different things. I said: 'What is the purpose of this?' One, are we trying to increase the number of people who support public ownership of water? Two, are we trying to increase the salience of the issue of public ownership of water? Or three, are we trying to lay down the argument, in advance of being in government, that these companies have built up masses of debt and therefore the price we should pay for them is lower? Or four, are we trying to just build into our overall narrative of being for the many, not the few, and this is a nice visible way of doing it? The reason why it shouldn't be numbers one and two is that there is already massive support for public ownership of water and, secondly, it's never going to be a top three issue. What's the most important issue facing you and your family? No one's ever going to say public ownership of water. We basically agree it's the latter two things. It's to popularize the arguments about how these companies went from public hands to private hands with no debt, now they are loaded up with debt, they haven't done the repairs, and just lined the pockets of shareholders with outsized dividends.

So, I said: 'If we want to do that, we don't need to have a big national campaign. We're just trying to get some attention – it's eyeballs on the issue.' Some activists, who aren't officially the Labour Party, should buy shares in Thames Water or some other privatized water company, turn up to the AGM, and do a big stunt. Then you, John [McDonnell], should be round the corner at the Bank of England having a meeting, and then you happen to go past them, the BBC happens to be tipped off this thing is happening, and then you're standing outside there giving an instant reaction, saying: 'I don't know everything about their tactics and all the rest of it, but their point is absolutely right, these companies have blah, blah, and that's why we should bring them back into public ownership.' It's a repeatable action because there are water companies everywhere and their AGMs are at different times, and you need very few people to be able to pull off that kind of stunt. There's your campaign. Anyway, John says, 'Brilliant', everyone seems very happy, and I walk out of the meeting dejected.

HW: Dejected?

JS: Dejected. One of John's staff says to me: 'That's a really good meeting, how's it going?' And I said: 'It's terrible. Because I guarantee you that come next summer there will be a million leaflets printed with the Labour Party logo and a leaky tap which activists will be asked to hand out on high streets.' Sure enough, that's what happened. Because the party machine would be horrified at the idea of helping to find some activists, getting them together, giving them a bit of training about how to do these things and letting them form their own group so they are then autonomous, but there is enough coordination so that these things can happen. It's set up to stop people doing these things and then to say: 'Well, no, if we're going to do a campaign we then need to deal with our stakeholders.' Of course, the trade unions are incredibly important, but that direct action should be the tip of the campaign. Then the next bit is when you involve all the trade unions on how you would actually run the publicly-owned water companies, then you start engaging the workers, and you run that whole process. But that is a process not for the attention economy, that's a process for how you're actually going to organize the industry. Again, how are you going to build the capacities within the industry to take it on to run it themselves?

HW: You could have a direct comms – attention economy – focus where the trade unions draw up a plan for Yorkshire Water, let's say, and then occupy Yorkshire Water's office.

JS: They demand a meeting, hold a teach-in …

HW: And reveal the plan.

JS: Exactly. That's absolutely fantastic.

HW: What structural constraints did such an idea come up against?

JS: The Labour Party's campaigns and elections team was almost entirely anti-Corbyn, a hangover from the Blair-Brown years. We didn't transform that at all. Even though we had the opportunity to put in an executive director at the top of the department, it didn't change that department's character one bit. It was a huge failure, frankly. The regional offices are all set up to prevent that kind of spontaneous action. It's the same thing in local party meetings. Did the Labour Party at the constituency level change very much under Jeremy? It changed in what kind of motions were debated, and the political character of the room changed. A party is its personnel, its policies, and its culture and practices. Obviously, we changed leader and, as time went on, we had more personnel change. The policies changed. But the culture and practices of the party remained rooted, I think, in that traditional top-down form.

There were a lot of participatory meetings on specific things like the Green Industrial Revolution, but there wasn't any commitment to the idea that: 'We will train every Constituency Labour Party (CLP) or borough organizer to go into each CLP and organize people and give them the skills and confidence to go out and do various things.' For example, we're sitting in Hackney South now. The London Renters Union (LRU) exists, the membership of Hackney South CLP is enormous. If you step back, it's bonkers that there wasn't a concerted campaign to get Hackney South CLP members going out and knocking doors, street by street, with LRU material, saying – 'This is for you'. Renters are a huge social base of Labour voters in an area like this.

Thinking over it, if we are to do it another time, you would pinpoint a few places with super-active memberships to do things which create positive case studies – and then put most of your actual resources into other places. Which would have its own benefits, because you would then be trying to build both the active membership, and the membership full stop, in electorally significant places with small Labour membership – and also trying to rebuild the working class there. The class for itself, class consciousness, are, in part, constructed by a party in the Gramscian sense. On that micro level of being part of people's daily struggles, we weren't really doing that. I think we were, on the macro level of opening space for socialist ideas and policies, but until 2018 we didn't have control of the machine.

HW: And now that sort of class-forming party isn't on the foreseeable horizon – what is to gain from being involved in the Labour Party, now that it seems to be reverting to a vacuous centrism?

JS: There are two defensive reasons and one potential offensive reason. The two defensive reasons are to keep open the possibility of the party as a vehicle for a socialist advance through (a) the selection of left MPs, and (b) not allowing the rules to be changed to keep the left off the leadership ballot. Those are the two vital things. If people stay in the party, they don't have to go to all the meetings or be deeply involved, but we need to have a form of organization where all the left people are able to turn out for anything that will prevent those rules changing. If those rule changes go through, then the Labour Party as a vehicle for socialism is closed for at least the time being. The third reason, which is potentially offensive depending on where people live, is that the rules for selecting local councillors are very open. There is mandatory reselection each cycle. There is an opportunity, I think, in lots of places where socialists in an organized fashion could go into local government and replicate the successes that we are seeing in Salford, in Preston, and so on – and build up an idea of local socialism.

HW. What are the strategic advantages of local socialism?

JS: There are several. First, it is a way to immediately improve the lives of some people in their neighbourhood. That is a significant prize if people are looking for meaningful political activity. Second, you begin to build up what a socialist programme would look like on a national level, based on some actually-existing local successes. You build homes, you create jobs, you expand services.

The third advantage of left strength in local government is that it will give some people, some cadres, experience in the state. We need this because, if we're going to get into national government, we need to have much more experience in operating – and fighting against, where necessary – the state machinery.

HW: Given your argument that the election to councils is open – or to nominations as a council candidate – why wasn't more achieved in that area in 2015-19?

JS: There are a number of reasons. The first thing to say is that some things were achieved. There was a natural churn, with each successive cycle, which brought in more left councillors than before.

HW: From what I've observed in many local councils, the Blairite-right is quite embedded at that level. So, I'm not sure how open it really is.

JS: That's all true and they will try to make it more difficult. They will try to hold on to their positions; and no idea of local socialism has been coherently developed. We didn't run on it in any local election campaigns where we could say: 'Vote Labour and this is what will happen in your town.' I think we were insufficiently imaginative and committed to it beyond: 'We will put more money into local government.' There are ways in which you could do it. You could imagine a way in which we came out with a blueprint for local socialism, 'local politics for the many not the few' or whatever it might be. And then said, 'We want to breathe new life into local government, so we need new candidates, new everything.' All of these things do involve picking a big fight with the established parts of the party. All of these things are a question of which fight you are going to pick.

NEW POTENTIALS

HW: How strong do you think the left is now to take on these fights?

JS: It's significant that the unions are no longer in decline. There is also an influx into the unions of a greater number of politicized socialists to form part of that re-politicizing trade unions at the base; and, at the level of the leadership, more people thinking that they are hugely political actors in their own right.

The amount of left-wing ideas through think tanks, books, intellectuals is also much larger. Momentum exists. If in parliament the left isn't big, it is bigger. Yesterday there was a by-election for one of the positions for Labour MPs on the National Executive Committee. Grahame Morris was the left candidate, and in a secret ballot he got 38 votes. It's only 20 per cent, he got absolutely hammered, but still that is more than it would have been five years ago. Then you have what I would say is a very firmly progressive common sense among big swathes of the population, which you see in polling, but also in the mobilizations for Black Lives Matter, for Extinction Rebellion, Fridays for Future, Sisters Uncut after Sarah Everard's murder, and against the policing bill. That is all a new politicization in Britain.

HW: Judging by the recent Palestine demonstrations in London they are a new generation. They are younger than your generation.

JS: And more radical. I remember it was the Friday before conference in 2019, there was the big Youth Climate Strike demo on Millbank and Jeremy went to speak to it. First of all, it's amazing, it's all kids, all teenagers. I see one of them with a clipboard who looks up and sees a camera crew moving along and says: 'No, not there! That's the pool cutaway from ITN, they need that shot.' I thought, 'Bloody hell, this is a 16-year-old who understands broadcast from the perspective of using it from the left.'

Okay, these recent demos I've been to are all in London, so a caveat is needed, but the crowds seem very young, majority female, and majority non-white – actually proportional to the real demographics of London 20-year-olds. Let's compare that to another big demo, the anti-austerity march of 2015, which was huge and really great and inspiring, but definitely felt less young, less representative. The left has clearly expanded, I think, and taken real root in parts of society. The problem is that the left can be very atomised. You can have a progressive common sense among a whole swathe of the population but if it's got no organizational vehicle to advance that, or articulate it, then it's worth less than the sum of its parts. That is the potential problem with people leaving the party, or the left failing to have a unified voice within, around and outside it.

Ultimately, the challenge for socialists is to knit together all of the potential progressive forces to create a historic bloc in the sense Gramsci wrote about, a social majority that can have the force to fight and therefore have the chance to win and make a transformative politics. What was so powerful about the Corbyn project was that all of the different types of lefts could see themselves in it and had a reason for being involved in the same project.

HW: Yes, so the question of being inside or outside the Labour Party was seamless. People did join, including people like me who had never joined before, but it was not an abandonment of previous commitments.

JS: And the danger of all these different sections of the left seamlessly going out is that the biggest organized base of socialists in Britain, right now, is in the Labour Party. Just because we had a political party that was trying to represent a class interest, and that was explicitly viewing itself in political terms – in the Marxist sense of political – and there was suddenly a mass engagement and the membership more than tripled in size, doesn't mean that the hollowing out of the party that took place under New Labour was entirely reversed. Part of that non-reversal is in people's minds. I've already mentioned a neoliberalization in how people engage with the party: from a collective vehicle that one has some ownership of, say, or control over, for whatever reason; it could be family, community, historical, trade union, to being something that expresses who I am as a person, and being more to do with individual choice. When you have that mindset, the fact that the Labour Party is doing bad things means, 'I don't want to be a member of the Labour Party, because it's not expressing who I am'. The Labour Party is an institution within society that has one foot within the progressive forces of society and one foot in the state, and therefore part of its role is to prop up the existing power structures of capitalist society and part of its role is to challenge that power. That conflict takes place within the party by definition. It's a site of struggle and it's a collective institution that we want to be able to use, in the same way we want to use other collective institutions. When you view the party that way it doesn't sum up who you are politically, and it doesn't put you in a position which means you are basically a cheerleader for whoever happens to be in the shadow cabinet at the time.

I'm not admonishing people at all, I'm saying let's see where people are and try to set up institutions or formations that engage with people where they actually are, and how they are feeling. The thought should be: is the Labour Party open as a vehicle for socialist advance? If yes, we should be in it, because that's where the greatest density of socialists is in society. If no, then leave, but it's not as an individual act of rebellion. It's a political act with other political actors. It's a collective, not an individual, thing.

Let's not forget how far we've come or that there is a nascent social democratic common sense in this country that the Corbyn project activated. It's hilarious to see all these Blairite retreads saying Labour needs to be the party of business and aspiration. Look at the polling. To the question, 'Are big businesses too powerful?', the majority say 'Yes'. 'Do businesses underpay their workers?' A majority 'Yes'. 'Do big businesses dodge taxes?', again a majority say 'Yes'. There are super-majorities on all of these things.

The so-called 'Red Wall' where Labour Party support has been impenetrable historically to Conservatives is another example. Non-traditional Tory voters who voted Leave in the Brexit referendum and then Tory in the general election have, on average, the most 'left-wing' opinions on economic questions. It is lunacy for the Labour right and supporters of Keir Starmer to say that Labour can only appeal to people by being more right wing. It doesn't matter what term they put on it – Mondeo Man, Worcester Woman, Workington Man, the Quiet Batpeople – whatever term they come up with, to say: 'This is the demographic we've really got to be going after', their conclusions are always the same. 'The way in which we do that is to combine centre-right economic policy with social authoritarianism, because that's really what these people want.' No, it's not, it's what you want to do, and you want an excuse to do it. It's always the same prescription. It's bollocks. It won't work. That kind of thinking will lead to further defeat. I saw a poll a couple of days ago which showed quite a lot more people think that the Conservatives are the agents of change than they do the Labour Party. That's a substantial shift.

HW: In a way it's a puzzle that Jeremy, who was so close to Tony Benn, never pursued democracy as the key issue. Benn drew up a whole bill on a democratic constitution.

JS: There are only so many things that could be proposed. I personally think that it's a shame. I think it's a double shame because it could have given us a narrative on Brexit that would have been very helpful. The vote to leave was motivated by concerns that were cultural, economic and democratic, or political. Obviously, we couldn't engage with the cultural ones, which were mainly reactionary. The economic one, most people voting for leave, if they were voting on economic things, they were voting against forty years of deindustrialization. We had a bit of that with 'left behind', 'levelling up' and so on. But we never really engaged with the sovereignty issue. One way we could have engaged with that was saying: 'We're leaving the EU so we're going to have some more powers, but this is going to be part of a wholesale democratization, real control in communities, you'll have oversight over policing, how your money is spent on the local council, we'll kick big money out of politics, scrap the House of Lords.' You could build a whole agenda off the back of it, which I think could have moved the Brexit debate on a bit, in a way that we were never really able to do.

HW: Radical political reform has rarely been on Labour's agenda. A distinctive feature of the Party has been its acceptance of the British state and the presumption that its job is to get into government and then steer it. But one of the many radical features of Corbyn and John McDonnell's approach was that it made the state and political reform an issue to be addressed. However, it was sidelined. Why and how was it then marginalized?

JS: Democratic reform was hugely underdeveloped in our programme, relative to other types of reform. If you look at the 2019 manifesto, there is a line about the House of Lords, there is a line about having a constitutional convention – which is a terrible framing – but beyond that democratic reform was not really taken seriously. I think that was, in part, due to the policy priorities of the policy team who were – I would say, in general – more interested in policies which would immediately improve people's lives. Clearly, transforming or reforming state architecture, or setting up alternative bases of power and so on, these are not things that are going to deliver improvements to people's living conditions in the immediate term. I think that's part of it.

So, we never had anything like the old Bennite concerns, which I think are very good ones, such as community oversight over local policing. Or things like bringing in participatory budgeting into local councils. There was more interest in getting more money to local councils, less in participation.

HW: How can we make it a live issue now? How can we, as the labour movement and the left, make it our issue in the absence of being in government?

JS: We need to develop and apply a narrative and a programme for democracy. I'm not saying I know exactly what the right framing is, but it needs to be non-technical and participatory. My fear always with talk of constitutional conventions is that you get a lot of liberal-left lawyer types who come and try to work out what they think would be a rational way to organize society – which is not what democratization is. I also think it needs to be more thoroughgoing. It needs to take in a number of different things. There are headline-catching things to do with Westminster: getting rid of the House of Lords, a cap on political donations, lobbying, all of that. And there's scope for pressing for funding for local government, and participating in local government. Where we have councils that we have influence over, we should be running those participatory experiments.

HW: Implementing them now?

JS: Yes, developing that knowledge and understanding of participatory democracy within the movement. Then there's the workplace. At a minimum that means workers on boards and so on, but there's a whole range of other, deeper forms of workplace democracy. That needs to be one of the major strands which, across the left, we push for. This is what control is, all these things, and this is our programme and our narrative for it.

But let's not be under any illusions. What we're pushing for is unlikely to become a major thing the public engage with politically, because we don't have a vehicle to force it forward. Not only is this not going to change people's lives immediately, were Labour in government with this programme, it's also that Labour is not going to be in government any time particularly soon. That doesn't mean don't develop it. We absolutely must. But what are the types of things that we should be doing now? I'd suggest this should be experiments through which we can build the various capacities you need to do these things. Part of that is: how do we get officials and politicians, at some point when we're in the state, who are able to construct new institutions? How are we going to get these new regional development banks? Part of that is a conscious and coordinated effort by socialists to go into the parts of local government, even though it's had its powers and funding dramatically reduced, and the parts of the state that are open to us to enter, to learn and build up those capacities. The other is, where possible, to use local government and open it up to a more democratic, participatory approach. Then there is another element that could apply across the left. There can be a tendency towards a fetishization of internal processes within our organizations, but we should have much more of a focus on participation. Participation and control, I think those are the two bits that are missing. There's accountability of a minimal kind: you can vote out governments every now and again; and there's a degree of transparency. That's the bit that is best served, basically because liberal lawyers are interested in that. Participation gets very little mainstream attention, neither does control, which is also especially important for public ownership, industry, industrial strategy, investment – very big issues which concern how economic and social power is structured.

HW: Maybe also the difference is that accountability can be consistently accommodated within a liberal framework of individual voting, whereas participation and control are collective.

JS: That's a very good point.

MOMENTUM – A NEW TYPE OF ORGANIZATION

HW: As you were talking about the structural limits of the Labour Party I was thinking: what about Momentum? Momentum was potentially a way of doing a lot of the things you are saying, autonomous from the Labour Party but yet connected with it. You were involved in the initial days of Momentum. Was that the initial conception, and could it have been more articulated and developed?

JS: I think probably the first thing to say is that there was just so much to do from May 2015 on. I wrote somewhere that the challenge was to bridge the gap between the moment's possibility and the movement's weakness – to fight within the party, to basically be the party for electoral mobilization, which we saw in 2017 and 2019. In 2017, why were the rallies suddenly massive? The rallies were being organized by the party in the usual way – members only, a small community room, ticking off the names you've got beforehand. We just got the postcodes, texted them to the local Momentum organizers who stuck them on Facebook or whatever, and boom – thousands of people, streets closed, and most people attending not actually being Labour members. It changed the social character of who was there and transformed it. That's why, as electoral events, those rallies were so successful. There is some LSE research on it, showing that Labour's vote in places where it held rallies went up 19.5 per cent – enormous. That's because – although rallies are being derided as preaching to the faithful – they were outdoors, anybody could come. Of course, they would appear on local news and everyone there was doing their social media, so lots of people in the area saw it – and it formed the backdrop to our message of the day.

HW: And it reached a lot of people who weren't the converted.

JS: That's what I'm saying. I remember very, very well one day when we were in a car park in Reading at eleven in the morning on a workday, and there are 2,000 or more people. I see people coming out of their offices, just coming down to have a look. You think: 'Oh, they are going to go back up and say this is the biggest thing that is happening in the town today, and that's going to ripple out.' Anyway, that should have been the party doing that, but Momentum did it. By 2019, Momentum's ability to mobilize people to campaign was even larger and, in technical terms, Momentum ran an even better campaign in 2019 than 2017. It was really very good on basically every single metric. Getting people to the right places, getting more people out knocking doors, more phone banking, better digital – the whole thing was very good. But that's what the party should be doing.

To come back to your question about whether there was this conception of Momentum at the beginning – yes, absolutely. A paper I wrote in August 2015 envisaged what became Momentum as an organization trying to construct a new social force in society, which would also be linked into the Labour Party. It would strengthen progressive social forces because it would organize tenants and carers, and have community campaigns – it would do all of these things and it would link them into the Labour Party. But also, it had to fight to win control and support for Corbyn in every CLP. There was just a huge amount of stuff that needed to go on.

Then there are contingent factors that prevented it from going on. We should have had a prototype for how the groups should be managed, or run, and handed it to each group when they set up. They wouldn't have to do it like that, necessarily, but it could have provided solidity and guidance. I don't know if this is your recollection, but I went to a lot of each local group's first meetings. Pretty much, wherever they were, they were similar. Let's say 200 people, most of whom had never set eyes on each other beforehand, many hadn't been to many political meetings, very excited, and just sitting in a big room with a real buzz. One by one someone stands up and says, 'We need to build more council houses', and everyone goes, 'Yeaaah!'. The person looks startled that they've got 200 people cheering and agreeing and sits down. Someone else stands up and says something else, everyone's like, 'Yeaaah!' Then it's: 'We need to do this, this and this.' It's fantastic and then they broke into far too many working groups. People say we'll do this, and we'll do that, and we'll try to prioritize it, etc. That was an amazing energy but then what happened very quickly was: 'Who is going to manage the mailing list.' Especially people who had much more formal political experience within the labour movement, or within different left groupuscules, said: 'We need a chair, we need a secretary, we need to do all of this stuff.'

That shifted power within the local groups, I think. Firstly, towards whoever was the best organized pre-existing left faction in any given area, and secondly towards people who were good at getting elected to a position rather than leadership through doing. I think it should be more horizontal. It comes more from an anarchist tradition of leadership being a temporary thing. If you say: 'I want to organize our group to try and organize tenants, who is with me?' And that person takes on some role of coordinating and leading that, their leadership is a temporary thing and it's specific to a project that other people have. Then you go back to the group and say: 'This is what we're doing.' It's really not about voting. It's democratic, it's participatory, but it's not primarily about voting.

HW: And it is more collective in the real sense – collaborative as well as collective. It depends on working together and creating a force, or power.

JS: Yes. We should have tried to do that more, but I can understand why people who had Labour Party experience – all over the country – and were now in Momentum groups were banging their head against the wall, saying: 'Do you not understand that if we aren't all turning up to branch meetings, we won't get elected to the constituency party general committee, which means we won't be able to elect delegates to conference, which means we won't be able to pass the policies, which means …' They were also one hundred per cent right. You could have done it with the same sort of model. Again, if we were thinking it through – we didn't have a formal agreed strategy at the beginning of Momentum, but if we had – that would have said, basically, part of being in Momentum is, if you're a Labour member, you go to your local party meeting and you vote. But that doesn't have to be how you mainly do your politics. You're doing that because that needs to happen, but it isn't the limit to your politics and organizing.

I'm not saying this in any critical way – except for, of course, a self-critical way – we didn't really know what we were doing. Momentum was a new type of organization. Jeremy was a new type of leader. The whole thing was novel and we were experimenting. We were trying something new, and it was all coming as a big, exciting surprise to everybody. What we needed was to have more of a conception of what it meant for Momentum to be a hybrid organization and to try to structure it a bit more.

HW: Yes, if it was going to be hybrid, everyone needed to understand the components. It also needed to be transparent.

JS: Yes. Take the national committee for example. We launched the organization without any governance structure. We were discussing and arguing a lot at the beginning about what that should be. One thing that I supported was that, in the same way we had the labour movement on the national committee – trade unions that wanted to be on plus Labour Party organizations like Compass, CLPD, and so on – we should have someone from Stop the War, CND (Campaign for Nuclear Disarmament), Sisters Uncut, etc. We should have these non-labour movement, and non-Labour Party orientated organizations as part of it. Momentum had to be a hinge between the two in some way.

Now, Momentum should change its membership rules back to having the same as the Fabians.

HW: What do the Fabians say?

JS: You don't have to be a member of the Labour Party but you have to be eligible to be a Labour Party member, i.e. not a member of another party – which was Momentum's original position.

HW: You are sketching a movement in which the unions slightly shift their relationship. They don't disaffiliate from the party, but they are involved in practical alliances with the left – whether the Labour Party left or just independent socialist activists. This can be difficult. What was the experience of Momentum? Is it that it didn't try to develop links?

JS: Some trade unions are affiliated to Momentum. The Communication Workers Union, the Fire Brigades Union, the Associated Society of Locomotive Engineers and Firemen, the Transport Salaried Staff Association, and the Bakers' Union are all affiliated. There was always a question of whether Unite would or wouldn't affiliate, and it never actually has. I was talking to an American friend about the Democratic Socialists of America (DSA), in part because I think the new leadership of Momentum takes the DSA as a model. I'm not saying this as a diss on either the DSA or on Momentum, but I think it's slightly mistaken. In some ways, Momentum is more developed than the DSA. Not one single union is affiliated to the DSA. The fact that five trade unions are affiliated to Momentum, and sit on its national coordinating group, is actually quite a significant thing.

HW. Another aspect of Momentum's work must be political education?

JS: Political education really happens through struggle. It doesn't happen through books and seminars. For a small proportion of the population, that stuff works. But political education is basically political exposure which encourages the development of confidence to act for yourself, and to act collectively. That's what political education really is. The books and the theory and everything else are in service of that.

For example, what's going on at British Gas-Centrica, that could be a way of teaching people about privatization, neoliberalism, and their impacts, but through an active struggle that people can be involved in, they can win and, through that, help to understand the world.

The left, over the past 45 years, because of defeat and being chased out of most mainstream places in society, has become more and more intellectual. Of course, I like a lot of the left intellectual stuff, but we're not going to change society by having the most nuanced analysis of capitalism or its injustices. It's combining those things. It's about how you embed political education into every campaign and turn political education efforts into campaigns. Within half a mile of this place, there probably is a Marxist reading group. There are probably ten people talking about Marx. How do we turn those out and link it into some campaign and some activity? Then how do you build upon people's experience of struggle? Let's take the bus drivers' strike in Manchester. That's more politically educational than a degree in political economy. Their understanding of the economy, politics, and society is going to be higher. But you could offer some political education organization to work with the union, to then deepen that in some way.

HW: But with these lessons learned, could Momentum become the hybrid organization you are now envisaging?

JS: Ideally it would have become the organization that we need, but it hasn't, and now alone it probably can't. It no longer has sufficient authority. That's not to say Momentum isn't a crucial organization with a big role to play. It is. But we also need something more.

This is something I have been calling for consistently now for a year – we need an organization that is a formal alliance between the left trade unions, Momentum, and the Socialist Campaign Group of MPs to begin with, basically making the MPs accountable to those bodies again. Then you bring in the organized left in the trade unions that are not led by the left. Then you bring in the other grassroots groups within the party – Stop the War, Sisters Uncut, XR, Youth Climate Strike, Kill the Bill, etc., and you build this left.

What would a thoroughgoing socialist organization be? Basically, it becomes a party in the Gramscian sense, not that it runs on a separate electoral line – its party is the Labour Party but it can provide political leadership. It can run campaigns. It has an autonomy. It has funds and resources. It can do political education. That means socialist perspectives and organizing can happen in a concerted and coordinated and effective way. But also, that's the weight within the party that will keep people in the party, because there is actually a pole of attraction. This way you've got the vehicle that would be strong enough to advance things in society, and at the same time to resist the obvious changes that the right will try to make to prevent there being a left leadership, and even prevent left MPs ever being elected again. Also, it makes it far harder for the present leadership to expel people or try to demoralize people bit by bit. If they started doing the mass expulsions, they would be expelling an organization that was a social force and that could become a rival electoral party.

HW: Partly as a consequence of demoralization – and also disillusionment after maybe completely unreal expectations around the 2019 election –a lot of people are leaving the Labour Party. But, at least from my experience in Hackney, they are not abandoning political activity – indeed they are very active in local campaigns around privatization and trade union rights. What do you think should be done in that context? How do we build on, or at least not lose, the politicization that undoubtedly occurred under Corbyn and has still a lasting legacy? What is your assessment of the forces at play, not just in the Labour Party but in society? How does the left get organized to consolidate what's moving on the left?

JS: I think this goes back to the creation of a formal alliance: an organized and identifiable, and therefore resourced and confident, socialist force in society that sits in the Labour Party but acts in society, and which is then a pole of attraction. Then, if you're a left member, why are you in the party? Because I'm part of this broader campaigning movement. I am going to do my politics through this movement, which means I can be part of national campaigns. I can do stuff in the party if I want. I can see socialist people on TV putting forward what the socialist line would be if the leadership of the party is going to refuse to do so.

We don't need a different party – in the Electoral Commission registration sense of the term – but we need to have a party in the Gramscian sense of the term: a political organization that stretches into society, that has real and organic links with different forms of ongoing struggle – trade union, environmental, feminist, anti-racist, and so on – and has some parliamentary representation and can speak in the country – it has the ability to communicate in a mass way.

It should be a Labour Party organization, in that Labour is its electoral vehicle, but it can operate in different ways. It's like adapting what the Working Families Party and DSA do in the US, by having their own organization but using the Democratic ballot line.

The Labour Party is a different beast: it's a political party, and the Democrats aren't – they are a state-backed political franchise. But we need to have an independent socialist voice within the party and an organization that unites the different parts of the movement where people are at.

SHIFTING THE GROUND

HW: Do you think that the left could develop a practical vision of democratization that's based on participatory collective reforms, rather than liberal reforms?

JS: It's all going to be very piecemeal, and that's fine. We're trying to intervene just now where we can stop things getting worse. We're trying to intervene to shift public attitudes and movement capacities. We're trying to shift the ground for whenever we have the next opportunity, in whatever form that will take – without trying to overdetermine what form that could take. It follows that it's not just one model that will emerge. Intervention needs to happen on all sorts of levels. There is the direct action-type movement populist comms I've spoken about before – occupying the private healthcare companies' offices, big attention-grabbing stuff in the way that Black Lives Matter and XR (Extinction Rebellion) have done very well. We need that. We also need people getting experience in local government.

We need to recapture the imaginative direct action of groups like UK Uncut, which I think did help shift attention on to tax-dodging and who was doing it. You can remember the companies they occupied and did teach-ins at, such as Vodafone and Starbucks, saying: 'they're not paying their taxes, so these services aren't being delivered by the state.' It was brilliant and had real impact. We need to get attention, and we need to drag the media to report on various things, which you can't just do by asking them to. You need to create the focus. If the Labour Party had been going on and on about government corruption for the last year, then the media would be covering it because they'd have to be. It would have appeared on the six o'clock news, which it hasn't. In the same way, privatization of the NHS – you're not seeing it on the six o'clock news. You've got to put it there.

Our plan needs to operate at all these different levels. The reason I keep banging on about this formal alliance of some sort, is just so that there is some coordinating thing, so that we are more than the sum of our parts – so that, if there is some group that is going to do direct action against private healthcare, the people who can get on broadcast are being booked to go on broadcast, they have lines and know the arguments to make about privatization. Then that works with the filmmakers who are making the short videos for social media and all that stuff with the trade unions active in healthcare. It should all be working in concert, but without creating a command-control operation, because you simply couldn't.

That's how coalitions and campaigns organize on a small scale. We're just talking about doing it on a bigger scale. We're describing what the Labour Party should have been able to do, in an ideal world, with Jeremy as leader.

HW: How would the priorities be decided?

JS: It depends which people and organizations come together, and in what formation, for how they would work it out. There's always going to be a relationship between the centre, or the leadership, and below. For example, the climate stuff was not a major focus, despite Jeremy being a major environmentalist. It wasn't a party focus, really. Then all this pressure comes from below, a big movement the Youth Climate Strike and XR, and suddenly that changes the dynamic within the leadership team and suddenly we can get loads of environmental stuff in. Then the end point is this really very good manifesto, probably the most advanced programme in the world, for climate. I'm not saying that just because something is now coordinated, you're handing over the decisions. People should do the things that they want to do, but the purpose of having some obvious national structure is that you see how you fit into it.

There is a huge incentive now, after the pandemic, to work together to create something. That's the thing we need to have – enough organization, enough potential, so that everyone doesn't go down their own rabbit holes.

There is a base on which we need to build further infrastructure. The Corbyn project gave us a big boost to build on. We're getting a little reminder of it now with how spineless and useless Starmer's Labour Party is. Austerity and anti-migrant politics might previously have just been the accepted political norm, but thanks to the Corbyn years they no longer are.

The Corbyn project first showed that we weren't losing because the majority of the population just loved the world as it was; quite the opposite. It's actually that the common sense in the country has remained broadly progressive, while not having political expression, while its organs were being defeated and crushed. The Jeremy surge has given us new strength and energy that pulls us out from the margins, and out from critique into organizing and proposals. That's very important. The incline of the left is up, even if the angle may not be very steep. There's a lot of rebuilding and new work that's going on.

We need to be doing that in every single conceivable area. We've moved from a war of manoeuvre to a war of position. We're trying to build the ground for the next time we have a surge, so it takes place on more propitious ground than what we had in 2015. That's the task.

NOTES

1   Including *Beyond the Fragments: Socialism and the Making of Socialism,* with Sheila Rowbotham and Lynne Segal, London: Merlin Press, 1980; *Labour: a Tale of Two Parties*, London: Chatto and Windus, 1987; and *A New Politics from the Left,* Cambridge: Polity 2018.

2   In Leo Panitch and Colin Leys, *Searching for Socialism*, London: Verso 2020, p. 217.

3   André Gorz, 'Reform and Revolution', in Ralph Miliband and John Saville, eds, *The Socialist Register 1968*, London: Merlin, 1968.

4   Tariq Ali, 'Why I'm Joining the Labour Party', *Socialist Review*, (38), 1981, pp. 20–21.

5   The Labour Group led by Ken Livingstone were elected on a radical mandate, the implementation of which was way beyond the powers of the GLC. For the group's manifesto to be fully carried through Councillors heading the most radical policy areas had to depend on the support of organized Londoners, and thus encouraged their empowerment. Hence the Council's Economic Policy Group, Racial Equality Unit, Women's Unit, Police Monitoring Unit, and the Inner City Planning Group, all made popular participation and grant support for citizens self-governing organizations central to their work. For the work of the Economic Policy Group in this respect see: Hilary Wainwright, 'The Economics of Labour: Robin Murray, Industrial Strategy and the Popular Planning Unit', Robin Murray, August 2020, available at: robinmurray.co.uk/glc-ppu; and M. Mackintosh and H. Wainwright, A *Taste of Power: The politics of local economics*, London: Verso, 1987.

Also Available

Socialist Register 2021: Beyond Digital Capitalism – New Ways of Living
Edited by Leo Panitch and Greg Albo

As digital technology became integral to the capitalist market dystopia of the first decades of the 21st century, it refashioned both our ways of working and our ways of consuming, as well as our ways of communicating. And as the Covid-19 pandemic coursed through the world's population, adding tens of billions of dollars to the profits of the high-tech corporations, its impact revealed grotesque class and racial inequalities and the gross lack of public investment, planning and preparation which lay behind the scandalously slow and inadequate responses of so many states.

Contents:

Ursula Huws: Reaping the whirlwind: Digitalization, restructuring, and mobilization in the Covid crisis

Bryan D. Palmer: The time of our lives: Reflections on work and capitalist temporality

Larry Lohmann: Interpretation machines: Contradictions of 'artificial intelligence' in 21st century capitalism

Mathew Cole, Hugo Radice & Charles Umney: The political economy of datafication and work: a new digital Taylorism?

Grace Blakeley: The big tech monopolies and the state

Tanner Mirrlees: Socialists on social media platforms: Communicating within and against digital capitalism

Derek Hrynyshyn: Imagining platform socialism

Massimiliano Mollona: Working-class cinema in the age of digital capitalism

Joan Sangster: The surveillance of service labour: Conditions and possibilties of resistance

Jerónimo Montero Bressán: From neoliberal fashion to new ways of clothing

Sean Sweeney & John Treat: Shifting gears: Labour strategies for low-carbon public transport mobility

Benjamin Selwyn: Community restaurants: Decommodifying food as socialist strategy

Pat Armstrong & Huw Armstrong: Start early, stay late: Planning for care in old age

Pritha Chandra & Pratyush Chandra: Health care, technology, and socialized medicine

Christoph Hermann: Life after the pandemic: From production for profit to provision for need

Robin Hahnel: Democratic socialist planning: Back to the future

Greg Albo: Postcapitalism: Alternatives or detours?

ISBN 978-0-85036-761-4 paperback
       978-0-85036-762-1 hardback

Socialist Register 2020: Beyond Market Dystopia – New Ways of Living
Edited by Leo Panitch and Greg Albo

How can we build a future with better health and homes, respecting people and the environment?

Connecting with and going beyond classical socialist themes, each essay in this volume combines analysis of how we are living now with plans and visions for new strategic, programmatic, manifesto-oriented directions for alternative ways of living.

Contents:

Stephen Maher/Sam Gindin/Leo Panitch: Class politics, socialist policies, capitalist constraints

Barbara Harris-White: Making the world a better place: restoration and restitution

Amy Bartholomew/Hilary Wainwright: Beyond the 'barbed-wire labyrinth': migrant spaces of radical democracy

Katharyne Mitchell/Key Macfarlane: Beyond the educational dystopia: new ways of learning through remembering

Birgit Mahnkopf: The future of work in the era of 'digital capitalism'

Michelle Chen: A new world of workers: confronting the gig economy

Yu Chunsen: All workers are precarious: the 'dangerous class' in China's labour regime

Ursula Huws: Social reproduction in twenty-first century capitalism

Alyssa Battistoni: Ways of making a living: revaluing the work of social
        and ecological reproduction
Nancy Holmstrom: For a sustainable future: the centrality of public goods
Karl Beitel: The affordable housing crisis: its capitalist roots and the
        socialist alternative
Roger Keil: Communism in the suburbs?
Owen Hatherley: The retroactive utopia of the socialist city
Nancy Fraser: What should socialism mean in the twenty-first century?

ISBN 978-0-85036-752-2 paperback
        978-0-85036-753-9 hardback

Socialist Register 2019: A World Turned Upside Down?
Edited by Leo Panitch and Greg Albo

Since the Great Financial Crisis swept across the world in 2008, there have
been few certainties regarding the trajectory of global capitalism, let alone
the politics taking hold in individual states.
This has now given way to palpable confusion regarding what sense to
make of this world in a political conjuncture marked by Donald Trump's
'Make America Great Again' presidency of the United States, on the one
hand, and, on the other, Xi Jinping's ambitious agenda in consolidating his
position as 'core leader' at the top of the Chinese state.

Contents:

Leo Panitch/Sam Gindin: Trumping the empire
Marco Boffo/Alfredo Saad Filho/Ben Fine: Neoliberal capitalism: the
        authoritarian turn
Ray Kiely: Locating Trump
Doug Henwood: Trump and the new billionaire class
Nicole Aschoff: America's tipping point: between Trumpism
        and a new left
Elmar Altvater/Birgit Mahnkopf: The Capitalocene: permanent capitalist c
        ounter-revolution
Alan Cafruny: The European crisis and the left
Aijaz Ahmad: Extreme capitalism and 'the national question'
Jayati Ghosh: Decoupling is a myth: Asian capitalism in the global disarray

Sean Starrs: Can China unmake the American making of global capitalism?
Lin Chun: China's New Internationalism
Ana Garcia/Patrick Bond: Amplifying the contradictions:
        the centrifugal BRICS
Adam Hanieh: The contradictions of global migration
David Whyte: 'Death to the corporation': a modest proposal
Umut Ozsu: Humanitarian intervention today
Colin Leys: Corbyn and Brexit Britain: Is there a way forward for the Left?

ISBN 978-0-85036-735-5 paperback
        978-0-85036-736-2 hardback

Socialist Register 2018: Rethinking Democracy
Edited by Leo Panitch and Greg Albo

This volume seeks a re-appraisal of actually-existing liberal democracy today, but its main goal is to help lay the foundations for new visions and practices in the development of socialist democracy. Amidst the contradictions of neoliberal capitalism today, the responsibility to sort out the relationship between socialism and democracy has never been greater. No revival of socialist politics in the 21st century can occur apart from founding new democratic institutions and practices.

Contents:
Sheila Rowbotham: Women: linking lives with democracy
Martijn Konings: From Hayek to Trump:
        the logic of neoliberal democracy
Alex Demirovic: Radical democracy and socialism
Dennis Pilon: The struggle over actually existing democracy
James Foley & Pete Ramand: In fear of populism: referendums and
        neoliberal democracy
Sharryn Kasmir: Cooperative democracy or competitiveness?
        rethinking Mondragon
Adam Hilton: Organized for democracy? Left challenges inside the
        Democratic Party
Natalie Fenton & Des Freedman: Fake democracy, bad news
Nina Power: Digital democracy?
Tom Mills: Democracy and public broadcasting

ISBN. 978-0-85036-733-1 paperback
        978-0-85036-732-4 hardback

---

www.merlinpress.co.uk